OREGON
STATE · PARKS

A COMPLETE
RECREATION
· GUIDE ·

SECOND EDITION

JAN
BANNAN

THE MOUNTAINEERS BOOKS

Published by
The Mountaineers Books
1001 SW Klickitat Way, Suite 201
Seattle, WA 98134

First edition, 1993. Second edition, 2002.

Published simultaneously in Great Britain by Cordee, 3a DeMontfort Street, Leicester,
England, LE1 7HD

Manufactured in the United States of America

Project Editor: Christine Ummel Hosler
Copy Editor: Chris DeVito
Cover and book design: The Mountaineers Books
Layout: Mayumi Thompson
Cartographer: Jennifer LaRock Shontz
Photographer: Jan Bannan

Cover photograph: *Cove at Miner Creek, Samuel H. Boardman State Scenic Corridor.* © Jan Bannan
Back cover photographs by Jan Bannan: *Atop spectacular cliffs with great wave watching, Shore Acres
    State Park features a botanical garden and garden house that were originally part of the Simpson
    Estate* (top); *Oregon iris is one of the beautiful wildflowers found near trails* (middle); *California
    sea lions are common along the Oregon coast* (bottom)
Frontispiece: *View of Humbug Mountain and surf to the south.* © Jan Bannan.

Library of Congress Cataloging-in-Publication Data

Bannan, Jan Gumprecht.
        Oregon state parks : a complete recreation guide / Jan Bannan.— 2nd ed.
        p. cm.
    Includes bibliographical references (p.) and index.
    ISBN 0-89886-794-0 (pbk.)
    1. Parks—Oregon—Recreational use. 2. Parks—Oregon—Directories. I. Title.
GV191.42.O7 B36 2002
333.78'3'09795—dc21

2001006490

CONTENTS

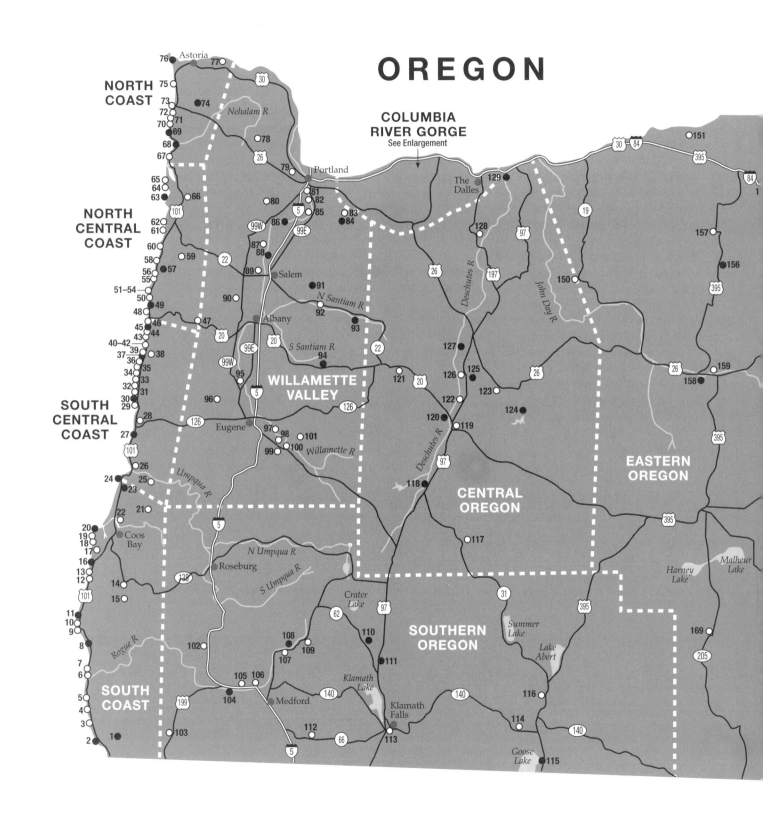

OREGON

NORTH COAST

COLUMBIA RIVER GORGE
See Enlargement

NORTH CENTRAL COAST

WILLAMETTE VALLEY

SOUTH CENTRAL COAST

EASTERN OREGON

CENTRAL OREGON

SOUTHERN OREGON

SOUTH COAST

Astoria

Nehalam R

Portland

The Dalles

Deschutes R

John Day R

Salem

Albany

N Santiam R

S Santiam R

Eugene

Willamette R

Umpqua R

Coos Bay

N Umpqua R

Roseburg

S Umpqua R

Rogue R

Crater Lake

Klamath Lake

Medford

Klamath Falls

Summer Lake

Lake Abert

Harney Lake

Malheur Lake

Goose Lake

Enlargement
COLUMBIA RIVER GORGE

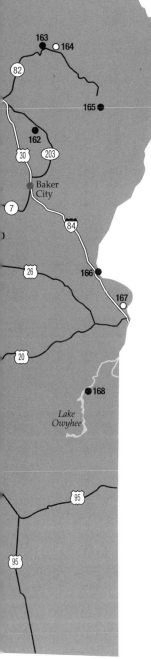

LEGEND

Interstate highway	Road
U.S. highway	Dirt road
State highway	Trail
Forest Service road	Park/region boundary

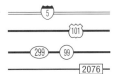

●	City or town	= Bridge
●	Campground park	Waterfall
○	Day-use park	Rapids
Ⓣ	Trailhead	Marsh or swamp
Ⓟ	Parking	River or stream
▲	Mountain or peak	Dam
★	Point of interest	Body of water
禾	Picnic area	Dock or pier
Λ	Campground	Sand/sand dunes
ʌ	Hiker/biker camp	Cliffs/bluffs
⌐\	Horse camp	Boat launch
■	Building	Boating
Ⓥ	Visitor center	Surfing
▰	Ranger station	Windsurfing
†	Cemetery	Waterskiing
♁	Church	Swim area
☀	Lighthouse	Hiking
♀	Springs	Horseback riding
👁	Scenic attraction/viewpoint	Bicycling
⚓	Marina	Fishing
▲	Forested area	Wildlife viewing
⁙	Tidepools	Birdwatching
⌐	Wildlife blinds	

A little exploring at Port Orford Heads State Park rewards visitors with surf booming off sea stacks.

ACKNOWLEDGMENTS

Many people helped me in many ways in the writing of this guidebook, whether they contributed from the pages of reference material or were people in the state park system that I talked to. Public Services Manager Craig Tutor helped me update information concerning the parks and other programs handled by the Oregon Parks and Recreation Department. Kevin W. Price, assistant area park manager of the Columbia River Gorge, was helpful in answering several questions, particularly concerning Government Island. At Farewell Bend, Chris Magallanes took time to give me a tour of the improvements in the park. Orrin P. Russie, photo/video services coordinator for the Oregon Department of Transportation, responded quickly to a request for a historic photo of the Twin Tunnels. M. G. Devereux, team leader at Tryon Creek and Milo McIver, took time to answer questions about the parks. Trails Coordinator Shawn Laughran responded to a map request, which Master Planner Kristen C. Stallman was kind enough to send me. John Forbes at La Pine sent me a new map of the park when it was revised. At Wolf Creek Inn, Executive Chef Dean Kasner spent time informing me about the dining room specialties. When I was a day too early to find Vista House open, volunteer Sally King answered questions for me. The staff at Frenchglen Hotel let me wander through the upstairs rooms to check out the furnishings. Information on both Collier Memorial and the OC & E State Trail was supplied by Jim Beauchemin. Tom Hill at Fort Stevens contributed informative material. Glen Andyke, the campground host at Deschutes River, let me disturb him off duty. Thanks also to many unnamed park rangers who were always willing to help.

Beginning with New Editions Coordinator Deb Easter and Managing Editor Kathleen Cubley, the staff at the Mountaineers Books has done a great job. Project Editor Christine U. Hosler has been very professional in keeping the book on schedule. Publicist Alison Koop and the marketing staff geared up early for the book's publication date. The copy editor, mapmaker, and so many others have done great jobs on the book's production. I thank them all.

When I took my last trip this April to revisit many of the parks, I was enchanted by the magnificence of springtime along the Columbia River Gorge and delighted to hike through the reopened Twin Tunnels. I thank all the people who contributed to the truly amazing construction of the Historic Columbia River Highway, one of our state's treasures. One delightful result of doing this second edition has been exploring more of Oregon's natural landscapes and biodiversity. And researching the state's rich history has been especially rewarding. Although I can only read about the Oregon Trail pioneers and the Lewis and Clark Expedition, such acquired knowledge makes me proud to be an Oregonian after searching many years for the right place to live.

Coast view south from Cape Lookout Trail in Cape Lookout State Park

INTRODUCTION

The landscapes of Oregon surpass imagination. They include some of the most spectacular and inspiring scenery created by natural forces: mountain ranges piercing the clouds, the magnificent Columbia River Gorge, the fertile Willamette Valley, lush temperate forests, high desert solitude, wild rivers, the blue magic of Crater Lake, and one of the most dazzling coastlines in the world. The recreational, aesthetic, and educational resources are unending amid this variety of landforms and waterways.

Many of these special places are protected as Oregon State Parks. Scattered throughout the state, these parks are places to picnic and camp, but many offer trails, waterfalls, lighthouses, mountains, lakes, rivers, beaches, sand dunes, boating, fishing, wildlife, wildflowers, and geologic formations that will tug at the visitor to linger, to ask questions, to learn, and to nurture a sense of wonder. Many parks include exhibits that impart a spiritual connection with the past, particularly memorializing pioneers along the Oregon Trail and the Lewis and Clark Expedition. Certain parks encourage quiet encounters. Others seem to invite large reunions or exuberant boating. Some are on main routes, some in isolated areas.

Oregon's weather is an eclectic affair, as if someone had programmed a computer to provide variations on a theme and put locations to the music, instead of words. Travelers can choose to spend summers on hot, dry deserts; temperate, breezy beaches; or cool mountain slopes; and winters skiing in the high country or watching winter surf during the often pleasant, warm coastal days. The shoulder seasons are peaceful, with exuberant lush growth in spring and autumn's calm and color.

Specific write-ups include 170 of the developed state parks, a greatly expanded number from the first edition, which did not include parks designated at that time as waysides and recreation areas. Incorporated are the many changes in the park system and in individual parks. To avoid conflict with information available from the Oregon State Parks and Recreation Department, except for incorporating the Portland Region into the Willamette Valley region, each chapter of this book covers one of Oregon State Parks and Recreation Department's designated regions. (Management areas differ from these regions.)

Because the state parks are stepping stones to discovering Oregon, a preamble at the beginning of each regional section presents an overview of the scope of that area. Following this is information about the features of each park: facilities and campground information, natural and human history, recreation possibilities, and nearby excursions. Maps will help in exploring; the many photos hint at what you will see.

HISTORY OF THE PARKS

Although Oregon officials early recognized the value of preserving and maintaining the natural scenery along its state highways and providing stopping places for travelers, the impetus for the development of a state park system was the increased mobility of wanderers.

In the late 1910s and early 1920s, motorized vehicles opened a new era in exploration, a way to get to a trailhead or waterway for self-propelled recreation. Tourists could purchase a Model T Ford for $500, equip it with food, cooking utensils, bedding, tents, etc., and take to the open road. They stopped to camp where they could find water. With few commercial places available for camping, and speeds of about 30 miles an hour, it was an economical way to travel. With the benefits of pleasure, health, and education, this mode of traveling became an antidote to ignorance.

The problem was that increased number of camping enthusiasts brought on more fenced private property and "no trespassing" signs. The demands for public camping grew. Governor Olcott made the comment in 1921 that "We are expending thousands of dollars in urging the tourist to come here. It is necessary that we care for him when he comes."

The need for land acquisition for parks—by donations, eminent domain, and purchase—was already underway. Various committees and commissions had met to further the formation of state parks, and some highway parks had been provided. Official sanction for the park program, however, occurred with the newly appointed State Park Commission on July 24, 1929. A policy statement was written and adopted:

> To create and develop for the people of the state of Oregon a state park system, to acquire and protect timbered strips on the borders of state highways, rivers, and streams, to secure in public ownership typical stands of the trees native to Oregon, to maintain the public right to the use of the sea beaches of the state, to seek the protection of our native shrubs and flowers and to preserve the natural beauty of the state.

The need for both recreational facilities and overnight camping by tourists escalated the development of more state parks. In 1913, Governor Oswald West had declared the wet-sand beaches a public highway and was backed by legislative action. The days of horses and buggies using the beach as a road soon passed with

A prime reason for the establishment of Oregon's state park system was to protect timbered strips along state highways, rivers, and streams.

the advent of travel by car. Today, many beaches are closed to motorized use. The result was that the public beaches became a playground strung with parks. One fine inland park arose early as a result of a historical meeting at Champoeg in 1843, site of the official birth of Oregon.

The original notion of parks involving beautification and extensive tree-planting at highway stops expanded to include the need to preserve special natural features of the state, not just easily accessible ones. Enthusiasm increased after several Oregonians attended the 1928 National Conference on State Parks in San Francisco.

Samuel H. Boardman served as Parks Engineer, or Superintendent, from 1929 to 1950. He has been called the "Father of Oregon State Parks" because of his furtherance of land acquisitions. During this period, 495 transactions secured 50,842 acres for parks, and in retrospect have saved many acres of old-growth forest.

Other agencies worked to develop these state parks. The Civilian Conservation Corps (CCC) in particular, under the technical supervision of the National Park Service and cooperating with other park agencies, employed youths who couldn't find work during the Depression. They constructed trails and bridges, rustic buildings, picnic areas, roads, parking areas, and viewpoint shelters, and did property-line surveys and marked corners. Seventeen of their camps were in Oregon State Parks, though improvements were made in forty-five parks. Many fine stone and wooden structures standing today attest to their good work.

Today, Oregon's large system of parks encompasses 228 properties and 94,330 acres of land; 170 of these have developed visitor facilities that include restrooms and parking areas, and most have water. More than thirty-six million people—local, national, and foreign—used the day-use facilities in the year from July 1, 1998, to June 30, 1999. More than two million used the campgrounds. The Oregon State Parks and Recreation Department also owns and manages ninety-two Willamette River Greenway properties, as well as many programs that include the management of the 362-mile ocean shoreline, state scenic waterways (with the highest number in the country), and Oregon recreation trails.

PARK CLASSIFICATIONS

Oregon's parklands are organized into nine regions: North Coast (eleven parks), North Central Coast (twenty parks), South Central Coast (twenty-three parks), South Coast (twenty-three parks), Willamette Valley (twenty-four parks), Columbia River Gorge (twenty parks), Central (thirteen parks), Southern (fifteen parks), and Eastern (twenty parks).

Within these regions, parks have the following classifications:

- *State Park:* An extensively scenic, outstanding natural setting for a variety of types of outdoor recreation
- *State Trail:* A linear park with miles of hiking, biking, and horse trails
- *State Recreation Area/State Recreation Site:* A location with facilities that provide access to a variety of recreational pursuits
- *State Heritage Natural Area/State Natural Site:* An outstanding natural resource that may offer opportunities to view unique plants and wildlife
- *State Scenic Viewpoint/State Scenic Corridor:* A scenic highway corridor or roadside spot that offers an outstanding view of natural features
- *State Wayside:* A small, sometimes isolated parcel of roadside land with a parking area, picnic tables, and restrooms

The official state park signs make it easy to find the parks, warning the visitor well in advance and then leading you to them.

PARK FACILITIES AND FEES

Fees are for 2001, both during the prime season and during Discovery Season, which is from October 1 to April 30. Changes may occur. Some campgrounds are open for a portion of Discovery Season; others are open year-round. Camper Bucks can be purchased during Discovery Season; these come in booklets of seven coupons that sell for $77 and buy seven nights in any type campsite (even a full hookup site), an additional savings over the already lower Discovery fees.

Day-Use Areas

Besides a scenic location and various recreation possibilities, most of the day-use parks provide picnic tables, restrooms (some of these are closed in winter) or vault toilets, and drinking water.

Group picnicking shelters. For a fee (depends on group size), group picnicking shelters can be reserved at twenty-nine parks (1-800-452-5687; a few are booked through the specific park):

- *Coastal Parks:* Bullards Beach, Cape Lookout, Ecola, Fort Stevens, Jessie M. Honeyman, Sunset Bay, William M. Tugman

- *Portland Area:* Champoeg, Mary S. Young, Milo McIver
- *Willamette Valley:* Cascadia, Elijah Bristow, Molalla River, Maud Williamson, Sarah Helmick, Silver Falls, Willamette Mission, Jasper, Lowell
- *Columbia River Gorge:* Benson, Dabney, Guy W. Talbot, Rooster Rock
- *Central Oregon:* Tumalo
- *Southern Oregon:* Collier Memorial, Joseph H. Stewart, TouVelle, Valley of the Rogue
- *Eastern Oregon:* Wallowa Lake

Meeting halls. Group meeting halls can be reserved for a fee (1-800-452-5687—free with rental of at least five campsites during Discovery Season) at these parks: Bullards Beach, Sunset Bay, Jessie M. Honeyman, South Beach, Beverly Beach, Cape Lookout, Nehalem Bay, Valley of the Rogue, La Pine, Champoeg, Silver Falls, and Emigrant Springs.

Day-use fee. Funding problems have necessitated the payment of year-round day-use fees ($3) for vehicle parking at twenty-six of the more popular state parks. If you are camping at any state park for that day, the day-use fee is waived; just display your receipt.

- *Coastal Parks:* Cape Lookout, Ecola, Fogarty Creek, Fort Stevens, Heceta Head Lighthouse, Jessie M. Honeyman, Nehalem Bay, Shore Acres
- *Western Valleys:* Champoeg, Detroit Lake, Fall Creek Reservoir (Winberry Area), Jasper, Milo McIver, Silver Falls, TouVelle, Willamette Mission
- *Columbia River Gorge:* Benson, Dabney, Mayer, Rooster Rock, Viento, Twin Tunnels (Hatfield Trailhead)
- *Central/Eastern Oregon:* Farewell Bend, Smith Rock, The Cove Palisades, Tumalo

An annual permit for unlimited use is available for $25, sold by merchants near the parks, at GI Joe's stores throughout Oregon, and at state park offices, or call the State Park Information Center, using a VISA or Master Card, at 1-800-551-6949.

Campsite Choices

Except in hiker/biker camps, the rock climbers' bivouac Smith Rock, and a primitive campsite on Government Island, campsites in fifty park campgrounds include a picnic table, fire ring, barbecue, or camp stove. Many campgrounds have restrooms with showers, accessible facilities, dump stations, public phones, firewood, campfire programs, and other amenities, which are listed with the individual park. Almost all of the campgrounds have paved vehicle parking at the sites (extra vehicles are $5 to $7). Twenty-nine campgrounds are open year-round, with heated facilities making this fun for those without RVs. Types of sites include:

- *Full hookup:* Sewer, electricity, and water available at the site—$15 to $20
- *Electrical:* Electricity and water available at the site—$12 to $20
- *Tent:* No utilities, but water at or near the site—$12 to $17
- *Primitive:* No utilities, with one water source, and generally there is no paved parking at the site—$7 to $13
- *Walk-in tent:* No utilities at regular tent sites, but water is nearby, with parking a short distance away—$13 to $14
- *Horse camps:* Primitive campsites with corrals are available at Bullards Beach, Cape Blanco, Emigrant Springs, Nehalem Bay, and Silver Falls—$13 to $14 plus $1.50 per animal

All of the above sites are discounted $2 to $4 during Discovery Season.

- *Hiker/biker:* Open areas with tables for walk-in, bike-in tent camping. Available at most coast parks and at Champoeg, Clyde Holliday, Tumalo, and Unity Lake inland—$4 per person

Specialty Campsites

- *Yurts:* Domed tent with lockable door, electricity, lights, heating, and beds with mattresses (bedding not provided); bunk beds sleep three and a fold-out couch sleeps two. A skylight allows stargazing. A deck is attached and a picnic table is outside. $27.
- *Cabins:* Fronted by porches, these structures vary from cozy one-room structures to deluxe two-room units with bathrooms; electricity, lighting, beds with mattresses, and a table and chairs are provided. Various types of these are found at Umpqua Lighthouse, Cape Blanco, Alfred A. Loeb, La Pine, Silver Falls, Emigrant Springs (a Totem cabin complex is included), The Cove Palisades, Prineville Reservoir, Farewell Bend, and Wallowa Lake. $35 to $65, with larger cabins discounted during Discovery Season.
- *Tepees and covered wagons:* Both structures have wooden supports covered with canvas, with mattresses and lighting. Tepees are found at Unity Lake (no electricity), Lake Owyhee (no electricity, but site includes two canoes and lifejackets), Farewell Bend, Tumalo, and Clyde Holliday. Covered wagons

Specialty campsites found in some parks include yurts, cabins, tepees, covered wagons, and houseboats.

are found along the Oregon Trail route at Farewell Bend and Deschutes River, with electricity, beds, stools, and an iron tripod with a coffeepot over an outdoor tripod. $27.

- *Houseboats:* The Cove Palisades has several options for renting a houseboat for groups of ten to twelve; they have all the amenities needed for renting by the week, for the weekend, or during midweek. Rates vary with time used and size, and are booked through the park.
- *Group tent camping:* Nineteen parks have group tent areas, with a common space, five picnic tables, a fire pit, and water source designed for twenty-five campers. $60; $40 in Discovery Season.

- *Group RV areas:* A large open space can accommodate five self-contained RVs, with tables, fire pits, and water source. May be reserved at Champoeg, Deschutes River, Silver Falls, and Willamette Mission. Call for fees.
- *Club camping:* If you reserve at least five traditional sites during Discovery Season and ten traditional sites during the prime season, your reservation fees can be waived. For details, call Reservations Northwest (see Reservations and Information below); a Club Camping packet is available.

Lodging

Several more developed lodging possibilities are available.

- *Officers' Inn Bed & Breakfast:* Rooms with Victorian elegance, private baths, and candlelight breakfasts are featured at Fort Stevens State Park.
- *Wolf Creek Inn State Heritage Site:* Period-furnished rooms with private bath and excellent dining choices in Southern Oregon.
- *Frenchglen Hotel State Heritage Site:* Historic bed and breakfast, plus family-style dinners, is near Steens Mountain in Eastern Oregon.
- *Silver Falls State Park:* Conference Center has four lodges, ten cabins, meeting rooms, jogging trail, volleyball court, and heated swimming pool. The Ranches, also in this park, are large buildings for up to seventy-five campers, with restrooms and a large kitchen. The park also has a rustic youth camp with eight cabins and all the needed amenities for recreation.

RESERVATIONS AND INFORMATION

Although many sites are available in campgrounds on a first-come, first-served basis, reservations at twenty-six of the busiest parks can be obtained by calling Reservations Northwest at 1-800-452-5687 from Monday through Friday, 8:00 A.M. to 5:00 P.M., and from 7:00 A.M. to 8:00 P.M. after May 1. You can also reserve online at *www.prd.state.or.us*. All group camping and special campsites are handled by Reservations Northwest's Special Facility Operators. Reservations can be made up to eleven months in advance, but no less than two days before your stay, with a $6 fee per site, plus the first night's rent. Reservations are rarely needed during Discovery Season. The following parks are reservable:

- *Coastal Parks:* Fort Stevens, Cape Lookout, Nehalem Bay, Beverly Beach, Devil's Lake, Beachside, Jessie M. Honeyman,

South Beach, Umpqua Lighthouse, William M. Tugman, Bullards Beach, Sunset Bay, Harris Beach
- *Portland area/Willamette Valley:* Champoeg, Silver Falls, Detroit Lake, Milo McIver
- *Columbia River Gorge:* Memaloose
- *Central Oregon:* Deschutes River, La Pine, Prineville Reservoir, The Cove Palisades, Tumalo
- *Southern Oregon:* Valley of the Rogue
- *Eastern Oregon:* Farewell Bend, Wallowa Lake

For information on any of the parks other than reservations, call 1-800-551-6949 or 1-800-858-9659 for the hearing impaired, or check out the official website (*www.prd.state.or.us*). Some of the major parks can be reached individually; if so, their phone number is included in the park write-up.

PARK RULES

Read the list of regulations posted in each park and become familiar with your responsibilities while visiting; they vary in different parks.

Litter. Consistently rated in the nation's top ten state park systems, Oregon's parks need the cooperation of users to maintain their attractive appearance. Please pitch all waste material into the proper disposal containers, even if it's not yours.

Pets. If kept on a leash up to six feet long, and if the owner is in control at all times, pets are allowed in the parks, although not on some trails. Walk pets in designated or isolated areas, and clean up any messes that land in other places; several parks provide doggie bags. If a pet creates a health hazard, a public disturbance, or is out of control, the owners will be asked to leave the park. Only seeing-eye dogs are allowed in buildings, including yurts, cabins, tepees, and covered wagons.

Quiet hours. From 10:00 P.M. to 7:00 A.M., quiet hours must be observed. Your neighbor may want to get up early to photograph a sunrise and not appreciate noisy late-evening entertaining, so please respect the rights of those around you. Don't leave your vehicle idling unnecessarily, and park only in designated areas. Any noisy, explosive substances (such as fireworks) are prohibited at any time. If noisy visitors threaten your enjoyment of the park, report them to park personnel—friendly, efficient professionals. It's best to avoid confrontations with unreasonable offenders. If a park ranger is unavailable, a list of local law enforcement telephone numbers is posted at campground registration booths.

Valuables. If you must bring valuables into parks, keep them with you if possible. The use of firearms is prohibited in parks.

Campfires. With frequent dry summers in Oregon and the resource value of the forests—and consideration of lives that might be threatened—careful control of campfires is required, and special regulations are sometimes imposed on campers.

Ocean beach recreation areas. Beaches along the ocean have additional rules, sometimes seasonal ones. Motor vehicles and horses are prohibited on certain beaches. No fires are allowed in driftwood piles. Firepits can be used for that beach party, but be sure to douse them later with wet sand or water. Permits are required for log and sand removal and any commercial activities.

SAFETY CONCERNS

In case of emergency, contact a park ranger or call 911. If you are prepared and use caution, your park visits should be safe—and enjoyable.

The beach. For those visiting parks along the ocean, the beauty of the scene sometimes overpowers a sense of caution. The surf is powerful and can throw huge logs onto the beach and roll them around; stay clear. Children, especially, should be warned not to walk on logs or play on them. Be aware of incoming tides, and don't become stranded on offshore rocks or while rounding headlands. Keep an eye on waves—they vary and occasionally send a sneaker wave ashore that could sweep you out to sea. It is better to grab onto some object, such as a rock, even if you get soaked, than be carried away. If you go into the ocean, be alert for outgoing currents. Very few, if any, Oregon beaches have lifeguards. Keep back from the edges of the many unstable cliffs. Giant sand dunes look like places for digging and tunneling, but this is hazardous and can cause avalanches that trap people.

Shellfish poisoning. At certain times, a public alert is issued against harvesting bivalves—clams, oysters, mussels, and scallops—because of a profusion of growth in a certain red algae in the ocean called *Gonyaulax catanella*. This is a toxic single-celled organism that is always present in small numbers. Certain environmental conditions cause rapid multiplication of this microorganism. Since bivalve shellfish feed by filtering water, they take in enough toxic organisms to threaten our health when numbers are high. Though called a "red tide," toxic conditions for us occur before growth is enough to cause this coloring. *Paralytic shellfish poisoning (PSP)* can cause serious illness, even death.

Shellfish are carefully monitored by state authorities, and notice is given to the public, usually in the specific area, if any danger is present by eating shellfish. Another potentially life-threatening chemical ingested by eating shellfish is domoic acid, which can cause amnesic shellfish poisoning. It appears that certain marine phytoplankton are responsible for this neurotoxin, possibly one not native to the West Coast. In addition to causing problems in bivalves, domoic acid is also found in Dungeness crab. It is carefully monitored, so be aware of any alerts. These are usually posted in the collecting area, but you can check with the Oregon Department of Fish and Wildlife.

Boating and water sports. Whether canoeing, kayaking, rafting, swimming, water skiing, or any way you choose to enter the water, make it a fun and safe experience. Match your skills to the local conditions, and consider the weather; it changes quickly in Oregon. Ask locally about specific water routes. Wear a life jacket and don't drink alcoholic beverages while enjoying these activities.

Hiking and walking. Certain regions in Oregon have rattlesnakes; be alert. It's always best to be prepared for the unexpected, whether it's a change in weather, getting lost, or whatever. Take along drinking water, map, walking stick, suntan lotion, sweater, insect repellent, sunglasses and/or sun hat, dry matches, compass, pocketknife, flashlight, a snack (add an extra high-energy bar just in case), and mini-first-aid kit (include forceps, for tick removal, and aspirin). One of the pleasures of outdoor recreation is a picnic at the foot of a waterfall or some other scenic spot. These items are easily carried, with hands free, in a knapsack on your back. Throw in an extra roll of film.

Oregon iris is one of the beautiful wildflowers found near trails.

RESPECTING NATURE

Fishing. All persons fourteen years of age or older (except certain disabled persons) require a valid angling license in their possession to take any fish except smelt for personal use. Special tags are necessary for salmon, steelhead, and sturgeon. The Oregon Department of Fish and Wildlife recommends the practice of releasing wild game fish—handled carefully—and only before a limit of fish is taken. Check with the Oregon Department of Fish and Wildlife for more information concerning limits and other restrictions; a detailed booklet is available.

Shellfish and marine invertebrates. No license is required to take smelt, shellfish, or other marine invertebrates. There are limits, however, and certain locations are closed to any takings. Check with the Oregon Department of Fish and Wildlife, or local authorities, for daily catch limits, harvest methods, locations, and special regulations. Some of the popular tidepool areas would soon lose their appeal if people indiscriminately took organisms. Some marine gardens are protected. Anyone enjoying the tidepool areas should also remember to treat the animals with respect. Please turn rocks back the way you found them after you look underneath.

Trails. There is nothing quite like the joy of hiking a trail in solitude or quiet company, watching for wildlife, and seeing what nature is doing at the moment. This joy is easily destroyed by the loud noises of other hikers or radios, or an unexpected, uncontrolled approach of a pet, just when you have discovered a fawn near the path. Please respect the enjoyment of others. "Leave nothing but footsteps," as they say, and they should not be heavy jogging ones on a muddy trail that can't recover. Even though orange and banana peels are organic, they are slow to decompose and unsightly. Pack out any garbage. Don't shortcut on switchbacks. It causes erosion and can send rocks down below and cause injury to others. Enjoy the vegetation; don't destroy or remove it. Instead, take a photo of that exquisite wildflower.

Wildlife. Many areas in Oregon offer excellent wildlife viewing, from marine animals to inland species. It's amazing how often travelers fail to respect the wildness of the animals they see, and want to approach them closely. Besides the possible danger, most animals are harassed by approaching them too closely, particularly when they have young. Survival in the wild is not easy, and your close approach may lower the odds of their survival. Please don't feed them.

California sea lions are common along the Oregon coast.

A lucky beach walker at Agate Beach State Recreation Site may be immersed in the movement of migrating sanderlings, and a few other species, as they fly north in spring.

PARK VOLUNTEERS

The Oregon Parks and Recreation Department receives hundreds of thousands of hours of service by volunteers who are key members of the staff team; these hours are equal to those of nearly 200 full-time employees. Some are park hosts in campgrounds; they assist in the popular Junior Ranger programs and evening campfire programs, and sometimes lead tours. Some volunteers assist at visitor centers, do maintenance chores, raise funds, and help with special events. Twelve parks have affiliated support groups called "Friends of the Park" that focus on educational and informative projects. The first of these was at Tryon Creek in 1969, followed by Fort Stevens in 1979, Champoeg in 1980, Crown Point in 1982, Shores Acres and Silver Falls in 1986, Collier Memorial in 1987, and Cape Blanco and Yaquina Bay in 1988. Banks-Vernonia Linear Trail, Cape Meares, and Sumpter Valley Dredge have been added more recently. Other volunteer projects include beach cleanups, Partners in Parks (Adopt-a-Park), and special opportunities, such as clearing storm damage.

A NOTE ABOUT SAFETY

Safety is an important concern in all outdoor activities. No guidebook can alert you to every hazard or anticipate the limitations of every reader. Therefore, the descriptions of roads, trails, routes, and natural features in this book are not representations that a particular place or excursion will be safe for your party. When you follow any of the routes described in this book, you assume responsibility for your own safety. Under normal conditions, such excursions require the usual attention to traffic, road and trail conditions, weather, terrain, the capabilities of your party, and other factors. Keeping informed on current conditions and exercising common sense are the keys to a safe, enjoyable outing.

—*The Mountaineers Books*

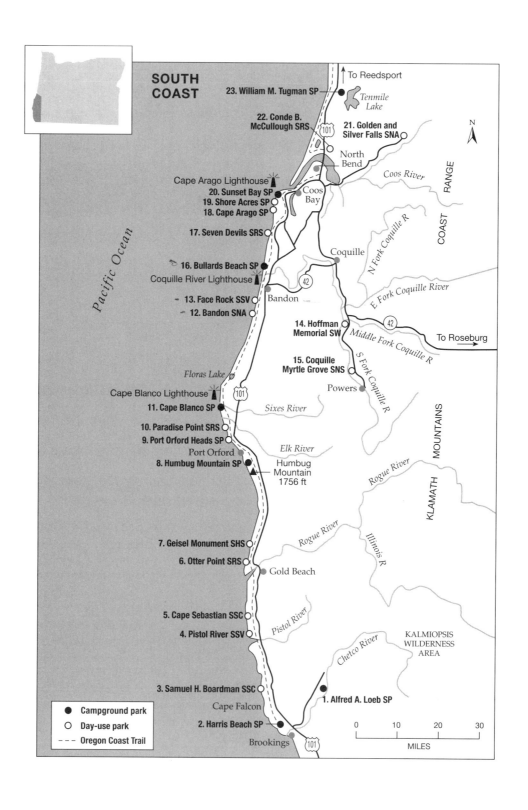

SOUTH COAST

↑ To Reedsport

23. William M. Tugman SP

Tenmile Lake

22. Conde B. McCullough SRS

21. Golden and Silver Falls SNA

US 101

North Bend

Coos River

COAST RANGE

N

Cape Arago Lighthouse

20. Sunset Bay SP

Coos Bay

19. Shore Acres SP

18. Cape Arago SP

17. Seven Devils SRS

Coquille

N Fork Coquille R

Pacific Ocean

16. Bullards Beach SP

Coquille River Lighthouse

E. Fork Coquille River

13. Face Rock SSV

Bandon

12. Bandon SNA

42

14. Hoffman Memorial SW

Middle Fork Coquille R

To Roseburg

15. Coquille Myrtle Grove SNS

S Fork Coquille R

Powers

Floras Lake

Cape Blanco Lighthouse

US 101

11. Cape Blanco SP

Sixes River

10. Paradise Point SRS

Elk River

9. Port Orford Heads SP

Port Orford

8. Humbug Mountain SP

Humbug Mountain 1756 ft

Rogue River

KLAMATH MOUNTAINS

Illinois R

7. Geisel Monument SHS

Rogue River

6. Otter Point SRS

Gold Beach

5. Cape Sebastian SSC

Pistol River

4. Pistol River SSV

KALMIOPSIS WILDERNESS AREA

Chetco River

3. Samuel H. Boardman SSC

Cape Falcon

1. Alfred A. Loeb SP

● Campground park
○ Day-use park
- - - Oregon Coast Trail

2. Harris Beach SP

Brookings

US 101

| 0 | 10 | 20 | 30 |

MILES

CHAPTER ONE

SOUTH COAST

From the rugged Oregon coastline at the California border, the South Coast region extends north past Coos Bay–North Bend to include the southern edge of the Oregon Dunes National Recreation Area (ODNRA). The interior of this region is so wild and unsettled that only one major road heads east. South of Bandon, the Coast Range to the east is soon replaced by the older Klamath Mountains, which have a trio of wilderness areas: Grassy Knob, the Wild Rogue, and the Kalmiopsis.

Except for traveling the east side of Humbug Mountain, the Pacific Coast Scenic Byway (US 101) follows a winding mix of cliffs, only occasionally dipping near the sea, as it travels north along the coast to Port Orford, where it swings inland a few miles, so even the drive is a high. Many of the self-reliant people who choose to live here believe this region embraces the Oregon coast's most spectacular scenery. Between Brookings and Gold Beach are state parks with stunning seascapes, wildlife viewing, and hiking trails: Harris Beach, Boardman, Pistol River, and Cape Sebastian. Situated in the "banana belt" of Oregon, the climate of the extreme south coast is temperate year-round, with rare freezing temperatures near the ocean. Even during winter, stormy days rub elbows with warm, sunny days and rainbows edging dynamic surf.

At Gold Beach, the legendary Rogue River ends its 210-mile journey to the sea from the slopes of Crater Lake National Park. Fishing is world class, as is rafting the wild river or hiking the adjacent trail. North of Gold Beach, Otter Point offers a park with unusual rock formations, and Geisel Monument is a heritage site.

The coast's oldest townsite and only natural harbor, Port Orford, has historic sites to visit, including Port Orford Heads, the former site of a valuable Coast Guard Lifeboat Station, now a hiker's dream place. Long stretches of walkable beaches are found south of town and north at Paradise Point State Recreation Site. South of Port Orford is the South Coast's only coastal mountain, Humbug, where a state park features a climb to the summit. The most westerly point in the state exists at Cape Blanco State Park, adjacent to the oldest active lighthouse.

The beaches near Bandon are some of the most beautiful along the coast, edged by sea stacks of all shapes and sizes, with numerous tidepool areas along miles of sandy oceanfront. Bandon State Natural Site and Face Rock State Scenic Viewpoint offer four access points south of the Coquille River. Along the northern bank of the river, where the historic Bandon Light is situated, is Bullards Beach State Park, a favorite camping base close to Bandon's Old Town attractions. North of town, Seven Devils State Recreation Site offers a more isolated beach location.

Several special tree species extend only as far north as the South Coast region: redwoods, Port Orford cedars, and myrtle trees. The popular wooden products of myrtle trees are found in many coastal shops, but three state parks feature the live trees: Alfred A. Loeb, near the border, Hoffman Memorial State Wayside, and Coquille Myrtle Grove State Natural Site.

The twin cities of Coos Bay–North Bend comprise the largest population center and shipping port along the entire coast. Three parks are a short distance southwest, near the fishing port of Charleston: Sunset Bay's protected ocean cove, Shore Acres's oceanfront, cliff-top botanical garden, and Cape Arago's tidepool areas and offshore marine life. To the east of Coos Bay, up the Allegheny River, is Golden and Silver Falls, where hiking trails through forest lead to waterfalls. At the northern end of the bridge over expansive Coos Bay is Conde B. McCullough State Recreation Site, honoring the designer of the bridge.

Across the bridge the coastline switches from cliffs and coves to flat terrain and allows winds to deposit sand from the ocean's reservoir. William M. Tugman State Park is a base for exploring these dunes, while offering water fun on Eel Lake.

For additional information on Oregon State Parks, call 1-800-551-6949, or check the official website: *www.prd.state.or.us.*

1. ALFRED A. LOEB STATE PARK

Hours/Season: Day use and overnight; year-round
Area: 320 acres
Attractions: Myrtle grove, redwood trees, wildlife viewing, hiking, swimming, fishing, rafting, drift boating, photography, picnicking, camping
Facilities: Picnic tables, campground (50 electrical sites, 1 accessible—maximum site 50 feet), 3 reservable log cabins, restrooms with showers, dump station, boat access, public phone, firewood
Access: Off US 101 at the south end of Brookings, 10 miles northeast via North Bank Chetco River Road
Contact: (541) 469-2021

Coastal residents know that summer warmth is only a few miles upriver. Alfred A. Loeb State Park invites a camping experience near the edge of the Siskiyou National Forest on the Chetco River, a waterway that flows seaward from the slopes of the Klamath Mountains.

Campsites are nestled among an outstanding grove of old-growth myrtle trees that flower in spring, with some sites fronting on the river, including the three new cabins. It is unusual today to find such a grove of these extraordinary trees, and the park was purchased to preserve them. A later purchase added a parcel with redwood trees, at the northern edge of their habitat.

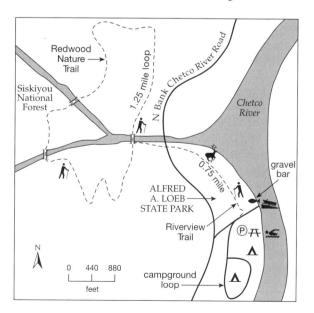

A boy and his shadow play along the Chetco River in Alfred A. Loeb State Park.

The picnic area is surrounded by more myrtle trees and edges a wide pebble beach, where drift boats can be launched by driving out onto the beach. Across the waterway is rugged forest land, where Emily Creek, the most important salmon-spawning tributary of the Chetco River, enters the water.

Trailhead parking for the Riverview/Redwood Nature Trail is along the entry road to the day-use area. Brochures with a hiking map and interpretive information are available. The 0.75-mile Riverview Trail is the connecting path to the Redwood Nature Trail. It climbs up from the river along a ledge and weaves through the forest, where a creek flows down a hillside.

A short distance after crossing the road, the Redwood Nature Trail begins. It can be traveled in either direction, a moderately steep up-and-down traverse of 1.25 miles. Along the trail are various ages of redwoods, from young ones growing out of old stumps to some large ones between 300 and 800 years old; one is over 33 feet in circumference and 286 feet tall. This forest also has myrtle, rhododendron, evergreen huckleberry, several species of ferns, salal, red alder, Douglas fir, bigleaf maple, tanoak, a carpet of wood sorrel, and the hanging lichen called grandfather's beard. Bridges cross a creek that runs through a deep gash in the land.

For a different hike in this vicinity, wilderness enthusiasts seeking the unusual might continue on the North Bank Chetco River Road another 5.7 miles to Forest Road 1909. Paved at first, this road becomes gravel and ends in 14.7 miles at the trailhead for 1.4-mile Vulcan Lake Trail. *(Trailers are not recommended.)* The trail switchbacks to a ridge and then drops down to the 4-acre lake, which fills a dramatic rock basin. This is the Kalmiopsis Wilderness, a region of unusual plant species that developed during the fifty million years that the Siskiyou Mountains were an island in the Pacific. Pre–Ice Age specimens that survived include the rare *Kalmiopsis leachiana,* carnivorous species, and weeping spruce. The topography is rugged and water is difficult to find. Hot and dry in summer, go in late spring when beargrass blooms and smell the flowering wild azalea along the path.

2. HARRIS BEACH STATE PARK

Hours/Season: Day use and overnight (reservations available); year-round
Area: 173 acres
Attractions: Beachcombing, hiking, biking, agate hunting, surf fishing, tidepools, photography, wildlife viewing, picnicking, camping
Facilities: Picnic tables, camping (34 full hookup, 52 electrical, 63 tent sites—1 accessible, maximum site 50 feet, cable TV at some sites), 6 yurts (1 accessible), hiker/biker camp, restrooms with showers, dump station, beach access, firewood, public phones, playground, laundry facilities
Access: Off US 101, 2 miles north of Brookings
Contact: (541) 469-2021

Huge rock sculptures of many shapes rise from the sandy beach of the day-use area of Harris Beach State Park and attract visitors like magnets. Some climb them; some graffiti and paint them; some photograph their enhancement of the beach landscape. It's a mystical sight to watch sunset atop these natural stone pieces of art as a full moon rises in the east and seagulls swirl in the colors of twilight.

Paths weave among picnic tables that sit on stone terraces overlooking the ocean and offshore rocky wildlife refuges. Ground squirrels scamper about, and gulls seem particularly argumentative. One large bird rookery is named "Goat Island" and a massive stone is called "Hunch Back." A fine sandy beach invites walkers and collectors. Storms have tossed ashore huge driftwood logs, and dynamic seas often leave a large tidal pool stranded on the beach, deep enough for children and dogs to jump in and play.

The campground is uphill and inland from the day-use area, in a wooded tract that contains azalea, shore pine, Sitka spruce, Douglas fir, red alder, salmonberry, Pacific wax myrtle, evergreen huckleberry, rhododendron, wild fuchsia, and Himalayan blackberry. Park animals include raccoon, Douglas' squirrel, opossum, brush rabbit, common crow, Steller's jay, California quail, and chestnut-backed chickadee. Unfortunately, only a couple of sites have an ocean view. The new yurt section is located at the rear of the camping area.

Several trails access different areas of the park. A short hiking trail across from the entrance to the campground switchbacks up Harris Butte to a vista point that looks north. En route to the top, there are fine views south. A nature trail begins near site C6 at the upper end of the campground, weaves through a wetland area, crosses the road, and connects with the South Beach Trail,

A boy and his dog explore a large tidal pool stranded on the beach at Harris Beach State Park.

paved downhill to good beach walking in front of oceanfront homes, with access to an intertidal marine garden. Collecting in the park is by permit only. Adjacent to site A12, the Rock Beach Trail crosses the entry road and heads toward the beach and day-use area, with several interesting side paths for getting the right camera angle for sunset shots. To reach the tidepools of North Harris Beach, head north on the beach.

The name of the park honors George Scott Harris, a native of Scotland, who obtained the property in 1871. His journey to this land was a long route, involving a stint in the British Army in India, trips to Africa and New Zealand, arrival in San Francisco, and work in railroad construction and mining before coming to Curry County. There he settled down to raise sheep and cattle.

Whale Watching

Gray whales migrate annually from the Arctic to lagoons off the west coast of southern Baja California, where some of them mate and others give birth. Their passage off the Oregon coast is south in winter and north in spring, though some linger here during the summer—probably young ones. For those who have never seen these charismatic animals, and for those who want to learn more about these fascinating marine mammals, a program is sponsored through the Hatfield Marine Science Center (HMSC) in Newport, Oregon State Parks, Oregon Coast Aquarium, and other cooperating agencies during the last week of the year and the week of college spring vacation. During these two weeks, signs pop up at many sites along the Oregon coast (plus one in California and one in Washington) that say "Whale Watching Spoken Here." Trained volunteers are present to help you spot whales, answer questions, hand out information sheets, and award First Whale stickers. Thousands of visitors from throughout the world stop each year to participate in these migration events. Films on gray whales are shown at HMSC. Information is available on boat and air charters that will take you whale watching.

Sites with Volunteers (South to North)
1. Crescent Beach Overlook, CA*
2. Harris Beach State Park*
3. Cape Ferrelo*
4. Cape Sebastian State Scenic Corridor*
5. Battle Rock Wayfinding Point*
6. Cape Blanco Lighthouse*
7. Face Rock State Scenic Viewpoint*
8. Shore Acres State Park*
9. Umpqua Lighthouse*
10. Sea Lion Caves Turnout*
11. Cooks Chasm Turnout*
12. Cape Perpetua Interpretive Center
13. Cape Perpetua Overlook
14. Devil's Churn Viewpoint
15. Yachats State Recreation Area*
16. Seal Rock State Recreation Site*
17. Yaquina Bay State Recreation Site*
18. Don A. Davis City Kiosk*
19. Yaquina Head Lighthouse*
20. Devil's Punchbowl State Natural Area*
21. Cape Foulweather*
22. Rocky Creek State Scenic Viewpoint*
23. Depoe Bay Sea Wall*
24. Boiler Bay State Recreation Site*
25. Inn at Spanish Head, 10th floor*
26. Cape Lookout State Park, 2.5-mile hike
27. Cape Meares State Scenic Viewpoint
28. Neahkahnie Mountain*
29. Ecola State Park*
30. Lewis & Clark Interpretive Center, WA*

*Disabled accessible

A gray whale mother and her calf migrate north in spring along the Oregon coast.

3. SAMUEL H. BOARDMAN STATE SCENIC CORRIDOR

Hours/Season: Day use; year-round
Area: 1,471 acres
Attractions: Viewpoints, hiking, tidepools, beachcombing, surf fishing, photography, wildlife viewing, picnicking
Facilities: Picnic tables, beach access, vault toilets
Access: Off US 101, along a 12-mile corridor north of Brookings

For 27 miles of weaving, jagged coastline south of Burnt Hill Creek, Samuel H. Boardman State Scenic Corridor encompasses the grinding edge of jagged, forested cliffs meeting the ceaseless energy of surf surging shoreward past the many offshore rocks. Every mile offers a different viewpoint, an unexpected bounty of geologic formations and sandy beaches hiding at the bottom of steep headlands. It is not exaggeration to call this one of the world's finest coastline corridors, and it is accessible by road and trail.

It is easy to see why Samuel H. Boardman, first state parks superintendent (from 1929–1950), conceived the idea of a great coastal park in Curry County. Boardman worked tirelessly to acquire the land. One gift of land was the first park grant by a foreign owner, Borax Consolidated, Ltd., of London, England. Boardman approached U.S. Department of the Interior Secretary Harold L. Ickes to propose that this should be a national park. Though federal officials toured the region, that idea did not take hold. Instead, it became a state park honoring Boardman. Perhaps that was best, since too much development has not spoiled the natural beauty and wildness of the park.

This unusual treasury of seascapes has a such a dramatic succession of areas to be explored on foot that using the overnight facilities of nearby Harris Beach State Park as a base would be a good idea.

The Boardman segment of the Oregon Coast Trail is not a sedate, windy beach walk, but an up-and-down excursion among many geologic happenings and natural history, including 300-year-old Sitka spruce. With recent extensions at both ends of the trail, the complete trail is approximately 15 miles, excluding connecting trails. With many highway access points and connecting trails, hikers can walk selected parts of the trail or the entire stretch, perhaps overnighting along the route. Check with state park information for allowable camping spots.

If you're heading north from Brookings to the park, the first area is Lone Ranch, a picnic area with restrooms at beach level in

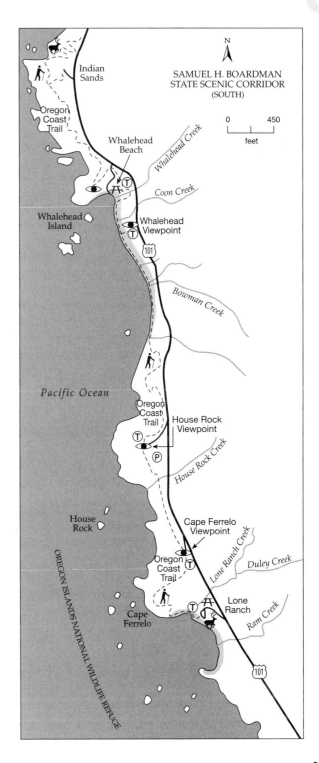

SAMUEL H. BOARDMAN
STATE SCENIC CORRIDOR
(SOUTH)

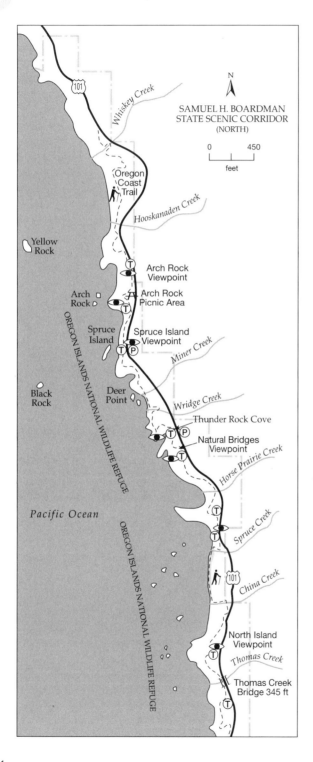

a wide cove south of Cape Ferrelo. An extensive intertidal region of fascinating organisms among overhangs, caves, and rocks has easy access from both ends of this large cove bracketed by hills. The Oregon Coast Trail begins at the north end of the cove and climbs moderately in about 1 mile to the Cape Ferrelo Viewpoint access point and then continues north through rolling grasslands overlooking the sea before crossing a wooded area, a small stream, and coming out into the open again. House Rock Viewpoint, with a commemorative monument honoring Boardman, and trail access are reached in 1.5 miles. Watch for black-tailed deer, peregrine falcons, gray whales, seabirds, and other varied flora and fauna.

From the northwest corner of the parking area at House Rock, enter a spruce-lined corridor where you might find chanterelle mushrooms, if the season is right. The open trail then crosses a sharp ridge and drops steeply to a grassy bench before taking to the beach at 1.5 miles. It's an easy 1.5-mile beach walk then—passing the connecting trail from Whalehead Viewpoint—to a crossing of Whalehead Creek at Whalehead Beach. Near the beach, an informative sign itemizes catch quotas for various fish and invertebrates. Whalehead Beach has picnicking and restrooms. A huge rock just offshore is aptly named Whalehead Island, as it looks like a beached whale frozen in stone. To find the trail continuing north, follow the spur road toward the

From the headland just north of the day-use area at Whalehead Beach along the Samuel H. Boardman State Scenic Corridor, hikers can see the 1.5-mile stretch of beach-walking to the inland trail to House Rock.

highway where you'll see the usual Oregon Coast Trail marker at the start of a path up to an awesome headland view. If it's spring, watch for a waterfall on the backside of the headland. A mile of hiking leads to Indian Sands, which has trail access.

Indian Sands is unique; shore pines edge sand dunes in the process of turning into sandstone high above the sea. A Native American midden—*it is a federal offense to disturb middens*—is seen on the south edge of the area, where seafood feasts have left a huge pile of shells and bones. Watch for showy rose-colored ice-plant blossoms in summer among the loose sand. The path continues north through a saddle overlooking a small cove, then twists and climbs around headlands with great views and continues to 345-foot-high Thomas Creek Bridge in 1.5 miles.

From Thomas Creek Bridge, it's a 2.8-mile hike to Natural Bridges, with a couple of short walks edging the highway. The trail first passes the North Island Viewpoint access point, and then continues to China Creek, before descending to a stretch of beach walking, if the tide is low enough. Near Spruce Creek, the trail heads inland to the highway, where the trail access for continuing to scenic rock formation at Natural Bridges is a short distance north.

From Natural Bridges Viewpoint, the path re-enters the woods, proceeds to parking at Thunder Rock Cove, and then continues on to a waterfall and beach access at Miner Creek, an idyllic spot with tree-topped offshore rocks and a cove surrounded by high cliffs. Watch for deer tracks on this isolated sandy beach. Some curiosity about paths off the main route on this stretch of trail will lead you to incredible spots. Bring a picnic lunch and linger with the view and the solitude while being alert for wildlife. A steep, abandoned roadway, formerly the northern trailhead, leads uphill to US 101. The trail now continues north past Deer Point to parking at Spruce Island Viewpoint in approximately 2 miles.

A short trek leads to Arch Rock Picnic Area, where a lush landscape and paved walkways access spectacular views of Arch Rock, other offshore islands, and Mack Arch. Surf colors vary considerably, depending on the direction of the sunlight hitting the water, and this walk reveals some waves rolling in with a soft green hue. From the north end of the area, a short trail drops down to cross a bridge before climbing to the pullover at Arch Rock Viewpoint, where surf rolls toward a crescent beach in a picturesque cove terminated by a point. A path along the end of the long pullover eventually connects to another couple of miles heading north.

If you've taken the time to sample much of this park, you'll probably agree with Boardman. It is mighty fine scenery, but many drive by and miss the added wonders of the trail.

4. PISTOL RIVER STATE SCENIC VIEWPOINT

Hours/Season: Day use; year-round
Area: 440 acres
Attractions: Beachcombing, windsurfing, horseback riding, hiking, birdwatching, dunes, exhibit information, fishing, photography
Facilities: Beach access, *no water*
Access: Off US 101, 11 miles south of Gold Beach

Few travelers can resist stopping along the long stretch of coastline included in Pistol River State Park once they've caught a glimpse of it while driving down the long hill south from Cape Sebastian. The parking area at Myers Creek Beach has beach access and features a walk along the sandy edge of this spectacular seascape, where it looks as if a giant has hurled massive boulders into the sea. You might prefer to ride horses amid this setting, or stay around for some sunset photography to observe how the sun peeks around various rock formations as it slowly sinks and washes color across the sand. Several additional pullovers provide viewpoints and beach access north of Pistol River for those wishing to hike down from Cape Sebastian and continue hiking to the river following the Oregon Coast Trail.

The park consists of three parcels. The largest portion lies between the highway and the ocean and extends from the river south to Crook Point, an area of rolling sand dunes with some scattered trees, beach grass, and shrubs. The other two parcels of land are located between the highway and the ocean north of the river, and these essentially protect beach land and some rare plants in the vicinity.

Another parking area just south of the river is reached via a short entry road. Although the river curves north before entering the sea, lagoons sometimes form in this area. On my most recent visit, a lagoon was south of the parking area and it was easy to walk across the sand to the beach, where hikers can walk to Crook Point. This patch of level, sandy shoreline includes rolling dunes with European beach grass. The beach just north of the river bridge cannot be reached due to the river's route. The river's estuary is a fine place to check out the birds that frequent the lagoons and estuary. Adventurous long-distance hikers might hike down

Lucky winter beach walkers might find a glass float with goose barnacles attached to it.

from Cape Sebastian, ford the river (rarely easy even in summer), and continue to do some exploring at Crook Point.

In the Rogue River Indian War, the Battle of Pistol River was fought here in March of 1856. Thirty-four minutemen under the command of George H. Abbott were attacked by a large number of Native Americans while in an improvised fortification of logs. After several days of hand-to-hand fighting, regular troops under Captains Ord and Jones drove away the Rogue River Indians.

The name of the park was adopted because James Mace lost his pistol in the river in 1853.

The Nature Conservancy recently acquired the 134-acre shoreline abutting Pistol River State Park at Crook Point from private ownership, which includes a mile of undeveloped shoreline, extensive rocky intertidal habitats, and a coastal grassland hosting rare native plants. The offshore islands in this vicinity host the second largest seabird nesting area on the Oregon coast, with more than 200,000 birds from March through October, a refuge that includes pupping grounds for marine mammals. Governor Kitzhaber called Crook Point "one of the most outstanding undeveloped areas on the spectacular Oregon coast," and added that "we are learning that the legacy of coastal Oregon will not be measured in acres of private development but in acres preserved for the public and for coastal wildlife that is increasingly under siege."

5. CAPE SEBASTIAN STATE SCENIC CORRIDOR

Hours/Season: Day use; year-round
Area: 1,104 acres
Attractions: Viewpoint, hiking, beachcombing, fishing, wildlife viewing, photography
Facilities: Beach access, *no water or restrooms (chemical toilets are sometimes available)*
Access: Off US 101, 7 miles south of Gold Beach *(entry road is steep and not recommended for trailers or motor homes)*

Most people visit Cape Sebastian to admire the superb views atop this headland, but many include a hike on the section of the Oregon Coast Trail found here. The entry road splits near the top to offer two viewpoint parking areas. The north view encompasses the seemingly endless scallops of surf hitting the 43-mile stretch of coastline, which includes the town of Gold Beach and views north to Humbug Mountain and Cape Blanco. From the south viewpoint, the offshore rocky sea sentinels at Pistol River State Park dominate the 50-mile seascape that is visible to Point St. George in California. The coast highway is seen winding south like a tiny ribbon carrying toy cars. Some days, fog lies below the cape and the place seems like an island in a sea of frothy egg white.

The first navigators to explore the Pacific Northwest coast were the Spanish, only fifty years after Columbus discovered the Americas, and it was Sebastian Vizcaino who named this cape after the patron saint of the day of his discovery in 1603.

A more recent tidbit of history occurred in 1942, when fog obstructed the view. A caretaker was checking the trail when he heard a foreign tongue being spoken below the cliffs. When a

Though often hazy, the view of the Pistol River State Scenic Viewpoint and the ridges of the Klamath Mountains to the south is impressive from the top of Cape Sebastian.

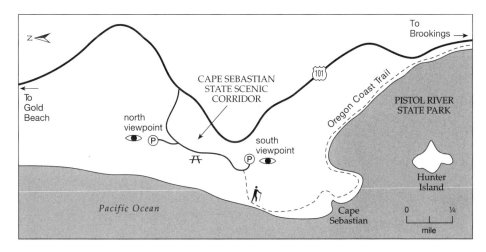

access point. A rutted road leads to parking in a short distance. The property was acquired to preserve scenic Otter Point and provide public beach access and viewpoints. The park includes a spectacular rocky point overlooking the ocean, which is backed by a heather and azalea prairie interspersed with shore pine and Sitka spruce. The area is in two separate sections and is developed with parking and trails.

The cliffs are high and unstable near the parking area, and it is not safe to try for the picturesque rock-strewn beach that can be seen to the north, where a headland called Hubbard Mound is visible. Instead, head south, just behind the railing and park regulation sign, where a trail begins. In a few yards, an Oregon Coast Trail sign branches off to the left (south). This level trail wanders past numerous animal tracks and occasionally wildflowers (I found a trillium) perhaps a mile along the edge of the cliffs before the path steeply descends some 60 feet, using a stairway of old tires and crossing a bridge over a creek before reaching

break in the fog layer opened up, he saw a Japanese submarine that had surfaced to recharge its batteries. He was soon on this way to tell the Coast Guard.

From the south viewpoint parking area, a paved path leads west through open meadows, where summer wildflowers bloom, to the cliff's edge, where a section of the Oregon Coast Trail begins. At first the path edges the cliffs at the tip of the headland, which drops off almost vertically to the water below. Trees lean from the force of the wind, which often roars here. Soon, however, the path descends through old-growth forest of Douglas fir, grand fir, and shore pine, and reaches the beach in approximately 2 miles. You can continue hiking along the beach to Pistol River to be picked up, or return via the same route.

6. OTTER POINT STATE RECREATION SITE

Hours/Season: Day use; year-round
Area: 85.5 acres
Attractions: Photography, hiking, beachcombing
Facilities: Picnic table, beach access, chemical toilet (sometimes)
Access: Off US 101, 4 miles north of Gold Beach on the old coast highway

Closer to the ocean in this area, the old coast highway accesses Otter Point State Recreation Site, a scenic stop usually missed along the newer highway. The road makes a short loop off the official highway, with the park only 0.2 mile from the northerly

Off the main highway, Otter Point State Recreation Site offers solitude and a fine view of a rocky stretch of coastline.

Bailey Beach. The wide beach in this area invites hiking approximately 2 miles south to the Rogue River jetty. This beach can also be reached from the north jetty of the river.

If you'd rather explore a fascinating area atop the cliffs near the parking area at Otter Point, head right or west from the sign along a path between vegetation to a point overlooking the sea. As you approach, notice the lone picnic table strategically placed to admire the panoramic view. Paths made by curious visitors lead to various viewpoints, where you should never stand at cliff's edge. Many of these coastal cliffs are undercut just beneath a smattering of vegetation, and chunks can easily break off. People unfamiliar with the coast have accidents every year; the view is just as fine a short distance from the edge. This is a fantastic area with curious geologic lines, textures, and rock formations, as well as an exciting stretch of coast seen below for long distances both north and south. Sounds are of surf crashing and aromas are of fresh sea breezes arriving from long distances. A little time spent here should include some wildlife viewing, perhaps some gray whale sightings.

7. GEISEL MONUMENT STATE HERITAGE SITE

Hours/Season: Day use; year-round
Area: 4 acres
Attractions: Historic exhibit information, picnicking
Facilities: Picnic tables, *no restrooms or water*
Access: Off US 101, 7 miles north of Gold Beach

A large grassy meadow in the midst of a forested area in Geisel Monument State Heritage Site has been developed for picnicking and day use. A separate area of the park contains the graves of John Geisel and his sons, who were killed during the Rogue River Indian War. Geisel's widow is also buried at this location.

A granite shaft is inscribed: *Sacred to the memory of John Geisel, also his three sons, John, Henry, and Andrew, who were massacred by the Indians, Feb. 22, A.D. 1856, ages respectively 45, 9, 7, and 5 years. Also wife and mother died Sept. 20, 1899, age 75 years.* There are individual grave stones and the plot is surrounded by an ornamental iron fence. The Geisel massacre was the outstanding tragedy in the early history of Curry County, described in Dodge's *Pioneer History of Coos and Curry Counties,* pp. 346–348.

In the forest behind the park, and nearby, are residential dwellings. Please do not trespass or disturb these places.

8. HUMBUG MOUNTAIN STATE PARK

Hours/Season: Day use and overnight; year-round
Area: 1,842 acres
Attractions: Hiking, mountain summit viewpoint via trail, beachcombing, fishing, wildlife viewing, photography, picnicking, camping
Facilities: Picnic tables, campground (35 electrical, 73 tent sites—2 accessible, maximum site 55 feet), hiker/biker camp, accessible restrooms with showers, amphitheater, dump station, firewood
Access: Off US 101, 6 miles south of Port Orford
Contact: (541) 332-6774

Mountain, beach, and forest landscapes meet in a wonderful trilogy at Humbug Mountain State Park. You can explore one or all of these scenic treasures.

The campground is a long, flat area bordered by the beach, Brush Creek, Humbug Mountain, and steep forest. Near the entry to the campsites is a wetland area signed Winter Haven, which is lush with vegetation. A walkway runs through the campground, with the beach access reached by passing under a highway bridge that leads to the 4-mile stretch of beach included in the park. This is a fine place for beachcombing or watching sunsets with the Redfish Rocks and Island Rock just offshore.

South of the campground, US 101 threads its way in sharp curves between Brush Creek and the back side of the mountain, through Humbug Canyon, to the separate day-use area located 0.75 mile south along the highway. A trail from the campground entry road also accesses the picnic area through an up-and-down path through the forest. At the day-use area, the town of Port Orford hides Easter eggs for its children in the lush grass of the meadows edging the forest.

Rising at the edge of the sea, Humbug Mountain is a landmark on the south coast of Oregon, the highest coast point at 1,756 feet. Originally called Sugar Loaf Mountain, it became known as Humbug Mountain after a scouting party sent by Captain Tichenor, founder of Port Orford, became disoriented in the area and dubbed it Tichenor's Humbug.

A fairly strenuous trail, part of the Oregon Coast Trail, switchbacks up to the summit. It passes through a pocket of temperate rain forest lush with vegetation. The temperate climate makes this an interesting and varied all-season hike. It is a rare day in a rare winter when there is snow, even on the summit.

The trail is accessed either from a signed parking space off

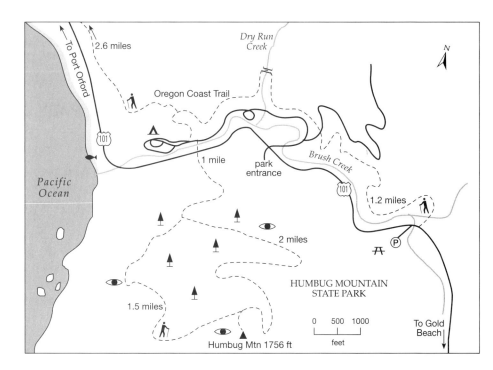

Continuing up on the 2-mile eastern trail, cross a small creek and then round a curve into hanging mosses on trees, with a small waterfall in the distance. The forest is mostly quiet, but you may hear a chickaree scold you, or see a varied thrush, a bird that Edwin Way Teale called "the true voice of the rain forest."

Sun flirts with the forests, sending shafts of light through the trees. A few openings in trees reveal views north up the coast past Cape Blanco, where Tututni Indian tepees on the beach were found in the early 1800s and handcrafted cedar canoes were launched into the sea.

Near the top of the mountain, the vegetation changes to madrone and tanoak trees. The summit is a small grassy slope, a perfect spot to sit with a picnic lunch and scan the panoramic view of the coast to the south, which includes the Sisters Rocks, Cape Sebastian,

US 101, just before it swings north of the mountain to follow the coast, or from the campground, near sites B1 and B53, where a walkway crosses Brush Creek and then passes beneath the highway to connect with the trail. Hiking begins by a creek bordered by enormous bigleaf maples and thick ferns. On a spring ascent, look for flowering trilliums, bleeding hearts, fairy lanterns, vanilla leaf, rhododendrons, and flowering myrtle trees among the huge Douglas firs, hemlocks, and Port Orford cedar. Port Orford cedar—a much-valued wood—is found only on the southern coast of Oregon and a short distance into California, not more than 40 miles inland. This hike is through the last uncut old-growth grove of timber along the coast between Redwood National Park and the Cummins Creek Wilderness north of Florence.

About a mile into the hike, a 1.5-mile trail branches off to the right (west). The Civilian Conservation Corps originally constructed this trail to the summit in 1934. This trail was drastically damaged by the severe Columbus Day storm of 1962 and subsequently closed, with hikers using the alternate trail I am describing until the original trail was reopened in 1993. Since both trails access the summit, choose either, or both as a loop trail of 5.5 miles round trip.

ridges of the Klamath Mountains, and on into California.

The park offers another, less well-known hike; both hikes are part of the Oregon Coast Trail. Take the campground walkway east, just past the fee booth, to a signed 2.6-mile Recreation Trail that follows the route of the old coast highway. The dirt path soon crosses a creek and then turns west and uphill on broken slabs of concrete, with steep forest on one side and sloping land on the other. Truckers dreaded traveling this narrow, high road in the old days, but it's an easy walk. Continue high above the campground and then north with good views of the ocean until the trail ends at the highway just south of Rocky Point, which has an excellent intertidal area, including the sessile jellyfish, *Haliclystrus,* and a small population of native littleneck clams, a popular clam-digging spot.

An easy place to re-access the Oregon Coast Trail to the north is at Hubbard Creek, where you walk past my favorite intertidal area on the entire coast along the way to Port Orford. You can even walk through a huge slot in a beach monolith. Intertidal organisms are numerous and varied, including sunflower sea stars, but it is also an easy intertidal area to explore, with lots of sand (summer only) between tidepools, not slippery rocks. In the distance is Oregon's only natural harbor; all the other ports have

A grassy summit on Humbug Mountain offers a great view south and a superb place for a picnic lunch; bring a book and enjoy the view longer.

river bars. Windsurfers and surfers frequent this area, and humpback whales occasionally come this far north.

Port Orford is the oldest townsite on the Oregon coast, founded by Captain William Tichenor because of the lure of gold mining in the area. The town's name is a result of Captain George Vancouver's naming of what is now Cape Blanco for his friend, the Earl of Orford, in 1792.

Stop at Battle Rock Viewpoint and climb the rocky island that projects into the water, a natural fortress where settlers fought the Native Americans and won. In earlier years, Russians, Yankee skippers, the British, and the French once hunted in the great kelp beds of this area for the world's most prized pelts, the sea otter, which were soon exterminated. Before the lighthouse on Cape Blanco was erected, a lamp was placed nightly in the window of the Knapp Hotel in Port Orford to warn sailors off the rocky Curry County coastline. The Knapps were noted for their hospitality to shipwrecked or stranded sailors.

The town's port is unique; it is the only place where commercial fishing boats are hoisted in and out of the sea daily during the storm season to avoid being capsized at anchor, which still happens occasionally. The port area is a favorite with both recreational and commercial scuba divers. A recent industry, harvesting sea urchins, has sprung up. The gonads are considered a delicacy by the Japanese and are flown overseas to them. Although Port Orford does not have as many commer-

cial fishers as it previously did, the angler will still find excellent fishing for cod, halibut, sole, and salmon, plus many rockfish you probably can't identify.

9. PORT ORFORD HEADS STATE PARK

Hours/Season: Day use; year-round
Area: 96.5 acres
Attractions: Historic Coast Guard Lifeboat Station, hiking, wildlife viewing, whale watching, wave watching, photography, picnicking
Facilities: Picnic tables, vault toilets
Access: Off US 101 in Port Orford; turn west on 9th Street and then left on Coast Guard Road to its terminus

Encompassing one of the most superb headlands on the Oregon coast, Port Orford Heads State Park is also one of the least known, being off the beaten track, a fact to be savored by the few who know it well.

Port Orford Heads was originally a Coast Guard Lifeboat Station. It was an important coastal installation for thirty-two years until its termination in 1966. The rugged wind and surf conditions on the rocky shoreline made it an appropriate place to establish a World War II training station. Commander Odell Flake, in charge from 1941 to 1949, told me about his secret orders during the war. His orders were to secure the coast against a surprise visit from a Japanese submarine, with the help of patrols with attack dogs on the beach. This particular station was headquarters for the coastline from Floras Lake south to the California border. The building that served as the Coast Guard living quarters still survives, and is a sort of museum, though not often open.

Picnic tables are situated in the midst of a spacious grassy meadow dotted with a few wildflowers and edged by lovely old Port Orford cedar trees and other tall conifers. Near the parking area are three possible entry points for hiking; the central and oldest one heads off on a concrete path near enormous Sitka spruce trees. The walkway gradually opens up and is edged with bushes laden with thimbleberries, red currants, and blackberries mingled with bush honeysuckle, pearly everlasting, fireweed, and wild cucumber. The sound of surf is soon heard as the path slopes downhill to a circular viewpoint where the old lookout tower for the Coast Guard stood until about 1980. This is just the beginning of great views dominated by

Humbug Mountain on these trails, and this spot often rewards with gray whale sightings, as they play in the nearby kelp beds.

Two options exist for continuing a loop trail back to the parking spot, both recently constructed trails that take you to more vistas. Both loops are under a mile and fairly easy. Take the path to the east and you'll return along the edge of headland near Nellie's Cove. Named after Captain William Tichenor's daughter because she enjoyed the area for fishing and picnicking, the somewhat sheltered cove later served as the harbor for the Coast Guard boats, complete with boathouse. Retired Commander Flake told the story of what was probably the worst wreck the Coast Guard was called to help, the *Willowpaw,* near Island Rock in 1941. Though winds of 85 miles per hour or more were recorded at Cape Blanco, all lives were saved. After the boathouse was no longer used by the Coast Guard, Oregon State University used the boathouse for marine research. Today, the stairs to access the cove are no longer available, and the boathouse is gone.

To take the return trail to the west of the lookout spot, back up a little and head north to see panoramic coastal views that soon reveal the distant coastline south of Cape Blanco and Port Orford's Garrison Lake. This direction may be quite windy in summer, with the usual northwest winds of this area. Not long before the trail turns to return to the picnic area, a spur has been extended to a viewpoint overlooking some of the nearby sea stacks that edge the headland. The park protects prehistoric archeological features and not too long ago included Native American trails that climbed the headland from the beach.

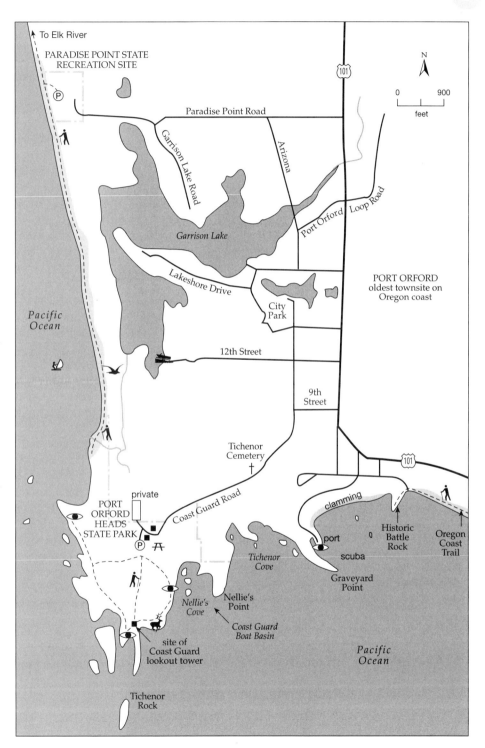

Black-tailed deer have long inhabited this headland, and it is laced with their confusing trails. Often they sleep along the open slope facing west, where the wind is so strong in summer that wildflowers grow profusely, but very small. Birds are easy to spot flying in the updraft or swimming in the coves. Killer whales sometimes pass nearby.

A Sitka spruce tree frames a colorful sunset at Port Orford Heads State Park.

10. PARADISE POINT STATE RECREATION SITE

Hours/Season: Day use; year-round
Area: 12 acres
Attractions: Beachcombing, hiking, photography, wildlife viewing
Facilities: Beach access, *no restrooms or water*
Access: Off US 101, 1 mile north of Port Orford and west on Paradise Point Road to oceanfront (no sign)

Although Paradise Point State Recreation Site is primarily used by locals, the small parking area has beach access at the northern end via a wide off-road-vehicle (ORV) track descending from the bluff that offers great beach hiking possibilities. With the main Port Orford beach located south of the Port Orford Heads, this is a quiet, introspective area, where wildlife sightings can be good. The ocean gets deep quicker here, so it is not as easy to walk, but it offers fine strolling at low tide. If you hike south, you can be below the Port Orford Heads in approximately a mile and a half. Brown pelicans can sometimes be found fishing very close to shore here, and their diving, which seems awkward yet is very productive, can easily be scrutinized. From summer into December, they swoop low across the sea and then fly higher to dive and catch fish in their huge, expandable bills.

The surf near the Heads is extraordinary, so take your camera. Deer have been known to play in circles on this beach, leaving their hoof prints as evidence. Sea lions also come in close to shore and seem curious about the few strangers they see. Some distance offshore are the protruding rocks of the Orford Reef, home to seals and Steller sea lions.

Behind the foredune along this stretch of beach is the edge of Garrison Lake, with a small creek draining into the sea at the southern end of the walk. The lake is accessible along Paradise Point Road, and a boat ramp is located near the western end of 12th Street. The lake is popular for fishing.

A walk north from Paradise Point finds driftwood and sandstone cliffs edging the beach and perhaps an osprey overhead. A fine hike takes you to the mouth of the Elk River, a bit over 2 miles away. If the season is right, fishing boats may be trolling near the mouth of the Elk River to catch chinook salmon before the fish head inland up the river to spawn in creeks such as Anvil, which is quiet and clear.

Most people, even the residents, don't know that Erle Stanley Gardner once owned approximately 100 acres of oceanfront

Fragile sandstone cliffs and driftwood edge the beach walk north to the Elk River from Paradise Point State Recreation Site.

property along this northern beach walk, adjacent to a large farm located along the river. Gardner never developed the property, leaving no trace when he left, but he brought a trailer here to do some quiet writing. It's a beautiful piece of land, but someone else no doubt owns it now, so don't trespass.

11. CAPE BLANCO STATE PARK

Hours/Season: Day use and overnight; year-round
Area: 1,880 acres
Attractions: Beachcombing, hiking, horseback riding, wildlife viewing, clamming, tidepools, boating, photography, river fishing, pioneer cemetery, historic Hughes House, adjacent to Cape Blanco Lighthouse, picnicking, camping
Facilities: Picnic tables, campground (53 electrical sites—1 accessible, maximum site 65 feet), 4 log cabins (1 accessible), horse camp (8 reservable sites, 6 corrals), reservable group RV/tent area, hiker/biker camp, restrooms with showers, firewood, public phones, boat launch on Sixes River, dump station, beach access
Access: Off US 101, 4 miles north of Port Orford, and then 5 miles west to park
Contact: (541) 332-6774

Occupying the most westerly point in Oregon, Cape Blanco State Park includes beaches and bluffs both north and south. The campground and horse camp are situated among a Sitka spruce forest with an undercover of huckleberry, salmonberry,

and thimbleberry. The campsites are fine places to look for mushrooms in autumn. The toxic, red-and-white amanita mushrooms are photogenic; others, such as the puffballs, are edible. *Be sure of your identification if you plan to indulge in eating wild mushrooms.* The cabins are the only sites with ocean views. The picnicking and boating areas along the Sixes River are reached by the spur road to the historic Hughes House.

Patrick Hughes, born in Ireland, came to the cape in 1860 and originally bought "Sullivan's Mine" to take advantage of the gold on the black sand beach to the south. Eventually the family's land expanded to almost 2,000 acres and became a prosperous dairy ranch. In 1898, P. J. Lindberg built the family a two-story, eleven-room Eastlake Victorian house, framed with Port Orford cedar, which had a chapel on the second floor. This home is all that remains of the ranch complex, occupied by the family for 111 years. It was restored by the Friends of Cape Blanco, and is now on the National Register of Historic Places. Open to the public from May through September, Thursday through Monday, 10:00 A.M. to 3:30 P.M., volunteers are available for tours and information. The pioneer cemetery and former church site are along the main road to the campground.

Hikers will delight in the park's many trails. A short walk on the road south of the campground leads to the beach and a 2-mile walk to the Elk River along the Oregon Coast Trail. The coast trail also heads north off this road and skirts the bluff for magnificent views south, which include Needle Rock, Blanco Reef, Orford Reef, Humbug Mountain, and fishing boats near

The oldest active lighthouse on the Oregon coast, on the state's most westerly point, is adjacent to Cape Blanco State Park.

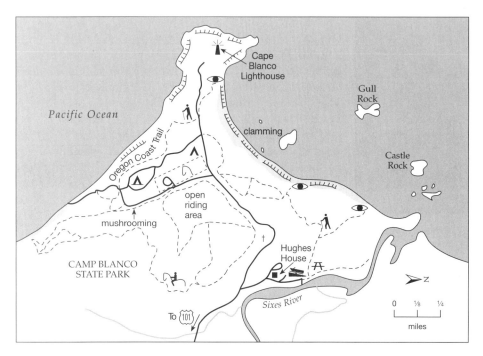

floats and erect triangular sails that allow them to tack with the wind. Pretty when fresh, by-the-wind sailors soon become a mass of slippery, smelly debris on the beach.

The Cape Blanco Lighthouse is a photogenic landmark easily viewed from the park, with regularly scheduled tours offered from April to October, Thursday to Monday, from 10:00 A.M. to 3:30 P.M. The oldest active lighthouse on the Oregon coast, it was built in 1870 on chalky cliffs named by Spanish explorer Martin d'Anguilar in 1603. The original Fresnel lens and apparatus, imported from France and costing $20,000, still flashes every twenty seconds from an elevation of 245 feet above the Pacific Ocean. Winter storms on this exposed point are often the most violent along the coast, with velocities of 100 miles per hour or more not unusual. These conditions, combined with dangerous offshore reefs, can prove a nightmare for ships at sea.

the mouth of the river during salmon spawning. Cross the road to a view of the lighthouse or jog east on the road to connect with a trail that reaches the mouth of the Sixes River on the north side of the Cape in about 2 miles. This route passes hillsides of wildflowers and descends to a good tidepool area and a favorite beach for digging razor clams. Gull Rock and Castle Rock are offshore bird-nesting refuges, and Blacklock Point is north of the Sixes River. The trail continues to the picnic area along the river and then follows the Sixes River estuary to the beach. This is an excellent birding area. The river is also a fine salmon-fishing river.

From the horse camp, 7 miles of equestrian trails and 150 acres of open riding range wander through open areas and woods, including one to the beach for a gallop to the Elk River.

If beachcombing in winter and spring, be alert for glass floats tossed ashore. Coming from lands across the sea, the prettiest of these floats are a clear aquamarine. Quick discovery—which is necessary—may find the indentation left from blowing these balls filled with wiggling gooseneck barnacles. These foreign treasures come ashore from their ocean floating in the same strong southerly or westerly winds that spin windrows of *Velella velella* (by-the-wind sailors) onto the beach. These small marine organisms of the open sea have round, bluish, cellophane-like

12. BANDON STATE NATURAL AREA

Hours/Season: Day use; year-round
Area: 879 acres
Attractions: Beachcombing, hiking, tidepools, fishing, photography, wildlife viewing, picnicking
Facilities: Picnic tables, accessible restrooms, beach access, *no water*
Access: Off Beach Loop Drive from US 101, 5 miles south of Bandon

Three entrances to parking areas in Bandon State Natural Area are strung out along the coast south of Bandon. They provide access to several beach areas, which are walkable for several miles. In fact, the Oregon Coast Trail is on the beach from the south jetty of the Coquille River in Bandon all the way south to Floras Lake, with tricky water crossings perhaps possible at low tide in summer at Four Mile Creek and New River (an interesting natural area).

The many rock formations along the beach and offshore provide intriguing distractions for beach walkers in Bandon State Natural Area.

The farthest wayside to the south accesses a gorgeous beach, but no other facilities. The second area has beach access up a steep dune, but no facilities. The third area is called Devil's Kitchen and has restrooms, picnic tables in a wind-sheltered area near a creek, benches on a hill overlooking the sea, and two paths to an excellent beach.

The town of Bandon was named for Bandon, Ireland, by George Bennett, who settled in the area in 1873. Bandon was twice almost completely destroyed by fire. The extremely flammable yellow-flowered and sharp-thorned gorse plant imported from Ireland, which covers much of the undeveloped land in the area, did not help the situation.

In a more positive vein, Bandon organized a group called the Bandon Storm Watchers in 1983 for the many locals and visitors who find the winter season exhilarating. Free talks and slide shows are given on Saturdays at 3:00 P.M. each week from mid-January through mid-April by experts on history, flowers, wildlife, tidepools, the cranberry industry, and other related subjects. Bandon is often called the "Cranberry Capital of Oregon."

13. FACE ROCK STATE SCENIC VIEWPOINT

Hours/Season: Day use; year-round
Area: 14 acres
Attractions: Beachcombing, hiking, wildlife viewing, tidepools, surf fishing, storm watching, photography, picnicking
Facilities: Picnic tables, accessible restrooms
Access: Off Beach Loop Drive from US 101, 1 mile south of Bandon; can be accessed in Bandon at 11th Street and then left on the drive

At Face Rock State Scenic Viewpoint, a parking area along a circular entry road overlooks Face Rock, a distinctive landmark of Bandon. According to Native American legend, the "face" is said to be that of a beautiful maiden named Ewauna, daughter of Chief Siskiyou, who swam alone in the sea and was caught by Seatka, the evil spirit of the ocean. After Seatka tossed her cat and kittens into the sea, they and Ewauna were all turned to stone.

The Face Rock area has picnic tables and a trail leading down some stairs and onto the beach area. The viewpoint features a scope for wildlife viewing, with more than 300 species of birds seen locally. Several species nest on the multitude of sea stacks

The huge rock to the right is called Face Rock and is said to be the face of a beautiful Indian maiden named Ewauna.

in this area, which are part of the Oregon Islands National Wildlife Refuge.

A short distance north of Face Rock along Beach Loop Drive, and left at 11th Street, is a relatively recent addition to the national wildlife refuges, and the only mainland portion of Oregon Islands National Wildlife Refuge. Located at Coquille Point, with a nice parking area, a paved hiking trail weaves across a level, grassy meadow past interpretive panels and strategically placed benches along the cliff overlooking the beach. Stairs connect the trail to beach access. It's a wonderful place to do some wildlife viewing.

14. HOFFMAN MEMORIAL STATE WAYSIDE

Hours/Season: Day use; year-round
Area: 4 acres
Attractions: River fishing, interpretive information, picnicking
Facilities: Picnic tables, river access, vault toilets, *no water*
Access: Off OR 42, 12 miles south of Coquille

Located along the South Fork of the Coquille River, Hoffman Memorial State Wayside is a small tract of bottomland given to the state by the heirs of Henrietta Hoffman in 1948. Nicely wooded with myrtle, maple, cottonwood, and willow, it is primarily a quiet place for fishing and picnicking, with access to the river.

Originating from the east flanks of 4,075-foot Iron Mountain, east of Port Orford in the Siskiyou National Forest, the South Fork flows 50 miles downstream to join with the main stem of the Coquille near Myrtle Point. Anglers can try for steelhead (best in January and February), wild cutthroat trout, and some fall chinook. The South Fork follows a paved road south past Powers into the wilds of the Siskiyou National Forest to near its headwaters, with two forest camps along the end of the paved road. The area near Iron Mountain has some of the unique flora found in this forest, one being the rare weeping spruce tree, which is only found in the Siskiyou area.

On the main stem of the Coquille River, the picturesque town of Coquille was once the head of navigation for river boats, with clumsy old stern-wheelers making regular runs, packed with merchandise and full of lively talk as laborers paddled to the wharves.

The river's name has been involved in endless speculation about its origin, although it is most certainly Native American with some French influence. An aging Native American wrote an editorial in the *Oregonian* that recounted the difficulties of spelling traditional names with "English letters," a difficulty for

While visiting Hoffman Memorial State Wayside, be on the lookout for Roosevelt elk, which are numerous in the area.

correct translation. *Oregon: End of the Trail,* compiled by the Writers Program of the Work Projects Administration, interprets the name as "small shell."

15. COQUILLE MYRTLE GROVE STATE NATURAL SITE

Hours/Season: Day use; year-round
Area: 7 acres
Attractions: Myrtle grove, fishing, swimming, picnicking
Facilities: Picnic tables, vault toilets, fishing access, *no water*
Access: Off OR 42, 14 miles south of Myrtle Point

The lovely stand of old myrtlewood trees in the bottomland habitat of the South Fork of the Coquille River was given to the state by Save the Myrtlewoods, Inc., in 1950. It is now the Coquille Myrtle Grove State Natural Site. An old, rutted dirt road winds down to the river for fishing access. There is also a secluded swimming hole, with a sandy beach.

Also called California laurel or Pacific myrtle—*Umbellularia californica*—these trees are prized for their hardwood, which is a rich, light brown that is hard, strong, and heavy. The cut wood is textured with varying shades of color and patterns that finish to a high polish and mellow wonderfully with age. Commercially, the tree is used for many items that are turned on a lathe—bowls, candlesticks, plates, and other specialty products—but it also makes excellent furniture and cabinets, as long-time residents of the growing area know. Many of the larger stands of myrtle trees have been cut, so there is only a limited quantity of large logs available for use today.

From lower California to as far north as Coos Bay, these slow-growing trees are found near the coast at low elevations. Although they tolerate many soil types and conditions, the largest trees are found in deep, rich soils such as those of valley bottoms. A couple of natural history guides give their maximum height as around 80 feet, but they exceed this height in more protected stands. The Oregon coast, with its rain and rivers, seems to produce the giant ones. In poorer soil, they are often multitrunked. The shape is often a rounded one; sometimes old ones have a gnarled appearance.

The deep-green evergreen leaves are lance shaped and about 10 centimeters long, with a strong pungent odor when torn reminiscent of bay leaves. Small yellow flowers are produced in clusters from December to early spring, followed by an abundant crop of spherical fruit of up to 2.5 centimeters that are yellowish green to purplish green, with a fleshy layer around one large seed. Visit the park in autumn and you'll walk on a carpet of myrtle fruit. Squirrels, other rodents, and some birds feed on the fruit and seeds.

16. BULLARDS BEACH STATE PARK

Hours/Season: Day use and overnight (reservations available); year-round
Area: 1,289 acres
Attractions: Coquille River Lighthouse, Bandon Marsh, exhibit information, hiking, biking, horseback riding, boating, surf and river fishing, crabbing, clamming, kite flying, beachcombing, wildlife viewing, photography, picnicking, camping
Facilities: Picnic tables, reservable picnic shelters, campground (102 full hookup, 83 electrical sites—2 accessible, maximum site 55 feet), 13 yurts (3 accessible), horse camp (8 sites with corrals), hiker/biker camp, restrooms with showers, dump station, river boat launch, meeting hall, playground, public phone
Access: Off US 101, 2 miles north of Bandon
Contact: (541) 347-2209

Just before the Coquille River empties into the Pacific, it takes a jog south and then turns sharply at the north edge of Bandon to aim straight for the sea. Bullards Beach is situated in this pocket bounded by river and 5 miles of ocean beach, and extends some distance north over level terrain to Cut Creek. Campsites are sheltered by forest from the windy weather by the sea.

Southwest of the campground, picnic tables are spread out near the river, where driftwood edges the water. Only a sandy foredune separates the horse camp and corrals from sunset rides on the beach, which stretches miles to the north.

The park was named for the Bullard family, who were early settlers in the Bandon area. Robert Bullard established a store and post office at the mouth of the river, and a ferry was operated at the location of the present bridge.

Several trails are open to various recreation uses. Equestrians can travel the 7 miles of trails. Hikers and bikers can access the beach by a 1.5-mile trail. A 3-mile path wanders through woods and then open fields to the historic Coquille River Lighthouse, located on the north jetty, where surf collides with the breakwater.

Built in 1896, the lighthouse was designed to serve as both a harbor and a seacoast light. Its fog trumpet sounded frequently. In those days, a large number of steam schooners and sailing vessels crossed the treacherous river bar to travel upriver, where timber and coal deposits were plentiful. In 1903, during a winter storm, an abandoned schooner rammed the lighthouse. The lighthouse was abandoned in 1939. Vandals streaked red paint on its exterior and graffiti collected on its walls until it was restored and listed on the National Park Service's Register of Historic Places in

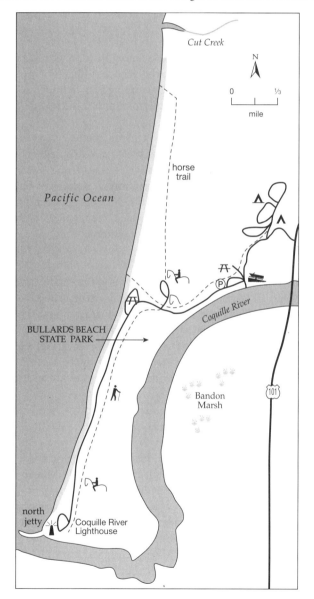

Along the Coquille River, the historic Coquille River Lighthouse is visited by RVers in Bullards Beach State Park.

1976. Today, as a museum, it is a much visited and photographed landmark, open daily to the public. The interior walls are decorated with dramatic photographs of old ships that have navigated the river (and some that have wrecked there). It is a great winter storm-watching spot. The power of the surf has lifted huge trees onto the end of the jetty, where views of Bandon are seen. Volunteer interpreters are available to answer questions and offer information from Memorial Day through September.

Though it can be quite windy near the lighthouse, the picnic area along the river is protected and boaters launch nearby.

There is good fishing for steelhead, coho and chinook salmon, and crabs can be caught using pots in the lower tidal section of the river. Clams are found on the estuary flats at low tide.

This wide estuary at the Coquille River is a national wildlife refuge, Bandon Marsh, with 289 acres of salt marsh. This wetland habitat lures 115 species of migratory birds, 8 species of mammals, 45 species of fish, and many invertebrate organisms. Native Americans settled this area by the marsh to use its resources: the fish, waterfowl, and shellfish. Their numbers equaled that of Bandon's population today. Bandon Marsh still provides clamming, fishing, and hunting activities.

17. SEVEN DEVILS STATE RECREATION SITE

Hours/Season: Day use; year-round
Area: 54.4 acres
Attractions: Beachcombing, fishing, hiking, picnicking
Facilities: Picnic tables, restrooms, beach access
Access: From Bandon, take US 101 3 miles north to Seven Devils Road and proceed 4.5 miles to the park entrance along ocean, or take Seven Devils Road south from Charleston and follow signs for the park

In this rather isolated location along the coastline, the large parking area at Seven Devils State Recreation Site is edged by meadows and backed on both sides by rolling hills with trees and thorny gorse that splashes the landscape with masses of yellow flowers in spring. Early explorers found the area rough going due to the rugged terrain and called the area south of Cape Arago "the Seven Devils." If you've approached the park from Charleston, you'll see what they mean. That drive is also along one of the most horrendous displays of recent timber harvesting.

Picnic tables are scattered about the meadows. The only route to the beach is near the south end of the bluff along the ocean, where it's low enough to descend to Merchant Beach near the outlet of a creek. Walk the beach in either direction, perhaps looking for agates, which are reportedly in the area. Whiskey Run Beach is 1.75 miles to the south, where black sand containing gold brought miners to the area, though not very profitably. People still pan for small amounts of gold in coastal creeks and rivers.

Five-mile Point, where tidepools exist, is between Merchant Beach and Whiskey Run Beach and cannot be rounded if the tide is too high. A link of the Oregon Coast Trail was constructed over this headland some years ago and it's all but abandoned now. I remember that it was not an easy crossing when it was first completed years ago, with ropes along the way for safety, so try it at some risk. If you can get to Whiskey Run Beach, the Oregon Coast Trail continues on the beach to Bullards State Park. A road also accesses Whiskey Run Beach from Seven Devils Road.

18. CAPE ARAGO STATE PARK

Hours/Season: Day use; year-round
Area: 134 acres
Attractions: Tidepools, wildlife viewing, photography, hiking, fishing, beachcombing, exhibit information, picnicking
Facilities: Picnic tables, restrooms, beach access
Access: From US 101 in North Bend or Coos Bay, follow signs 14 miles southwest to park on Cape Arago Highway

At road's end, Cape Arago State Park is backed by high cliffs, forest, and a roadless area to the south. If you look in that direction in the spring, you'll be rewarded with ribbons of seasonal waterfalls cascading down notches in the sandstone bluffs.

Cape Arago is a 200-foot-high, partly forested promontory that juts out into the wild ocean surf. Picnic tables are scattered around the edge of the cliff for viewing wildlife or surfers while picnicking. Simpson Reef and Shell Island are just offshore, a stretch of rocks that often break the water surface and are home to harbor seals, California sea lions, and Steller sea lions—part of the Oregon Islands National Wildlife Refuge. The islands are also the northernmost pupping area in the world for northern elephant seals and the largest marine mammal haul-out site on the Oregon coast. Black oystercatchers are year-round residents, and pelagic cormorants are seen during the breeding season. A pullout located 0.4 mile north of the cape offers the best view of the offshore refuge.

This headland was originally called Cape Gregory by English navigator James Cook, in honor of the saint of the day of sighting, March 12, 1778. After the 1850 U.S. survey, the cape was renamed to honor French physicist and geographer Dominique F. J. Arago (1786–1853). It is reported that Sir Francis Drake anchored in the South Cove in June of 1579.

The park was originally part of the Simpson Estate (see Shores Acres State Park) and was given to the state in 1932. The Civilian Conservation Corps did improvements in the park; a

Sunlit cliffs in South Cove at Cape Arago State Park have ribbons of waterfalls in spring; the cove is excellent for tidepooling.

few of these remain. After the Coast Guard and the U.S. Army used the location as a radio station and lookout during World War II, it was reopened for public use in 1945.

Three coves—North, Middle, and South—provide tidepool and beach access, although Middle Cove is more for mountain goats. A paved path easily leads you to North Cove for a short stretch of beachcombing and grand views along the way. North Cove is closed between March 1 and June 30 each year to protect seal and sea lion pups. South Cove is the destination for serious tidepooling. Guided walks are available in summer, down a steep paved trail and over a curve of sandy beach that meets a rocky shoreline surrounded by high cliffs. During a minus tide, negotiation over an expanse of slippery rocks will take you horizontally to the various zones of intertidal organisms. Each of the small pools among the rocks is exuberant with life of intricate designs and adaptive mechanisms. In addition to the ubiquitous sea stars and anemones, look for black turban snails and tiny porcelain crabs, and try to find three species of chitons. The seaweeds will certainly challenge your identification skills as you move west. Near the treacherous surf, notice the sea urchin homes, circular holes carved out of rock. Great blue herons and seals are often seen near the beach during the tidal drainages in the cove. Permits are required for collecting in this marine garden.

A 3-mile section of the Oregon Coast Trail can be accessed by following the road for a short distance to the north. The final portion to this park has been eroded by wave action and is now unsafe. The trail to Shore Acres is not hiked much, though it is quite special and provides a nice measure of quiet introspection. (See Sunset Bay State Park for a map of the trail and park.)

Few people other than the local residents know of the other trail that starts at Cape Arago, the signed 2.25-mile Cape Arago Pack Trail, which was formerly a wagon road. Accessed near the south end of the park, the trail leads east up a forested hillside. After an ocean view at a higher elevation, it drops down into lovely coastal rain forest and crosses a creek before climbing again and curving back downhill to the road. You can easily return via the road to Cape Arago in about an hour. The trail can also be accessed from along Cape Arago Highway a short distance south of Shore Acres, where a small pullover is across the road from the trailhead.

A hermit crab inhabits an empty shell among the tidepools at Cape Arago State Park.

19. SHORE ACRES STATE PARK

Hours/Season: Day use (fee); year-round
Area: 743 acres
Attractions: 7-acre botanical garden, exhibit information, hiking, wildlife viewing, storm watching, sandy cove, photography, picnicking, Christmas light display
Facilities: Picnic tables, observation shelter, gift shop, information center, accessible restrooms, beach access
Access: From US 101 in Coos Bay–North Bend, take the signed road 13 miles southwest to the park, located off Cape Arago Highway
Contact: (541) 888-3732

It's difficult to imagine that the stretch of spectacular coastline that includes Shore Acres State Park was once the family estate of California shipping magnate, Louis J. Simpson. Although his impressive home is gone, much of the magic remains.

Crawling through dense brush, Simpson discovered this rocky headland while on a timber cruise in 1905 and thought it a wonderful place for a country home. He purchased 320 acres for $4,000 of inherited cash from Jake Evans, who lived alone there in a cabin after his Native American wife died.

In 1906, Simpson began to build a Christmas present for his wife, Cassie Hendricks: a mansion, which was located in what is now Shore Acres State Park. Much of the land was cleared and 200 acres were cultivated. The sprawl of coastal acreage that Simpson owned included a dairy and farm to the south. North of the house, beyond the stables and carriage house, were concrete tennis courts, now being eroded by wave action.

A glass-enclosed observation building occupies the homesite now. In it, and at the entrance to the garden, are exhibits showing the history of this place. The stunning procession of spruce-topped sandstone cliffs weaving among wild coves is the same view that was seen from the windows of the Simpson mansion.

The rich peat soil found by logging crews (once an oceanside bog) was one good reason for planting extensive gardens; the temperate climate was another. Hydrangeas were the first specialty; then roses, rhododendrons, wisteria, and exotic trees and shrubs began arriving by Simpson ships from faraway lands. The meadow in front of the house was bordered by red and white hawthorns. The gardens have been kept in beautiful condition.

Except for a short period in winter, the geometrical flower beds splash lavish colors against the connecting carpets of green grass

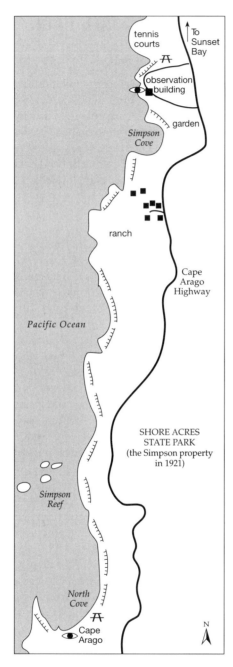

through mid-May, roses from June through September, and dahlias from August through mid-October. Hummingbirds nest here to be near their nectar supply. Walk among the multitude of rose hybrids and choose your favorite, if you can select just one.

Linger in the sunken Oriental garden where Simpson placed ocean-washed rocks from the cove below. Cherry trees blossom near a lily pond where two sculptured bronze herons create shadows on the water. Stone lanterns and bamboo stands add to the quiet, refined atmosphere, called *shibusa,* that is a goal of the Japanese garden.

Shore Acres is along the 3-mile section of the Oregon Coast Trail between Cape Arago and Sunset Bay. You can access it easily by walking north along the cliffs, or behind the Japanese garden on the path to Simpson Cove. The year-round trail meanders up from the beach, where the Simpsons once sunbathed and swam in a bowl of seawater edged by cliffs. Be alert along the trail for the unexpected. One winter day, I walked the trail north in Shore Acres and flushed a bald eagle from his perch only a few feet away, a wonderful experience. South along the trail, boisterous barking of seals is heard from Simpson Reef (see Sunset Bay State Park for a map of the entire trail).

Geology buffs will want to take time to observe the sandstone cliffs and varied formations north of the observation building. Layers of rock are exposed, some tilted sideways, some thrown flat with long creases. Punched groups of holes and rounded knobs add patterns and textures. Take care, though; there are many places to see the geology without accessing steep, slippery, and eroding limestone cliffs. More geologic features are found continuing along the trail.

Wave watching is a good reason to visit in winter. Shore Acres is one of the premier spots to see the fury of a winter storm as it booms high when it hits the magnificent rock formations. A 75-foot seawall is not high enough to contain the surf splash during a stormy period, but the observation building will let you stay dry and see 180-degree views.

In July, as part of the Oregon Coast Music Festival, a garden concert is usually held on the lawn of Shore Acres. People spread blankets and unload picnic baskets as music fills the outdoor space. Music, flowers, and the coastal environment—what luncheon ambiance!

A beautiful annual custom was started in 1986 by the newly formed, nonprofit Friends of Shore Acres. During the last three weeks of December, colored lights decorate trees and outline plantings all over the botanical garden, and it becomes a fantasyland. Arrive before dusk, and perhaps find a fine ocean sunset, so you can photograph the luminous colors and the garden

that stretch between giant spruce trees thriving in the salty sea air. Planning provided staggered seasonal blooming peaks: spring bulbs and daffodils from February through March, tulips from March through April, rhododendrons and azaleas from April

Atop spectacular cliffs with great wave watching, Shore Acres State Park features a botanical garden and garden house that were originally part of the Simpson Estate.

when a hint of light in the sky shows both these subjects at their best. The festively lit garden house, with its antique furnishings and old photographs on the walls, is then open to visitors. Volunteers answer questions about the park and its history while refreshments are served. Thousands of people from all over the world see this impressive display.

20. SUNSET BAY STATE PARK

Hours/Season: Day use and overnight (reservations available); year-round
Area: 395 acres
Attractions: Beachcombing, hiking, swimming, wildlife viewing, fishing, photography, boating, picnicking, camping
Facilities: Picnic tables, group picnic reservations, campground (29 full hookup, 36 electrical, 66 tent sites—3 accessible, maximum site 47 feet), 8 yurts, 2 group tent areas, hiker/biker camp, restrooms with showers, boat launch, beach access, fish-cleaning station, doggie bag machine, Junior Ranger activity area
Access: Off US 101 in either North Bend or Coos Bay; follow signs 12 miles to park on Cape Arago Highway, past Charleston
Contact: (541) 888-4902

The day-use area of Sunset Bay State Park is an unusual, wind-protected cove and beach area just south of the inlet to enormous Coos Bay. Its charm is that steep sandstone bluffs on the north and south of the sandy beach leave only a narrow passageway to open sea, mellowing the shallow water of the cove into a quieter area that warms in the summer sun and permits some swimming, though watch out for tricky currents.

The protective nature of the cove was discovered long ago; it is rumored that it was once a haven for pirate ships. Since those days, fishing boats and shallow draft vessels have occasionally entered this tiny harbor as a refuge from dangerous ocean conditions. The park was part of the Simpson Estate. After their home was built at Shore Acres, the Sunset Bay Inn was constructed at the edge of this cove.

The day-use area not only fronts the beach along the cove, but spreads out on spacious lawns to the south along Big Creek. Shelters and nets for badminton or volleyball are found in this area.

The forested campground is on the east side of the road, with the waters of Big Creek weaving through its campsite loops. The yurt village is located along the creek. To access the picnic area from the campground, follow the walkway that leads under the road just south of the Big Creek highway crossing.

Today, one of the reasons for visiting the park, besides the stunning landscape and colorful sunsets, is the 3-mile section of the Oregon Coast Trail. The north trailhead is at the footbridge at the south edge of the beach, where the trail heads south along the forested cliffs and through meadows until the path edges the paved road. After the path re-enters a wooded area, the trail splits. The left spur roughly follows the path of the old entry road to the Simpson Mansion. Take the right spur to continue along the coast trail, which is now in Shore Acres State Park.

More fascinating geology is seen along this stretch of the trail, with steep-walled coves of striated rock and massive stone slabs gouged, flipped sideways, and stood on end. Some knobs protruding from the walls have become shattered rock balls strewn

The sun flashes a starburst as it sets behind a rock formation at Sunset Bay State Park.

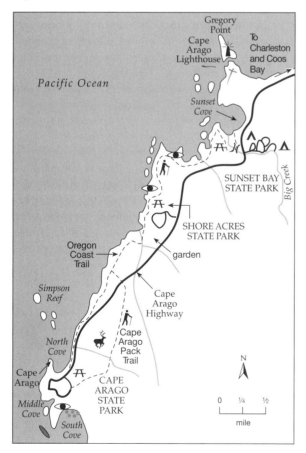

about the beach. Swirled patterns in beige, gray, and gold form steep-sloped rock perches for oystercatcher birds with their red bills and black bodies. The surf booms off the many rocky interruptions in the shoreline, backed by good views of the Cape Arago Lighthouse.

The lighthouse is situated on a small islet called Gregory Point, north of the park. It perches on a section of sandstone cliffs eroded by tremendous surf action. The light guards a dangerous section of the coast near the shipping center of Coos Bay—North Bend. The first lighthouse here was built in 1866, but with continual encroachments on the land, the third structure, 44 feet high, now sits 100 feet above the water. The public is denied access via the footbridge to the islet.

While in the area, visit the South Slough National Estuarine Reserve by traveling south from Charleston for 4 miles on

Seven Devils Road. The 4,400-acre reserve is located in the southern half of South Slough and includes a visitor center, hiking trails, fishing, educational workshops, marine research, and canoeing, which is one of the best ways to see this estuary ecosystem with its varied wetlands. The canoe launch is just east of the Charleston Bridge, but the trip is tricky, so it needs some planning. Go with the tide: south and up the slough at, or shortly after, low tide, with your return at, or shortly after, high tide.

21. GOLDEN AND SILVER FALLS STATE NATURAL AREA

Hours/Season: Day use; year-round
Area: 157 acres
Attractions: Hiking, waterfalls, old-growth forest, fishing, photography, picnicking
Facilities: Picnic tables, vault toilets, *no water*
Access: From US 101, at the south end of Coos Bay, follow signs to Allegany and then 10 more miles to the park, 24 miles northeast of Coos Bay

For views of two stunning waterfalls and old-growth wilderness habitat, Golden and Silver Falls State Natural Area will serve nicely. Be warned, however, that the last 5 miles are on a gravel road and the last 2 miles of that are quite narrow, so please don't attempt

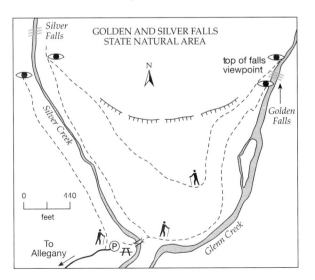

the drive with an RV. Logging trucks use this road, so one is advised to visit on weekends or holidays. Then the drive is a pleasant one, first along the Coos River, where boaters and anglers are out in numbers, then skirting the Millicoma River and passing a series of farms before reaching a scattering of homes. The final miles of the road follow Glenn Creek, a feeder stream into the Millicoma, just past the southern boundary of the Elliot State Forest.

The road ends at the picnic area of the park, a shaded piece of bottomland along Silver Creek and Glenn Creek. Great blue herons feed along the water as it flows over boulders and through small pools. Fishing for cutthroat trout is reportedly good in Glenn Creek. Beyond the creeks lies a lovely forest canyon.

As you hike, consider the road that once continued through the park area, skirting the falls. One information source said that a "tortuous road crossed the base of Silver Falls and followed a narrow ledge to leave the park above Golden Falls." Another source said that the bridge across Silver Creek collapsed and it was decided not to rebuild the steep, narrow portion of the road around the falls. Even in the mind's eye, it is difficult to envision this road. Is that the remains of a bridge in the creek at the bottom of Golden Falls?

Three hiking trails let you choose, or you can easily hike all three. Taking off to your left is the 1,550-foot path that climbs gently to a view of 100-foot-high Silver Falls. In the past, a narrow path descended through vegetation to let one approach closer to the water, but a slide of several trees has blocked the path and this is no longer possible. In open sunshine, the water falls like silver strands of hair from a round "head" of dark basalt rock, though the flow is more vigorous in a wet spring. The water catches on another notch lower down before cascading onto rocks. To the side, another ledge of rock forms another small waterfall. All in all, it's an unusual waterfall in appearance, not fitting into any specific type.

Golden Falls can be viewed from two trails accessed via a bridge over Silver Creek. An easy 1,375-foot walk through old-growth forest of Douglas fir, myrtlewood, alder, and bigleaf maple takes you to the bottom of the falls. This woods is all that remains of the ancient forest that covered this 25-mile valley, saved because it is a state park. This is in the midst of what was once the "Timber Capital of the World," but most of the forest was logged in less than a human lifetime.

To reach the top of the Golden Falls, and a grand overview of the old forest and the landscape to the west, take the 1-mile trail to the left after you cross the bridge. This climbs moderately to a

A short trail leads to Silver Falls, where silver strands of water plunge down huge boulders, in Golden and Silver Falls State Natural Area.

close view of Silver Falls and then switchbacks up to the top of Golden Falls. The last portion of the trail is a ledge midway between huge rocky cliffs topped with a few trees, and a straight drop to the forest below. *Please use caution.* The waterfall cascades down from Glenn Creek into a wedge of rock, sliding over more ridges of rock before it hits bottom. The forest is lush with mossy trees and dew-sprinkled ferns, with mushrooms popping up in spring and fall. Huge fallen leaves of bigleaf maples soften the path in autumn, beautiful artistic artifacts.

22. CONDE B. McCULLOUGH STATE RECREATION SITE

Hours/Season: Day use; year-round
Area: 23 acres
Attractions: Viewpoint
Facilities: *No restrooms or water*
Access: Off US 101, 1 mile north of North Bend

At the north end of the McCullough Memorial Bridge over Coos Bay, it is easy to miss the pullover at the side of the road where Conde B. McCullough's name is found on this wayside. The recreation site apparently consists of an acreage of spruce-forested tract with boating available in Coos Bay, although its location is not obvious. The wayside is a place to ponder the beauty of the bridge over immense Coos Bay.

Conde B. McCullough (1887–1946) was a bridge engineer for the Oregon State Highway Department from 1919 to 1935 and was responsible for the design of the Coos Bay Bridge, as well as four other magnificent concrete arch bridges built with federal assistance across rivers and estuaries on the Coast Highway in the 1930s. From 1937 onward, McCullough was assistant state highway engineer. The Coos Bay Bridge was renamed in his honor following his death in 1946.

23. WILLIAM M. TUGMAN STATE PARK

Hours/Season: Day use and overnight (reservations available); year-round
Area: 560 acres
Attractions: Freshwater lake, fishing, swimming, wildlife viewing, boating, paddling, sailing, hiking, photography, picnicking, camping
Facilities: Picnic tables, group picnic reservations, campground (108 electrical sites—2 accessible, maximum site 50 feet), 5 yurts (1 accessible), hiker/biker camp, accessible restrooms with showers, firewood, dump station, boat launch, accessible fishing dock, play area, public phones, firewood
Access: Off US 101, 8 miles south of Reedsport
Contact: (541) 888-4902

Situated along the southwest shore of Eel Lake and just across the highway from Oregon Dunes National Recreation Area (ODNRA), William M. Tugman State Park offers a base for a vast number of recreation choices. The Lakeside airstrip is within a half-hour hike of the park. In the day-use area, picnic tables dot the spacious lawn, where you can choose sunny or shady locations, and a gazebo-style picnic shelter edges the sparkling waters of this freshwater lake. Adjacent to the boat launch is a walkway to a large, T-shaped fishing dock (modified for use by anglers with disabilities) that spreads out above the water.

Near the boat launch, a 5-mile trail heads north along the water's edge for hiking away from any development and doing some wildlife viewing. Besides the mallards and geese that often hang out here, osprey, heron, eagle, or deer might be sighted. Coastal mountain forest rims the lake to the east.

A pullover on the north end of the McCullough Memorial Bridge in North Bend honors the designer of this impressive bridge over Coos Bay.

William M. Tugman State Park is near the impressive Umpqua Dunes, where explorers can see transverse dunes form in the summer winds.

Eel Lake extends about 2 miles to the north for a surface area of 350 acres and is 60 feet deep in the center channel. Anglers can fish for trout in spring and summer, catch largemouth bass from the shoreline, fly fish, or bait fish. Boaters can explore the many inlets (10 mph speed limit). Swimming, canoeing, and sailing are also popular water sports. This is one of a series of lakes formed long ago when sand dunes blocked the flow of inland waterways to the sea.

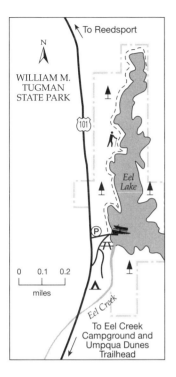

A walkway connects the day-use area with the campground, with sites among the pines, Sitka spruce, cedar, salal, alder, and evergreen huckleberry. Tiny Eel Creek drains from the south end of Eel Lake, just east of the campsites, and then turns southwest to cross into the dunes.

The park was named after a prominent newspaperman of Eugene and Reedsport, William M. Tugman (1894–1961), who headed Governor Paul Patterson's State Park Advisory Committee. That committee made the important 1956 citizens' report and recommendations on state parks. Tugman became the first chairman of the State Parks and Recreation Advisory Committee, formed in 1957, and was known as a "rugged character" who championed wise use of Oregon's natural resources.

Some of the best hiking in the ODNRA is across the highway from the park in the Umpqua Dunes, an area where off-road vehicles are not allowed and the dunes are some of the highest and most spectacular. The designated Umpqua Dunes Trail begins in Eel Creek Campground. For hikers who like to do their own orienteering, this is the perfect place for exploring (with a map). Creeks, forested islands in the sand, sparkling circles of water, flowers blooming in sandy soil, valleys, and huge oblique dunes are some of the landmarks to guide your way. The golden hills extend for some 2 miles to the ocean and stretch many miles north and south. It's a great place for aerobic exercise and natural discoveries in a unique landscape. Photographers will love the textures and patterns and the sunsets. Check the visitor center in Reedsport for other hikes.

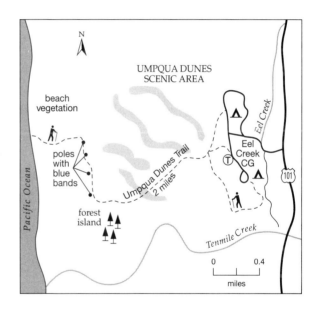

In the day-use area, a T-shaped, accessible fishing dock draws anglers at Eel Lake in Tugman State Park, where camping is available.

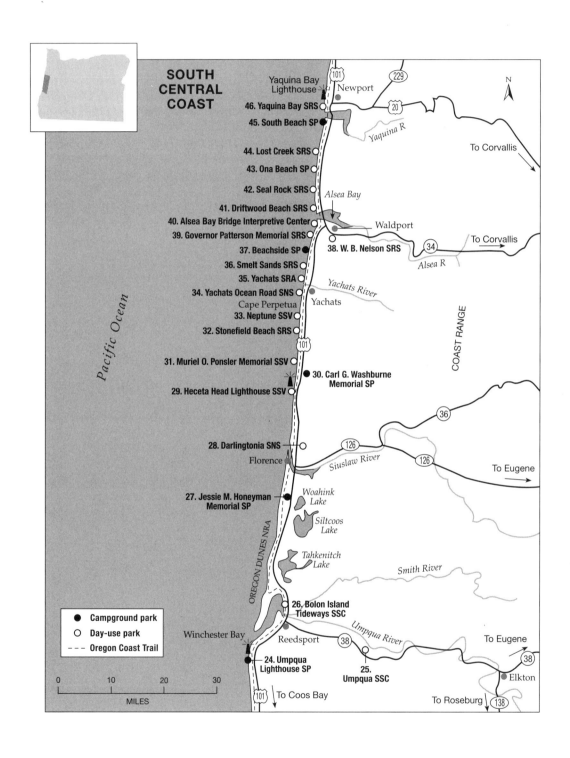

SOUTH CENTRAL COAST

Yaquina Bay Lighthouse
Newport
46. Yaquina Bay SRS
45. South Beach SP
44. Lost Creek SRS
43. Ona Beach SP
42. Seal Rock SRS
41. Driftwood Beach SRS
40. Alsea Bay Bridge Interpretive Center
39. Governor Patterson Memorial SRS
37. Beachside SP
38. W. B. Nelson SRS
36. Smelt Sands SRS
35. Yachats SRA
34. Yachats Ocean Road SNS
Cape Perpetua
33. Neptune SSV
32. Stonefield Beach SRS
31. Muriel O. Ponsler Memorial SSV
29. Heceta Head Lighthouse SSV
30. Carl G. Washburne Memorial SP
28. Darlingtonia SNS
Florence
27. Jessie M. Honeyman Memorial SP
26. Bolon Island Tideways SSC
Winchester Bay
Reedsport
24. Umpqua Lighthouse SP
25. Umpqua SSC
Elkton

Pacific Ocean

Yaquina R
Alsea Bay
Waldport
Alsea R
Yachats River
Yachats
COAST RANGE
Siuslaw River
Woahink Lake
Siltcoos Lake
Tahkenitch Lake
Smith River
Oregon Dunes NRA
Umpqua River

To Corvallis
To Corvallis
To Eugene
To Eugene
To Coos Bay
To Roseburg

● Campground park
○ Day-use park
- - - Oregon Coast Trail

0   10   20   30
MILES

CHAPTER TWO
SOUTH CENTRAL COAST

The South Central Coast region encompasses parks that are close to the coast, from the dune area near the Umpqua Lighthouse north to the Yaquina Bay Lighthouse in Newport. The Umpqua Lighthouse edges the Umpqua River, where schooners sailed upriver with supplies for mining camps a little over a century ago. Sand dunes continue north to Florence. Visitors might be intimidated by all that sand and the conflict with beach access, but they offer a rare kind of open-space orienteering. At the northern end of Florence, a park focuses on a rare plant species, *Darlingtonia*, with boardwalks giving views of multitudes of this wetland flora.

The dunes vanish abruptly as the highway climbs a high, broad headland where a famous sea lion cave occupies a huge cavity in the ocean side of the rocks. One of the coast's most photographed lighthouses is perched above a cove on Heceta Head, with park trails that access the lighthouse.

The highway then drops down almost to sea level where four state parks—Carl G. Washburne, Muriel O. Ponsler, Stonefield Beach, and Neptune—offer access to varied beach walks before another rocky headland area, Cape Perpetua Scenic Area, causes a stretch of winding road and more recreation. The resort town of Yachats (pronounced *YAH-hots*) lies on the downslope of Perpetua and is known for its smelt catches. In fact, one park is named Smelt Sands; it has a spectacular coastal hike edging a rocky seafront. Two other parks are found in Yachats: Yachats Ocean Road and Yachats, on opposite sides of the Yachats River.

Many of the names on the coast are legacies of the Native Americans and the rich lives they lived in this land of plenty, before they were moved to reservations. The Siletz Indian Reservation once occupied 125 miles and 1,300,000 acres along the central coast, but after forty years their land had shrunk to 47,000 acres and the reservation held only a few hundred residents. Some still live on their land in the town of Siletz, inland a few miles, where they still perform rhythmic powwows in historic traditional dress. Recently they opened the Chinook Casino in northern Lincoln City.

In 1991, an exciting event occurred at Waldport's Alsea Bay: a new bridge was completed, and the old one dynamited into oblivion—an awesome sight. The Alsea Bay Bridge Interpretive Center is nearby. The bay offers fine crabbing and windsurfing. South of Waldport is the only overnight park, Beachside, with oceanfront camping sites. Governor Patterson Memorial offers a view of the new bridge, while Waldport's W. B. Nelson wayside is along a freshwater lake with good birding and fishing.

The beach north to Newport is lined with state parks: Driftwood, Seal Rock, Ona Beach, Lost Creek, and South Beach. All offer beach walks, but they vary. Seal Rock has views of varied rock formations. Ona Beach includes a wide paddling and boating creek, and picnicking space for reunions. South Beach edges the south side of Yaquina Bay with trails and camping.

Many long-distance bikers travel the length of the Pacific Coast Scenic Byway (US 101) during the summer. The smart ones go with the wind, heading north during spring and south as the wind shifts to the northwest in the summer months. Bicycling lets travelers savor natural history, with the many hiker/biker camps in state parks allowing overnights.

Newport is the coast's second largest city, with a major port and a long stretch of beach. Amenities include the Performing Arts Center, the Visual Arts Center, and many shops and galleries. The city's working bayfront area is a fun place for a stroll, with its restaurants, wildlife, and many attractions. In fact, *Sunset* magazine recently awarded Newport the distinction of "Best Waterfront" under the "West's Best Cities," a result of research and reader response involving cities of less than 600,000 population. The Yaquina Bay Lighthouse is no longer active, but now houses a museum and gift shop in the state park. Its scenic location and beach access make it one of the most visited day-use parks.

For additional information on Oregon State Parks, call 1-800-551-6949, or check the official website: *www.prd.state.or.us.*

24. UMPQUA LIGHTHOUSE STATE PARK

Hours/Season: Day use and overnight; year-round (reservations available)

Area: 450 acres

Attractions: Hiking, boating, fishing, swimming, photography, sand dunes, adjacent lighthouse, wildlife viewing, exhibit information, picnicking, camping

Facilities: Picnic tables, campground (20 full hookups, 43 tent sites—maximum site 45 feet), 2 yurts, 2 log cabins, restrooms with showers, firewood, public phone, boat launch, beach access (use dump station at Tugman campground a few miles south)

Access: Off US 101, follow Discovery Drive to park, about 1 mile south of Winchester Bay

Contact: (541) 272-4118

In a wooded basin between the highway and the ocean, Umpqua Lighthouse State Park is centered on small Lake Marie and bounded by sand dunes thrown ashore by the wind and the wave action of the Pacific Ocean. Located on the southern shore of the mouth of an important river named after the local Umpqua Indians, the park and adjacent lighthouse have also taken that name. This was once a larger park meant to include preservation of the adjoining sand dunes, but 2,265 acres in the dunes were exchanged with Oregon Dunes National Recreation Area in 1981 for potential parkland in other areas.

In summer, Lake Marie is a favorite water playground for youngsters, who float around kicking on small rafts near the sandy beach. It is also a nice lake for canoeing. Visitors have easy access from the day-use area and parking found along Discovery Drive. The campground is located above the lake, where recently built cabins have lake views. Steep paved paths lead downhill to the lake from the three loops of the campground. These paths connect to the 1.3-mile hiking trail that circles Lake Marie. By turning north and going counterclockwise on this path, a series of picnic spots on the lake are reached. Continuing, hikers pass through a tunnel of huckleberry and rhododendron until a spur branches off that climbs to a dune overlook and access point. A huge expanse of dunes called the Punch Bowl is found here, though this area receives heavy off-road vehicle traffic at times. This is a convenient place, however, to watch the annual Oregon Dunes Mushers Mail Run in March when dog sleds on wheels traverse the dune hills from Coos Bay to Florence. To get to the beach, it's a bit of a walk over dunes, then through vegetation, to the sand by the ocean. The lake loop continues to the south past this dune spur, where multiple springs feed the lake and nourish the lush vegetation of fir, Sitka spruce, hemlock, lodgepole pine, and cedar.

The Umpqua Lighthouse is seen from the day-use area by the lake and can be reached by an easy walk. It is fenced, however, and visitors are not allowed in the structure without special arrangements. This is not the original Umpqua River Lighthouse, which was completed in 1857. That one stood as a sentinel on its sand foundation at the mouth of the river for only four years before erosion of its unstable foundation toppled it. In 1894, a light again flashed from the new lighthouse wisely built up and away from the river entrance to the sea. The light at the top of the 65-foot tower is now at an elevation of 165 feet and is visible for 19 nautical miles.

Across from the lighthouse, on a bluff overlooking the sea, is a whale-watching area with exhibit information concerning behavior, migration, birthing, and different species. An enclosed triangular area at the mouth of the Umpqua River is used for farming oysters and mussels.

The Umpqua Lighthouse overlooks the Pacific Ocean at the edge of Umpqua Lighthouse State Park.

To take advantage of the fine area fishing, a marina is just north of the park at Winchester Bay, where other services are found.

25. UMPQUA STATE SCENIC CORRIDOR

Hours/Season: Day use; year-round
Area: 110.8 acres
Attractions: Rest stop, picnicking, boating, fishing
Facilities: Picnic tables, boat launch, vault toilets, *no water*
Access: Off OR 38, 9 miles east of Reedsport

Five separate tracts from 7 miles east of Reedsport to 6.6 miles west of Elkton, mostly located between the highway and the Umpqua River, make up this property, which is designated the Umpqua State Scenic Corridor. The developed area, at 9 miles, is a quiet riverside picnic area overlooking the wide Umpqua River, with a boat launch available for anglers. The acreage was acquired to protect the fine stands of myrtle trees, maples, and other native species that contribute, along with intriguing rock walls and seasonal cascading waterfalls, to make this highway between Reedsport and Interstate 5 one of the most scenic river roads in Oregon.

The park is a few miles east of the Dean Creek Elk Viewing Area, which was developed and is managed by the Bureau of Land Management. It is a reliable stretch of highway to consistently sight many elk, including fine buck specimens, in the area. Restrooms, exhibits, wetlands, and off-road parking are located near the highway.

26. BOLON ISLAND TIDEWAYS STATE SCENIC CORRIDOR

Hours/Season: Day use; year-round
Area: 11.4 acres
Attractions: Hiking, viewpoint, fishing
Facilities: Memorial, exhibit information
Access: Off US 101, immediately north of the bridge over the Umpqua River on the northern edge of Reedsport, a short distance south of the Smith River Road

This is one of the few state parks missing an official state park sign. It is undeveloped except for limited parking and a hiking trail. What catches the eye of an observant traveler, however, is the highway marker with historic exhibit information about the mountain man and explorer, Jedediah Smith. This intrepid explorer made the first recorded overland trip by a European-American from California along the Oregon coast in 1828. His party was attacked by the Lower Umpqua Indians while encamped on the Smith River, less than a mile northeast of the wayside. Though several of the party were killed, Smith and other survivors were able to reach Fort Vancouver.

This wayside was a gift to the state from William L. and Jenny Chamberlain in 1934 as a memorial to their children. The land was once an island in the Umpqua River, but the lowlands to the north were filled in for a sawmill and dock facilities. The property is part of a tree-covered hill overlooking the Umpqua River estuary and the mouth of the Smith River. Although this island was a traditional occupation site of Native Americans, the island was named Bolon for an early settler in the vicinity. The name used by the park donors for their portion of the island was Tideways. To avoid confusion, the name Bolon Island Tideways was adopted for the park.

A trail leads west from the parking area with a huge stone memorial at the beginning of the path with information about the park's origin. The trail is at the edge of the forested hill, which rises above the trail. Below are tidelands, railroad tracks, and an abandoned industrial building. Some distance to the north is the mouth of the Smith River. After approximately a half mile of easy walking, the hiker is at the edge of the Umpqua River, near the large, abandoned remains of a docklike structure—a quiet fishing spot.

27. JESSIE M. HONEYMAN STATE PARK

Hours/Season: Day use (fee) and overnight (reservations available); year-round, except group tent camping areas at Woahink Lake are open May through September
Area: 522 acres
Attractions: Hiking, sand dunes, three lakes, boating, water skiing, fishing, swimming, nature study, ORV exploring in dunes, birdwatching, photography, picnicking, camping
Facilities: Picnic tables, 4 day-use areas with boat launches, group picnic reservations, campground with 3 accessible sites (44 full hookup, 122 electrical, 193 tent sites—maximum site 60 feet), 10 yurts (1 accessible), hiker/biker camp, group tent camping (6 areas), accessible restrooms with showers, 2 meeting halls, nature center, paddle boats, playground, slide programs, firewood, dump station, swimmer's float at both Cleawox and Woahink Lakes, bathhouse and concession store and deli at Cleawox, hikers' dune access from campground and day-use area, ORV dune access (seasonal)
Access: Off both sides of US 101, 3 miles south of Florence
Contact: (541) 997-3641

Jessie M. Honeyman State Park has long been one of Oregon's most popular parks. In the late 1950s, *Life* magazine listed it as one of the outstanding state parks in the United States. Besides having a campground and picnic area nestled against dramatic sand dune formations, the park has lovely lakes for water sports, trails for exploring, and nature study of the fascinating dune formations and ecosystems.

On the east side of the highway, 350-acre Woahink Lake has tent group camps, a meeting hall, boat ramps, a roped-off area for swimming, and a vast lawn sprinkled with picnic tables. Besides native cutthroat trout and largemouth bass, the lake is stocked with rainbow trout, so anglers are attracted to this area of the park. In autumn, a gaggle of tagged Canada geese takes over the waterfront lawn and wild ducks land on the lake.

Lake Cleawox, the campground, and the dune environment are west of the highway. This lake, though considerably smaller than Woahink, also has swimming, fishing, and boating, but in a totally different environment, with tall dunes sliding into the lake on one side. Picnic tables edge the dune parking area and are placed along the shore of the lake in several areas.

The Civilian Conservation Corps was busy here from 1935 to 1940, designing and constructing improvements adapted to the surroundings. The concessions building on the north shore of Lake Cleawox—originally a bathhouse—is listed in the National Register of Historic Places; the stone and log caretaker's house and garage is now the park office; and there are several rustic kitchen shelters. Stone curbs edge landscaped roadways.

The park honors Jessie M. Honeyman of Portland (1852–1948), a leading advocate for roadside beautification, scenic preservation, and Oregon parks. She was a staunch supporter of and guide for Sam Boardman.

A visitor wanders along the edge of Cleawox Lake, among the dunes in Jessie M. Honeyman State Park.

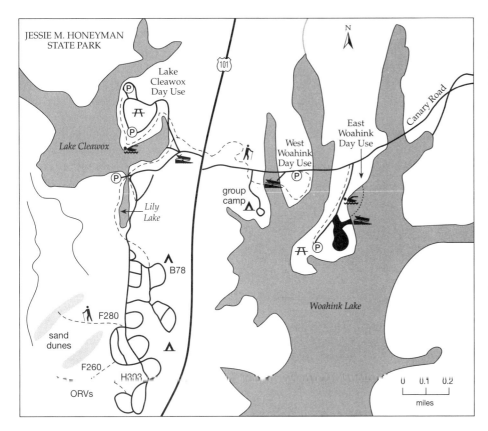

ORVs where they are allowed; these vehicles are restricted in some areas, including vegetated dunes. Most of the dunes west of Cleawox are now part of the ODNRA.

The huge long dune formations that waddle toward the beach are called oblique dunes, a unique type found only on the Oregon coast. Take a long walk on top of one of these dunes where the sand is packed for easy hiking and the views are panoramic. Look for the succession of small transverse ridges that form at right angles to the summer northwest winds, with steep slip faces where the sand blows over the edge. If it's windy, hike the still valleys between dune hills.

It is interesting that the dunes are also a great place to study plant succession, from pioneer plants that grow on open sand, to intermediate vegetation, and eventually to forest. Some orienteering in the dunes will reveal all of these stages. This 32,000-acre recreation area has 426 species of wildlife. Some animals are difficult to spot, but it is easy to find their tracks in the patterned sand. Birds are the most numerous species. The number and density of songbirds is greater here than in the coastal mountain forests.

Different areas of Honeyman can be accessed by several paths. The Sand Dune Trail connects the dune parking area with the campground as it follows a wetland area along the third park lake, Lily, which lives up to its name. Another lakeside trail leads from the dune parking area around the edge of Cleawox to the north day-use and concession area. A trail branches off from this one near the entry road and leads across the highway to Woahink Lake. These trails are mostly through wooded areas of fir, spruce, hemlock, salal, and thimbleberry. Outstanding areas of old rhododendrons border the lakes and dunes, blooming in late spring as they contrast colorfully with the dunes and tall conifers. Nearby Florence holds an annual Rhododendron Festival in mid-May.

Hikers can access the dune formations from the day-use parking area or near sites F260, F280, and H393 in the campground. During Discovery Season in winter, the H loop is open to off-road-vehicle (ORV) users and these vehicles are allowed on the road in that loop to access the dunes near site 382. Hikers should be alert for

28. DARLINGTONIA STATE NATURAL AREA

Hours/Season: Day use; year-round
Area: 18.4 acres
Attractions: Botanical area, exhibit information, hiking, picnicking
Facilities: Picnic tables, restrooms
Access: Off US 101, 5 miles north of Florence

An unusual botanical area located in a bog has been protected at Darlingtonia State Natural Area. The star attraction is the California pitcher plant, or cobra plant, *Darlingtonia californica*,

Seen along a boardwalk at Darlingtonia State Natural Area is a single Darlingtonia californica *flower blooming among a multitude of these hooded plants that capture insects.*

which can be found in sphagnum bogs in extreme northern California, in the Siskiyou Mountains, and along the coast of Oregon as far north as this particular location. This amazing plant is the only western representative of the pitcher-plant family. They are abundant here in the park and make a nice display.

To maximize the public view of the pitcher plants, an interpretive boardwalk and observation platform provide access to the bog area where these strange plants resembling tiny alien creatures are found. Skunk cabbage is also abundant in the bog area. In the sandy lowland nearby are Sitka spruce, shore pine, rhododendron, evergreen huckleberry, and associates. Picnic facilities are available, and many red cedar trees near the trailhead are impressive.

A bog is not just another marsh or swamp. It is a specific situation, characterized by high acidity, a poverty of nutrients, and a distinctive assemblage of plants. First, there must be sphagnum mosses, which draw up water by capillary action, as well as absorbing water that falls as rain. One of the more unusual flowering plants characteristic of lowland bogs in this area is the *Darlingtonia.* Its leaves, which can be more than 50 centimeters tall, arise from the creeping stem. It is the remarkable design of the leaves that is responsible for their ability to trap insects. Essentially tubular, the

leaves become gradually wider toward the hood, which lies just above an opening and has a number of glassy "windows." Hanging just beneath the opening is an appendage that looks like a mustache. Nectar glands are located on this appendage, as well as within the tubular cavity, where downward-directed hairs tend to keep insects that have been lured moving toward the bottom of the trap. The leaf secretes the fluid into the trap, and the trapped insects drown and are then digested by bacteria. Some of the soluble products of digestion are absorbed and used by the pitcher plant.

A spring visit may reward the visitor with a view of the flowering of the *Darlingtonia,* when purple petals, surrounded by long, creamy sepals, are borne singly on stalks a little taller than the largest leaves. Flowers are about 5 centimeters across, followed by fruit capsules approximately 3 centimeters long.

29. HECETA HEAD LIGHTHOUSE STATE SCENIC VIEWPOINT

Hours/Season: Day use (fee); year-round
Area: 546 acres
Attractions: Heceta Head Lighthouse, beachcombing, hiking, wildlife viewing, fishing, exhibit information, picnicking, photography
Facilities: Picnic tables, restrooms
Access: Off US 101, 13 miles north of Florence
Contact: Phone (541) 563-3211 for reservations for bed and breakfast rentals and facilities for groups

Heceta Head Lighthouse State Scenic Viewpoint embraces spectacular Cape Cove and is bounded by 1,000-foot-high Heceta Head on the north and a steep, craggy cape to the south called Devil's Elbow. Cape Creek flows under the high, reinforced concrete deck arch bridge—another of Conde McCullough's engineering designs—that connects these headlands as its waters join the Pacific in the midst of Devil's Elbow Beach. Picnic tables are scattered around the edge of the sea in terraces to provide visual pleasure while lunching, with lots of human and natural action often occurring on this popular beach.

At the tip of the north headland, 205 feet above the ocean, is the active Heceta Head Lighthouse, one of the most photographed features of the Oregon coast. Its name honors the Spanish navigator Bruno de Heceta, who first sighted the headland in 1775. Built in 1894, the lighthouse has a rotating Fresnel lens with 640 glass prisms, mounted in a 56-foot tower

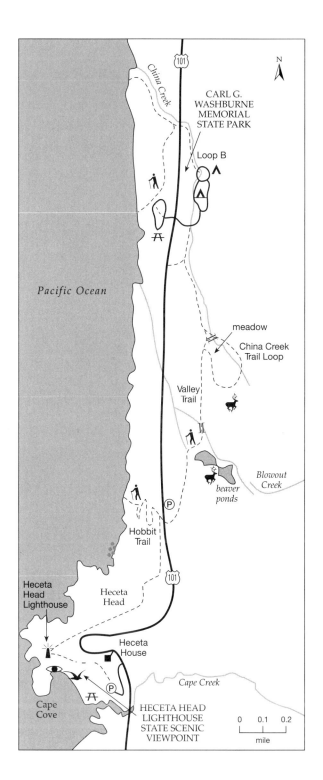

that is visible 20 miles out to sea. Now operated automatically, the lighthouse is managed by the Oregon Parks and Recreation Department, with seasonal guided tours of the lighthouse starting at the beach parking area. The most scenic photographs of the lighthouse are taken from turnouts south of the tunnel.

Although the main keeper's residence is gone, the remaining residence is in fine shape. This historic building now offers bed and breakfast rentals and facilities for groups (call for reservations). Called Heceta House, it is an 1893 Queen Anne–style residence that is now a Historic Landmark. In the past, rumors were circulated that it was haunted. I doubt today's visitors will encounter any ghosts, but they will observe magnificent scenery and sunsets.

A trail of approximately 0.5 mile leads visitors to close-up views of both structures. Several places reveal excellent seascapes south, which include the bridge, park, and rocks. You can walk around Heceta House before continuing on to the lighthouse. Seabirds are abundant and include cormorants, surf scoters, and tufted puffins. A recently constructed trail continues north from the lighthouse and curves inland to reach US 101 near the Hobbit Trailhead in 1.2 miles. (See Carl G. Washburne Memorial State Park for more information.)

The Heceta Head Lighthouse and Cape Cove are best viewed from the headland to the south, where the rhythmic flow of waves are seen washing onto Devil's Elbow Beach.

A visit to nearby Sea Lion Caves, on the headland to the south, reveals some of the aspects of the lives of wild Steller sea lions. An underground elevator accesses views of them inside a huge cave, where they spend most of the winter months. During spring and summer, when they are breeding and birthing their young, they can be observed on outside rock ledges.

30. CARL G. WASHBURNE MEMORIAL STATE PARK

Hours/Season: Day use and overnight (reservations available only for yurts); year-round
Area: 1,089 acres
Attractions: Hiking, beachcombing, clamming, tidepools, fishing, wildlife viewing, picnicking, camping
Facilities: Picnic tables, beach access, campground (58 full hookup sites, 1 accessible—maximum site 45 feet), 2 yurts, 7 walk-in tent sites, hiker/biker camp, restrooms with showers, dump station, sand box in campground, public phone
Access: Off US 101, 14 miles north of Florence
Contact: (541) 997-3641

Step out onto the sand at the day-use area of Washburne and you will often see wispy ribbons of fog on at least one of the capes that bracket the 5 miles of beach included in the park. Beach strollers can walk as far south as Heceta Head and north to the scenic bridge over Big Creek. Cape Perpetua is visible in the distance. Those who search the sands of the beach may find agates and other colorful rocks. Though the day-use area is on the ocean side, most of the picnic tables are set among thick dune vegetation.

This vast park of gently rolling hills—really ancient sand dunes—are covered with Sitka spruce, shore pine, and much evergreen huckleberry, particularly near the ocean frontage. This area has been called "the Persian Carpet" because of the vivid bronze-colored new growth on the huckleberry in spring.

Carl G. Washburne Memorial State Park is a memorial to a Eugene businessman who was OR Commissioner from 1932 to 1935. The original tract for the park was a gift from the estate of his wife, Narcissa. Their modest home was once on the northeast corner of the property.

The campground is east of the highway near China Creek, which flows through the interior of Loop B. A trail heads off to

Beaver ponds and wetlands are seen along the Valley Trail in Carl G. Washburne Memorial State Park.

the beach from the north end of Loop B, or visitors can cross the highway and follow a trail through the day-use area.

A nice 4-mile loop trail, through several habitats, can be hiked in the park by combining two specific trails with a beach walk. The north trailhead for the Valley Trail is by the creek along the entry road to the campground. (Park your car in the day-use area, if you are not camping.) The trail climbs gently for 1.5 miles to the highway. A dirt path branches off to the west, heading for the beach, at about 0.25 mile, but stay left and you'll soon come to a meadow and wetland area where China Creek comes in from the east. A bridge at this location accesses the China Creek Trail, an easy loop trail through a typical inland forest of firs, maple, and hemlock. The Valley Trail continues on what was once a wagon road constructed in 1895 between Yachats and Florence, now being partially reclaimed by new growth and mossy-green forest floor. A short path branches off to the left to access a beaver pond, with water lilies, great blue herons, and lush tall

WILD BERRIES

Travelers, especially hikers, can experience the delectable satisfaction of eating wild berries from June through November as they explore outdoor Oregon. First found, in early June, are the salmonberries, named for their color. Their flowers are magenta or light purple. Ripeness of the berries is crucial, and the reason many find these berries not to their taste. Look for plump, deep orange-red specimens that slip easily from the vine. These are found in wet areas.

The picturesque white blossoms of thimbleberries produce bright red berries in sunny locations. When ripe and sweet, this fruit literally squashes in your hand as it detaches, unless you are gentle. One well-known cook of the Pacific Northwest did a taste test with all the local berries in small pie tarts, and thimbleberries were rated best.

Both salmonberry and thimbleberry are members of the raspberry family. Blackcap raspberries also grow wild, but they aren't as numerous. Their vines sprawl on the ground and their small black berries are delicious.

Another early berry is the wild strawberry that spreads across foredune areas and hummocks near the beach. Their vines spread horizontally on the sand with red berries following the white flowers. They are very tiny, and you need several to get a good taste of them, but the ripe ones are sweet.

Salal berries seem to be everywhere in summer. This purplish black fruit is edible, though not very juicy. Don't eat too many, however, as they seem to have a laxative effect. Native Americans used them often, as did pioneering botanist David Douglas.

The native blackberry, the dewberry, is a small black fruit from vines that hug the ground with many prickly stickers. It ripens much earlier than the imported blackberries. The most ubiquitous berries are the Himalaya blackberries, large, plump berries that quickly fill containers and are tasty to eat and use in breads, cobblers, pies, and jams. These ripen in late August in most places. Blue elderberries ripen in late August or September and are fine for cooking and eating. Red elderberries, however, should be avoided.

Late fall, huckleberries are profuse on their evergreen branches. Small and shiny black, they are edible and make fine pies, though picking enough berries for a pie is slow. Edible blueberries are often nearby. The deciduous red huckleberry grows in moist coniferous woods. They are too sour to become a favorite. A fool's huckleberry is very similar to the red huckleberry, but it has dry fruit.

The purplish blue berries of the state flower, Oregon grape, look tempting, but they are too sour even for animals. One should always be sure of berry identification before indulging, but most of the mentioned ones are easy to distinguish.

A showy white flower is prelude to the ripe, red thimbleberry that will follow, a tasty treat for wanderers.

grasses, or you can continue to the right and come to an observation platform overlooking the wide pond. The park staff initially fought the efforts of beaver construction along the creek, but eventually rerouted the trail and let the beaver get on with their survival. Such beaver ponds have recently been shown to improve salmon habitat. The park is also home to at least two elk herds and an occasional black bear.

A parking area is seen upon reaching the highway at the terminus of the Valley Trail. Walk across the highway to find the signed 0.75-mile Hobbit Trail. A path was first blazed to the beach by those going to the fine clam digging and mussel collecting on the north side of Heceta Head. It plunges downhill in a tunnel-like affair that suggested its name to someone in the 1970s, when J. R. R. Tolkien's fantasy books about gnomelike creatures called hobbits, who favored underground dwellings, were so popular. The park staff upgraded the trail and eased the sharp descent into switchbacks that weave through the thick growth of rhododendrons, salal, stunted shore pines, and Sitka spruce. Mushrooms, especially studded puffballs, are numerous on the trail in autumn. The loop continues by walking north on the beach for 1.5 miles to the day-use area. You can, alternatively, park at the southern trailhead and hike north on the Valley Trail first. It depends whether you prefer to end or begin with an uphill section.

A new trail branches off at the Hobbit Trail trailhead and climbs 1.2 miles through nice forest to coastal views as you approach the Heceta Head Lighthouse, where it meets the uphill trail from Heceta Head Lighthouse State Scenic Viewpoint (see preceding park for that description). To hike the Valley Trail from the campground and then the Heceta Head Trail is approximately 6 miles round trip.

31. MURIEL O. PONSLER MEMORIAL STATE SCENIC VIEWPOINT

Hours/Season: Day use; year-round
Area: 2 acres
Attractions: Beachcombing, fishing, picnicking
Facilities: Picnic tables, beach access, *no restrooms*
Access: Off US 101, 16 miles north of Florence

The land for Muriel O. Ponsler Memorial State Scenic Viewpoint was a gift from J. C. Ponsler to honor his wife. The entry is a curving in-and-out road edged by parking spaces and picnic tables. The cobble beach is just a few steps away, just north of the mouth of China Creek and the northern end of the Washburne park. The creek spreads out in winter to form a pondlike area before it spills into the ocean. The lowland of Ponsler is covered with low, wind-swept Sitka spruce, shore pine, and salal. Initial developments show the handiwork of the Civilian Conservation Corps, with the stone entry sign predominant.

32. STONEFIELD BEACH STATE RECREATION SITE

Hours/Season: Day use; year-round
Area: 19.3 acres
Attractions: Beachcombing, fishing
Facilities: Beach access, *no restrooms or water*
Access: Off US 101, 6 miles south of Yachats

Stonefield Beach is an open, grassy flat on both sides of the mouth of Tenmile Creek. No developments are found here except beach access on either side of the creek, which is sufficient reason for people to visit and see what some beachcombing produces, or simply to explore a quiet area along the river and coast. Anglers can scout both sides of the creek for fishing possibilities, as well as the ocean for surf fishing. A picturesque bridge that includes a walkway crosses Tenmile Creek, for access to either side of the river. The south-side entry road is sometimes closed because of parking limitations in winter, but a year-round parking area on the north side allows a walk along a rutted, often muddy road to the beach.

Tenmile Creek flows down from the Coast Range in the Siuslaw National Forest, and the ancient-forest habitat of this area is so valued that two designated wilderness areas bracket the creek: Cummins Creek and Rock Creek. Upstream from the park, along Forest Road 56, 200 acres of prime habitat along the creek has been preserved as Audubon's Ten Mile Creek Sanctuary. Such streams in prime forest areas are important as salmon spawning habitat, and this sanctuary is a focal point in protection and restoration of critical habitat for salmon, the marbled murrelet, and other threatened species. Although the sanctuary is closed to the public, those travelers wanting to camp in a nearby secluded forested area along this creek will find Tenmile Forest Camp along this forest road, approximately 5 miles from the bridge.

33. NEPTUNE STATE SCENIC VIEWPOINT

Hours/Season: Day use; year-round
Area: 302 acres
Attractions: Tidepools, hiking, ocean windsurfing, exhibit information, photography, beachcombing, wildlife viewing, saltwater fishing, spouting horn, picnicking
Facilities: Beach access, picnic tables, restrooms
Access: Off US 101, 3 miles south of Yachats

The violent wave action on the basalt rock formations along the shore in this area suggested the park's name, Neptune, after the Roman god of the sea. Although it is not obvious from the state park signs, four developed areas are part of Neptune State Scenic Viewpoint. The sign that reads Neptune, just south of Cape Perpetua Scenic Area, accesses picnicking and restrooms edged by woods that overlook a rocky shoreline backed to the east by the steep forested slopes of the Cummins Creek Wilderness. Possibly because of the fact that this park area straddles Cummins Creek as it enters the ocean, another parking area with picnicking facilities is north of the creek—no sign here. This area is more open, with excellent views and access to a wide sandy cove that invites strolling and other beach play. Windsurfers find suitable waves for ocean sailing and wave riding, and they provide entertainment when conditions are right. The parking area is fronted by a bluff with good views for wildlife viewing. Below the low terrace, the beach is a mixture of cobble rock with sand closer to the sea. Short trails access the beach from both sides of the creek for wandering along the rocky shore and exploring the tidepools at low tide.

Divided by the highway, more than 2 miles of ocean frontage in the park extend south of Cape Perpetua to Bob Creek. A third parking area, signed Strawberry Hill, is south of the other two,

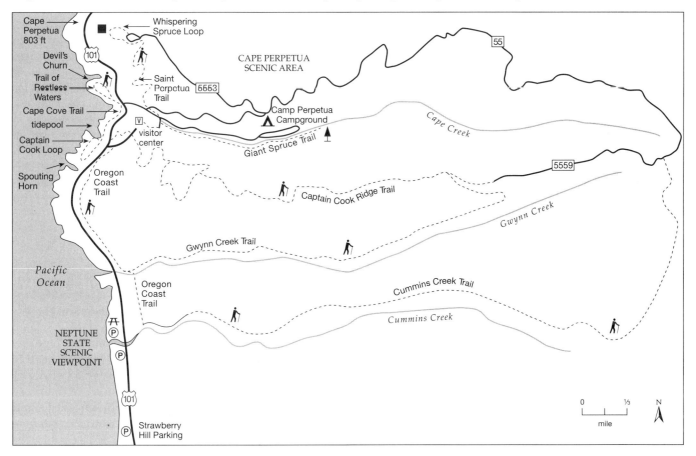

The most northerly area of Neptune State Scenic Viewpoint has great views, a nice beach, and attracts windsurfers, who ride the waves. Cummins Creek separates this area from the central area of the park.

with a half-circle entry and exit road that has limited parking. In addition to the scenic vistas of headlands in both directions, the best tidepools of the park are found here, where a steep trail leads downhill from the bluff to the beach. This rocky, sometimes sandy area has most of the common species of intertidal animals, plus abundant algae and surf grass. Continuing south along US 101, the fourth developed area, called Bob Creek, offers a large parking area and picnicking along a flat lowland area with open views and a longer sandy beach.

Although Alsi Indians came to camp in this area in the summer for the bounty of the shellfish beds and left behind shell middens, the first white visitor to view this coast was Captain James Cook. When he sighted the nearby cape on Saint Perpetua's Day on March 7, 1778, he named the cape after this saint.

Where Neptune State Scenic Viewpoint ends to the north, the 2,700-acre Cape Perpetua Scenic Area begins, a great recreation area to visit. The rock of the cape is old bedrock sea floor (which extends into Neptune) formed from lava flows that erupted underwater some fifty million years ago, during Eocene time. Among the solid lava flows are several zones of broken and fragmented rock. The restless sea has sought out any weaknesses in the rock and made coves and fissures, leaving the more resistant basalt as headlands and sea stacks.

A visitor center staffed by the Siuslaw National Forest Service has information about Cape Perpetua and its history, along with trail maps for the many hiking possibilities that connect Neptune with the scenic area. A section of the Oregon Coast Trail begins just across the highway from the signed area of Neptune State Scenic Viewpoint. This 1.3-mile trail with ocean views goes between this park and the visitor center and is part of the 7-mile loop made by the Gwynn Creek Trail and the Captain Cook Ridge Trail.

Short trails along the rugged coastline begin across from the visitor center. The 0.6-mile Captain Cook Loop includes a spectacular close-up view of a spouting horn. The surf roars into Cook's Chasm—a fissure in a rocky headland—and finds a cave that traps the water momentarily and ejects it violently after mixing it with air. The 0.3-mile Cape Cove Trail continues north along the shelf above the craggy rocks to the next trail. The 0.4-mile Trail of Restless Waters loops around at the edge of the sea to give visitors a view of Devil's Churn, a deep gash eroded along a fracture. Paths provide access to tidepools and saltwater fishing.

The 1.3-mile Saint Perpetua Trail climbs from the visitor center, or the nearby Cape Perpetua Campground (a possible overnight), up the south face of the 803-foot cape. Climbing through coastal forest, the trail switchbacks past views of the coast and ends with the impressive seascape view that motorists see after driving to the top and taking the 0.3-mile Whispering Spruce Loop. On a clear day, you can view headlands as far south as Cape Blanco and north to Cape Foulweather. Along the loop is a scenic rock shelter built by the Civilian Conservation Corps, used as a lookout for ships during World War II, and now an official whale-watch site.

The 1-mile Giant Spruce Trail is an inland hike through forest that climbs gently above Cape Creek to a 500-year-old Sitka spruce tree that grew from a nurse log, now rotted away. Once 225 feet tall, it is now about 190 feet high after losing its top, with a diameter of 15 feet—a splendid tree. This trail begins by the visitor center, or is accessed from the Cape Perpetua Campground in two places.

34. YACHATS OCEAN ROAD STATE NATURAL SITE

Hours/Season: Day use; year-round
Area: 79 acres
Attractions: Beachcombing, tidepools, exhibit information, picnicking
Facilities: Beach access, picnic tables, chemical toilet
Access: Off US 101, from south end of Yachats River Bridge in Yachats

Yachats Ocean Road State Natural Site is a spruce-forested tract of land backed by oceanfront homes along the road edging the river and ocean. Sandy beach edges the south side of the river near the

A daring surfer prepares to hurl himself from the rocks into a wave at Yachats State Recreation Area; he successfully rode the wave.

strollers, anglers, surfers, photographers, and those who simply enjoy the wildness of the dynamic sea and the wildlife to be sighted. Seabirds are plentiful in the rocky area where the surf booms and keeps them on the move. Ruddy turnstones, with their harlequin dark and light patterning, provide a flash of beauty as they take flight. Between aerial maneuvers, gulls line up in rows along a fence. Concrete steps that led downhill to tidepools in the midst of surf and basalt rock were recently ripped apart by the sea's energy—along with coast frontage—but a new route has been built with reinforced sandy steps. There is only a smidgen of sandy beach to be seen in the midst of the many rock formations. I watched a surfer climb across these rocky expanses and plunge into an incoming wave, which looked pretty dangerous.

Several viewing benches edge the long strip of frontage here that curves around from riverfront to oceanfront. Sunlit silver waves enter the river before it flows under the highway bridge. Blowholes are seen on the south side of the river as rocks capture water and then toss it high, similar in appearance to a geyser. It's hypnotic to just stand or sit and watch how each wave is driven ashore by the wind in a slightly different fashion, some booming higher, curling first into a blue-green roll-over of surf. The observer learns to watch farther out as the waves approach shallower water to notice which ones will be large and more dramatic when they hit rock. The lawn on the opposite side of the drive is expansive, with picnic tables and restrooms in this area.

Both salmon and steelhead migrate up the river from the sea. Many fishing spots are found along the high banks and rocky bluffs, and anglers catch blueback and trout in the river.

bridge, and visitors have a little playground here that varies in area with the tidal changes. A few picnic tables are strung out along the road and offer good views. A beach-access path is near the bridge, and another access is a little farther along the road, where a stairway heads down to the beach near the beginning of the rocky tidepool area. Parking is wherever a pullover is found along the narrow road. Local residents probably walk to the park.

The Native American name for the river and community, *Yachats,* means "at the foot of the mountain," appropriate since this area lies downslope from Cape Perpetua.

35. YACHATS STATE RECREATION AREA

Hours/Season: Day use; year-round
Area: 93.6 acres
Attractions: Tidepools, fishing, surfing, wildlife viewing, wave watching, picnicking, photography
Facilities: Picnic tables, benches, restrooms
Access: Off 101 in Yachats, at the mouth of the Yachats River

Within the artistic, resort community of Yachats, Yachats State Recreation Area preserves the rocky junction of the Pacific Ocean and the north side of the Yachats River, allowing public use to prevail over private development. It is enjoyed by mothers walking

36. SMELT SANDS STATE RECREATION SITE

Hours/Season: Day use; year-round
Area: 3.9 acres
Attractions: Hiking, annual smelt run, tidepools, wave watching, nature study, fishing, beachcombing, exhibit information, photography, picnicking
Facilities: Picnic tables, viewing benches, restrooms, beach access
Access: Off US 101, at the north end of Yachats

Smelt Sands State Recreation Site was so named because the beach in this area provides fine spawning ground for surf smelt when they come ashore to lay their eggs in gravelly sand during

A bronze fish sculpture marks the trailhead for the Yachats 804 Trail in Smelt Sands State Recreation Site, where smelt are caught in season.

the summer. Approximately 10 inches long, these fish are light brown to green on their backs, with a silvery band along their sides, and silver to white on their bellies. Spawning males may have golden tones. Dip nets and a special A-frame net are used in this fishery. Smelt fries follow good catches.

An entry road leads to a circular drive with parking along its edge. Exhibit information and a few picnic tables are nearby. This wayside is remarkable because a county road right-of-way platted on maps became a wheelchair-accessible 0.75-mile walkway along the oceanfront. This happened because local citizens pursued saving this right-of-way for public use for fifteen years until the Oregon Supreme Court granted access for trail use in 1986. It was dedicated as the Yachats 804 Trail in 1990 after the state parks completed the paved walkway. When the coast was first settled, towns often platted roads right up to—and sometimes into—the edge of the ocean, not being very realistic about erosion at the coast or simply not checking where the squares on paper were really located. For a long time, a path for anglers took advantage of this publicly owned strip of land.

Beginning near a tall sculpture of fish, the walkway is unusual because it edges the dynamic happenings along a rocky shore. The park is one of Oregon's special places to watch energetic winter surf on scallops of ragged basalt rock formations. Some places are more spectacular than others, and this is one of them. Daring visitors walk out on the rocks and get close to the action, which requires constant vigilance.

The trail meanders atop an ancient, rocky beach that was formed by wave erosion before the last Ice Age and is again being eroded, though the resistance of the basalt rocks and old lava flows has slowed erosion. The sandstone elements, however, are less resistant. Short, sandy pocket beaches are intermittent. The rocks are part of the Yaquina Formation, which is about twenty-five million years old.

The trail is a fine nature walk, vibrant with demonstrations of the tenacity of nature. Salal roots hold soil from falling off banks. Other vegetation includes bog anemone, leathery grape fern, ladies' tresses, and golden-eyed grass.

At the northern end of the trail, hikers can access a stretch of sandy beach in front of oceanfront homes.

37. BEACHSIDE STATE PARK

Hours/Season: Day use and overnight (reservations available); the park is closed December through February
Area: 16.7 acres
Attractions: Beachcombing, fishing, hiking, picnicking, camping
Facilities: Picnic tables, campground (33 electrical, 49 tent sites—maximum site 30 feet), 2 yurts, hiker/biker camp, restrooms with showers, firewood, public phone, beach access
Access: Off US 101, 4 miles south of Waldport
Contact: (541) 563-3220

The campground at Beachside is the only Oregon State Park with oceanfront sites where you can walk right out onto the beach. The recent addition of two yurts adds to the park's appeal. This is a small, cozy campground where reservations are a good idea

Waterfowl are varied and numerous on Eckman Lake, where W. B. Nelson State Recreation Site provides access and facilities.

during summer, but you may be lucky to find an oceanfront site without reserving one during the shoulder seasons in spring and fall. All of the sites, however, are not far from the beach.

A small creek separates the campground from the day-use area, with beach access on either side of the creek. The hiker/biker camp is near the registration booth and adjacent to the day-use restroom. Across the highway is a small airstrip at Wakonda Beach.

The park is situated roughly midway along the approximately 8-mile beach section of the Oregon Coast Trail between Yachats and Waldport, so round-trip day hikes could go in either direction. The wide beach is smooth, hard sand and offers easy strolling and beachcombing.

38. W. B. NELSON STATE RECREATION SITE

Hours/Season: Day use; year-round
Area: 2 acres
Attractions: Freshwater lake, birdwatching, fishing, scenic wetlands, picnicking
Facilities: Fishing pier, picnic tables, vault toilets
Access: Off OR 34, 2 miles east of Waldport

Named for the donator of the property, W. B. Nelson Recreation Site is a small spruce-forested piece of land edging the west end of Eckman Slough, which branches off from the Alsea River just across the highway from the wayside.

Although picnic tables are inviting under tall, sheltering trees near the water, the wayside area is more popular for its birding and fishing. A rather dilapidated pier extends out some distance into a wide expanse of this freshwater lake, where anglers can throw out lines, or boaters can enter and find favored spots where trout or bass are found.

The birding is especially fine, particularly during migrations, but also throughout the year. A variety of ducks and other birds are scattered over the water's surface, paddling along and taking wing if disturbed. If you walk along the road through this small residential area, resident ducks are sometimes found splashing at water's edge. The nearby wetlands are obviously rich with nutrients and food for them. On the north side of the highway, wide Alsea Bay has narrowed into a good-sized river that flows down from the Coast Range. Many birds and fish populate the estuary system. Alsea Bay is popular for its crabbing, and also for

the sand shrimp fishery, which is used as bait. Steelhead and salmon enter the bay to go upriver to spawn.

39. GOVERNOR PATTERSON MEMORIAL STATE RECREATION SITE

Hours/Season: Day use; year-round
Area: 10 acres
Attractions: Beachcombing, picnicking, hiking, surf fishing
Facilities: Picnic tables, restrooms, beach access
Access: Off US 101, 1 mile south of Waldport

The many long stretches of beaches interspersed between the headlands on the central coast allow for a number of coastal parks with access to surf, beaches, wildlife viewing, and scenery. Governor Patterson Memorial State Recreation Site, near the mouth of the Alsea River, is among these. The fairly new Alsea Bay Bridge, however, is an unusual part of the vista from this park.

Picnic tables overlook the beach on the low bluff of this wooded oceanfront tract that commemorates Governor Isaac L. Patterson, who was a strong believer in scenic area preservation

Sunny winter days at Governor Patterson Memorial State Recreation Site provide fun for visitors with kite flying and other activities on the beach.

and advocated park development. He appointed the first Park Commission in 1929 and died in office that same year.

The easiest beach access, a wide one, is just north of the restrooms. Even during the winter, beach strollers, kite flyers, and perhaps someone riding a tricycle while flying a kite and pedaling up and down the beach might be seen. At low tide in summer, it's possible to walk north along the beach at the edge of the bay to Waldport. At this water level, several sandy shoals are seen in the bay, and seals haul out on certain ones. A sand spit on the north side of the bay serves as a resting spot for brown pelicans in summer. The wide bay often includes a scattering of boats with anglers and crabbers, who pull up their pots to collect their catch of Dungeness crab. The view walking south from the park stretches past Yachats to Cape Perpetua.

Hikers of the Oregon Coast Trail can resume beach walking after crossing the Alsea Bay Bridge and proceeding to this park. Except for small creek crossings, almost 8 miles can be hiked, to a headland just north of Yachats.

40. ALSEA BAY BRIDGE INTERPRETIVE CENTER

Hours/Season: Day use; 9:00 A.M. to 5:00 P.M. daily during summer and "spring break"; 9:00 A.M. to 4:00 P.M. Tuesday through Saturday during fall, winter, and spring
Attractions: History of transportation and bridges of Oregon, video, gallery, shell collections, bridge walks, "fishing" demonstrations
Facilities: Exhibits, restrooms
Access: Off 101, in Waldport, on the south end of the Alsea Bay Bridge
Contact: (541) 563-2002; email: mjrivers@teleport.com

The Alsea Bay Bridge Interpretive Center was built, after the dedication of the new Alsea Bay Bridge on August 24, 1991, to tell the story of the history of transportation along the Oregon coast from the year 1800 to the present. This history highlights the construction of the original bridge, which was designed and supervised by the famous bridge engineer Conde B. McCullough, and completed in 1936. The center's displays pay tribute to McCullough.

US 101, the Pacific Coast Scenic Byway, was nearly complete when McCullough joined the highway department, but the problem of crossing five major estuaries existed. Ferries slowed traffic and were inconvenient. The Works Progress Administration

Walk out the door of the Alsea Bay Bridge Interpretive Center for a view of the recently completed bridge over the bay.

funded the five coastal bridges: Yaquina Bay Bridge in Newport, Siuslaw River Bridge in Florence, Umpqua River Bridge near Reedsport, Coos Bay Bridge near North Bend, and the Alsea Bay Bridge. McCullough had earlier designed the Depoe Bay Bridge and the Rogue River Bridge. Many other bridges in the state and even in Costa Rica are McCullough designs.

McCullough was the first to use a certain European design in this country, a reinforced-concrete, tiered-arch structure, and the Alsea Bay Bridge was the largest of these on the coast. He was able to combine function, innovation, and aesthetics in his bridges. A failing foundation and rusting steel "rebar" lessened the useful life span of the Alsea Bay Bridge and it was replaced with the new, dramatic bridge in 1991. For a time, travelers watched from the old structure as the new design took shape. In a spectacular final event, the old bridge was dynamited—after careful consideration of the bay's ecosystem—which was a sight to behold. Exhibits show the details on the structural damage of this bridge. Other historic coastal bridges have also suffered corrosion-related damage, caused by salt. Though the old Alsea Bay Bridge was beyond saving—other factors were involved—it is hoped that structural rehabilitation of the other bridges will make replacement unnecessary.

Today, outside the visitor center, visitors can see the final result that spans Alsea Bay so majestically. Inside, exhibits include a scale model of the 3,000-foot new bridge, a video alcove that shows the history of the Alsea Bay Bridge, covered bridge models, and a gallery with international bridge photos. There are even toy bridges constructed of pieces that fit together.

The building of the Pacific Coast Scenic Byway, originally called the Roosevelt Coast Military Highway, was conceived during World War I to aid defense along the coast. It's a rugged coastline, so this was not an easy or speedy project. Fascinating historic photographs from the Oregon Historical Society include old camping photos along the Oregon coast and one of numerous old vehicles on the beach by today's Nye Beach Turnaround. The highway certainly aided transportation. In 1800, it might have taken thirty days to travel the Oregon coast, a feat that can be done in one day now, though you would miss a lot by not stopping often.

The museum also includes numerous exhibits that feature coastal ecosystems. A few aquariums contain organisms of the bridge area: small steelhead fish, sand shrimp (fish bait), small fish and sea stars, and others. Wood-carved wall hangings are of adult steelhead and Dungeness crab. An enormous shell collection, some mounted on cotton, framed, and wall hung, are seen throughout the building—a gift to the park from Mrs. Marceil Howells. There is also a photo of the *New Clarissa* wreck, which drifted just south of the bridge here and caused anxiety in 1999.

The name for the river, bay, and bridge comes from the tribe of Alsi Indians who lived in this area. An old, well-worn utility canoe used by these Native Americans is on display.

The interpretive center invites people to join their bridge walks, usually offered daily from Fourth of July through Labor Day at 2:00 P.M. A schedule for crabbing, clamming, and fishing demonstrations is usually posted during the visitor season. Call to confirm these activities. This is also one of the official "Whale Watching Spoken Here" locations. The center also welcomes school groups for educational use of the facility, which includes a bridge model computer.

41. DRIFTWOOD BEACH STATE RECREATION SITE

Hours/Season: Day use; year-round
Area: 36.7 acres
Attractions: Beachcombing, kite flying, hiking, fishing, photography, picnicking
Facilities: Picnic tables, beach access, restrooms
Access: Off US 101, 3 miles north of Waldport

Driftwood Beach is one of the many beaches that invite locals and travelers to spend some time. Picnickers will find tables and benches scattered about near the parking area. Winter storm watchers can park at the edge of the slight bluff, unobstructed by trees, and observe the energy absorbed by the surf in comfort. Coast pines grow in the sandy soil surrounding the area.

A path leads to the wide beach, where driftwood is scattered at the high tide line. It's easy walking in both directions; a small creek requires little effort to wade or step across. Sunny days bring kite flyers, people tossing Frisbees to dogs, and beachcombers. Hikers can walk a short distance north, where the view is of the Seal Rock area. The Oregon Coast Trail can be hiked from the park to Alsea Bay and then across the bridge to Waldport, a nice excursion that includes some good birding along the coast and the bay.

42. SEAL ROCK STATE RECREATION SITE

Hours/Season: Day use; year-round
Area: 5 acres
Attractions: Photography, tidepools, geology, wildlife viewing, hiking, beachcombing, fishing, picnicking
Facilities: Beach access, exhibit information, picnic tables, restrooms
Access: Off US 101, 10 miles south of Newport

Professional photographers visit Seal Rock because of its stunning scenery, but travelers pull over at Seal Rock State Recreation Site for several reasons, which vary with the weather, the time of year, and the tides. The park site has taken advantage of a wooded bluff

Surf curves into the cove that Seal Rock creates along the Oregon coast.

that has room for facilities that include sheltered picnic tables among the coast pine, spruce, and salal. Near the parking area, historic exhibit information reveals that the small community here called Seal Rock was platted in 1887 and a large hotel built in the hope that this would become a summer resort, but inaccessibility caused development to lag. The Chinook jargon for this area was *Seal Illahe*, which meant seal place or seal home.

A recent addition to the park is an accessible, wooden platform at the edge of the cliff that provides a viewpoint of the scenic coastline on the north side of Seal Rock, which includes several offshore sea stacks. Any explorer, however, will head down the loop trail on the south side of Seal Rock to another fine viewpoint with benches and natural history exhibit information. From there, a steep paved walkway continues to the cove below and to beach access, where cobbles at the vegetation line give way to a sandy stretch of beach. The park was named for the enormous rock that juts out from the land to form the cove, with its rhythmic sweep of curving surf. The striated columnar surface of Seal Rock is very picturesque when washed by sunlight. To the north of the walkway is a sandy, vegetated hill that is a restricted nesting area for birds.

Exploring can continue with a walk on the beach, best at low tide, where a line of jagged basalt rocks—shaped like sharp giant teeth—are just offshore. Part of the photogenic appeal is the crashing surf as it booms off the rocks; sunsets and sunrises are often spectacular. The offshore basaltic rock formations are the habitat of seals, sea lions, seabirds, and other marine life, including intertidal organisms. Large rocks in the park called "Castle," "Tourist," and "Elephant" were obtained from the federal government in 1928.

43. ONA BEACH STATE PARK

Hours/Season: Day use; year-round
Area: 237 acres
Attractions: Beachcombing, tidepools, fishing, boating, paddling, swimming, wildlife viewing, photography, picnicking
Facilities: Boat launch on Beaver Creek, beach access, picnic tables, restrooms
Access: Off US 101, 8 miles south of Newport

From inland pastoral wetlands, Beaver Creek empties into the Pacific at Ona Beach. As it flows beneath the low highway bridge, it edges an expansive lawn fringed with picnic tables strung along

Beaver Creek is a placid waterway for paddling canoes in Ona Beach State Park.

the water and then turns back in an S-shaped meander before it enters the ocean. From calm, deeper waters, the wide creek that approaches river status spreads out over a wide sandy estuary that ripples as it meets the tidewater of the sea. Shore pine and beach grass grow between the curves of the creek. It's a fine place for picnic reunions combined with several recreation choices.

Ona is a Native American word for "razor clam" and doubtless they were successful at collecting these on the sandy beach here, as it once offered good clamming. In the days before the highway was constructed, this beach was used as an access road at low tide by motorists. The only barrier between Newport and Seal Rock was at Beaver Creek; following the mailman revealed the best place to cross its waters.

Hiking paths lead through the picnic area and along the creek to a footbridge arching across the water to beach access. Many varieties of ducks are seen throughout the year in the creek area. A path branches off from the paved trail just before the bridge crossing that provides an access for anglers. In autumn, vivid-red amanita mushrooms are seen in this area.

The wide beach stretches south for a couple of miles to Seal Rock. Chunks of rock, some shaped like bowling balls, have been tossed onto the beach and cause sunlit pools of water to accumulate where sea gulls float about. Children have fun where the creek meets the sea, sometimes trying to raft about at the edge of the sea. Strollers can head south to the picturesque sea rocks below enormous Seal Rock. The walk is backed by tall, crumbling cliffs of pocked sandstone with precarious homes perched on top.

Sanderlings rush along at the edge of the surf as they feed. During spring and fall migrations, these birds are often present in large numbers. In autumn, brown pelicans wing south swiftly as they alternately skim and dive into the sea and then repeat the curving up-and-down process. At the same time, Canada geese head south in V-formation.

The beach is vastly different in winter and summer. In winter, rocky terraces are exposed as the sand moves offshore and these are speckled with tidepools at low tide. Then it is an interesting, though more difficult walk to maneuver past the changing, rock surfaces. In summer, when sand covers the rock terraces, it's a sandy beach with only a small number of rocks projecting above the deep sand.

Paddlers can easily play in the placid creek. Fishers will find the boat launch on the east side of the highway. River otters are occasionally spotted there.

The Oregon Coast Trail is on the beach from Newport to Seal Rock if the hiker wants to do the entire 8-mile section. If the tide is in, a quick jog to the highway, rather than crossing the creek, provides an interesting diversion through the park before reaccessing the beach.

44. LOST CREEK STATE RECREATION SITE

Hours/Season: Day use; year-round
Area: 34 acres
Activities: Picnicking, surf fishing, beachcombing, wildlife viewing
Facilities: Picnic tables, beach access, vault toilets, *no water*
Access: Off US 101, 7 miles south of Newport

Lost Creek State Recreation Site capitalizes on having access to a long, straight stretch of sandy beach. From the large parking area situated on an ocean bluff, a path drops downhill past oceanfront picnic sites to views of Yaquina Head and Seal Rock in the distance. Lost Creek enters the Pacific at the terminus of the path. Though there are no sea stacks to enhance the view, fishing boats dot the ocean frequently, brown pelicans may glide above the surf, and wave watching is always enticing, particularly in the fall and winter months.

This narrow strip of park shoreland occupies both sides of the highway and includes a portion of the right-of-way of the abandoned Pacific Spruce Corporation Railway. The need for lightweight spruce timber in building aircraft during World War I precipitated the harvest of Sitka spruce along the Pacific Northwest coast. Several railroads were built to transport the logs. This particular railroad was in operation from 1918 to 1920 and ran from Yaquina Bay to south of Waldport.

Lost Creek State Recreation Site is along a beach section of the Oregon Coast Trail that can be hiked on the sand from the south jetty of Yaquina Bay to Beaver Creek in Ona Beach State Park. Those who want to hike the long distance as shorter hikes will appreciate this access point.

45. SOUTH BEACH STATE PARK

Hours/Season: Day use and overnight (reservations available); year-round
Area: 434 acres
Attractions: Nature trail, beachcombing, agate hunting, fishing, clamming, crabbing, hiking, views of bay and lighthouse, picnicking, camping
Facilities: Picnic tables, beach access, campground (238 electrical, 6 primitive sites—maximum site 60 feet), 16 accessible yurts, group tent (3 areas), hiker/biker camp, restrooms with showers, meeting hall, dump station, program area, firewood, volleyball and basketball courts, play area, horseshoe pits, yurt visitor center, gift shop, public phones
Access: Off US 101, 2 miles south of Newport
Contact: (541) 867-4715

South Beach State Park offers a camping base that is close to lots of action and recreation in its location on the southern edge of Yaquina Bay. The south jetty and a long stretch of sandy beach form the north and west sides of the park. Between the high beach foredune and campground are vast areas of marshes, wetland ponds, grassy meadows, and trees that shelter campers from winter winds and provide summer warmth. Though the large wetland ponds become dry during the summer, they offer large waterways for ducks in spring and fun for birders.

A few picnic tables are found at the day-use area, where it is only a short climb over the foredune to good walking on the beach in both directions. To the north, the south jetty of Yaquina Bay is only a mile away and, at low tide, passes the remains of a beached fishing boat, which intertidal organisms have selected as habitat. A short walk east along the dirt road edging the jetty

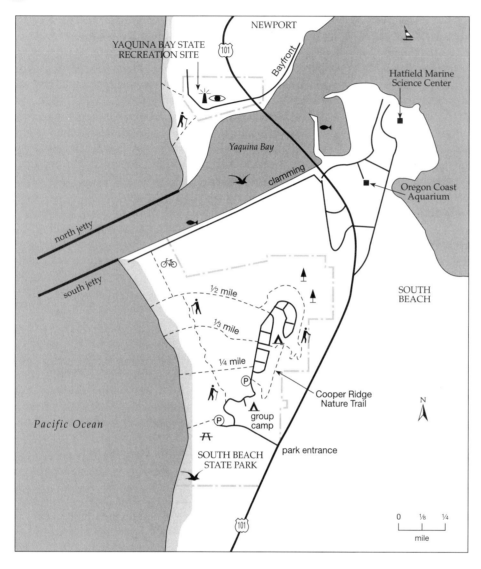

NEWPORT

YAQUINA BAY STATE
RECREATION SITE

Hatfield Marine
Science Center

Yaquina Bay

clamming

Oregon Coast
Aquarium

north jetty

south jetty

SOUTH
BEACH

½ mile

⅓ mile

¼ mile

Pacific Ocean

Cooper Ridge
Nature Trail

N

group
camp

SOUTH BEACH
STATE PARK

park entrance

0   ⅛   ¼

mile

the Yaquina Bay Bridge, Yaquina Bay Lighthouse, and Yaquina Head Lighthouse to the north, all framed by the waters of the river and the ocean. Each of these beach-access trails is crossed by the paved walking/bicycling path.

The 1-mile Cooper Ridge Nature Trail begins near the registration booth of the campground and winds through a young forest of shore pine and spruce, thickly packed with rhododendrons, salal, and evergreen huckleberry. The land along this trail is rolling country, constantly going up and down, so one gets some aerobic exercise. A couple of wetland ponds are glimpsed through the trees. Many side trails go to different loops of the campground, and it gets a little confusing. The park staff puts signs along the nature trail but they keep getting removed. The Cooper Ridge Nature Trail can be also be reached by a trail from the jetty, where parking is available, though it takes a bit of exploring to hike it.

The beach near the south jetty was used as a life-saving station in the late 1800s. Visitors found it exciting to watch the lifesavers practice their maneuvers in the surf, but this dangerous sea coast also demanded some real rescue work. The unexpected has a way of happening on Oregon's wild coast. During the winter of 1993, a large commercial shrimp boat ran aground near

offers views of boats going to and from the Port of Newport, birds and marine mammals, and rocks where anglers can toss out a line. This walk soon accesses a wide, paved walking/bicycling path that heads back to the day-use area for a loop trail option. A separate horse path from the jetty area accesses the beach. South of the day-use area are 8 miles of beach walking on the Oregon Coast Trail to Beaver Creek.

In the campground area, three pathways lead from the campground to the beach, ranging from to mile. The most northerly, and longest, path has a panoramic view that includes

the day-use area, but is no longer there.

The bay offers a possible harvest of Dungeness crabs, salmon, ling cod, sea bass, and perch. Gaper, butter, and cockle clams are found at low tide, plus a small population of razor clams on the beach south of the jetty. Check with the locals for the best spots. Charter boats and crab pot rentals are available at the Newport marina. Sailboats are numerous on fine days in the bay—some heading out under the bridge to the ocean—and races are often held on summer weekends.

Just across the highway from the park is the Hatfield Marine

The walkway from South Beach State Park to the south jetty offers views of sailboats and commercial fishing boats going to sea, as well as good birding. Campers can charter a boat for fishing or whale watching at the nearby marina.

Science Center (HMSC), an affiliate of Oregon State University, with research facilities and a renovated public wing with aquariums and interpretive exhibits on marine research projects. The chaos machine is particularly fascinating. This is your chance to touch a live octopus, watch it change color, and perhaps see it devour a crab. The touch pool is popular because of its hands-on aspect. Feel the surface of sea stars, watch giant green anemones contract at your touch, or pet one of the fish. The many exhibits will increase your knowledge of coastal environments and how to be a good steward of its resources.

Near the HMSC is a world-class interpretive center, the Oregon Coast Aquarium. On 23 acres along the Yaquina Bay Estuary, the aquarium theme, or "storyline," allows visitors to follow the journey of a drop of rain from the coastal mountains to the ocean. Inside the 40,000-square-foot building, four galleries are filled with the lives and sounds of sandy shores, rocky shores, coastal waters, and wetlands, plus the Whale Theater. Outdoor exhibits are set in forest, cliffs, bluffs, and beaches where you will find a trout-filled mountain stream, a sea otter pool, an octopus in its cave, seals and sea lions, a wave-raked tidepool, and a vast walk-through aviary of seabirds. Although the charismatic killer whale, Keiko, is now gone from the aquarium and returned to the sea, new exhibits continue to be added. The "Passages of the Deep" is an exciting addition, with a clear underwater tunnel that lets visitors walk in an environment surrounded by sharks, rays, and thousands of other fantastic fish, then past a shipwreck, and through surging surf.

46. YAQUINA BAY STATE RECREATION SITE

Hours/Season: Day use; year-round
Area: 36 acres
Attractions: Historic lighthouse, beachcombing, birdwatching, fishing, kite flying, hiking, photography, wildlife viewing, picnicking
Facilities: Picnic tables, museum and interpretive store, restrooms, exhibit information, beach access, play area
Access: Off US 101 in Newport, at north end of bridge over Yaquina Bay
Contact: (541) 265-5679

Several aspects of this park have made Yaquina Bay State Recreation Site one of Oregon's most visited state parks. One reason is the splendid location in a popular coastal city, where it occupies a 100-foot bluff overlooking the merging of the Yaquina Bay with the Pacific Ocean, so there is easy access to wave watching, beachcombing, and bay fishing. The restored lighthouse is the icing on the cake that pulls in even more people. Even a winter weekend finds the parking lot and the lighthouse full of visitors.

Picnic tables are scattered among the shore pine and spruce woods edging the lighthouse. Walkways meander north to a play area and gently climb to the lighthouse if you choose to avoid the stairs in front of the lighthouse. In fact, walkways lead to many private spots set amid a jungle of rhododendron and salal vegetation, and then disperse into the residential area of Newport, but most visitors are too intrigued by attractions of the ocean and bay to explore these paths. Exhibits overlook the view and parking area that edges the bluff. This steep bluff overlooking the sea is one of the official whale-watch sites during migration times. It is also a great spot for watching winter storms from your car.

Two paved stair-step walkways lead down to an expanse of low windblown sand dunes, piled up by the obstruction of the north jetty, and to the ocean. It's fun to watch ships going to and fro between the bay and the ocean. Besides sailboats and sport-fishing boats, the astute observer will pick out the various types of commercial fishing boats that include bottom trawlers, double-rigged shrimpers, longliners, and salmon trollers with their outstretched arms. What you see will depend on the weather and ocean conditions.

In 2001, an octagonal structure was constructed as a Fishermen's Memorial Sanctuary in the park. The interior is similar to an amphitheater, with rows of seats facing front where a large desklike affair, at which a speaker could stand, is fronted with the names of those lost at sea, a tragic element that can occur in the lives of commercial fishers on this often stormy coast. Four east-facing sides are open, but protected by the adjacent woods and the tall ceiling complete with skylight. Four-windowed sides facing the sea are enclosed, a nice tribute to courageous workers.

The original lighthouse was not a success story. Erected in 1871, when carpenters were paid fifty cents an hour for its construction, it was soon realized that Yaquina Head, 3 miles to the north, blocked the light for ships past that point. After a lighthouse was built on that headland, the Yaquina Bay Lighthouse was abandoned in 1874, only three years after its construction.

After the lighthouse keepers moved out, the building stood empty for fourteen years until it was used as living quarters by the Army Corps of Engineers while constructing the north jetty of Yaquina Bay. Later the U.S. Life Saving Service (now known as the U.S. Coast Guard) used the building as both a lookout station and living quarters until 1933. In 1934, the area surrounding the lighthouse was given to the state by the U.S. Lighthouse Service. Ignoring the building, the day-use area of the state park was developed by the Civilian Conservation Corps.

Several years later, the state scheduled removal of the lighthouse for safety reasons, but with the active participation of local historians and the formation of the Lincoln County Historical Society, aided by the Oregon Historical Society, the lighthouse was preserved as a historical landmark. For many years, it was leased to the society as a county museum. In 1974, however, a visit by state park personnel made them realize that the lighthouse should be preserved and renovated for its historical value.

The renovated lighthouse is the only surviving one in Oregon of its type. Rather than building a separate house for the light-keeper's family, which was the usual plan, this light was perched above the house structure, a majestic Cape Cod design. Many of the rooms on the first and second floors have been nicely done with furnishings that seem appropriate to that period. Incredible ocean and bay views are seen from most rooms. The narrow, winding stairs to the third floor access the watchroom, where the lightkeeper was on duty, climbing up the ladder to tend the light as needed from that small cubbyhole. The basement houses the gift shop. Volunteers answer questions and show a video. Exhibits include actual Coast Guard apparel plus drawings, photos, and information about all coastal lighthouses, old ships and wrecks, wildlife, and Coast Guard drills. This is supposedly the oldest surviving building in Newport.

The lighthouse museum is open daily from 11:00 A.M. to 5:00 P.M. from Memorial Day through September, and from 12 noon to 4:00 P.M. on weekends during the winter. In the past, the lighthouse has donned colored lights on its exterior and a special indoor gathering celebrates the Christmas season. Because of structural concerns, future lighting may be discontinued. A high viewing tower in front of the old lighthouse was built in 1936.

Beachcombers can walk the beach north all the way to Yaquina Head, with only a few creeks to cross, which is easiest at low tide during summer. To visit Newport's working bayfront, with many new murals adorning buildings, it's a short walk from the park east edging the water and the Yaquina Bay Bridge. No other port on Oregon's coast matches the ambiance of this stroll. The smells are of the sea and the fishing industry with boats unloading their catch. Sea lions dive for fish debris in the bay; gulls and brown pelicans join in the action. Great blue herons, loons, ducks, cormorants, and a variety of seabirds are often spotted in the bay, which also offers fine crabbing, so you might want to try it, or go clamming on the south side of the bay. During the spring, killer whales sometimes enter the bay. Upriver is oyster country, the marine resource that was responsible for the founding of this city. Art galleries are numerous along this walk, with crafts and paintings of remarkable quality. The smell of fish and chips is in the air, and people stroll around with ice cream cones. Restaurant choices are many, with seafood naturally the specialty. Docks access the fleet of commercial boats along the walk, and sailboat slips and charter boats front the Embarcadero, where the walk ends.

The unique lighthouse built above living quarters at Yaquina Bay State Recreation Site is no longer active and is now a renovated museum for park visitors.

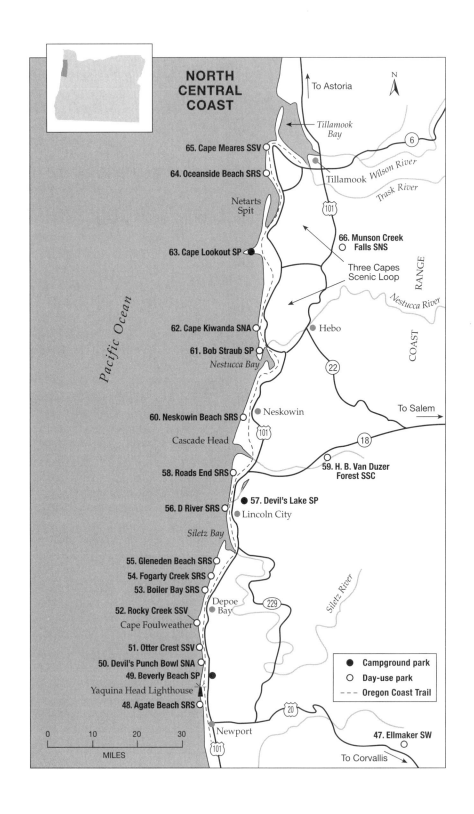

NORTH CENTRAL COAST

To Astoria

N

Tillamook Bay

6

65. Cape Meares SSV

64. Oceanside Beach SRS

Tillamook *Wilson River*

Trask River

Netarts Spit

101

66. Munson Creek Falls SNS

RANGE

63. Cape Lookout SP

Three Capes Scenic Loop

Nestucca River

62. Cape Kiwanda SNA

Hebo

COAST

61. Bob Straub SP

Pacific Ocean

Nestucca Bay

22

60. Neskowin Beach SRS

Neskowin

To Salem

101

Cascade Head

18

59. H. B. Van Duzer Forest SSC

58. Roads End SRS

57. Devil's Lake SP

56. D River SRS

Lincoln City

Siletz Bay

55. Gleneden Beach SRS

Siletz River

54. Fogarty Creek SRS

53. Boiler Bay SRS

Depoe Bay

229

52. Rocky Creek SSV

Cape Foulweather

51. Otter Crest SSV

50. Devil's Punch Bowl SNA

49. Beverly Beach SP

Yaquina Head Lighthouse

● **Campground park**

○ **Day-use park**

--- **Oregon Coast Trail**

48. Agate Beach SRS

20

Newport

47. Ellmaker SW

0   10   20   30

MILES

101

To Corvallis

CHAPTER THREE

NORTH CENTRAL COAST

From the northern edge of Newport, the North Central Coast region reaches north to the Tillamook Bay area. Inland, it includes a highway wayside at Ellmaker, a highway forest corridor at H. B. Van Duzer, the tallest waterfall in the Coast Range at Munson Creek Falls, and numerous salmon-rich rivers. Coastal parks, however, dominate the region, each with its own distinctive allure. Agates can be found on the beach below the Yaquina Head Lighthouse at Agate Beach while camping at Beverly Beach campground, where a forest nature trail edges Spencer Creek.

Atop Cape Foulweather, the Devil's Punch Bowl—named after an unusual geologic formation—is a coastal park with an outstanding marine garden. Otter Crest features a coastal viewpoint from this cape named by Captain Cook while exploring the coast. It is not difficult to guess what the day was like, but rain along the coast does have pluses. Trees and vegetation are lush and green. Mushrooms abound. Groups of enthusiasts get together to learn safe species for eating, and commercial pickers have their secret chanterelle patches. On the northern edge of the cape, the Rocky Creek park is an awesome place for winter wave watching, as is Boiler Bay, north of Depoe Bay.

Depoe Bay is promoted as the world's smallest navigable harbor—just 6 square miles—but that doesn't seem to inhibit the many charter boats that often go to sea to fish or whale watch. The town is also noted for gray whales that swim near its waterfront walk, where blow holes are exuberant in their watery displays. Fogarty Creek offers a sheltered beach cove, while Gleneden Beach is near Siletz Bay, where great blue herons feed and then nest adjacent to the Siletz National Wildlife Refuge.

Another superlative attaches to the D River, which connects Devil's Lake to the ocean in Lincoln City. Is it really the world's shortest river? Nearby Devil's Lake State Park provides a natural setting for camping in the midst of a touristy city. Lincoln City is a composite of five smaller towns that ran together. On fair days, the skies near the beach are often filled with kites. Roads End is a quiet wayside at the north end of the city.

The Salmon River carves a wide estuary frequented by Roosevelt elk south of 1,600-foot-high Cascade Head, which is a special place with its botanical research area and outstanding coastal viewpoint from wildflower-dotted slopes. A forest road atop the headland traverses an arm of the Siuslaw National Forest and accesses a special forest trail to Hart's Cove. A view of Cascade Head's northern cliffs is a feature of Neskowin Beach.

The Three Capes Scenic Loop is an alternate to US 101 that heads north of Pacific City near the coast. The first of the capes is Kiwanda, near Pacific City, the home of the dory fleet, where fishers launch their boats from the beach, motor right through the incoming surf, and farm the sea. A huge sand dune hides a spectacular wave-watching and photography spot. Cape Lookout State Park features year-round camping along the ocean and miles of trail. A long spit projects north of Cape Lookout and encloses most of Netarts Bay, a favorite clamming area where multitudes of people come wearing high boots and carrying shovels. Three Arch Rocks National Wildlife Refuge is offshore, an important seabird nesting area. Oceanside Beach offers another view of the refuge with beach walking to Netarts. The coast's shortest lighthouse is located at the tip of Cape Meares, with trails to the unique Octopus Tree and a giant Sitka spruce. Trails connect to an inland wildlife refuge bordering the park to the north, and a branch descends to the Tillamook Spit along the bay. In 1907, a real estate developer from Kansas City decided to build a resort town on the spit called Bayocean Park—complete with a natatorium that housed a swimming pool, waterfall, and wave-making machine. Alas, the sea has a great claim on the land that touches it and its dynamic actions swept away the transitory structures of man. Tillamook Spit is now a place for birdwatching.

For additional information on Oregon State Parks, call 1-800-551-6949, or check the official website: *www.prd.state.or.us.*

47. ELLMAKER STATE WAYSIDE

Hours/Season: Day use; year-round
Area: 77 acres
Attractions: Picnicking, rest stop on highway
Facilities: Picnic tables, restrooms
Access: Off US 20, 31 miles east of Newport

On the highway between Newport and Corvallis, 1 mile west of the community of Burnt Woods, this land gift of Harlan D. Ellmaker works well as a highway rest stop that protects trees. The donor, who had worked for the U.S. Forest Service, called it his "Garden of Eden."

Although the acreage is split by the highway and the Tumtum River, the developed area is on the north side of the road, with a scattering of picnic tables bordering a large grassy meadow. A small stream flows from the northeast through the fir forest to join the river.

48. AGATE BEACH STATE RECREATION SITE

Hours/Season: Day use; year-round
Area: 18.5 acres
Attractions: Beachcombing, kite flying, photography, birdwatching, surfing, clamming, fishing, agate hunting, picnicking
Facilities: Beach access, picnic tables, restrooms
Access: Off US 101, 1 mile north of Newport on NW Ocean View Drive
Contact: Yaquina Head Outstanding Natural Area, (541) 574-3100

Situated between the old and new routes of the Oregon Coast Highway, Agate Beach is a popular recreation spot along the northern edge of Newport. The large parking lot on the east side of NW Ocean View Drive borders the restrooms and picnic tables, which are scattered along the edge of tree-lined Big Creek. A bridge allows access to a path on the other side of the creek. This walkway, and another one at the east side of the parking area, allows access from US 101. Beach access is via a tunnel under Ocean View Drive, but beach strollers usually park at the parking area edging the beach.

Although Agate Beach was named for the many agates found there in the past, visitors are more likely to find surfers riding the waves.

Big Creek—the city's water source—flows under the road and empties onto Agate Beach. In doing so, it spreads out into a lake before meandering north and into the Pacific, changing its route frequently with the season and the rainfall. Fortunately, the small amount of water that branches off to the south is not difficult to cross to access the beach.

It is not just the route of the creek that changes with the seasons. This particular beach accumulates a wide expanse of transverse dunes that form due to the northwest winds of summer as the ocean throws ashore lots of sand. In winter, the beach is flat as the sand is pulled back into the ocean reservoir.

The park was named for the abundance of agates once found in this area. Though beachcombers still find varied and pretty stones, numbers are fewer because of the popularity of the wayside. Jasper, fossilized wood, fossilized clams, and a few shells are also found by strollers not hypnotized by the views and wave watching. During the frequent minus tides in summer, which occur in early morning at this time of year, the wide stretch of patterned sand attracts people digging for razor clams.

Easy walking distance to the north terminates at the long arm of Yaquina Head. This is best done at low tide when the mouth of Big Creek is shallow enough to cross. Surfers are frequently seen riding the waves in the curve of the headland. Tidepools are found at low tide where the basalt rock jogs out into the sea. Pigeon guillemots nest in the rock crevices and fly near the water. The Yaquina Head Lighthouse is easily seen at the tip of the headland.

A longer beach walk heads south, and during low tides in summer hikers can walk along a beach segment of the Oregon Coast Trail all the way to the north jetty of the Yaquina River (approximately 6 miles round trip), where two walkways access the Yaquina Bay Lighthouse. Several sea stacks and offshore basalt terraces are exposed along this walk, particularly near Nye Beach, where a side trip invites a visit to the changing shows at the Newport Visual Arts Center, restaurants, and several shops.

Lucky beach walkers might walk through multitudes of flying sanderlings (mixed with a few other species) on their northern spring migration. In summer, brown pelicans, surf scoters, and other shorebirds can be spotted. The lakelike creek area is a favorite swimming and bathing place for sea gulls.

Photography possibilities are excellent with the striated rocks, low tide patterns on the sand, shore birds, the lighthouse backing an expanse of waves, and the tangerine wash of color on Big Creek at sunset.

Yaquina Head is the location of Yaquina Head Outstanding Natural Area (a fee area), which is managed by the Bureau of Land Management and includes an interpretive center. It is a rare place to view sea birds on offshore rocks so close to land that newborn sea gulls walk about a few feet away. During mating season in spring, several bird species can be seen nearby in breeding plumage. Common murres are almost solid on some of the offshore rocks. Harbor seals are numerous on several sea stacks. Tours through the historic lighthouse are available. Stairs lead down to a protected marine garden on a cobble beach. A new road accesses parking for ocean viewing and a unique barrier-free walkway through a rocky intertidal area, which was reclaimed in 1992–1994 from a rock quarry by the Bureau of Land Management. Gray whales are occasionally spotted quite near the headland, and the tip of the headland is an official whale-watching site. Interconnecting trails and exhibit information are found throughout the area.

49. BEVERLY BEACH STATE PARK

Hours/Season: Day use and overnight (reservations available); year-round
Area: 130 acres
Attractions: Beachcombing, hiking, nature trail, fishing, wildlife viewing, kite flying, photography, surfing, picnicking, camping, summer programs and movies
Facilities: Picnic tables; beach access, exhibit information, campground (53 full hookups, 76 electrical hookups, 129 tent sites, 21 yurts—reservations available, cable TV hookups in yurts and selected campsites, accessible campsites, maximum site 65 feet), restrooms with showers, group tent camping, hiker/biker camp, yurt meeting hall (with sink, counter range, and many chairs), visitor information center, playground, amphitheater, dump station, newspaper dispensers, pay phones, nearby laundromat and grocery store
Access: Off US 101, 7 miles north of Newport
Contact: (541) 265-9278

With its proximity to lots of activities in the Newport area, Beverly Beach State Park has been one of the most heavily used of Oregon's state parks since its construction in the post–World War II era. The day-use area, with picnic tables, restroom, parking, and yurt meeting hall, is west of the park's entry station. It borders Spencer Creek and provides beach access beneath an overpass of US 101. Although this area is protected from summer winds, tables have no ocean view. A bridge across the creek allows campers to walk to the beach. A paved walkway begins near information exhibits and ends with a recently constructed ramp to the beach near the mouth of the creek. Autumn finds the beach a combination of cobbles and sand, with less sand in winter. Directly west is a long, narrow offshore rock that inspired the name Otter Rock.

The long expanse of beach extends from Yaquina Head, views of the lighthouse north to the headlands of Otter Rock. On good days, kites color the air and whip in the wind, and sand castles are built. Surfers use the north end of the beach. Part of the Oregon Coast Trail, this 5-mile stretch of beach can be hiked by wading the creek—best done in summer—and timing the walk at low tide to round a promontory just north of Yaquina Head. It is 1.2 miles to the north headlands, where Devil's Punch Bowl can be visited by climbing a long stairway. To the south, the

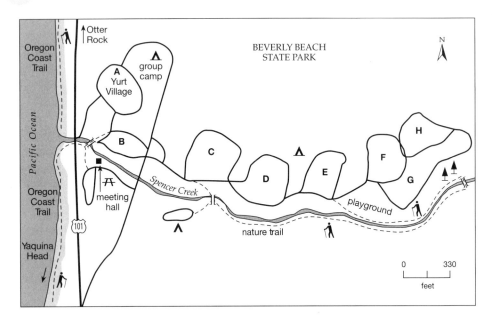

habitat. Huge old stumps, giant wind-sculptured trees, and nurse logs are seen. If you're not familiar with the plants of the temperate rain forest, look for ferns, western azalea, twinberry, giant horsetail, skunk cabbage, great hedge nettle, deer fern, false lily-of-the-valley, and other species. The nature trail is beautiful year-round, with mushrooms in autumn, berries in season, and skunk grass flowering in spring. Amid the campground area are several interesting wetland areas. A photo taken in 1961 shows the campground area as flat and devoid of shading trees. Today, it is a beautiful forest environment.

The park is adjacent to the small community of Beverly Beach, which Florence and Curtis Christy initially owned and founded. They let their small daughter name the settlement after her favorite doll, Beverly.

Oregon Coast Trail exit to the highway is via a primitive road to the north of Moolack Shores Motel. The beach to the south is narrow in winter and best walked at low tide since the cliffs provide no escape.

The day-use area was once a pond at the mouth of Spencer Creek. A fish hatchery was located here and a farm was above the pond. The road into the park was once part of the Roosevelt Military Highway. During World War II, guard dogs patrolled the beach.

Most of the many campground loops edge the north side of Spencer Creek, with lovely treed sites along the waterway. Two loops, Yurt Village and RV spaces, and a group tent camping area are north of the entry station. A visitor information center staffed by volunteers (with books and other items for sale) and the park host are located between the two campground areas.

A self-guiding 0.75-mile nature trail begins between campsites C3 and C5, with a spur to the hiker/biker camp—for foot traffic only. Cross the bridge over Spencer Creek and follow the creek until another bridge recrosses the water at the end of the campground and follows the other side of the creek to just past the playground. Several access paths lead from individual sites on the north side of the creek. Though logged in the past, the forest has grown back and this hike reveals an excellent example of rain forest shaped by coastal winter storms, as well as riparian wetland

Visitors at Beverly Beach State Park enjoy a picnic on the north side of Spencer Creek, with a view of Otter Rock at the north end of the long beach.

50. DEVIL'S PUNCH BOWL STATE NATURAL AREA

Hours/Season: Day use; year-round
Area: 4 acres
Attractions: Unusual geology, marine gardens, exhibit information, whale and wave watching, beachcombing, hiking, photography, picnicking
Facilities: Picnic tables, wheelchair-accessible restrooms, small playground, paved trail
Access: Off US 101, 8 miles north of Newport, on the Otter Crest Loop

During winter storms, water from the restless sea pours with a thundering roar into a hollow rock formation shaped like a punch bowl. The surf churns, foams, and swirls as if the Devil were mixing some violent brew. This natural landmark of intriguing geology, composed of sedimentary rock and basalt, juts out into the sea just west of the small community of Otter Rock and is the centerpiece of Devil's Punch Bowl State Natural Area.

The punch bowl was probably created by the collapse of the roof over two sea caves, and shaped by wave action. The ocean enters the bowl from tunnels on opposite sides. It empties and fills with the tides. Views to the north are of the rocky headlands of Cape Foulweather.

Walkways circle and cross a scenic picnic area situated amidst vegetation and trees south of the punch bowl, atop an undulating rocky shoreline that consists of soft sedimentary rock. These diverse formations make for varied wave watching as the surf bounces off the cliffs. The site is also an official whale-watching site during whale migrations.

A wooden stairway, across from the restroom parking lot, descends to the long stretch of sandy beach to the south that ends at Yaquina Head Lighthouse. Light-colored deposits of volcanic ash

can be seen along the cliffs at the bottom of the stairs.

To visit the marine gardens, follow the street about two blocks north of the restrooms to a parking lot which accesses a trail that descends to a nice area of tidepools. The last section is hazardous at high tide when the waves inundate the marine garden, but during a minus tide it is a wonderland for exploring. A sandy beach then edges a varied terrain of sandstone shelves and rock formations with channels and pools of water. Sea urchins lives in round holes carved out of underwater rocks. Tiny sculpin fish dart around in pools. Sea anemones and sea stars hang onto rock in the surge of waves. It takes time to see and learn to identify the diverse intertidal inhabitants. They vary as you get closer to the sea, but there is a good collection of species here. The floor of the punch bowl can be entered from the south end of this beach, and you can see the tunnels where the water enters the bowl. Offshore some distance is a large sea stack called Gull Rock.

The best time to visit the tidepools is near the summer solstice

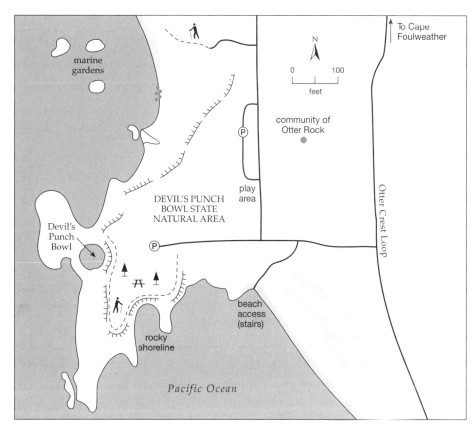

Oregon Islands National Wildlife Refuge

More than 1,400 islands, rocks, and reefs scattered along the Oregon coast, from Tillamook Head to the California border, comprise the 762-acre Oregon Islands National Wildlife Refuge. Off limits to humans, they are essential real estate for birds and marine mammals. These rocky homes provide nesting habitat for more than 1.1 million seabirds, more birds than all the nesting birds along the combined California and Washington coastlines. In addition, seals and sea lions choose these wave-battered refuges for resting, pupping, and molting sites.

Thirteen species of seabirds nest in this refuge. How do so many different seabirds share this environment to raise their young? The answer is that each species chooses a different food resource and nest site. Black oystercatchers make a pebble-lined hollow on the lower rocks. Western and glaucous-winged gulls prefer to nest on rocks and islands that are flat or have gentle slopes; they often prey on young of other birds. Rhinoceros auklets dig burrows into grassy slopes and are mostly active at night, so are rarely seen in colonies. Tufted puffins also dig burrows and lay a single egg 3 to 6 feet underground; they are active during the day, near the tops of vegetated islands. Pigeon guillemots nest in rock crevices or burrows. Pelagic cormorants nest on steep cliff ledges where their nest of vegetation is cemented together with their droppings. Brandt's and double-crested cormorants prefer to rest on flat rocks or slopes. The most numerous seabird along the Oregon coast is the common murre; they lay a single egg on exposed rocks. Murres can share 1 square foot of space with six others; they use distinct body language in order to get along in crowded nesting colonies.

With all this seabird nesting, spring is one of the best times to check the closest offshore rocks with binoculars, when breeding plumage, nesting, and even chicks might be sighted. In summer, from mid-July to late August, seal and sea lion numbers peak. In spring and fall, watch for migrating birds. Sea ducks and waterbirds are most abundant during winter: surf, white-winged, and black scoters; harlequin ducks; common and Pacific loons; and western, horned, and red-necked grebes.

The behavior of refuge inhabitants is often intriguing. For instance, the male Steller sea lion is the only North American sea lion that roars, and it is much larger, up to 2,200 pounds, than the California sea lion. If you notice cormorants resting with their wings spread out, that's because they lack the water-repellent oil present on feathers of most waterbirds and their wings must be dry to be able to fly.

These islands, and other refuges, protect some species that have been threatened. These include brown pelicans, who spend time from late spring through early fall along the Oregon coast, after breeding further south. About 3,000 Steller sea lions use these islands as haul-out and pupping sites.

A few of these islands are close enough for good wildlife viewing from coastline viewpoints. These include Harris Beach, Cape Blanco, Cape Arago, Heceta Head Lighthouse, Yaquina Head, Haystack Rock in Cannon Beach, and Ecola State Park. The seabird aviary at Newport's Oregon Coast Aquarium is a great place to watch tufted puffins fly underwater and observe the antics of black oystercatchers and other seabirds, as well as several species of marine mammals, including sea otters, seals, and sea lions.

To ensure that inhabitants remain undisturbed, the Oregon Islands National Wildlife Refuge is closed to all public entry; all watercraft must stay at least 500 feet from the islands.

Tufted puffins nest in the Oregon Islands National Wildlife Refuge.

After exploring the varied intertidal life found at the marine gardens at Devil's Punch Bowl State Natural Area, visitors can enter the punch bowl through this rock formation at a good low tide.

in June, when good minus tides occur. Check a tide book for times. Go an hour before the lowest tide and remember to watch for the incoming tide; leave the area before you're stranded by incoming water. No collecting of marine life is allowed in this much-visited intertidal area by anyone, even scientists and educators. Explorers should wear boots and proceed with caution, especially where slippery seaweeds flourish.

51. OTTER CREST STATE SCENIC VIEWPOINT

Hours/Season: Day use; year-round
Area: 1.48 acres
Attractions: Photography, whale watching, exhibit information
Facilities: Viewpoint parking, gift shop with telescopes outside
Access: 10 miles north of Newport along the Otter Crest Loop

Otter Crest State Scenic Viewpoint occupies the high point of a picturesque headland called Cape Foulweather, a complex of volcanic rock, with an excellent view of the Devil's Punch Bowl environs and the coastline south to Yaquina Head. From the Otter Crest Loop, pull into a large parking area and walk to the paved viewpoint at cliff's edge for an aerial perspective of the geology in this area of the Oregon coast. It is easy to distinguish the cove where marine gardens are frequently hidden by ocean waves, as well as the rocks that form the punch bowl just beyond, followed by a long stretch of beach. The elevation is excellent for scanning for gray whales and shoreline birds. Kelp beds are numerous offshore and indicate a healthy marine habitat. Sea otters were once found in these waters, and local Native Americans made capes of their skins. Their value to whites in the fur trade to the oriental market eventually depleted their numbers.

This view of the Devil's Punch Bowl area and the marine gardens can be seen from Cape Foulweather.

Captain James Cook sighted and named the cape when he sailed back from his discovery of the Hawaiian Islands with two ships, the *Resolution* and the *Discovery*. It was a stormy March 7th of the year 1778; hence the name Cape Foulweather. Cook continued north as far as Vancouver Island—where he traded with Native Americans for furs—in his search for a northern passage from the Pacific to the Atlantic.

The land for the viewpoint was given to the state by Wilbur S. and Florence Badley in 1928 with the provision that concessions not be allowed. The state was to maintain the wayside for the public. The Badleys, however, built a gift shop at the edge of the cliffs called "The Lookout." It is still privately owned and replete with fascinating items relating to the natural beauty of the area.

52. ROCKY CREEK STATE SCENIC VIEWPOINT

Hours/Season: Day use; year-round
Area: 58 acres
Attractions: Wave watching, whale watching, picnicking, trail on cliffs, offshore rocks with bird life
Facilities: Picnic tables, restrooms
Access: Off US 101, 2 miles south of Depoe Bay

Between Whale Cove and Rocky Creek, Rocky Creek State Scenic Viewpoint occupies an excellent stretch of coastal bluff. On a day in early fall following the first storm of the year, when the sun shines and the blue sky is textured with ribbons of white clouds and there is little wind, the park is a glorious place to explore. Parking along the loop road allows easy access to viewing the concatenation of coves and rocky projections. The surf crashes noisily on the rocks and offshore sea stacks, with each cove exhibiting its special wave action as the water angles in on a slightly different approach. Walk along the grassy edge and scan for whales as you gaze north and south to see high tide climbing the rocky walls in a never-ending, exuberant rhythm. Picnic tables are positioned near these views, and a bench invites relaxing to take in the panoramic events.

This park, however, is a fine stopping place at any time of the year, on a windy summer day—when you can find a sheltered picnic table among the woods—or a stormy day while sitting in your vehicle. In spring, birds nest on the offshore rocks. North of the restroom, a path through the woods edges the cliffs for more views, and also wanders into the coastal shore pine woods.

Charter boats are popular at nearby Depoe Bay.

From a viewpoint at the far end of the trail, you can see the golden sandstone cliff walls of Whale Cove that are pocketed with eroded caves.

The park actually continues south along the Otter Crest Loop as far as the historic bridge over Rocky Creek (recently renovated), where salmon have historically gone upstream. A parking space overlooking the Pacific is available near the beginning of the road.

The Civilian Conservation Corps did the original park developments between 1934 and 1936, with later improvements for day use by the park system.

For more surf watching, visit nearby Depoe Bay, with its

oceanfront walkway through town. Charter boats will take you out through the narrow channel of the "world's smallest harbor" for fishing or whale watching. It's a very busy place in summer, with some fine seafood at local restaurants.

53. BOILER BAY STATE RECREATION SITE

Hours/Season: Day use; year-round
Area: 33 acres
Attractions: Photography, wildlife viewing, picnicking, wave watching
Facilities: Picnic tables, restrooms
Access: Off US 101, 1 mile north of Depoe Bay

The popular viewpoint at Boiler Bay State Recreation Site is located at the north end of Depoe Bay, where parking along the large paved loop surrounds a flat, grassy meadow. The scenic magic is a few steps away at the edge of the steep, rocky bluff that faces the ocean and a small bay to the north, where surf sweeps toward the rocks in great swells until it booms on the rocks. The half circle of land that forms the coastline here projects out near the midpoint to what is known as Government Point, where a dirt path continues to a fenced-in area where visitors can scan for whales and other wildlife. Picnic

Boiler Bay State Recreation Site often has spectacular surf watching.

tables rim the bluff for fine picnicking views. Below the bluff are exposed beds of volcanic ash, some arriving from the air and others from currents in the water.

Boiler Bay was named for the remains of a ship's boiler that were visible at low tide. These maritime remnants are from the freighter *J. Marhoffer,* which was wrecked off this point in 1910.

54. FOGARTY CREEK STATE RECREATION SITE

Hours/Season: Day use (fee); year-round
Area: 142 acres
Attractions: Picnicking, beachcombing, fishing, hiking, photography
Facility: Beach access, picnicking, group picnic area, restrooms
Access: Off US 101, 2 miles north of Depoe Bay

Fogarty Creek flows into the sea at an enchanting ocean cove in Fogarty Creek State Recreation Site. In the afternoon sun, its waters are a fluid silver ribbon that curves often as it turns to the south, changing course with the vagaries of the season. Many of the ingredients that make the spirit soar are found here. A jumble of rocks at the edge of the sea bounces the surf in all directions on both sides of the mouth of the creek. Seabirds swim near the rocks. Gulls frequent the creek. To the north, a sweeping line of golden scallops of cliffs edges the beach. Beach walkers scan the sand for agates. As the surf sweeps into the cove in bright sunlight, leaving a curve of white surf momentarily edging the azure water, a resort atop the cliffs completes a scene that is reminiscent of a postcard of Mexico's west coast.

Fogarty Creek State Recreation Site is accessed from US 101 by forested entry drives from both the north and south that lead to separate parking areas. To get to the beach, the access is through the main area of the park on the east side of the highway, where walkways on either side of Fogarty Creek go under the highway to the beach.

Inland, the park fans out in a broad, level expanse of natural terrain that is sometimes a surface of cushioned moss. Three arched footbridges cross the wide stream at several points as it flows lazily through the park, and paths offer considerable walking to discover the essence of the park. Perhaps you'll spy a muskrat or a beaver swimming in the creek in a quiet area. A forest of shore pine, Sitka spruce, western hemlock, red cedar,

A sandy beach edges the mouth of Fogarty Creek and forms a cove for agate hunting.

and alder has regrown after being logged in the past. It is a pleasant stop along the highway, a place for individual or group picnicking, with tables spread out in all directions, each with considerable choice in scenic locations or privacy among the trees and by the creek. The creek and park are named for John Fogarty, a native of Ireland who became a Lincoln County judge.

55. GLENEDEN BEACH STATE RECREATION SITE

Hours/Season: Day use; year-round
Area: 17.5 acres
Attractions: Beachcombing, fishing, picnicking, wave watching
Facilities: Picnic tables, group picnic area, beach access, restrooms
Access: Off US 101, 7 miles south of Lincoln City

Gleneden Beach fronts the Pacific Ocean in the small community by the same name, where the post office was established in 1927. The park is situated on a bluff that gently slopes downhill at its northern end. Picnic tables and a sheltered group-picnic area are found in the woods edging the parking area, with more tables at the edge of the spacious meadow on the bluff overlooking the ocean, where a walk along the edge offers fine views of the wave action. Paths lead downhill through the woods to the beach.

To the north is the 3.5-mile finger of the Siletz Spit that encloses Siletz Bay, so the beachcomber can cover a great distance on foot while looking for debris and treasures tossed ashore by the sea. To celebrate the new millennium, Lincoln City released specially made, colorful glass floats that some people have come long distances to find, though only a few succeed—the ocean currents are capricious about where they bring these treasures to shore. Many luxurious homes are located along the spit, and one wonders how long nature will allow these structures to remain.

The approach to the park along US 101 has spectacular wetlands south of Siletz Bay where great blue herons can be seen flying to their roosts across the highway. Birdwatching is fascinating in the midst of scenery that consists of patches of picturesque logs dotting the shallow estuary area that changes with the tides, and is particularly spectacular at sunset. Several areas of the Siletz Bay National Wildlife Refuge are in this region. Established in 1991, the refuge is developing public use opportunities.

D River State Recreation Site is in the midst of Lincoln City.

A premier resort, The Weston Salishan Lodge, in Gleneden Beach features a golf course and various cultural events during the year. The Marketplace on the west side of the highway offers fine galleries and shops.

56. D RIVER STATE RECREATION SITE

Hours/Season: Day use; year-round
Area: 4 acres
Attractions: Kite flying, beachcombing, hiking, photography, fishing, picnicking
Facilities: Beach access, picnic tables, restrooms, exhibit information, pay telescopes
Access: Off US 101, in the middle of Lincoln City near 1st Street

The busiest beach area in touristy Lincoln City is D River State Recreation Site. Even in the midst of winter—when the weather is cooperative—crowds of people visit to fly kites, toss Frisbees, walk their dogs, build sand castles, or just to saunter along the sandy beach. A few people, especially the children, run quickly out through an incoming wave to see what fun it can be—even though the water is cold at any time of year. Seagulls congregate near the river and are often fed by the visitors, creating some lively action. Geese fly past in V-formation, and shorebirds are seasonal.

A walkway rims the often crowded parking lot. Exhibit infor-

mation, a couple of picnic tables, a telescope, and a bench are near the walkway, and concrete steps lead to the beach, as does a sandy approach near the restrooms.

The D River flows along the northern edge of the parking area, quite exuberantly in winter. Less than 1 mile from its source in Devil's Lake, it is one of the shortest rivers in the world.

A multitude of restaurants and shops are a few steps away.

57. DEVIL'S LAKE STATE PARK

Hours/Season: Day use and overnight (reservations available); year-round
Area: 104 acres
Attractions: Fishing, boating, scenic lake, wildlife viewing, wetlands, nature study, swimming in freshwater lake, water skiing, picnicking, camping
Facilities: Picnic tables, campground (32 full hookup, 1 electrical, and 54 tent sites—2 accessible, maximum site 45 feet), 10 yurts (2 accessible), hiker/biker camp, restrooms with showers, dump station, 16 boat moorage slips, fishing dock, boat launch, program area, firewood
Access: The park is in two separate units on opposite sides of Devil's Lake: the campground is off US 101 in Lincoln City, ast off NE 6th Drive; East Devil's Lake day-use area is 0.75 nile east from US 101 via East Devil's Lake Road
Contact: (541) 994-2002

Devil's Lake State Park is the only campground on the Oregon coast located in the midst of a city, although Lincoln City is a resort area rather than a large metropolis. To balance that, the campground is on the west shore of 678-acre Devil's Lake, although no campsite has a lake view. A swatch of wetlands separates the sites from the lake, but the lake is easily approached on foot via a narrow roadway to the boat slip area, where moorage is available by reservation. Changing views of the forest and Coast Range across the water are quite scenic, and even spectacular if there's a fine sunrise. Trees—shore pine, alder, and crabapple—provide a parklike setting for the campground. A hiker/biker camp is to your left just before reaching the registration booth. Yurts are found in the B and C loops of the campground. A program area is centrally located.

The wetlands, with channels of water amid lush vegetation, entice the naturalist for birding and nature study. Wildlife is

abundant with coots, cormorants, and ducks on the lake. A pair of great blue herons and mallard ducks were startled at the lake's edge by this visitor in winter, and birding is good in all seasons. The freshwater lake is popular with anglers.

Whether you enjoy the beach, the city attractions, nature, or fishing, the park offers a good base for it. A stay in winter reveals the spectacular surf of that season, when the rainy days are interspersed with sunny ones that have moderate temperatures. You can walk to D River State Recreation Site, restaurants, shops, and galleries.

Devil's Lake was named because of numerous legends, such as the Native American tale of a giant fish or marine monster that lived in the lake and occasionally came to the surface to attack some unlucky person. One evening when the Siletz tribe's Chief Fleetfoot sent his warriors across its waters, the placid, moonlit lake suddenly erupted into turmoil. Legend says the frail canoe was grasped by gigantic tentacles and pulled below the surface. Some boat occupants crossing the moon's reflection in the center of the lake have reported a strange chill of fear. Even today, festivals are held on the shores of the lake to pacify its spirit, though boaters now seem little affected.

The day-use area and boat ramp for the park are located across the lake at the East Devil's Lake unit, directly across from the boat slip area of the campground unit, so you could launch your boat from there and then store it in a slip on the west side. Large alder trees border the boat launch area, where nearby shallow water contains lake tules. Bald eagles often perch on nearby trees, and ducks and waterfowl are abundant. This is a designated wildlife viewing area.

Wetlands with fine birding edge Devil's Lake near the campground.

A large strip of tall lush forest exists between East Devil's Lake Road and the lake. Shaded picnic tables overlook the water near the fishing dock and boat launch. A swimming area is available in summer. This large lake spreads out mainly to the north and edges all of Lincoln City in that direction, so there is room for waterskiing. East Devil's Lake Road continues to the north of Lincoln City, where it connects with US 101 and offers a quiet bypass to a busy tourist city. A small community at the north end of Devil's Lake is called Neotsu, another Native American name for the lake.

An interesting piece of historical information ties Lincoln City with Willamette Mission State Park in the valley. Jason Lee, who set up that first Native American mission, came with his bride of one month, and another missionary couple and guide, over the Old Elk Trail to camp on the Oregon coast in 1837. It is believed they were the first to vacation on this scenic coast.

58. ROADS END STATE RECREATION SITE

Hours/Season: Day use; year-round
Area: 4.7 acres
Attractions: Beachcombing, wildlife viewing, tidepools, picnicking, hiking, photography
Facilities: Exhibit information, beach access, picnic tables, restrooms
Access: From US 101, on the north end of Lincoln City, turn at the light and follow Logan Road to the park

From a low bluff overlooking a long ocean beach, Roads End State Recreation Site provides a paved path that descends a draw edging Logan Creek to miles of beach activities. Two quite different walking opportunities exist. For quiet strolling, head north across the small creek past oceanfront homes for over a mile to the rocks at the foot of the headlands on the south side of Salmon River, where tidepools are found at low tide. For a more urban environment, walk the beach south past Chinook Winds Casino and Convention Center, oceanfront inns, and various developments.

Exhibit information at the beginning of the beach-access walkway features tsunamis and wildlife viewing. A few picnic tables overlook the ocean. Seafood is featured at adjacent Dory Restaurant.

The coastline edging the long stretch of Lincoln City is seen from Cascade Head.

The Oregon Coast Trail continues the length of Lincoln City to the mouth of the Siletz River, a distance not quite 6 miles from the wayside, though you can choose to sample any distance.

Any naturalist or hiker in the Lincoln City area should not miss hiking in the Cascade Head Natural Area to the north. The lower trailhead is accessed via Three Rocks Road, just north of the Salmon River. En route, if it's winter, be alert for Roosevelt elk crossing the Salmon River or in the adjacent meadow. The upper trailhead is found by following Forest Service Road 1861 (closed during spring nesting season), which goes west at the crest of Cascade Head on US 101. Although the trail has forest and wetland habitat, much of the trail is an open walk on the sloping grassland of this sheer promontory that rises from the sea. This is a rare remnant of coastal prairie with native grasses and beautiful wildflowers in summer. The premier coastal seascape seen to the south includes the estuary of the Salmon River, offshore Three Rocks, and the headland north of Roads End State Recreation Site. Please follow the guidelines in this fragile area, a Nature Conservancy project.

59. H. B. VAN DUZER FOREST STATE SCENIC CORRIDOR

Hours/Season: Day use; year-round
Area: 1,487 acres
Attractions: Rest stop, picnicking, fishing
Facilities: Picnic tables, restrooms, trails to river
Access: Along OR 18, 15 miles east of Lincoln City

Not far from the Pacific Ocean, on the most direct route between Portland and Lincoln City, 12 miles along the highway between Grande Ronde and Rose Lodge is a splendid forest (located in three counties) that the state was astute enough to buy and preserve between 1935 and 1942, with some later adjustments. This is now the H. B. Van Duzer Forest State Scenic Corridor.

The two units of the corridor display a range of coastal Douglas fir forest, from forty-four-year-old second growth to virgin forest containing trees more than 200 years of age, including some of the finest remaining examples of ancient Douglas fir, western hemlock, western red cedar, and Sitka spruce to be found in the Coast Range. Since the land adjoining this narrow strip has been logged, protection from strong winter winds is somewhat limited, and trees blown down by the wind have required periodic salvage operations to permit safe highway travel.

Observant travelers will notice glimpses of the Salmon River along this route, but a stop at the scenic rest stop on the south side of the highway—and a little exploring on short trails—reveals river access for anglers, but anyone should enjoy the lovely forest edging this stretch of the river. An immense stump is an example of logging here before the forest's protection. Fallen trees, shaded pools, and riffles illustrate good salmon habitat. And it's not unusual to spot a dipper, the underwater scavenging bird, flitting from stone to stone after a swim.

A looping road into the rest stop edges a large meadow with a scattering

CASCADE HEAD NATURAL AREA

Pacific Ocean

north viewpoint

south viewpoint

grasslands

Cascade Head

Three Rocks

Salmon River

Upper Trail

1861

To 101

Lower Trail

Crowly Creek

Sitka Center

Three Rocks Road

N

0   800
feet

of trees that was the historic location on the Salmon River Toll Road operated by John and Julia Boyer from 1908 to 1920. The Boyer Post Office was also located here. The early wagon road followed a previous Native American path called the Old Elk Trail.

The corridor is named for Henry B. Van Duzer (1874–1951), a member of the Oregon State Highway Commission, vice president of the Inman Poulsen Logging Company of Portland, and a strong supporter of the Oregon State Parks. He promoted the protection of roadside stands of native forest.

60. NESKOWIN BEACH STATE RECREATION SITE

Hours/Season: Day use; year-round
Area: 8 acres
Attractions: Beachcombing, hiking, picnicking, photography, fishing
Facilities: Beach access, restrooms, picnic tables
Access: Off US 101, in Neskowin

At the northern foot of Cascade Head, Neskowin Beach State Recreation Site is located in the small community of Neskowin. At the edge of the large parking lot are restrooms and two picnic tables, with tree-lined Hawk Creek flowing along the west side. The attraction here is beach access, with a paved trail that immediately crosses a bridge over the creek and connects to a short corridor trail that soon reaches a nice swatch of sandy beach. In a short distance, Hawk Creek joins larger Neskowin Creek and curves toward the sea, which it enters just north of a huge sea stack, Proposal Rock, at the edge of the beach.

Proposal Rock has scrambling trails through salal vegetation to its top. According to Alexandria L. Rock, who came to this area in the 1880s, her recollections on file at the Oregon Historical Society reveal that Proposal Rock became so known after Charley Gage proposed to her daughter about the turn of the century.

The desire is great to cross Neskowin Creek and walk the beach to the south, which has a spectacular view of the basalt cliffs of Cascade Head. The creek is too deep to cross easily in autumn, though it might be possible in summer. A long stretch of beach heads off north, however, and initially passes ocean-front homes and sea gulls surfing the ocean waves. The Oregon Coast Trail follows the beach for more than 4 miles past Daley Lake to Camp Winema, across the bay from Nestucca Spit.

Neskowin Beach State Recreation Site features views of Neskowin Creek, Proposal Rock, and Cascade Head.

Neskowin Creek, with its history of excellent fishing, was known to early settlers as Slab Creek. Appointed postmaster of this community in 1887, Mrs. Sarah H. Page wrote the *Oregonian* in 1925 that *neskowin* was a Native American word that meant "plenty fish." The creek and town name arose after a ship wrecked on the coast and a quantity of slabwood washed up on the beach. Mrs. Page, however, heard a native call the creek Neskowin and give the reason why. In 1925, the U.S. Board of Geographic Names changed the name of the stream to Neskowin, which resulted in the present name of the town. A deli, a restaurant, and an inn are adjacent to the park.

The Oregon Coast Trail begins again 1 mile south of Neskowin, off US 101, and climbs over Cascade Head to Three Rocks Road in 6 miles.

61. BOB STRAUB STATE PARK

Hours/Season: Day use; year-round
Area: 484 acres
Attractions: Horse and hiking trails, fishing, picnicking
Facilities: Picnic tables, beach and river access (by trail or boat), restrooms
Access: Off the Three Capes Scenic Loop, continue straight one block after crossing the bridge over the Nestucca River in Pacific City; then south on Sunset Drive to the end of the road at the beginning of the Nestucca Spit

Originally called Nestucca Spit State Park, it was renamed in 1987 for former Oregon Governor Robert Straub, a strong

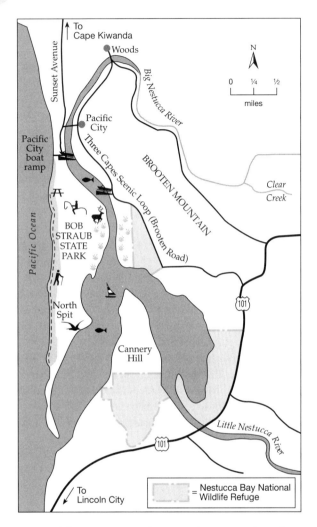

from the south edge of the parking lot. Picnic tables are found among the vegetation.

The Nestucca River curves south from Pacific City and winds around the eastern side of the spit until it spreads out to form Nestucca Bay and then enters the Pacific at the end of the spit. This is a rather wild and lonely area, where exploring can only improve with acquired knowledge. Since both ocean and bay water surrounds the spit, fishing and boating possibilities are numerous.

Several sections of the Nestucca Bay National Wildlife Refuge edge the bay area, habitat (riparian wetlands, salt marsh, wooded uplands, and managed pastures) for a variety of fish and wildlife, including waterfowl, shorebirds, raptors, small mammals, and amphibians. The bay supports the only coastal population of dusky Canada geese and a wintering population of 100 to 150 Semidi Islands Aleutian Canada geese. The bay and its tributaries support large runs of chinook and coho salmon, cutthroat trout, and steelhead.

There was a time when the Highway Commission proposed a relocation of the Pacific Coast Scenic Byway along the spit and across the mouth of the Nestucca River. Fortunately, wise opponents resisted this plan, the obvious shortcomings of which were revealed when, in 1978, the spit was breached by the ocean about one-half mile north of the Nestucca River. History has repeatedly shown that spits are unstable landforms.

In summer, brown pelicans wander along the Oregon coast scouting for fish.

supporter of the Oregon Beach Law and conservation of natural resources, and is now known as Bob Straub State Park. The park encompasses all of the sand spit at the mouth of the river south of the platted limits of Pacific City. The park is a lowland coastal tract with sand flats up to one-half mile wide, with the spit extending more than 2 miles to the south and narrowing at its extremity. The park preserves the river entrance, sand spit, and ocean shore for public use.

Near the parking area, a paved walk begins the climb up the large foredune that fronts the ocean and is punctuated with European beach grass. Visitors can explore this area and find a route to the beach for a walk to the south end of the spit. Horse and hiking trails lead off through vegetation and small trees

62. CAPE KIWANDA STATE NATURAL AREA

Hours/Season: Day use; year-round
Area: 185 acres
Attractions: Photography, wave watching, beachcombing, tidepools, dory boat launching from the beach, ocean fishing, surfing, ocean kayaking, wave-sculptured cliffs, wildlife viewing, sand dunes, hiking, hang gliding
Facilities: Beach access, restrooms
Access: Off Three Capes Scenic Loop, 1 mile north of Pacific City *(no signs for the park, but there is one for Cape Kiwanda)*

The beach that hugs the southern side of Cape Kiwanda is the launch pad of the dory fleet of ocean fishers that call Pacific City home. Getting their boats off the sand and into—and through—the surf is no easy matter, requiring frequent pushes, jumps into boats, quick engine starts, and skilled maneuvering to avoid capsizing. It's a wild but wonderful experience if you have a chance to try it, but it's also fun to watch. Sheltered from northwest winds by the cape in summer, this is the place to watch fishers, both men and women, in their struggle to ride the sea.

Why would fishers want to go to sea where there is no protective harbor or boat basin? Because the fish are there and it's a good place to live. Nearby Nestucca River is a famous spawning region for salmon. The double-ended design of the dory has been used for ocean fishing since the early 1900s, when horses and wagons and then Model A automobiles hauled boats through the drifting sand. In the 1970s, about 300 boats fished for salmon here. Fishing restrictions and fewer fish have reduced the number of boats, but many still dory fish at Cape Kiwanda. If you want to experience the thrill of this surf entry, charter boats will take you out.

Most summers, the Pacific City Dory Derby is held here in July, an exciting event to watch as contestants launch boats, circle Haystack Rock, and return with a fish caught almost in the blink of an eye.

When the surf is wild, surfers come to ride the waves, and it's not unusual to watch a kayaker doing the same thing.

Cape Kiwanda is a photographer's paradise, particularly in winter after a storm, but the geology is a wonder in any season. Although you can easily photograph shots of dory boats, Haystack Rock with its jug handle, the tidepools at the foot of the cape, and the cape itself, the awesome surf-action photos demand a climb up the dune to the top of the cape. This is accessed at the north end of the beach. Follow the footprints in the soft sand. At the top, explore—with caution—in several directions, except where signs forbid it. The succession of sculptured sandstone cliffs is truly impressive, as is the wave action that collides with them and continues to shape this soft rock. In spring, the basin here is a favored spot for brown pelicans and sea birds.

The park on the north side of the cape can be accessed by climbing the sand dune on the back side of the cape or, more easily, by driving north and parking by the road where the bluff ends. A walk south from there on the beach for more than a mile takes you to the enormous sand dune that climbs the cape. For some aerobic exercise, climb to the top of this dune. That is what hang glider pilots do, carrying heavy wings that weigh between fifty and eighty pounds. This dune is rated as one of the best for beginners in hang gliding, and lessons, which are important in this sport, are frequently given here. With winds deflected up cliffs, the coast often provides good lifts.

The park goes north along the strip of beach to Sand Lake. The Oregon Coast Trail is on the beach between the lake and Cape Kiwanda. From the south side of the cape, beach walkers can hike to the end of the Nestucca Spit.

The popularity of the outdoor activities at Cape Kiwanda has encouraged commercial development along the highway here, with shops and lodging available across from the beach parking area. The RV park located a block away has made recent improvements in its amenities. Pacific City also holds frequent art celebrations and exhibits.

Sandstone cliffs and surf at Cape Kiwanda are impressive.

63. CAPE LOOKOUT STATE PARK

Hours/Season: Day use (fee) and overnight (reservations available); year-round
Area: 2,014 acres
Attractions: Beach access, hiking, nature study, wildlife viewing, beachcombing, kayaking, clamming, fishing, photography, picnicking, camping
Facilities: Exhibit information, picnic tables, meeting hall, group picnic reservations, campground (38 full hookup, 1 electrical, 176 tent sites—maximum site 60 feet), 10 yurts, hiker/biker camp, group tent (4 areas), wheelchair-accessible restrooms with showers, dump station, summer slide program, firewood
Access: Off Three Capes Scenic Loop, 12 miles southwest of Tillamook
Contact: (503) 842-4981

Cape Lookout is an outstanding example of the many coastal headlands preserved by the state park system that contain fine examples of ancient forest. In the endeavor to create more designated wilderness areas, we sometimes forget how farsighted the state has been. When they lock up pristine coastline for recreation, it's a double blessing. This vast park extends from the tip of the 5-mile Netarts Spit (which encloses Netarts Bay) south past the developed area to include the rocky headland named Cape Lookout, so recreation opportunities are varied.

The cape was named by John Meares, sea captain. He intended this name for what is now Cape Meares, but charts put it in the wrong place and it stuck. The original land for the park was a 1935 gift from the U.S. Lighthouse Service, although it was later concluded that a more accessible site for the lighthouse was on Cape Meares.

On a map, Cape Lookout resembles a dagger jabbed into the sea. The wave action on the cliffs has exposed a sequence of lava flows, some of which cooled on dry land and others that are pillar basalts which erupted under water. Gradually—but oh, so slowly—the surf is pounding this volcanic peninsula into sand and mud.

The park facilities are on low land along the ocean, reached by a road past gurgling creeks and wetland habitat. To prevent erosion along such low areas along the Oregon coast, European beach grass was planted over a period of several years to stabilize and halt the inland sweep of sand along the coast. This grass is an introduced plant that has built our coastal foredune system,

At sunset at Cape Lookout State Park, a child with a sand bucket walks the beach.

an unnatural formation that can provide protection from inland surges of water in winter where necessary. A few years ago, storm damage near the campground area required new plantings of this beach grass to stabilize the foredune. A path through the foredune allows beach access. Visitors in winter can see how high tides cover the beach areas of the park. The campground area itself is quite safe in winter, however, and yurts and a meeting hall are recent additions. The short Jackson Creek Loop Trail is accessed to the rear of the campground.

Trails connect the various areas of this large park. For a better understanding of the ecology of the temperate rain forest, hike

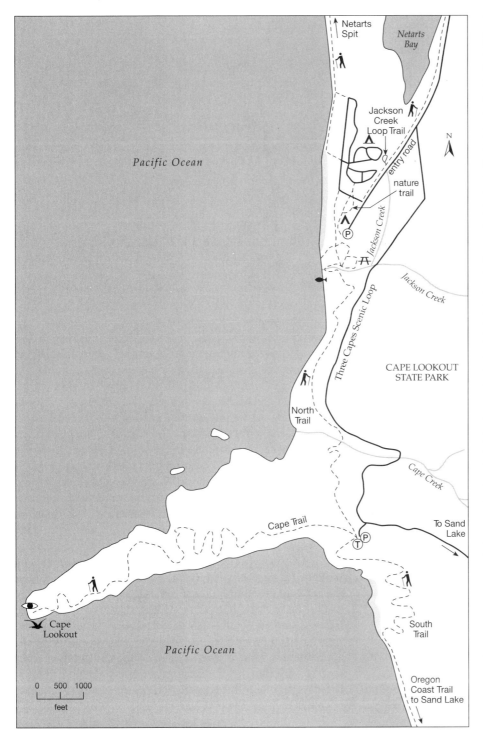

the nature trail between the campground and hiker/biker camp, which is located near the day-use area to the south. Cape Lookout averages over 100 inches of rain each year and the temperatures are moderate—ingredients for the success of native plants. Along the path, you can count tree rings, see ferns rooted to spruce trees, a springboard notch used by loggers, natural grafting of trees, and western red cedar—once the most useful tree to the north coast Native American, who used it to make canoes, nets, homes, and clothing.

Picnic tables in the day-use area are scattered beneath windblown spruce trees near the ocean, close to where Jackson Creek flows out to the sea. At several points, trails access the beach. Wildlife is easy to spot even in the developed area. Raccoons are almost tame, deer are seen, and squirrels are numerous. Steller's jays make their presence known, and red-tailed hawks scout above the cape.

For a longer trail, hike some of the Oregon Coast Trail that traverses the park. It enters from the north along the entry road—with a connecting trail from the campground—and then heads south along the North Trail of the park as it climbs in 2.3 miles through the forest to the top of the 800-foot ridge summit of the cape. It emerges there at the parking area for those hiking west to the tip of the cape. Those parking here might be confused by the trails. Of the two trails, the south one goes to the tip of Cape Lookout; the north one comes from the campground. Another confusion might arise in a short distance when a trail branches off to the south. This trail is the continuation of the Oregon Coast Trail, which descends in 2 miles to the beach and then proceeds south to Sand Lake, where it continues on the beach—if Sand Lake can be crossed—to Cape Kiwanda.

The popular trail is the 2.4-mile hike that drops slowly down to the rocky terminus of the cape. It initially edges the southern portion of the cape, with views down steep cliffs to tree-framed azure water below. Level at first, the path is not difficult, with alternate up and down portions, and it then jogs into an ancient forest of Sitka spruce and western hemlock, with undercover of sword and maidenhair ferns, in the center of the cape. Along the trail is a plaque in memory of the crew of a B-17 bomber on coastal patrol that crashed on the cape on October 12, 1943, with only one survivor. A little past halfway, the trail reaches the north side of the cape, with a view of Cape Meares, Three Arch Rocks, the spit, and Netarts Bay. After winding through the middle forest again, the path descends along the south edge to a tiny clearing on the rocky point. Though this is a year-round trail, it can have muddy sections in winter, and caution is especially required on the last area where the trail is edged by a sheer drop-off. This final view is to the south, and includes Cape Kiwanda with its huge sand dune. The cape is a good wildlife viewing area, with 154 species of birds being recorded. One can watch them fly from nesting and resting places. It is also an official whale-watch site, and must be a fairly good one since quite a few people make the hike out, even in late December, to watch whales migrating. Viewing these cetaceans is always easier from a lofty elevation directly above the sea.

Netarts Bay draws crowds of people who wade in with hip boots for clamming and even pick up steamers on the mud flats without much effort. Others launch kayaks to paddle across the bay to the end of the spit for some mostly solitary beach strolling. Humans, kingfishers, and great blue herons all enjoy the fishing.

64. OCEANSIDE BEACH STATE RECREATION SITE

Hours/Season: Day use; year-round
Area: 7.3 acres
Attractions: Wildlife viewing, beachcombing, fishing, clamming
Facilities: Beach access, restrooms
Access: Off the Three Capes Scenic Loop, 11 miles west of Tillamook

Oceanside Beach State Recreation Site fronts the resort community of Oceanside, where homes are spectacularly stair-stepped

A scenic beach walk curves south from Oceanside Beach State Recreation Site to Netarts.

up the steep slope just south of Cape Meares, precariously, but perfectly situated to take in the view west. And it is stunning! The ocean vista is highlighted by offshore Three Arch Rocks and bracketed by the headland to the north and Netarts Bay to the south. Jutting out into the sea beyond that is Cape Lookout.

Some visitors just park facing the ocean and inhale the view, or step outside to throw food to the seagulls, who are happy to eat and entertain them. A short path accesses the sandy beach, where a short walk north ends at Maxwell Point, which stretches out into the sea. The first tract given for the park by Orin and Lorraine Rosenburg included Maxwell Point with a tunnel for beach access, but only an intrepid explorer will locate it, and probably at low tide. The agate hunting is reported to be prime in this beach area. Walking south, you can stretch your legs a bit more by hiking a 2-mile section of the Oregon Coast Trail via the beach to the community of Netarts.

One-half mile offshore, Three Arch Rocks is part of the Oregon Islands National Wildlife Refuge, a designated National Wilderness Area, so binoculars would be helpful in observing the action, which is definitely better in spring and summer when seabirds are nesting. This refuge supports Oregon's largest breeding colony of tufted puffins, the largest breeding colony of common murres (about 75,000) south of Alaska, in addition to pigeon guillemots, storm petrels, cormorants, and gulls. Sea lions share this habitat. It is the only breeding site for Steller sea lions on the northern Oregon coast. Three Arch Rocks became the first national wildlife refuge west of the Mississippi River in 1907, and was designated by Theodore Roosevelt. Protection was urged by William Finley and H. T. Bohlman after they found that weekend fun in this area involved tourist boats riding around these rocks and shooting birds for sport.

65. CAPE MEARES STATE SCENIC VIEWPOINT

Hours/Season: Day use; year-round
Area: 233 acres
Attractions: Historic lighthouse, photography, hiking, wildlife viewing, Octopus Tree, giant Sitka spruce, Cape Meares National Wildlife Refuge, paddling, picnicking
Facilities: Picnic tables, information center, exhibit information, restrooms
Access: Off Three Capes Scenic Loop, 10 miles west of Tillamook

Most humans visit Cape Meares State Scenic Viewpoint to see the lighthouse and the spectacular ocean views, perhaps having lunch on the lawn or at the few picnic tables. Others come with binoculars for the offshore wildlife refuge at Three Arch Rocks. Smart ones include some hiking on the trails. The entry road passes through the 138-acre mainland Cape Meares National Wildlife Refuge, whose boundaries are contiguous with the park.

Although now inactive, the Oregon coast's shortest lighthouse (38 feet high) was built in 1890, and its beacon of red and white alternating light shone until 1963, when it was replaced by an automatic beacon. The hand-ground French lens came around Cape Horn and was lifted onto the 200-foot cliff and onto its tower by a hand-operated crane made from local spruce trees. From May through September and during the Christmas season, the gift shop and lighthouse, with its spiral staircase, are open to visitors.

It seems appropriate that this cape was named after John Meares, eighteenth-century British naval officer, fur trader, and explorer. He had named it Cape Lookout, but that name was misplaced on maps and this cape needed a name.

Hiking options are varied. From the ocean parking lot, a loop

The Oregon coast's shortest lighthouse (38 feet high) is reached by trail on Cape Meares.

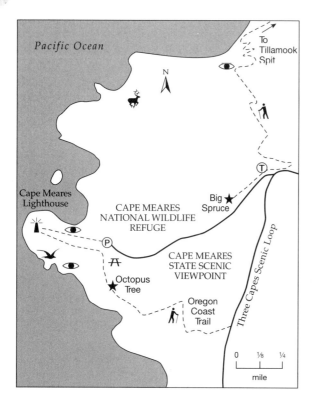

Pacific Ocean

To Tillamook Spit

N

Cape Meares
Lighthouse

CAPE MEARES
NATIONAL WILDLIFE
REFUGE

Big
Spruce

CAPE MEARES
STATE SCENIC
VIEWPOINT

Octopus
Tree

Oregon
Coast
Trail

Three Capes Scenic Loop

0   1/8   1/4
mile

beginning of the entry road where there is a trail map exhibit, however, a short segment west is still open that leads to a giant spruce tree. This tree is truly impressive, a straight, majestic specimen that has a crown of gnarled limbs—a good example of this protected old-growth spruce and hemlock forest. This is in the Cape Meares National Wildlife Refuge, which protects one of the remaining stands of coastal old-growth forest in Oregon. It was designated a Research Natural Area in 1987. It is habitat for threatened and endangered bird species, including northern spotted owls, bald eagles, and marbled murrelets.

At this trailhead, a spur also heads north for 6 miles to the end of the Tillamook Spit. It descends gently through woods until it opens into sunlight and mind-elevating views of waves pounding the spit and Tillamook Bay beyond. Good birding is found by walking on the spit, but it is worthwhile just to hike the first short distance, less than 0.5 mile, to the view. The trail to Cape Meares can also be accessed from the community of Cape Meares, at the end of 5th Street.

Tillamook Bay offers good paddling possibilities combined with wildlife viewing. Several rivers empty into the bay, and traveling up these quiet river inlets allows the paddler to get close to many ducks and hawks that would normally be frightened away—a great experience.

When winds blow from the southwest, keep an eye out for hang gliders over the cape. Nearby 500-foot Maxwell Mountain offers opportunities for hang gliders to lift their wings and glide north.

66. MUNSON CREEK FALLS STATE NATURAL SITE

Hours/Season: Day use; year-round
Attractions: Waterfall, photography, hiking, picnicking
Facilities: Picnic tables
Access: Off US 101, 6 miles south of Tillamook, then 1.5 miles east from sign to gravel parking area

Long known to Tillamook area residents as a county park, Munson Creek Falls State Natural Site features an easy 0.25-mile trail through northwest forest to a view of the highest waterfall in the Coast Range, 319 feet high. The trail leads to a picnic area at the base of the falls. In the past, a precipitous trail accessed a higher viewpoint of the falls, but mud slides have obliterated it. Visit in spring when the falls are energetic from winter rain and spring snowmelt from the mountains.

trail descends to the lighthouse on the tip of the headland via a wide paved path, with a spur going a few steps north at one point to a picnic table and a view that includes a steep-walled rocky cove with seasonal, ribbon waterfalls. A loop back to the parking lot hugs the southern edge of the headland where benches and natural history exhibits let you linger to view the fantastic seascape, which includes a broad wave-swept cove, the hillside town of Oceanside, and Three Arch Rocks National Wildlife Refuge. This trail continues past the restrooms and passes the Octopus Tree, a large Sitka spruce on a point facing southwest that one assumes has been configured by the force of winter winds. Native American legend, however, holds that natives shaped the young tree for a sacred burial tree so that it would hold the canoes of their deceased leaders. This portion of the Oregon Coast Trail continues to the highway in less than 1 mile through forest that skirts fine views south near its terminus.

In the past, these trails were contiguous with the Oregon Coast Trail north through the park, but storms and erosion plus a bald eagle nest have caused closure of the trail from the parking lot north for some of the way. If one parks near the

Forested Munson Creek Falls State Natural Site features a trail to a 319-foot-high waterfall, the highest one in the Coast Range.

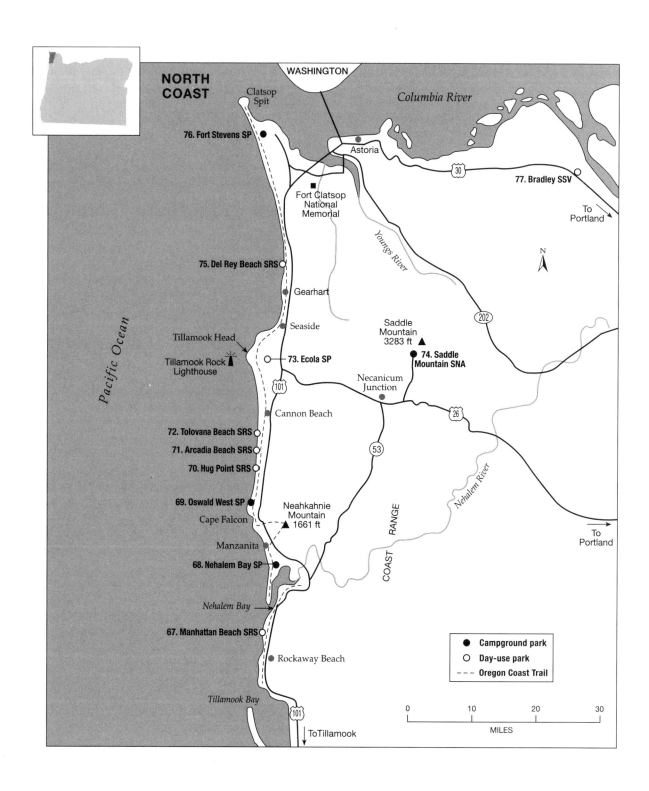

NORTH
COAST

WASHINGTON

Columbia River

Clatsop
Spit

76. Fort Stevens SP

Astoria

30

77. Bradley SSV

To
Portland

Fort Clatsop
National
Memorial

Youngs River

N

75. Del Rey Beach SRS

Gearhart

202

Saddle
Mountain
3283 ft ▲

Seaside

Tillamook Head

**74. Saddle
Mountain SNA**

Tillamook Rock
Lighthouse

○ **73. Ecola SP**

Necanicum
Junction

Pacific Ocean

101

Cannon Beach

26

72. Tolovana Beach SRS

71. Arcadia Beach SRS

53

70. Hug Point SRS

69. Oswald West SP

Neahkahnie
Mountain
1661 ft ▲

Cape Falcon

COAST RANGE

Nehalem River

To
Portland

Manzanita

68. Nehalem Bay SP

Nehalem Bay

67. Manhattan Beach SRS

Rockaway Beach

● **Campground park**
○ **Day-use park**
- - - **Oregon Coast Trail**

Tillamook Bay

101

To Tillamook

0   10   20   30

MILES

CHAPTER FOUR

NORTH COAST

From Tillamook Bay north to the mouth of the mighty Columbia River, and inland to the forested peaks of the Coast Range, the North Coast region encompasses varied landscapes. Scenic dairy farms surround Tillamook, and the drive through town might include stops at the cheese-making plants, and a dip (or two) of excellent Tillamook ice cream.

Several rivers flow from the inland mountain terrain to empty into Tillamook Bay and Nehalem Bay. North of Tillamook, Garibaldi has excellent charter boat facilities and the fishing is good—salmon, perch, halibut, rock fish, or longer trips for albacore tuna. Charter boats also take tourists out for excursions to watch wildlife and see the coastline from a different perspective. Restaurants feature local oysters along with the fresh marine bounty harvested by commercial boats.

Manhattan Beach features beachcombing. Nehalem Bay offers a playground for visitors, where paddling canoes or kayaks and digging clams or surf fishing is fun. Nehalem Bay State Park even caters to fly-in visitors and has camping facilities for equestrians. Windsurfers challenge the surf at nearby Manzanita.

From Nehalem Bay north to Seaside, the coastline is a concatenation of bluffs, coves, headlands, beaches, and the north coast's only mountain that slopes into the Pacific Ocean. A large share of this wild paradise is included in Oswald West State Park. The park attracts the outdoor enthusiast with surfing coves, mountain streams, old-growth forest, and a trail up 1,661-foot Neahkahnie Mountain.

Beaches become more numerous and accessible north of Arch Cape, with three waysides—Hug Point, Arcadia Beach, and Tolovana Beach—providing access to an incredible variety of views and beach walking. Oregon's beaches were originally needed for public access because they were used as a pioneer wagon road. Hug Point is noteworthy because of the challenge of rounding this point, even at low tide.

Cannon Beach is the cultural center of the north coast. Its long stretch of beach competes with Bandon Beach as the most scenic in the state. Just north of town, Ecola State Park provides awesome vistas everywhere you look. Tillamook Rock Lighthouse, now inactive, is offshore. The park's Indian Beach is along the historic trail traveled by the Lewis and Clark Expedition. Today, park visitors hike the same trail within the park.

Inland from Cannon Beach and Seaside, Saddle Mountain State Natural Area preserves a mountain rich in geologic and plant interest, and a trail for experienced hikers. North of Seaside, the land along the coastline is flat coastal plains that extend to the Columbia River. Midway along this route, Del Rey Beach provides beach access for hikers, off-road vehicles (ORVs), and equestrians.

The north coast of Oregon ends at the mouth of the Columbia River, an area rich in history that was the terminus of the Lewis and Clark Expedition. During the winter of 1805–1806, they stayed at the inland fort they constructed. Fort Clatsop National Memorial, their reconstructed fort, is now a tourist attraction. Historic Astoria, Oregon, at the mouth of the Columbia River, became the first permanent European-American settlement west of the Mississippi.

Historic Fort Stevens State Park includes both the river and ocean sides of Clatsop Spit. It was originally a fortification built during the Civil War that continued to be active through World War II. The northern trailhead to the Oregon Coast Trail is just south of the river, and it can be hiked from Fort Stevens to Tillamook Bay. This huge park is great for bicycling, hiking, and camping. East of Astoria, along the river, is a high viewpoint of the river and into Washington State at Bradley State Scenic Viewpoint.

The climate changes somewhat as one travels north on the coast. Winters are cooler, though still temperate; summer temperatures vary less. Inland terrains are colder in winter and hotter in summer.

For additional information on Oregon State Parks, call 1-800-551-6949, or check the official website: *www.prd.state.or.us.*

67. MANHATTAN BEACH STATE RECREATION SITE

Hours/Season: Day use; year-round
Area: 41 acres
Attractions: Beach walking, surf fishing, kite flying, picnicking
Facilities: Beach access, picnic tables, restrooms
Access: West off US 101, 2 miles north of Rockaway Beach

The road branching off from US 101 to the ocean crosses the tracks of the Southern Pacific Railroad before accessing the level beach tract of property that is Manhattan Beach State Recreation Site. Just north of the summer resort community of Rockaway Beach, picnicking and a rest stop are reasons to stop, but the beach is an even better one.

The name of the park is a curious one. The postmaster of the community wrote in 1926 that promoters gave it this name because it was a watering place. The Native American word *manhattan,* as applied to the island in New York, is reported to describe that city as a place of drunkenness, but this Manhattan is quite a different place.

Situated between Tillamook and Nehalem Bays, an easy path leads through coastal vegetation to 7 miles of sandy beach that is far from the madding crowd. Almost midway between looming bluffs in either direction, you can stroll out in either direction for a day hike while doing some wave watching, or traverse this entire stretch of the Oregon Coast Trail. Offshore to the south are scenic sea stacks called Twin Rocks. Less than 2 miles south is Rockaway Beach Wayside, further south is Twin Rocks Wayside, and the beach ends at Barview County Park at Tillamook Bay, also the end of the first 64 miles of the trail to be completed from the trailhead at the Columbia River.

68. NEHALEM BAY STATE PARK

Hours/Season: Day use (fee) and overnight (reservations available); year-round
Area: 890 acres
Attractions: Hiking, biking, and equestrian trails, boating, paddling, fishing, clamming, crabbing, beachcombing, windsurfing, wildlife viewing, exhibit information, picnicking, camping
Facilities: Several beach access paths, picnic tables, exhibit information, campground (4 full hookup, 277 electrical sites—3 accessible, maximum site 60 feet), 12 yurts, accessible restrooms with showers, horse camp (17 primitive sites with corrals), hiker/biker camp, fly-in camp (6 primitive sites), meeting hall, amphitheater, playground, boat launch, dump station, public phone
Access: Off US 101, 3 miles south of Manzanita Junction, 2.5 miles via spur road
Contact: Nehalem Bay State Park, (503) 368-5154; for ferry service across Nehalem Bay, phone Jetty Fishery at (503) 368-5746

With a 2,400-foot airstrip, Nehalem Bay State Park offers the unique opportunity of a fly-in camp, a great way to view the coastline near Neahkahnie Mountain and Nehalem Bay from an aerial perspective. The park lies between the bay and the ocean, and includes the long sand spit to the south that edges the river estuary. Step off the plane or out of your vehicle, arrive by bicycle, or on foot via the Oregon Coast Trail, and recreation is just a few steps away. You can watch the wild surf from the edge of the beach or travel upriver to calm canoeing. The bay has excellent crabbing and a good supply of bay clams. In the past, Native American used weirs, or fish traps, to catch salmon going upriver.

A foredune with European beach grass separates the campground from the beach, but many paths lead over this to the ocean. The horse camp is south of the main campground. Picnic choices include three day-use areas: just west of the boat ramp with a path to the beach, near the overnight camp overlooking the boating activity on the bay with a backdrop of coastal mountains, and at

Ocean windsurfers may be seen on a beach stroll from Nehalem Bay State Park to nearby Manzanita.

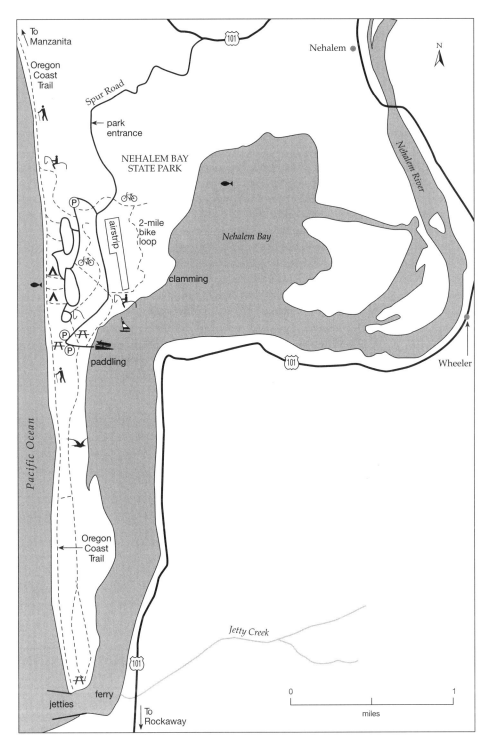

Oregon
Coast
Trail

Spur Road

← park
entrance

NEHALEM BAY
STATE PARK

P

airstrip

2-mile
bike
loop

Nehalem Bay

clamming

P

P

paddling

Pacific Ocean

Oregon
Coast
Trail

Jetty Creek

Nehalem

Nehalem River

N

101

Wheeler

101

0   1

miles

101

ferry

To
Rockaway

jetties

the end of the spit (reached by foot, horse, or boat—*no potable water*).

The spit was formed by continued sand deposition where the outward flow of the Nehalem River meets incoming waves. The growth of the spit is to the south because it is influenced more by the southward longshore currents of the summer winds.

The park has a curious history of people finding chunks of beeswax, marked with shipping markings and religious Latin symbols, in fields about a mile south of the entrance. The theory is that a ship (perhaps the Spanish ship *San Francisco Xavier*) wrecked on the spit in 1705. The ship remains are no longer visible. At least six galleons left the Philippines for Acapulco, Mexico, and were lost at sea. Besides finding several uses for the beeswax, the Native Americans and early settlers appropriated the teak planks of the ship and used them for furniture.

Hikers can walk the Oregon Coast Trail 1.1 miles north to Manzanita, at the foot of Neahkahnie Mountain, where windsurfers often tack back and forth through the waves. Or they can head south for 3.7 miles to the spit's end. With advance reservations, hikers can cross the bay by boat to continue hiking south on the beach to Tillamook Bay. Native Americans used to ferry pioneers across the mouth of Nehalem Bay in cedar canoes with the horses swimming behind.

Trails that weave through the interior of the park include a 1.5-mile hiking trail, a 6-mile equestrian trail, and a 2-mile bike loop. Equestrians can ride on the beach, where photographers should be alert for good silhouettes at sunset. Equestrians are restricted from the campground and day-use areas.

Oregon Coast Trail

The first explorers of what is Oregon today were those who came by sea. It is no wonder that the Oregon coast—a vital connection between sea voyagers and coastal inhabitants—has long been an area of many trails. Native Americans followed the paths made by Roosevelt elk and black-tailed deer; Lewis and Clark took advantage of the same trails. Today, many of the surviving trails are used for recreation as a way of personal discovery, of witnessing up close the beauty of our surroundings and its wildlife inhabitants, and of simply enjoying outdoor exercise.

Government and other agencies have greatly extended the construction of new and connecting trails. The Civilian Conservation Corps did their part in the 1930s. Then, in 1971, the Oregon Legislature created the Oregon Recreation Trails Advisory Council to promote development of long-distance trails throughout the state, an ongoing project today.

In 1959, Samuel N. Dicken, who researched pioneer routes and taught geography at the University of Oregon, conceived the idea of a hiking trail extending the full length of the Oregon coast. For a decade, the idea was discussed by hiking clubs, the press, and state park personnel, and in 1969 the state park system began a study of the concept that involved using what trails remained intact, and solving problems, such as ownership, safety, and water crossings. Another feasibility study, undertaken in 1972, brought more solutions to the trail possibility.

With his wife, Dicken explored the proposed route for this hiking trail, and his dream finally became reality. Since 1972, the first 64.4 miles of the Oregon Coast Trail, from the Columbia River to Tillamook Bay, was completed, along with other sections farther south. Today, the trail is more than two-thirds complete.

The Oregon Coast Trail is a concatenation of trails on headlands, up mountains, past creeks and rivers, past lighthouses, and along beaches that provide endless variety and beauty. Truly, Oregon's coastline is one of the world's finest.

Besides the 64.4-mile northern segment, spectacular sections are found in Ecola, Oswald West, Cape Lookout, Carl G. Washburne to Heceta Head Lighthouse, Sunset Bay to Cape Arago, Humbug Mountain, and Samuel H. Boardman state parks. Many other parks have long beach stretches and interesting day hikes. Distinctive Oregon Coast Trail signs are found on posts near trail access points. Camping is allowed in some areas along the trail for backpackers, and many state park campgrounds have hiker/biker camps.

Whether you're interested in hiking, geology, coastal history, wildlife sightings, wave watching, whale watching, or ocean windsurfing, you'll find it along this fabulous trail.

A brochure is available from the Oregon State Parks and Recreation Department—call the information number—that covers the entire trail, though more detailed maps and information are needed. Trail information and several detailed maps are included in this book, since so much of the trail is accessed in the seventy-seven coastal state parks.

One highlight of the Oregon Coast Trail is the hike to the summit of Neahkahnie Mountain in Oswald West State Park.

69. OSWALD WEST STATE PARK

Hours/Season: Day use and overnight; campground facilities closed November through February
Area: 2,474 acres
Attractions: Hiking, ancient forest, photography, fishing, surfing, wildlife viewing, picnicking, camping
Facilities: Picnic tables, campground (28 walk-in tent sites—wheelbarrows provided), restrooms, beach access
Access: Off US 101, 10 miles south of Cannon Beach

Oswald West State Park preserves a spur of the Coast Range that sits on the coastline and encompasses Arch Cape, Neahkahnie Mountain, Cape Falcon, and Smuggler's Cove—an incomparable 4 miles of shoreline geology, ancient forest, and majestic views.

The park honors Governor Oswald West, in office from 1911 to 1915. The park is also a monument to the acquisition efforts of Park Superintendent Samuel H. Boardman, who negotiated with the highway engineer to realign US 101 south of Arch Cape on the shoulder of Neahkahnie Mountain. This conserved the enormous swatch of forest on both sides of the highway. In doing this, no other roads were necessary within this vast acreage, yet the most spectacular attractions are accessible via self-propelled energy, some quite easily, others demanding greater effort. The result is the experience of wildness.

The campground is a 0.25-mile walk-in affair for tenters via a downhill, paved trail. Just toss your gear into a wheelbarrow and roll it to the campground's lush setting among red huckleberry, salmonberry, salal bushes, and towering trees. The campsites are located between Short Sand Creek and Necarney Creek, just before they merge in the middle of Smuggler's Cove, an unusual phenomenon. The word "Necarney" comes from the Spanish name for meat, *carne* (which the native thought synonymous with elk), to which the Native Americans added *ne*, which means "the place of," since this is the place to find Roosevelt elk.

Steller's jays and chickarees are notorious camp robbers, so don't leave food out. Kingfishers catch their own fish, hairy woodpeckers peck into trees, and dippers go underwater in the streams for food.

Along the east side of the highway is a day-use area, with trails leading under the road and into the canyon along Short Sand Creek to an ocean picnic area and driftwood-edged Smuggler's Cove. Surfers put boards into the Pacific and sea lions are curious about human activities. Fishing boats sometimes anchor in the cove in bad weather. The cove is edged by Cape Falcon to the north and Point Illga to the south, named for a Tillamook Indian woman. Tidepools are at both ends of the cove.

With 13 scenic miles of the Oregon Coast Trail in the park (mostly constructed by the Civilian Conservation Corps from 1939 to 1941), visitors might want to sample some of the varied hiking, or take a backpacking trip, using the campground for overnighting. (Although the campground restrooms are closed in winter, hiking is possible year-round.) One might consider hiking through the ancient forest during the rainy season, when

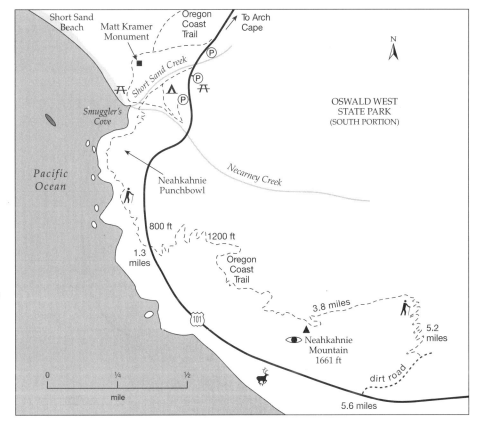

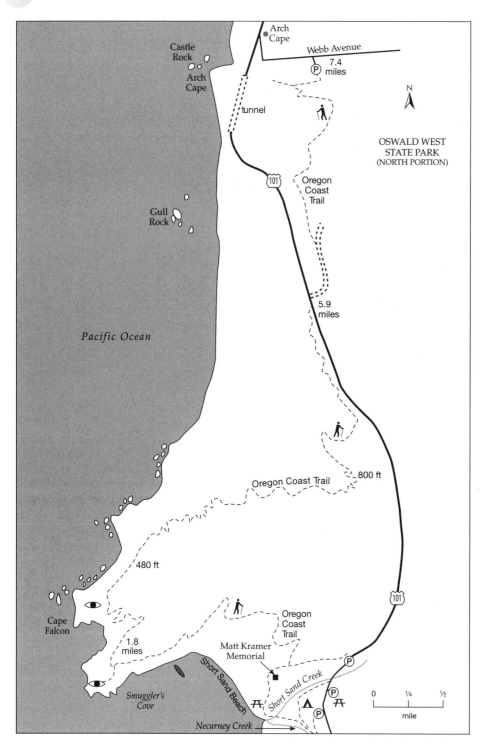

Arch
Cape

Webb Avenue

P 7.4
miles

N

Castle
Rock

Arch
Cape

tunnel

OSWALD WEST
STATE PARK
(NORTH PORTION)

101

Oregon
Coast
Trail

Gull
Rock

5.9
miles

Pacific Ocean

800 ft

Oregon Coast Trail

101

480 ft

Cape
Falcon

Oregon
Coast
Trail

1.8
miles

Matt Kramer
Memorial

P

Short Sand Beach

Short Sand Creek

P

*Smuggler's
Cove*

P

P

0   ¼   ½

mile

Necarney Creek

a drizzle is hardly felt under the giant trees and the wind is subdued. Sounds are of overflowing creeks; green leaves form small cups of water. You can witness winter storm damage and windswept litter that nourishes the forest throughout the year. Summer is not the best time to feel the mystique of the temperate rain forest.

It is thought that Cape Falcon was discovered and named by Captain Bruno Heceta in 1775. The 1.8-mile trail to the 750-foot-high cape begins just west of the picnic grounds by the cove. Near the beginning is a split in the trail that goes to a memorial for Matt Kramer, an Associated Press journalist whose articles were important to the passage of the 1967 beach bill. The trail continues through ancient green forest of ferns and Sitka spruce, western hemlock, cedar, and fir. At one point, a broken, old-growth tree that split a few feet above the ground edges the trail. Its remaining trunk looks like a mammoth shell rooted to earth, yet the unmistakable artistry of wood grains edge curves in the break. At the tip of the cape, a fork leads west to a vegetated knoll beside the sea, with south views of the cove and mountain, which are often strung with fog ribbons. Listen to the sounds of surf against the steep slice of cliff as black sand beach is slowly formed. Wander the paths to see the scallops of cliff to the north, with views of the columnar basalt joints where lava cooled in straight lines. Watch for seals, sea lions, and whales below. (The official whale-watching site, however, is south along the highway.)

To continue north on the Oregon Coast Trail, return from the tip of the cape to the main trail and continue north past more ocean coves and then east for 4.1 miles through dense forest.

The terminus of the popular Cape Falcon Trail in Oswald West State Park is viewed from the whale-watch site on US 101.

Little light reaches the forest floor on this trail to a highway crossing. East of the highway, the trail follows the mail route of the late 1880s to early 1900s. A story is told of how a mail carrier guided a man on horseback over the mountain trail who was so frightened that it was necessary to blindfold him and tie his feet under his horse. The trail descends Arch Cape through the only ancient forest left in Clatsop County on the east side of US 101. In 1.5 miles, the trail leaves the state park just south of the town of Arch Cape, soon crosses a small suspension bridge (check to see if this has been repaired), and reaches Webb Avenue.

To hike to the summit of Neahkahnie Mountain, cross Necarney Creek and travel through woods to Neahkahnie Punchbowl, a broad meadow at the edge of sheer cliffs on the west side of the highway. In 1.3 miles, the highway is reached (you might begin there), and the 2.5-mile trail up 1,661-foot Neahkahnie Mountain begins through a profusion of wildflowers and then climbs in switchbacks, with a moderate grade of 7.5 percent. The Tillamook Indians called Neahkahnie Mountain "the place of the Fire Spirit" and considered it a special place. It is for hikers, too, with the soaring vista of the coast, Nehalem Bay, and sea views that span 50 miles.

From the top of the mountain, the trail continues south for 1.8 miles, through forest and many good views of mountain ridges, to a dirt road that leads to the highway. You can make a loop hike by returning north along the highway. Rumors have long circulated that Neahkahnie Mountain has buried treasure, and stones with curious letters have been found, but no treasure as yet.

70. HUG POINT STATE RECREATION SITE

Hours/Season: Day use; year-round
Area: 43 acres
Attractions: Historic stagecoach trail, natural caves, seasonal waterfall, beachcombing, hiking, surf fishing, photography, picnicking
Facilities: Beach access, restrooms
Access: Off US 101, 5 miles south of Cannon Beach

The name for Hug Point relates to the historic fact that pioneers used the beach as a highway in the late 1800s and they had to "hug" this particular point even at low tide to get around it. This was possible only after a wagon road was blasted out of the rock. Patience and planning were required in those days, as it is today for those walking the Oregon Coast Trail in this area. Hikers

This narrow rocky ledge was historically a wagon road traversed at low tide, now on the Oregon Coast Trail in Hug Point State Recreation Site.

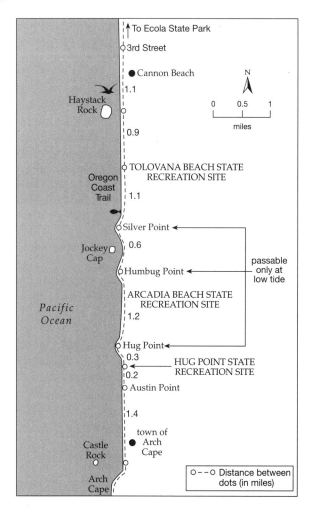

To Ecola State Park
3rd Street
● Cannon Beach
N
1.1
Haystack Rock
0   0.5   1
miles
0.9
Oregon Coast Trail
TOLOVANA BEACH STATE RECREATION SITE
1.1
Silver Point
0.6
Jockey Cap
Humbug Point
passable only at low tide
ARCADIA BEACH STATE RECREATION SITE
1.2
Pacific Ocean
Hug Point
0.3
HUG POINT STATE RECREATION SITE
0.2
Austin Point
1.4
Castle Rock
town of Arch Cape
Arch Cape
○--○ Distance between dots (in miles)

lands are backlit by a sparkling sea or washed by a setting sun.

This section of the Oregon Coast Trail is a scenic one and can be hiked on the beach between 3rd Street in Cannon Beach to the inland route over Arch Cape, a distance of 6.8 miles. Day hikers could walk in either direction from Hug Point State Recreation Site. It is 10.4 miles round trip north to 3rd Street and 3.2 miles round trip south to Arch Cape. Haystack Rock (yes, there are two of them on the Oregon coast) is 4.1 miles one way to the north, an excellent destination; consider being picked up there by fellow travelers. *Please don't attempt this destination except at low tide.*

71. ARCADIA BEACH STATE RECREATION SITE

Hours/Season: Day use; year-round
Area: 19 acres
Attractions: Beachcombing, hiking, surf fishing, picnicking
Facilities: Picnic tables, beach access, restrooms
Access: 3 miles south of Cannon Beach

Trees edge the parking lot at Arcadia Beach State Recreation Site where a trail leads downhill to a sandy cove that stretches for more than a mile between two headlands. The park includes forested Humbug Point, which is a short distance to the north. To the south is Hug Point. Humbug Point was named because pioneers mistakenly thought they had reached Hug Point, but they had farther to go and a more difficult point to round.

Off Humbug Point is Lion Rock, and 0.6 mile farther north, past an offshore rock called Jockey Cap, is Silver Point, so named for the color of the weathered spruce trees on the bluff. If you look east between these two points, you'll notice a slide area. The hike between Arch Cape and Silver Point is a good place to see hardened sediments in cut-away places of the bluffs. These sandstone bluffs were once under water and only recently uplifted. The pressures exerted on them can be observed in the tilted and twisted patterns of layered rock. In addition, wind, sea, and rain have eroded them, and continue to do so, a reason to leave these cliffs undeveloped. The Native Americans understood these natural forces and used more stable inland elk trails for their travels.

The beach widens by the time Tolovana Beach is reached in another 1.1 miles. Backpackers will find "unofficial" camps on the south side of Silver and Austin Points.

rounding this point on the rock road will feel some of the emotion that the incoming surf evokes on this narrow ledge.

The entry to the park accesses a large parking area that slopes downhill past a few picnic tables and connects to a walkway to the beach. This oceanfront area is backed by hills vegetated by salal, other shrubs, and Sitka spruce. The beach area is a lovely sandy cove midway between Austin Point on the south and Hug Point to the north. It is a beautiful private place with a seasonal waterfall on the south side of Hug Point where caves have formed from erosion of the golden-layered walls of sandstone. Jellyfish and sand dollars are often seen on the sand. Austin Point has more of this tilted sedimentary rock. This area is one of those special locales that appeals because of its scenic beauty, and is particularly photogenic when the inundations of curving head-

72. TOLOVANA BEACH STATE RECREATION SITE

Hours/Season: Day use; year-round
Area: 3.3 acres
Attractions: Kite flying, beach walking, beach horseback riding, surf fishing, picnicking, birdwatching, nature study, photography
Facilities: Picnic tables, restrooms, beach access
Access: 1 mile south of Cannon Beach, off US 101

Tolovana is a Native American name, and the park is in the midst of the small community of Tolovana Park, which was named after a town in Alaska. This subdivision was the historic setting of a rustic oceanside hostelry known as Warren Hotel.

At the south edge of touristy Cannon Beach, Tolovana Beach offers access to miles of strolling on this scenic beach. Offshore rocks and various basalt structures along the beach are highlighted to the north by enormous Haystack Rock, a formation resulting from an active volcanic period more than 20 million years ago.

This park provides excellent parking near restrooms and picnic tables, away from crowded parking in the main area of Cannon Beach, and the opportunity for a 2-mile walk to Ecola Creek at the north end of town, with options for side trips to galleries, shops, or a snack before returning to your vehicle. Along the way, you'll be entertained by kites flying, dogs playing with Frisbees, surf fishers, or perhaps picturesque equestrians. Sunsets are spectacular in this area with the colored surf and silhouetted sea stacks. Oregon Coast Trail hikers can also walk south on the beach for 5 miles to Arch Cape, at low tide.

Part of the Oregon Islands National Wildlife Refuge, Haystack Rock and neighboring rocks called the "Needles" are particularly intriguing when you can view the intertidal inhabitants of the protected marine garden. Organisms are organized by niches in different horizontal zones. Sea stars, anemones, tiny crabs, sea snails, urchins, seaweeds, barnacles, chitons, and tiny sculpin fish darting among the tidepools are just a few of the possible sightings.

The area above the mean high water level of rocks of the refuge is closed to all public use to protect the wildlife. Native Americans and early settlers gathered bird eggs and young seals to eat. Now the entertainment is to observe the sea birds arrive in spring, mate, and nest on these rocks. At Haystack Rock, tufted puffins and western gulls choose the upper northeast grassy slope; pelagic cormorants nest on the south face; pigeon guillemots find crevices for their eggs in various nearby rocks. Common murres nest in dense colonies on rocks north of Haystack. At mating time, the sea birds are in their breeding plumage. In winter, the sea birds head for the open sea.

After an outing on the beach, hungry visitors will find an oceanfront Mo's restaurant, with its famous clam chowder, adjacent to the parking lot. If you're visiting in late spring, check out when Cannon Beach's famous Sandcastle Contest is scheduled and join the fun.

73. ECOLA STATE PARK

Hours/Season: Day use (fee area) and hiker camp; year-round
Area: 1,304 acres
Attractions: Photography, hiking, birdwatching, whale watching, offshore lighthouse, geology, fishing, ancient forest, surfing, beachcombing, picnicking
Facilities: Picnic tables and reservable covered shelter, restrooms, hike-in camp at Indian Creek, beach access
Access: Off US 101, via north entrance to Cannon Beach, turn north 2 miles on signed entry road
Contact: (503) 436-2844

When you drive into Ecola State Park via the twisting, narrow entry road and then walk to the viewpoint south, you will no

From Tolovana Beach north past Cannon Beach, walkers pass many rock formations, Haystack Rock, and side trips for an ice cream cone or visiting art galleries.

doubt recognize the scene from the many published photographs of it. It is a seascape to savor and remember. From the main parking area, the view south from Ecola Point reveals a long stretch of beach and incoming surf punctuated by offshore sea stacks and Haystack Rock. Backing the town of Cannon Beach are ridge upon ridge of the Coast Range. On sunny days, the scene is dominated by an azure blue ocean. Sunset brings a unique view when the last light of day flickers on the whitecaps and the town's lights become pinpoints on a canvas of mountains washed blue in the dusky light.

The southern end of the park begins just north of Chapman Point, which pairs with Ecola Point to bracket Crescent Beach. The path that once led to this beach was washed out in 1995, and the park access now is via a steep 2-mile trail that begins on the road past the restrooms and weaves downhill through the forest. Paved walks are scattered around Ecola Point for a variety of magnificent views that include Sea Lion Rocks and Tillamook Rock Lighthouse. Picnic tables dot the meadow and are perfect for enjoying the beauty and the offshore wildlife.

The storm-battered lighthouse is more than a mile offshore on 100-foot-high Tillamook Rock. Inactive now, the lighthouse is privately owned and used as a columbarium, a place to entomb urns of cremated ashes. The offshore chunk of basalt rock was once part of the mainland.

Ecola was developed originally by the Civilian Conservation Corps, and in the early 1950s a campground was developed. However, this was abandoned in 1954 as being inappropriate to the setting. The name of the park comes from the Chinook Indian word for

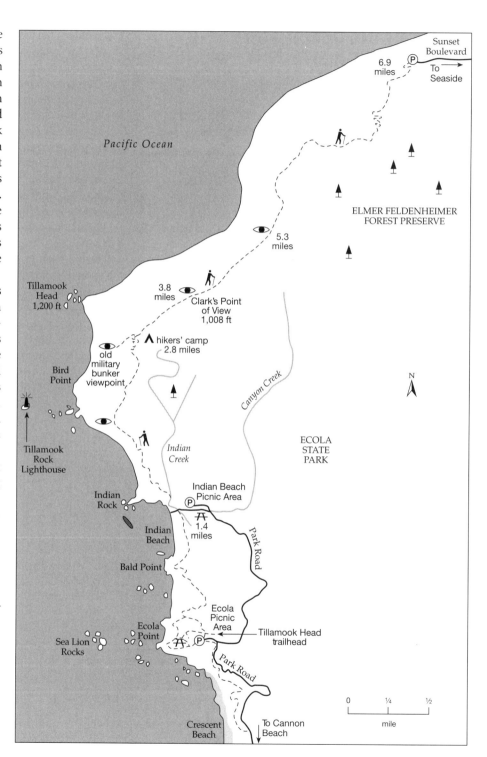

Equestrians take a ride at Crescent Beach in Ecola State Park.

whale, *ekoli*. William Clark and members of the Lewis and Clark Expedition passed this way on January 8, 1806, and saw burial canoes of the Tillamook Indians when they followed an elk trail south from Seaside to Cannon Beach to a village on what is now Elk Creek. They bartered for 300 pounds of blubber from a beached whale to vary their winter diet.

The park road continues north to Indian Beach, which also has day-use facilities and beach access to a cove bounded by basaltic Indian Rock to the north and Bald Point, the toe of an old landslide, on the south. This cove, where Indian Creek enters the sea, is popular with surfers. A village was located at Indian Beach when Lewis and Clark came this way.

Included in the park north to road's end in Seaside is the vast undeveloped acreage of 1,200-foot-high Tillamook Head, for a total of 9 miles of coastline. This volcanic spur of the Coast Range has a large intrusion of basalt rock sandwiched between layers of mudstone. Tillamook Head exists because the basalt was fortuitously positioned to resist the pounding surf. Landslides of the softer rock have frequently caused damage in the park.

The Oregon Parks and Recreation Department has sought to preserve this fragile headland from wind and storm damage by maintaining a wide swatch of forest. The donation of the Elmer Feldenheimer Forest Reserve, which adjoins the northeast section of the park, has increased the cushion of trees, including old-growth Sitka spruce and western hemlock, that is habitat for elk and deer. Wildlife viewing is increased by the many offshore rocks that are national wildlife refuges, and the gray whales that migrate past this official whale-watching park.

Today, hikers can follow roughly the same route that Clark took over Tillamook Head. This path was dedicated as a National Recreation Trail in 1972, a scenic 6.9-mile hike that is part of the Oregon Coast Trail. It's not a difficult trail, but it is often quite muddy, even in summer, so boots are advised.

The trail begins from the north side of the main parking lot near the entrance. Good ocean views are seen on the 1.4-mile hike along the marine terrace to Indian Beach. A fault zone near Bald Point reveals where earth layers have slipped out of alignment. Another 1.4 miles of hiking leads to a hikers' camp—helpful for backpackers doing longer sections of the Oregon Coast Trail—at the top of Tillamook Head. A fork in the trail at this point leads to an old military bunker viewpoint. Clark's Point of View (1,008-foot elevation), where Clark thought the view was "the grandest and most pleasing," is 1

mile past the camp. The last 3.1 miles of trail includes a couple of good viewpoints on the north side of the headland. At one of these, the view includes the mouth of the Necanicum River, the town of Seaside, Clatsop Point, South Jetty, and Cape Disappointment. This area traverses some ancient forest. Parking at the north trailhead is reached by following Sunset Boulevard south in Seaside.

74. SADDLE MOUNTAIN STATE NATURAL AREA

Hours/Season: Day use; overnight (closed December through February)
Area: 2,911 acres
Attractions: Hiking, photography, rare plants, wildlife viewing, summit viewpoint, picnicking, tent camping
Facilities: Picnic tables, restrooms, primitive campground with 10 tent sites (RV camping not allowed)
Access: From Cannon Beach, 3 miles north on US 101 to US 26, 10 miles east (1.5 miles east of Necanicum Junction) to park road, and 7 miles uphill to developed area

Saddle Mountain State Natural Area was for a time the largest Oregon State Park, and is one of the few located off the main highway system. The entry road and trail were constructed by the Civilian Conservation Corps. A Registered Natural Heritage Site, this 3,283-foot double peak attracts cautious, experienced hikers and botanists to its wild setting. For some of the 301 identified species of flora, this is their only Coast Range habitat. The mountaintop was a refuge for plants from the north during the Ice Age. Saddle Mountain bittercress, Saddle Mountain saxifrage, alpine lily, pink fawn-lily, hairy-stemmed sidalcea, sedge, and trillium grow on the mountain. It is also habitat for bird species that include great horned owls, nuthatches, and rufous hummingbirds, as well as coyotes, squirrels, and Roosevelt elk; there were once reports of an albino elk.

The saddle of the mountain can be seen from the picnic grounds, which is situated in an alder grove. Its craggy appearance is impressive. Camping is allowed only for tenters at individual campsites adjacent to the parking area. Water is available.

Saddle Mountain was a sea-floor volcano that erupted about twenty million years ago, and pillow basalt lava is exposed on the

Look for sidalcea among the many interesting plants found on a hike up Saddle Mountain.

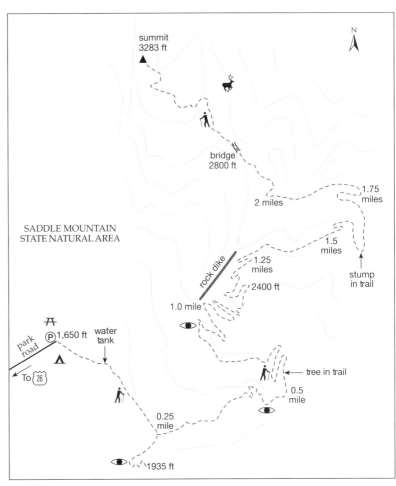

SADDLE MOUNTAIN
STATE NATURAL AREA

peak. The Coast Range has been slowly rising from the sea floor for some thirty-five million years.

The modern name of the mountain came from Lt. Charles Wilkes, U.S. Navy, in 1841, obviously because of the shape. According to Native American legend, however, it was once called *Swallalhoost,* in honor of a chief who was killed by enemies, became an eagle, and created thunder and lightning on the peak.

Saddle Mountain can be hiked to its summit, an elevation gain of 1,600 feet from the trailhead, but it is a treacherous and hazardous climb above timberline, and people are warned not to attempt it unless they are in good condition and surefooted. Recent years have seen some erosion of the path and upkeep has

not kept pace with its condition, but it is only moderately difficult to hike up to some of the interesting flora.

The 2.5-mile trail begins at the campground and first travels through alders, vine maples, mossy trees, Oregon grape, and sword ferns before entering a conifer forest of Douglas fir and hemlock. (Mileage for the trail varies according to several sources of information. The state park guide gives the length as 2.5 miles, whereas other guides list it as 3 or even 3.4 miles. My description is based on the state's 2.5-mile map, although the park staff admits it seems more like 3.4 miles.) A side trail at 0.25 mile goes to a steep rocky viewpoint, but there are good views on the main trail shortly before 0.5 mile and 1 mile. Between these two viewpoints, an open trail along a steep vertical face is traversed.

Though the surrounding countryside has been logged, there is good regrowth of forest. At 1.5 miles, a small meadow has a rich diversity of wildflowers, many rare or endangered. The path becomes steep here, and narrow rock ledges must be traversed. The trail has been worn by storms, elk, and hikers. At 2-plus miles, a bridge spans the saddle and the trail climbs to the higher summit, where a lookout cabin once stood. Those who reach the top tell of the wonderful views of northwest Oregon, southwest Washington, the Pacific Ocean, the Columbia River, and the Cascade Range to the east. It is not unusual to see surefooted black-tailed deer climb up past the saddle on the steep cliffs.

75. DEL REY BEACH STATE RECREATION SITE

Hours/Season: Day use; year-round
Area: 18.7 acres
Attractions: Beach access
Facilities: Equestrian and other vehicle parking
Access: Off US 101, head west to beach on entry road 2 miles north of Gearhart

Del Rey Beach State Recreation Site offers a huge parking lot where equestrians can unload their horses and take the short path to a scenic ride on this nice stretch of beach. Hikers can enjoy the same views. Beach walkers and equestrians should take the left spur of the road near the road's terminus; vehicles aiming to drive onto the beach (which is legal here) go straight ahead where the road splits, but are not allowed to park in that area. Driving on dunes is prohibited.

From the northern trailhead of the Oregon Coast Trail to the town of Gearhart, which is 1.5 miles south of this wayside, there are 16 miles of beach walking. Overnight camping, however, is prohibited on this stretch of the trail. East of the beach is the Clatsop Plains, a strip of land 2 to 3 miles wide that Clark named after the inhabitants of the area. This landscape consists of a series of sand ridges running parallel to the shore, the only location where a parallel ridge system is found on the Oregon coast. Dune vegetation is varied, with seaside tansy, coast strawberry, beach morning glory, beach pea, and American sea rocket easily discovered. The most extensive sand dune stabilization of the coast occurred here on the Clatsop Plains in the 1930s by the planting of European beach grass, scotch broom, and shore pine. The first two were imported plants. Settlers found the area

desirable since it was easy to clear the limited vegetation. Later settlers discovered that the lush Tillamook Valley to the south was a more fertile region. The park site was acquired in 1970 as a gift from Clatsop County.

76. FORT STEVENS STATE PARK

Hours/Season: Day use (fee in some areas) and overnight; year-round
Area: 3,763 acres
Attractions: Hiking, biking, northern trailhead for Oregon Coast Trail, exhibit information, beachcombing, windsurfing, surfing, wildlife viewing, fishing, freshwater swimming, freshwater lake, boating, longhouse replica, self-guiding tour of historic military fort and artillery batteries, historic military museum, *Peter Iredale* shipwreck, photography, Labor Day weekend Civil War encampment and reenactment
Facilities: Ranger station, picnic tables, 2 reservable group picnicking shelters, campground (171 full hookups, 304 electrical, 43 tent sites—4 accessible, maximum site 50 feet), group tenting (4 areas), 15 yurts (7 accessible), hiker/biker camp, dump station, accessible restrooms with showers, amphitheater, natural history programs, boat launch, fishing dock, observation tower, espresso stand/ice machine, Officers' Inn Bed & Breakfast
Access: Off US 101, 10 miles west of Astoria; follow separate signs from US 101 when coming from the north or the south; from the north, signs direct you along Harbor Street to Fort Stevens Highway (Warrenton Drive) until you turn left at Lake Drive, which turns into Ridge Road; from the south (north of Seaside), take a left at the sign and soon take the left spur onto Columbia Beach Road, which intersects with Ridge Road; all three entrances to the park are found along Ridge Road
Contact: Fort Stevens State Park, (503) 861-1671; Officers' Inn Bed & Breakfast, phone (503) 861-0884 for reservations

The third largest of Oregon's state parks, Fort Stevens State Park includes sand flats, shallow lakes, spruce and pine forest, wetlands, and stabilized dunes fronting the Pacific Ocean and the mouth of the Columbia River.

An unusual park feature is the fort, built during the Civil War. It was named for Territorial Governor General Isaac Ingalls Stevens, who was killed at Chantilly, Virginia, in 1862. The fort

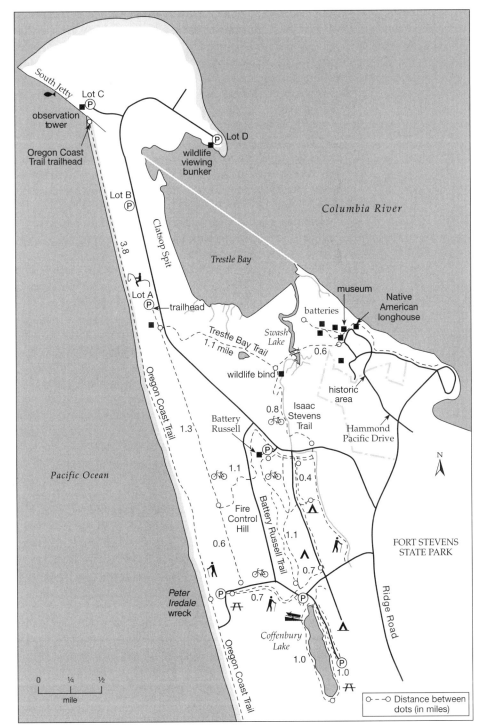

South Jetty

Lot C

observation tower

Oregon Coast Trail trailhead

Lot D

wildlife viewing bunker

Columbia River

Lot B

3.8

Clatsop Spit

Trestle Bay

museum

batteries

Native American longhouse

Lot A

trailhead

Trestle Bay Trail
1.1 mile

Swash Lake

0.6

wildlife bind

historic area

Hammond Pacific Drive

0.8

Isaac Stevens Trail

1.3

Battery Russell

N

1.1

0.4

Pacific Ocean

Fire Control Hill

Battery Russell Trail

0.6

1.1

FORT STEVENS STATE PARK

0.7

Peter Iredale wreck

0.7

0.7

Ridge Road

Coffenbury Lake

1.0

1.0

Oregon Coast Trail

0   ¼   ½

mile

⊙– –⊙ Distance between dots (in miles)

continued to be developed and was active through World War II. During the Civil War, it was used to protect the mouth of the river from Confederate gun boats. As a defense facility in World War II, the fort was actually fired on by a Japanese submarine, but the sub was too far away to cause damage and no fire was returned.

The Historic Area entrance (fee) is the most northerly of the three park entrances. It's a good idea to stop first at the Musuem/War Games Building to view the artifacts of the three wars and view the scale model of the fort; then pick up a detailed brochure of the self-guiding trail of the extensive military structures. Two tours, with a total of thirty-six sites, are suggested as walking trails. Along these routes are the command station, numerous batteries (minus the guns), rifle range, steam plant, officers' quarters, guardhouse, hospital, commissary, searchlight stands, torpedo loading room, and various other essential components of the fort. A recent addition to the grounds is a replica of a Native American longhouse, an easy 200-yard walk from the museum.

If you have a reservation for the Officers' Inn Bed & Breakfast, it is adjacent to the military area of the state park, in Hammond. The 8,000-square-foot inn originally housed army officers, but is now owned by the park system and offers eight rooms with Victorian elegance and modern conveniences.

The middle entrance (no fee) to the park accesses Battery Russell, which was built in 1904. A trail leads uphill via a path or a long stairway to this structure, where birds hang out in the uninhabited shelters. The trail continues uphill past remarkably varied vegetation (many

The sun sets over the Peter Iredale *wreck in Fort Stevens State Park.*

fishing access along the Columbia River, which Captain Robert Gray entered and named after his ship more than 200 years ago in 1792. The first sighting of the river was made by the Spanish navigator Bruno Heceta in 1775. Cape Disappointment, in Washington, can be seen across the water.

At the penultimate parking area, Lot C, an observation tower (the official whale-watching site) overlooks the Pacific and provides a fine view of the South Jetty and the surf. Along the beach here is an entry path for surfers and surf fishing. A cedar post marks the northern trailhead of the Oregon Coast Trail. From here, the trail is on the sandy beach for 19 miles, except for diversions through the towns of Gearhart and Seaside. Consider a day hike to the *Peter Iredale,* 3.8 miles from Lot C.

Another quiet area for beach access and fishing is at Lot B. Equestrian beach-access parking is found at Lot A, where riders can enjoy a ride on the coastal edge.

The south park entrance leads past the ranger station to the camping areas, Coffenbury Lake, and the road to the wreck of the *Peter Iredale.* With the highest number of campsites in the state park system, camping loops head off both south and north of this road. Although several of the yurts are scattered throughout the campground, seven of the yurts make up Yurt Village, in the south loop area. Tom and Glori's Espresso stand is at the beginning of the road to the south campground loop, next to an information building. Throughout the campground are detailed exhibits on the many habitats of the park and what lives in them.

The largest of the lakes is Coffenbury Lake, a short walk from the campground. Besides a boat launch and fishing dock, a 2-mile trail circles the lake, past pond lilies and fishing spots for the numerous trout and perch.

A 1-mile trail from the campground to the beach emerges near the wreck of the *Peter Iredale,* a four-masted, 278-foot British bark that went aground in a heavy southeast wind in late October of 1906, on its way to Portland to load wheat. All hands were rescued. During World War II, the wreck anchored barbed wire that was used as a coastal defense against invasion from Japanese submarines.

Beachcombers might find the remains of sand dollars, with the distinctive design left by scars of their many tube feet. Lucky people might find a glass float after a storm, swept to shore via the *kuroshia* current.

Although one can drive to many of the attractions in this park, the fact that the land is mostly level and open to exploration, added to the availability of 14 miles of hiking and biking trails, offers considerable incentive for self-propelled commu-

trees, shrubs, and wildflowers) and a variety of wildlife, with easy sightings of squirrels and chipmunks, for a true wild experience. The battery commander's station is along the trail, which continues on to the Kestrel Dune Trail.

The road past Battery Russell continues all the way to the wide tip of the Clatsop Spit that edges the mouth of the Columbia River and the Pacific Ocean. At the end of the drive is Lot D, with a planked walk leading to a wildlife viewing bunker, for rainy-weather birding, and a path through the beach grass to a long stretch of beach walking. In spring and autumn, look for migrating birds. Locals have discovered the quiet of this area, as well as nication with the natural surroundings. In fact, the only way to explore the interior of the north edge of the park is via the trail system, which connects to Trestle Bay, Swash Lake and its nearby wildlife-viewing blind, a small lake, and the military museum. Fort Stevens has a 14-kilometer Volksmarch hike that includes a section of the beach, passes the wreck of the *Peter Iredale*, the wildlife viewing platform, and the museum and fort area.

Fort Stevens is well situated for some sturgeon or salmon fishing on charter boats out of Warrenton, where you might slip past deer in the Skipanon River and into the lower Columbia River at early light. These charter captains know how, when, and where to find the fish. Even novices can have good luck.

Several historic sites are found east of the state park. Fort Clatsop National Memorial is a reconstruction of the log stockade

A lush island in the Columbia River and a bridge into Washington are seen from Bradley State Scenic Viewpoint.

built by the Lewis and Clark Expedition during the winter of 1805–1806, a place chosen by canoe along what is now the Lewis and Clark River. During the stormy winter season, they reworked their journals and organized their scientific data.

Astoria, founded in 1811, has some fine museums, including the Columbia River Maritime Museum, and historic buildings. Of special interest is the Astor Column, a monument on Coxcomb Hill decorated with scenes of Native American culture, western settlement, and the Lewis and Clark Expedition. The 164 steps to the top of this tower reward with a panoramic view of Astoria, the shoreline, and the bridge over the Columbia River.

77. BRADLEY STATE SCENIC VIEWPOINT

Hours/Season: Day use; year-round
Area: 18 acres
Attractions: Columbia River viewpoint, picnicking
Facilities: Picnic tables, restrooms
Access: Off US 30, 22 miles east of Astoria

High above the Columbia River, at the Clatsop Crest, Bradley State Scenic Viewpoint features a panoramic view from the Oregon border along the Columbia River into Washington State. Originally given to Clatsop County by the heirs of Nathan Bradley, the park was transferred to the state in 1922. It was developed as a concession area for motorists that included a caretaker's cottage, but today those are gone and it is now a forested rest stop with picnic tables.

The view offers a perspective of the offshore Lewis and Clark National Wildlife Refuge, which includes a scattering of islands in the lower Columbia River accessible by boat. The refuge encompasses 35,000 acres of mostly tidelands and open water. Habitat consisting of 8,313 acres of island and sandbars provides wintering and resting areas for up to 1,000 tundra swans, up to 5,000 geese, and up to 30,000 ducks. Bald eagles and shorebirds are included among the other species sighted in the refuge. Channels of water weave among the lush vegetation on some islands. The salty estuarine waters here near the mouth of the Columbia River provide vital food resources for juvenile salmon as they slowly make the passage from freshwater to the saltwater of the Pacific Ocean. Sturgeon, trout, and warm-water fish are sought by anglers.

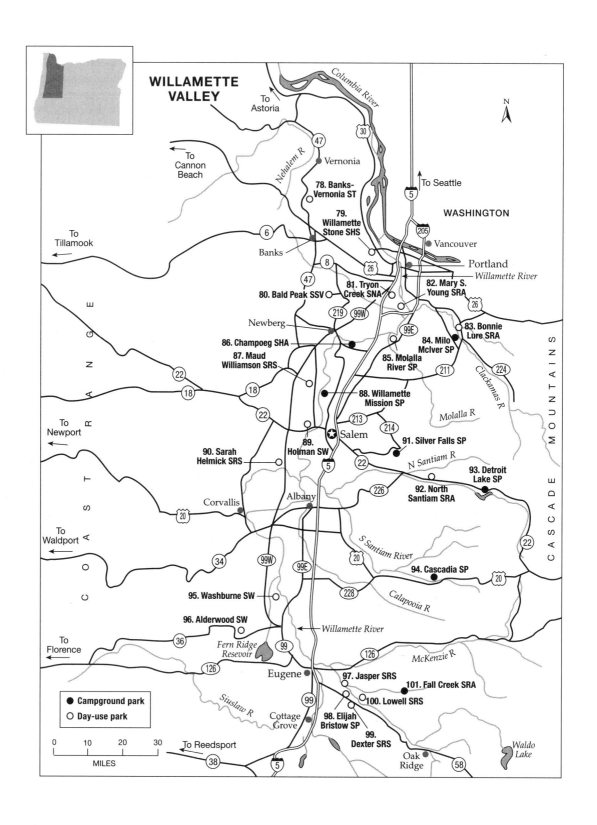

WILLAMETTE VALLEY

To Astoria

Columbia River

To Cannon Beach

Nehalem R

Vernonia

To Seattle

78. Banks-Vernonia ST

79. Willamette Stone SHS

WASHINGTON

Vancouver

To Tillamook

Banks

Portland

Willamette River

81. Tryon Creek SNA

82. Mary S. Young SRA

80. Bald Peak SSV

Newberg

83. Bonnie Lure SRA

86. Champoeg SHA

84. Milo McIver SP

87. Maud Williamson SRS

85. Molalla River SP

Clackamas R

88. Willamette Mission SP

Molalla R

89. Holman SW

Salem

91. Silver Falls SP

90. Sarah Helmick SRS

93. Detroit Lake SP

92. North Santiam SRA

N Santiam R

Corvallis

Albany

CASCADE MOUNTAINS

To Newport

To Waldport

94. Cascadia SP

S Santiam River

95. Washburne SW

Calapooia R

96. Alderwood SW

To Florence

Willamette River

Fern Ridge Reservoir

McKenzie R

Eugene

97. Jasper SRS

101. Fall Creek SRA

● Campground park
○ Day-use park

Siuslaw R

Cottage Grove

100. Lowell SRS

98. Elijah Bristow SP

99. Dexter SRS

0 10 20 30
MILES

To Reedsport

Oak Ridge

Waldo Lake

COAST RANGE

CHAPTER FIVE
WILLAMETTE VALLEY

When pioneers moved west on the Oregon Trail, the Willamette Valley was the usual destination. It was getting there that was not so easy, yet many succeeded, and historic buildings throughout the valley trace the founding of the oldest settlements. One state park, Champoeg, is of particular historic value. It preserves the site of the establishment of the first Provisional Government in the Pacific Northwest. Another unusual historic park, site of a former railroad, is now a hiker, biker, and equestrian path: the Banks-Vernonia State Trail.

Named after the Willamette River, which slices through its lowland middle, the valley is a broad piece of farmland that stretches south of the Columbia River from the metropolitan area of Portland almost to Roseburg. With its rolling hills, checkered agriculture, rivers, and buttes, the countryside offers picturesque touring and varied recreation. Optimal growing conditions provide a bounty of crops of fruits, vegetables, and nuts. Two mountain ranges border the region, the Coast Range to the west and the majestic Cascade Mountains to the east.

This lowland is the population and commercial center of the state. The state's capitol, Salem, is a swift hour south of Portland. Within the city are two state parks: Tryon Creek State Natural Area features many miles of hiking, biking, and equestrian trails; Mary S. Young offers recreation along the Willamette River. Near the urban area, Milo McIver offers a campground and recreation along the Clackamas River. Nearby Bonnie Lure offers fishing along the same river.

The Willamette Valley is crisscrossed by many rivers that flow out of the Cascades. Ferries were originally used to cross these waterways, and stern-wheelers plied the Willamette and some of the larger tributaries. Two state parks are adjacent to ferries still operating along the Willamette River: Mollalla River and historic Willamette Mission, a diverse recreation site.

Before the waterways of the valley became transportation routes, they provided habitat for beavers in this once wild land,

a major reason for the early development of the area after beaver hats became the fashion. Beaver numbers declined sharply by the 1840s and the fashion passed.

In the 1930s, more than 300 covered bridges were built over Oregon streams from hand-hewn timber to provide transportation for the horse-and-buggy era and later for automobiles. By covering the bridges, the builders ensured that the trusses and plank decking lasted longer, sheltered from the rainy weather. Today, fifty-three covered bridges still exist in Oregon, the largest number west of the Mississippi.

The largest of Oregon's state parks is in the Willamette Valley, Silver Falls, and it is a unique one with an incredible trail past a series of waterfalls, amid other attractive elements.

Flowing down from the Cascade Mountains, both the North Santiam and South Santiam Rivers feature state parks: Detroit Lake edges a reservoir with a campground; North Santiam is an angler's and river runner's choice; Cascadia on the South Santiam features a waterfall, hiking, and playing in the boulder-dotted river.

Throughout the valley, several state parks provide quiet, picnicking waysides, often along rivers: Maud Williamson, Holman, Bald Peak, Sarah Helmick, Washburne, and Alderwood.

The Middle Fork of the Willamette River, east of Eugene, offers four choices of state parks along its edge: Jasper is great for reunions; Elijah has miles of trails for hikers and equestrians; Dexter and Lowell feature reservoir water sports. Fall Creek Reservoir is the location of a state recreation site with camping.

If it gets too hot in the lowland, a jaunt to the mountains lets you select an elevation with the right temperature. In the Coast Range, a drive up 4,097-foot Mary's Peak has views from the Pacific to the Cascades. To get higher, go east to the Cascade Mountains where green forests, clear lakes, and hiking trails are found in national forests and wilderness areas.

For additional information on Oregon State Parks, call 1-800-551-6949, or check the official website: *www.prd.state.or.us.*

78. BANKS-VERNONIA STATE TRAIL

Hours/Season: Day use; year-round
Area: A 21-mile-long, 8-foot-wide abandoned railroad bed
Attractions: Hiking, horseback riding, bicycling, jogging,
    wildlife viewing, fishing, picnicking
Facilities: Picnic tables, restrooms, several trailheads
Access: Off OR 47, between Banks and Vernonia; Vernonia
    Trailhead is in Anderson Park; Beaver Creek and Tophill
    Trailheads are south of Vernonia along OR 47; Buxton
    Trailhead is accessed from US 26 by heading north on
    Bacona Road; Manning Trailhead is northeast off US 26,
    a short distance along Pihl Road
Contact: (503) 324-0606

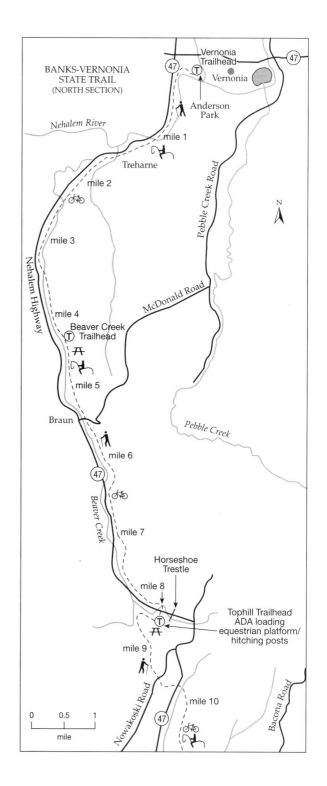

Between Banks and Vernonia, along an abandoned railroad bed in northwest Oregon, the 21-mile Banks-Vernonia State Trail traverses a stretch of varied scenery and terrain. Hikers, equestrians, and bikers share the route with families pushing strollers on the paved, level section near Vernonia. The town of Vernonia has contributed a 2-mile addition that extends to the pond bordering the city. Formally dedicated in late 2000, the long-distance trail offers a gentle grade for users who enjoy the scenic mountains, fields, numerous creeks, and forests of Washington and Columbia Counties. A horse path runs parallel to the hiking and biking trail.

Originally developed by the Portland, Astoria, and Pacific Railroad, the railroad between Banks and Vernonia served the area from 1913 onward for hauling logs, finished lumber, freight, and passengers. In 1960, after mill closures, the railway line was operated for five years as a steam excursion train. In 1973, the line was abandoned and the rails salvaged. The next year the State Highway Department purchased the right-of-way, and it was officially transferred to the Oregon Parks and Recreation Department in 1990. Considerable time and effort led to the planning and development of a linear trail with several trailheads and a few facilities along the route.

The linear trail features twelve bridges crossing the many creeks and two 600-foot-long, 80-foot-high railroad trestles near the trail, scenic subjects for photography. Several trailheads allow individuals to hike the long trail in shorter segments. Choices can be made between easy paved sections with gentle grades and more strenuous unpaved sections through rugged forested areas and rolling hills.

From Vernonia Trailhead, the trail is paved for the first 7

miles as it heads south just east of OR 47. Initially, the easy terrain roughly follows the meandering flow of the Nehalem River, but that stream soon heads off west for the coast and the trail now closely follows Beaver Creek. A short distance past mile 4, the Beaver Creek Trailhead offers parking. A walk across the highway allows access to the paved trail via one of the twelve bridges along the trail. A picnic table and accessible vault toilet are situated in this lovely treed location. The walkway edges open views to the east, a delightful easy segment for strolling.

At the end of mile 7, the trail continues unpaved for a mile and then heads west at mile 8 across Beaver Creek and the highway to the Tophill Trailhead. Facilities here include parking, an accessible equestrian loading platform, vault toilet, and hitching posts. The continuing trail jogs north for a short piece as it climbs a hill and then continues south. Horseshoe Trestle is just south of this trailhead as it rises high above the creek and the highway.

The trail continues from Tophill to the Buxton Trailhead, approximately one-half mile past mile 13. The park office is located here, as well as parking, accessible vault toilet, volunteer staging area, picnicking, and an interpretive trail that loops east of the Buxton Trestle in a jog of parkland edging Mendenhall Creek. South of Buxton, paved trail exists to mile 15 at Pongratz Road, followed by almost a mile of unpaved path and crossing Whitcher Creek, to the Manning Trailhead at mile 16.

From the parking area at Manning Trailhead, the remaining linear trail is paved as it closely follows OR 47 to the present terminus at the end of mile 20, 1,300 feet northwest of the town of Banks at Dairy Creek.

Obey these park regulations while hiking the trail:

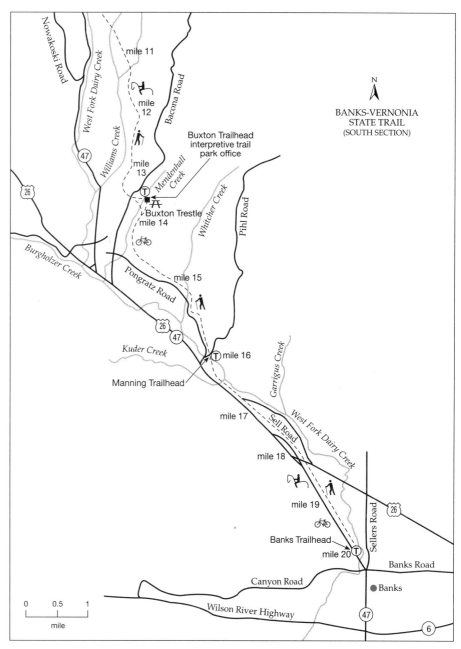

1. Stay on the trail.
2. No camping, smoking, or fires.
3. Hikers and bicyclers use gravel or paved trail.
4. Equestrians travel single file on the horse trail.

At the Beaver Creek Trailhead of the Banks-Vernonia State Trail, a bridge crosses the creek to access an easy, paved section of the trail.

5. Bicyclists call out when approaching hikers or equestrians from the rear.
6. Park only in designated areas.
7. Pets must be leashed and their waste removed appropriately.
8. Do not litter.
9. No motorized vehicles on the trail.

Those not living in the area and wishing to spend more days on the trail can camp at a county park among trees near the Nehalem River, just north of Vernonia along OR 47.

79. WILLAMETTE STONE STATE HERITAGE SITE

Hours/Season: Day use; year-round
Area: 1.6 acres
Attractions: Willamette Meridian focal point, exhibit information
Facilities: *No restrooms or water*
Access: 4 miles west of Portland on Skyline Boulevard

Willamette Stone State Heritage Site has geographical significance. It preserves and makes available to the public a small forested tract of land that contains an important survey stake in a concrete apron. This stake marks the intersection of the Willamette Meridian and the Willamette Baseline, the point from which all lands in Oregon and Washington were sectioned. The townships and ranges on local property descriptions all relate to this initial origin point. In this way, surveyors can accurately locate a parcel of land.

This point was established by the first Surveyor General of Oregon, John. B. Preston, on June 4, 1851. It was rededicated in 1988. A trail leads from the parking area to the monument.

80. BALD PEAK STATE SCENIC VIEWPOINT

Hours/Season: Day use; year-round
Area: 26 acres
Attractions: Picnicking, photography, viewpoint
Facilities: Picnic tables, vault toilets
Access: Off OR 219, 4 miles north of Newburg, take signed road for 5 miles to park

Views of the Coast Range through the trees are visible on the paved drive to the summit of Bald Peak. This is the high point of the Chehalem Hills at an elevation of 1,633 feet. From the northeast-facing bald area of the park, good views of the Cascade spine are seen with Mount Hood, Mount Adams, and Mount Saint Helens in the distance. The foreground view drops down to the agricultural land of the Tualatin Valley and the north part of the Willamette Valley. Unfortunately, some days there is a smog line up to the height of Mount Saint Helens' peak that can wreck any attempt at sharp photography of this fine view. The southwest side of the peak is forested, with a meandering path that swoops downhill a short distance before it loops back to the grassy summit area.

In 1939 the park was considered for a memorial to the pioneer women of the Oregon country, but when Parks Superintendent Boardman brought an inspection group to the site, the idea was rejected for various reasons.

81. TRYON CREEK STATE NATURAL AREA

Hours/Season: Day use; year-round
Area: 645 acres
Attractions: Hiking, bicycling, equestrian, and all-abilities barrier-free trails; nature study, wildlife viewing, annual Trillium Festival and native plant sale
Facilities: *No picnic tables or fire rings,* Jackson Shelter (pack out what you bring), accessible restrooms, nature center, exhibit information, gift shop
Access: At 11321 SW Terwilliger Boulevard, 6 miles south of downtown Portland; 2 miles south of Exit 297 off Interstate 5; or northwest from Interstate 205 off OR 43
Contact: (503) 636-9886

Portland is an excellent example of a city where residents can find refuge from the noise and pace of metropolitan life in its

The beautiful trillium flower is celebrated in the Trillium Festival at Tryon Creek State Natural Area in Portland.

expansive natural parks. Tryon Creek State Natural Area is one of the special ones. Shortly before it joins the waters of the Willamette River, Tryon Creek flows through a shallow, forested canyon bordered on the east by SW Terwilliger Boulevard and on the west by SW Boone's Ferry Road. Logged in the past, the forest has reasserted itself and joins with shrub areas, grassy meadows, and marsh to provide the landscape for an extensive trail system complete with a nature center and the Jackson Shelter.

The park is a legacy of the Carter administration and the concept of urban parks. In the 1960s, when local people realized that this large undeveloped tract would soon be developed by real estate interests, they sought to preserve it as an untouched ecosystem for native plants and animals, and a place for people to enjoy and to observe nature.

Multnomah County began the park process by its purchase of 45 acres in 1969. This spurred the organization of The Friends of Tryon Creek in the same year—the first such group—who raised funds for more land and, with tremendous community support, appealed to the state for help, with the result that a state park was established.

The Friends of Tryon Creek helped design and then finance the nature center and Jackson Shelter. The group continues to work with the Oregon Parks and Recreation Department to maintain the center, assist staff, give educational programs, organize a summer concert series, and host the annual Trillium Festival and native plant sale. The nature center has seasonal exhibits on varied topics and a nature-oriented gift shop. Two other affiliations are the Tryon Creek Photo Club and the Day-trippers Hiking Club.

Eight miles of hiking trails, 3.5 miles of horse trails, and a 2.6-mile paved bike path offer many route possibilities since, except for the bike path, they intersect frequently. A map is necessary to see the numerous ways to enter the park by trail, and to keep you on course.

The Trillium Trail is two easy loops totaling 0.35 mile for wheelchair riders. Three short, easy nature trails—Maple Ridge, Center, and Big Fir—are 0.5-mile loops by the nature center that let you view the canyon but do not descend to the creek. Other trails connect and lead to the creek from Maple Ridge and Big Fir Loops in about 1 mile. From Tryon Creek, trails continue to the Northwestern School of Law of Lewis and Clark College, to SW Boone's Ferry Road, to surrounding suburban areas, or let you loop around on the west side of the creek and return to the nature center.

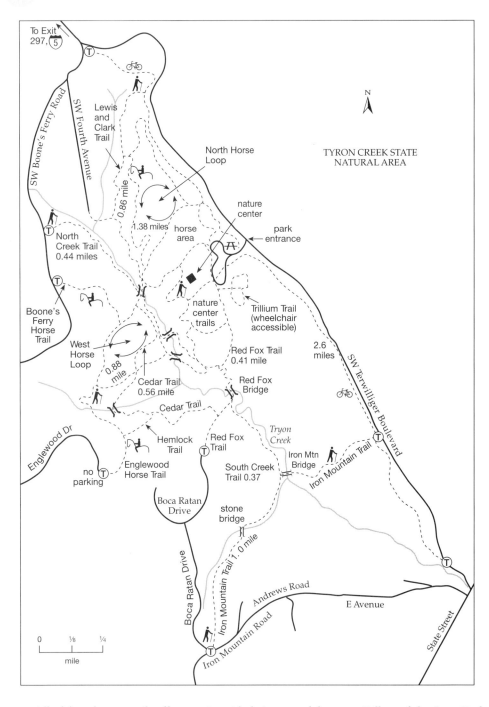

To Exit
297, I-5

SW Boone's Ferry Road

SW Fourth Avenue

Lewis
and
Clark
Trail

North Horse
Loop

0.86 mile

1.38 miles

horse
area

nature
center

park
entrance

TYRON CREEK STATE
NATURAL AREA

N

North
Creek Trail
0.44 miles

nature
center
trails

Trillium Trail
(wheelchair
accessible)

Boone's
Ferry
Horse
Trail

West
Horse
Loop

0.88
mile

Cedar Trail
0.56 mile

Cedar Trail

Red Fox Trail
0.41 mile

Red Fox
Bridge

2.6
miles

SW Terwilliger Boulevard

Englewood Dr

no
parking

Hemlock
Trail

Englewood
Horse Trail

Red Fox
Trail

South Creek
Trail 0.37

Red Fox
Trail

Tryon
Creek

Iron Mtn
Bridge

Iron Mountain Trail

Boca Ratan
Drive

stone
bridge

Boca Ratan Drive

Iron Mountain Trail 1.0 mile

Iron Mountain Road

Andrews Road

E Avenue

State Street

0   ⅛   ¼
mile

All of these longer trails offer exercise with their ups and downs going to the creek, crossing the various bridges, and climbing

again to the ridge. Though the trails near the nature center are maintained for year-round hiking with bark dust, longer excursions may be muddy or slippery.

Douglas fir dominates the forest, which includes western red cedar, grand fir, western hemlock, bigleaf and vine maple, red alder, Oregon ash, and black cottonwood. Seasonal finds might be oyster mushrooms, buttercups, waterleaf, false Solomon's seal, yellow violets, wild ginger, and trilliums—the park treasure, which blooms in early spring. If you're unobtrusive, perhaps you'll glimpse beaver, raccoon, skunk, opossum, squirrel, black-tailed deer, jay, woodpecker, thrush, hawk, or owl.

Horseback riders can choose from the North Horse Loop or the West Horse Loop, or combine them for a longer ride from the equestrian parking lot near the park entrance. The North Horse Loop round-trip mileage from the parking area is 2.1 miles. The round-trip mileage using the West Horse Loop from Boone's Ferry access is 1.7 miles, or 3.1 miles from the equestrian parking lot. These graveled trails are passable even in wet weather. They begin near the ridge line and travel down to the creek, across it, and back.

The 3-mile bicycle trail parallels the eastern edge of the park, near the road. It starts at the Northwestern School of Law, just outside the park, and continues to the intersection with OR 43, a fine option for transport. In 1975, on the day the park was dedicated, an impromptu bicycle race resulted in victory for Highway Commission Chairman Glenn Jackson over David G. Talbot of the State Parks Agency, U.S. Congressman Al Ullman, and Governor Straub.

82. MARY S. YOUNG STATE RECREATION AREA

Hours/Season: Day use; year-round
Area: 133 acres
Attractions: Hiking, fishing, photography, bicycling, picnicking
Facilities: Picnic tables, accessible restrooms, athletic fields
Access: Off OR 43, 9 miles south of Portland

Urban dwellers living in nearby residential areas spend many a pleasant day in this chunk of natural terrain along the southwest bank of the Willamette River. Most of the park is level land on a bench above the water. The south side of the park, near the road, is a largely cleared area that was cultivated for grass and now provides a play area. This city park was a gift of Thomas E. Young and his wife, Mary S. Young.

A 0.5-mile biking trail and a 2-mile hiking trail are part of the recreational improvements. These trails descend through a forest of Douglas fir, cedar, alder, bigleaf maple, oak, and cottonwood to the riverfront. Hikers can walk a loop by going along the river to reconnect with another trail. An alternate wooden-staired path over a creek can be taken from the west paved path up to parking and the bike path.

Although it is quiet enough in some areas to glimpse great blue herons at water's edge, the river is a great expanse of activity on fine days as kayaks, jet skis, and motorboats launch from the opposite side of the water. The waterfront is varied terrain with rocks for fishing spots, undulating water sloughs, and points of land projecting into the Willamette River.

Rules are stringent here, with *no fires, no pets, and no beer in kegs* allowed in the park.

83. BONNIE LURE STATE RECREATION AREA

Hours/Season: Day use; year-round
Area: 94 acres
Attractions: Fishing, hiking, boating, picnicking
Facilities: Picnic tables, restrooms, river access
Access: 6 miles north of Estacada, west off OR 224 at the Eagle Creek intersection onto Burdett Road, and continue to County Road 24028; follow this to the park

Bonnie Lure State Recreation Area has no sign and is mostly used by local residents who know where it is. You will notice a parking area and picnic tables just past a one-lane bridge across Eagle Creek. The land was purchased from the Nature Conservancy in 1976, which indicates that the acreage has natural appeal. A level trail leads to the easily accessible Clackamas River, and paths wander along the river and into the woods at various spots. It's an appealing forested riparian area to explore, with chatterbox orchids and blackberries growing among a profusion of vegetation.

84. MILO McIVER STATE PARK

Hours/Season: Day use (fee) and overnight (reservations available); campground open March 15 to November 1
Area: 951 acres
Attractions: Equestrian, bicycle, and hiking trails; guided horseback rides, fishing, rafting, wildlife viewing, radio-controlled (RC) airplane flying, fish hatchery, photography, disc golf, picnicking, camping
Facilities: Picnic tables, equestrian parking and concession, group picnic reservations, campground (44 electrical, 9 primitive sites—1 accessible, maximum site 50 feet), 2 group tent areas, hiker/biker camp, accessible restrooms with showers, dump station, firewood, boat launch, model airplane strip, 18-hole disc golf course
Access: Off OR 211, 4 miles south of Estacada, take Springwater Road northwest to park
Contact: (503) 630-7150

This spacious park is mostly gently sloping land on a long stretch of the southwest bank of the Clackamas River that preserves river access and habitat only 20 miles from Portland. Campground sites and most of the park are up and away from the water on a series of natural terraces, offering few river views, though a pond and wetland area are centrally located. Rather, it is a place for social gatherings where picnic and play areas on large lawns can accommodate hundreds of visitors. An unusual feature is the model airplane strip, where RC clubs and individuals can enjoy flying planes.

The park and a viewpoint near the entrance are named after Milo K. McIver, a member of the OR Commission from 1950 to 1962, and a strong supporter of state park activities. From the viewpoint, you can sight past the partly forested park across the valley to the foothills of the Cascades and a distant view of Mount Saint Helens, Mount Adams, and Mount Hood.

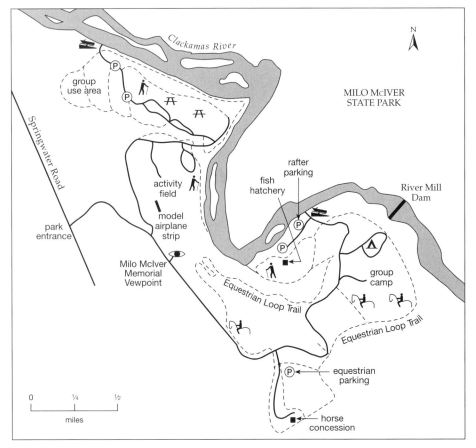

rabbits, squirrels, songbirds, and osprey. Hikers are welcome along this trail. Hiking-only trails are located in the north day-use area, with connecting trails to the south area.

Rafting the river in the park is possible for experienced boaters most of the year, according to the Willamette Kayak and Canoe Club. The put-in is at the boat ramp by the fish hatchery, below River Mill Dam. This 2.5-mile section starts with the first and largest drop, followed by twistings, small rapids, a pass through a rock garden, a play spot with standing waves and eddies, more bends, and small rapids, to the park take-out at the northern picnic area. River runners can continue another 5.5 miles to a take-out at Barton Park. This area is rated class 2+, but requires caution at the first drop in high water.

85. MOLALLA RIVER STATE PARK

Hours/Season: Day use; year-round
Area: 567 acres
Attractions: Pond nature trail, fishing, boating, water skiing, wildlife viewing, radio-controlled airplane flying, picnicking, Civil War reenactment in August
Facilities: Picnic tables, group picnic reservations, boat launch, restrooms
Access: Off US 99E, 2 miles north of Canby, follow signs to ferry on Holly Street

Molalla River State Park was developed as part of the Willamette River Greenway. It is primarily used as a recreation area by local residents. The acreage includes the confluence of the Molalla with the Pudding River in the southern area of the park, and extends to where these waters join the Willamette River to the north.

The developed area is gently rolling land to level, river bottom-land, and is surrounded by flower and vegetable farms. It is at the easterly edge of the historic French Prairie, where agriculture

Picnicking with shelters, fishing, a boat ramp, disc golf course (begins near the Riverbend picnic area parking), and several interconnecting nature trails are located in the northern day-use area. The southern area of the park includes the activity field, hiking and equestrian trails, the RC airplane strip, more picnic tables, the boat/rafter access ramp, fish hatchery, and camping areas. The fish hatchery, operated by the Oregon Department of Fish and Wildlife, annually raises and releases chinook salmon.

Seven miles of hiking and equestrian trails are found in the park. Equestrian parking is off the entry road in the southeast corner of the park, with a nearby horse concession. Horseback riders will find many miles of trails that wander through lush vegetation of Oregon grape, sword fern, cedar, maple, and Douglas fir. Wildlife is plentiful and viewers can observe deer, started in Oregon about 1830. The land was originally the ancestral home of the Molalla Indians.

The park is a sunny, warm valley location in summer that urges water sports and fishing in the calm waters of the river. It is not unusual to see motorboats zooming past or water-skiers zigzagging back and forth across the water. Some boaters pull young children on huge, brightly colored rubber tubes that emulate the ride of the water-skier.

A 0.75-mile, flat, graveled hiking path borders the river along the high tree-covered riverbank before it gradually descends, winding through the soft dirt of the woods, to a beach on the river. You can fish from the muddy beach here, but there are no picnic tables.

Plenty of picnic tables are available, however, near both of the parking areas. One of these is near a vegetated wetland region. Paths circle this large area and tables are spread out under the trees. The other picnicking area is close to the river. Between the two areas is a large open field where radio-controlled airplanes are often flown.

Bring your binoculars and see if you can find the great blue heron rookery. These huge birds are most easily seen flying to their nests in tall trees from late spring through July, when they are busy providing food for their young. If you watch carefully when you spot a heron fishing in the wetlands or by the river,

The Molalla River is a place for fun on the water. Here one visitor uses a child's substitute for waterskiing.

and then follow it with your binoculars, you may learn the location of the rookery.

86. CHAMPOEG STATE HERITAGE AREA

Hours/Season: Day use (fee) and overnight (reservations available); year-round

Area: 615 acres

Attractions: Visitor Center, Newell House Museum, Pioneer Mothers Cabin Musuem, Manson Barn and Farmstead, Pioneer Memorial Building and Pavilion, historic sites, hiking, bicycling, exhibit information, boating, fishing, wildlife viewing, disc golf, picnicking, camping, nature walks and bicycle tours, Earth Day Celebration in April, "Founders Day"celebration on first Sunday in May, Bluebird Festival in mid-May, Indian Summer Folklife Festival in late September

Facilities: Picnic tables, reservable group picnic areas, campground (8 full hookups, 65 electrical sites—5 accessible, maximum site 50 feet), 6 pull-through electrical sites in club-camping loop, 6 yurts (1 accessible), 6 cabins, 6 walk-in tent sites, 3 group tent areas, RV group camping loop with meeting hall, hiker/biker camp, restrooms with showers, dump station, amphitheater, courtesy boat dock, food concession sales in summer, public phone, firewood

Access: From US 99W in Newberg, follow signs 7 miles southeast to park; or from Interstate 5, take Exit 278 and follow signs 5 miles to park

Contact: (503) 678-1251

Champoeg State Heritage Area is a park for the imagination, a place to visualize history along the south bank of the Willamette River, where Kalapuyan Indians lived in the village Champooick and harvested camas roots, fished, and hunted. In 1811, their lives changed when the site was first visited by hunters and fur traders of the Hudson's Bay Company and the company built a warehouse and gristmill in this location. Retired French Canadian trappers established the first white settlement of Champoeg, taking Kalapuyan mates, and sowing wheat after fashionable beaver hats were no longer the prime industry.

The park site was chosen by the early settlers as a meeting place. Initial "Wolf Meetings" about area predators developed into government concerns. On May 2, 1843, 102 settlers voted 52–50 to organize a provisional government, the first American government

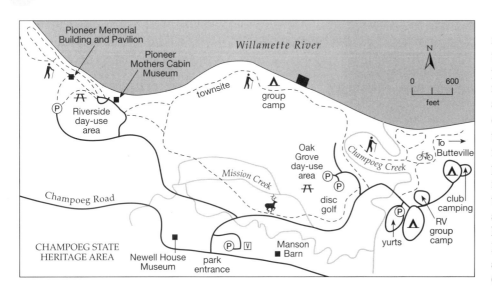

Hiking and biking trails connect many of the park's attractions. From the westerly Riverside area, a bicycle path traverses the south prairie for 1.5 miles and then hugs the riverbank for another 2.5 miles to Butteville. A hiking-only trail separates from this path near the DAR Cabin and borders the river for 1.5 miles, passing through diverse plant and animal habitat of both prairie and woods before rejoining the bike trail near the Oak Grove day-use area and the campground area. Side trails lead to the Visitor Center, west of the Pioneer Mothers Cabin, to viewpoints along the river, and along Champoeg Creek, where colorful wildflowers are numerous.

While walking or biking in the park, be alert for wildlife sightings. Birds are especially abundant. Great blue heron and osprey are impressive species, but numerous western bluebirds—threatened due to habitat loss in the valley—have also found

on the Pacific Coast and a spur to orderly settlement.

By the late 1850s, the town boasted fifty buildings and a population of 200. Stern-wheelers on the river were announced by their steam whistles. The 1861 flood, however, swept away most of the town buildings, and in 1892 the townsite was abandoned. A few buildings are reminders of the past: the Manson Barn, the Pioneer Mothers Cabin, and the restored Newell House.

The Manson Barn was erected in 1862, a building salvaged from the original townsite after the flood. The Newell House was originally built in 1852, and later reconstructed by the Daughters of the American Revolution (DAR). Edging the river, the Pioneer Memorial Building and Pavilion (which is being renovated) commemorates the 1843 vote. The nearby Pioneer Mothers Cabin Museum is a hand-hewn log structure that was established in 1931.

The Riverside day-use area is located at the western end of the park, while the Oak Grove day-use area, situated under one of the oldest groves of whiteoak trees in Oregon, is more centrally located. The campground area is at the east end of the park.

The disc golf course is a short distance west of the camping area. This intriguing game combines some of the aspects of discus-throwing with golf. A Frisbee-like disc is launched from tee-offs to 12 numbered basket-like holes a few feet above ground, and is scored as in golf, with most holes par 3. Distances are given at the tee-off sites. Teams schedule play-offs with enthusiasts from Dabney and Milo McIver parks.

A view of the Willamette River, near the site where the first American government on the Pacific Coast was organized, Champoeg State Heritage Area.

homes in the park. Volunteers and the park staff have been responsible for erecting some fifty bluebird boxes since 1993, and as many as fourteen pairs now nest here.

Once the Willamette Valley was mostly prairie, with both "wet prairie" and "dry prairie" (upland prairie or grassland), and the park area was named French Prairie by the early settlers. Today, with much of the valley's prairie converted to agriculture use, Champoeg is undergoing a series of projects to restore both types of prairie.

The Visitor Center has an array of information and artifacts. Exhibits feature Native American culture, Willamette Valley and Pacific Northwest history, the Oregon Trail, archaeological artifacts, pioneer life, stern-wheelers, and state park history. Outside, a recent addition is the nineteenth-century kitchen garden, which has about fifty species of vegetables and flowers.

The Sesquicentennial Celebration of the provisional government vote was observed in 1993. The Friends of Historic Champoeg produce living history programs and special events throughout the year.

87. MAUD WILLIAMSON STATE RECREATION SITE

Hours/Season: Day use; year-round
Area: 23.9 acres
Attractions: Picnicking and rest stop
Facilities: Picnic tables, restrooms
Access: Off OR 221, 12 miles north of Salem

Maud Williamson State Recreation Site is primarily a rest stop and picnicking area that also preserves many old trees. Overnight camping was once available here, but it is now open only for day use. Tall second-growth Douglas fir trees provide plenty of cool shade. A sharp line separates these woods from open, cultivated farmland to the west of the park.

A historic farmhouse still stands on park land in good condition, once the home of the park donor, Maud Williamson, and her brother. She gave the land for park purposes in memory of her mother, Ruby T. Williamson. Across the highway from the park is the road that accesses the Wheatland ferry, which once was a shipping point for wheat grown in the Willamette Valley.

This historic farmhouse was once the home of the park donor, Maud Williamson, and her brother.

88. WILLAMETTE MISSION STATE PARK

Hours/Season: Day use (fee) and overnight; day use is year-round
Area: 1,686 acres
Attractions: Hiking, jogging, bicycling, and equestrian trails; historical site, exhibit information, boating, paddling, fishing, wildlife viewing, nation's largest cottonwood tree, picnicking, camping, annual Fourth of July Civil War reenactment
Facilities: Picnic tables, playfields, 3 reservable group picnic areas, volleyball courts, horseshoe pits, 2 reservable Beaver Island group tent/RV areas, equestrian center, 4 overnight horse camps with corrals and water, horse and kayak rentals (summer), guided trail rides, dinner moonlit ride, boat launch, accessible restrooms, 2 fishing piers (1 accessible)
Access: From Interstate 5, take Exit 263 and drive 1.75 miles west on Brooklake Road, then turn north on Wheatland Road for 2.5 miles; or travel 12 miles north of West Salem on OR 221 to Wheatland Road and across the ferry (fee) to the park
Contact: To reserve park rides, phone (503) 393-1611

In 1834, Reverend Jason Lee viewed this fertile landscape along the Willamette River, and set up the first Indian Methodist

Mission School in the Willamette Valley. Initially, a one-room log Mission House served as a school, chapel, hospital, kitchen, and living quarters. Later a barn was added and another log room to the mission. Approximately twenty Native American children were being cared for by the mission by 1836, and the farm was becoming self-sufficient. Among a small party of reinforcements that arrived by ship in 1837 was the first white woman to enter the valley, Anna Maria Pittman, and she soon married Jason Lee. More buildings were added: a blacksmith shop, granary, hospital, and later a combination school and dining hall. The Willamette Mission moved from this site on a flood plain to Chemeketa (now Salem) after 1840. This turned out to be a fortunate move as the former mission site was severely damaged by the great flood of 1861.

A more permanent event occurred in 1844 when Daniel Matheny purchased land on the west bank of the river and acquired a ferry built by Lindsay Applegate. In the same year, he operated the first ferry to carry a wagon and team across the Willamette River. A ferry still operates at this site, an interesting way to travel to what is now Willamette Mission State Park, one of the major state parks along the Willamette River Greenway. Just north of the ferry landing is the park's boat launch to the river. The major unit of the park is a fertile river bottomland acreage reached by taking Wheatland Road to the park entrance. A nature-viewing platform is reached by turning right just before the toll booth. This platform overlooks what is probably wetland during part of the year. Two blinds are helpful in observing the many species of birds found here, which include finches, nuthatches, robins, grosbeaks, and towhees.

Past the pay station, the road passes agricultural management areas, some planted with tall sunflowers and other colorful blooms that are a butterfly garden. Private farmers lease part of the park to grow corn, beans, filbert, or cane berries in a cooper-

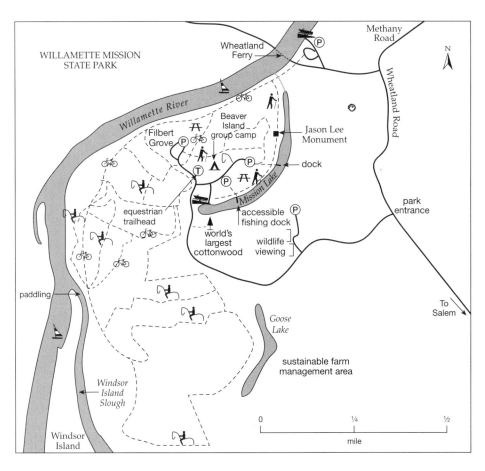

ative management to sustain wildlife habitat. One quickly gets the impression that this park is appealing to both wildlife and people. Mount Hood can be seen in the distance, and skeins of hundreds of geese fly over in autumn.

The expansive Mission Lake day-use area is near a long, narrow strip of water left by an old channel of the river during the 1861 flood—called an oxbow because it is cut off from the river—and includes a walnut orchard, two fishing piers (one is wheelchair accessible), and a boat ramp. Come in the fall and harvest the walnuts that have fallen to the ground. A hiking-only trail follows the riparian area along Mission Lake to the Jason Lee Monument, where the mission once was located. Watch for the "Mission Rose." Though wild now, a cutting of this subtle violet rose was given to Anna and Jason Lee as a wedding gift by the blacksmith's wife, Rachel Beers. It still blooms once a year. Wildlife is abundant, with red-tailed hawks circling above, great blue herons fishing, blue jays squawking, and squirrels scampering about. Deer, coyote, raccoon, and osprey also find habitat here.

From the accessible fishing pier, an enormous cottonwood tree can be viewed across the water. This wonderful old tree has been growing since approximately 1735, is 155 feet high with a 110-foot spread, and is 26.25 feet in circumference. It can be reached by hiking a short, signed trail from the park road.

A second slough in the park, Goose Lake, offers a more adventurous fishing excursion. Some trail blazing is required to find a route to this lake; a map is helpful. A float tube is suggested for this area, where the fishing is reported to be fine.

The Filbert Grove day-use area is along the Willamette River. This sizable grove of filbert trees drops a large number of nuts in autumn, but most of the ones I found had been devoured by some pest (perhaps the filbert worm) that leaves tiny holes drilled in them. A hiking and bicycling trail, accessible to those with disabilities, circles the filbert grove.

In addition to the historic walkway along Mission Lake, the park has 4 miles of bike paths, 5 miles of horse trails, and a 1-mile jogging loop near the camping area. All of the trails are accessible to hikers. Horseback riders will find level trails that wind in and out of thick foliage as they provide views of the Willamette River, Windsor Island Slough, meadows, and farmlands in the southwest area of the park. Biking trails border the river for some distance before looping back near the beginning of Windsor Island Slough. Long-distance bikers can arrive via

Walkways in the Filbert Grove day-use area access the Willamette River in Willamette Mission State Park.

One of the major parks along the Willamette River Greenway, Willamette Mission State Park, can be accessed by a ferry established by Daniel Matheny in 1844.

the ferry and immediately connect with the bike path to the west of the ferry landing.

Besides grasslands and farmland, about half of the park has a natural forest of maples, cottonwoods, ash, and willows. Ancient broadleaf forest is seen and explored by paddling the sloughs of the river. Paddlers can enter the water at the boat ramp by the ferry landing and paddle upriver to enter Windsor Island Slough along the main unit of the park. Other entry points for paddlers exist along OR 221, or boaters and paddlers can travel downriver to Lambert Slough, adjacent to another unit of the park to the north that is accessible by boat from other put-in points.

Salmon are moving along this portion of the Willamette River year-round, but are more commonly fished in the tributaries. Summer steelhead are occasionally taken near the Wheatland Ferry. The primary resident fish are bass and panfish. Sloughs offer refuge for largemouth and smallmouth bass, crappie, bluegill, and catfish. Boaters can use the park ramp to go downstream to Lambert Slough or motor upstream to Windsor Island Slough and drift back. At high water, the cut-off oxbow lakes in the park refill with fish from the river, including bluegill, bass, bullhead, crawfish, and crappie. The park also offers bank fishing. A copy of the *Willamette River Recreation Guide* is helpful for boaters.

Willamette River Greenway

In a time when Americans were beginning to value their rivers for uses other than transportation, governors Tom McCall and Bob Straub supported a program that was endorsed by the Oregon Legislature in 1967 and 1973 called the Willamette River Greenway. The aim was "to protect, conserve, enhance and maintain the natural scenic, historical, agricultural, economic and recreational qualities of lands along the Willamette River." The Greenway consists of a 255-mile strip of river frontage (50,000 acres) from the river's mouth upstream—and the Multnomah Channel—to the Dexter and Cottage Grove Dams. Although the Oregon Parks and Recreation Department has no regulatory authority over land use and development in the Greenway, it manages more than 8,000 acres of riverfront land contained in more than ninety separate units ranging from several fully developed state parks to small, undeveloped parcels.

In the early days of pioneer settlement of the Willamette Valley, being near water, especially this major river that bisected the region, was essential, particularly for commercial transportation of supplies. By 1851, several small steamboats worked the area above Willamette Falls, near Oregon City, but the first steamboat for hauling passengers and freight was the steam-powered *Canemah,* a 135-foot-long side-wheeler. As a result, boat landings, ferries, and small towns sprang up along the river. The steamboats ruled the Willamette for about seventy years, as it was a natural main route. After 1887, the steam locomotive began vying for commerce transport, and most of the steamboats were no longer operating after World War I. Some ferries are still in use, a nostalgic way to cross the Willamette River.

The Willamette River has long been a place of boating and fishing, but the development of public accesses, boat launches, and primitive camps for boating groups under the Greenway program has

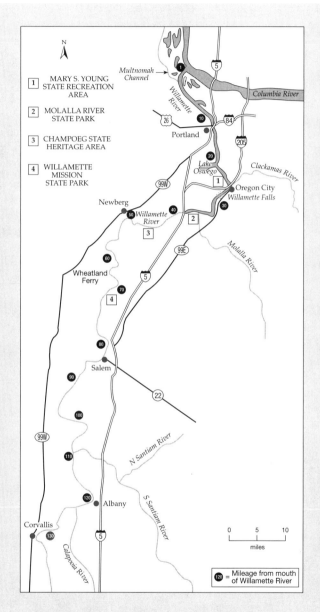

increased recreational use, as has the effort to clean up the river.

The river once meandered through grassy meadows and woodlands nourished by black alluvial soil, and groves of fir and cedar once lined the river above the

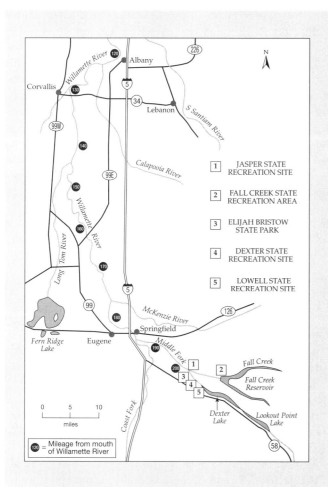

JASPER STATE RECREATION SITE

FALL CREEK STATE RECREATION AREA

ELIJAH BRISTOW STATE PARK

DEXTER STATE RECREATION SITE

LOWELL STATE RECREATION SITE

120 = Mileage from mouth of Willamette River

flood water. Progress has changed some of the riverine area, but preservation has saved other areas. Many of the original plant species still exist, including some rare ones. If you visit, look for willow, camas, reedgrass, wappato, and many other species. Along the river, Sauvie Island (mile 1), Oaks Bottom (mile 15), Candiani Bar (mile 59), and Wells Island (mile 106) are accessible areas to view these in natural ecosystems.

More than 130 species of birds are sighted in the riverine habitat, so birders will find diverse viewing that includes tree swallow, green heron, common yellow-throat, red-tailed hawk, and great blue heron, with their rookeries found in some areas.

89. HOLMAN STATE WAYSIDE

Hours/Season: Day use; year-round
Area: 10.2 acres
Attractions: Bicycling, picnicking
Facilities: Picnic tables, restrooms
Access: Off OR 22, 4 miles west of Salem

Adjacent to busy urban traffic, this parcel of land lying on a hillside forested with Douglas fir, Holman State Wayside, at first seems just that, a wayside for picnicking. A paved bicycling path diverts bikers from the bike lane edging traffic as it detours through the park, where they can stop to have lunch or just enjoy the change of scenery. Picnic tables are scattered about, and a sink with water and preparation table are furnished for visitors. A trail heads uphill among trees to the street above, with access from neighboring residents. The Willamette River can be glimpsed across the highway.

Historic reasons exist for the location of the park, which is located between OR 22 and the old Doak's Ferry Road. Historically, the old territorial road of the 1850s passed through the wayside en route to Dallas and points south. Though the wayside property was owned by Thomas and Cora Holman, the presence of a spring on the tract resulted in it being traditionally used as a watering stop by travelers and their livestock. Because of the Holmans' willingness to allow public use of the spring and their long ownership of the property, the Highway Commission approved the commemorative name for the wayside.

90. SARAH HELMICK STATE RECREATION SITE

Hours/Season: Day use; year-round
Area: 79 acres
Attractions: Fishing, picnicking, reservable group picnicking, wildlife viewing
Facilities: Picnic tables, restrooms
Access: Off US 99W, 6 miles south of Monmouth, follow spur road a short distance to park

Majestic old trees shade picnic tables along the Luckiamute River at Sarah Helmick State Recreation Site. Something about such mature trees lifts the spirit. In the early days of the park, it was an overnight spot for travelers along the old route of Pacific

Highway 99W, and before that it was a camping place for Native Americans. Today it is a day-use area.

This valley park includes the first land given to the Oregon State Highway Commission for park purposes, in 1922, by Sarah Helmick and her son James. The park expanded as others gave more land at later dates. Sarah and her husband Henry came to Oregon with their oxen-drawn wagon via the Oregon Trail in 1845 from Burlington, Iowa, but it is said that they lost all of their possessions at Cascade Rapids on the Columbia River. In

1846, they settled on a 640-acre Donation Land Claim on the Luckiamute River. Sarah was known as "Grandma" to all her friends and acquaintances.

The park is along the flood plain of the river with flat to gently sloping land that sometimes floods in winter. Spacious lawns beneath huge trees circle a wild central area with snowberry, salmonberry, and thimbleberry complementing the Douglas fir, grand fir, ash, cottonwood, willow, red cedar, and bigleaf maple. Paths form diameters to the opposite side of the park. A rough trail is found at the edge of the high bank by the river, and a path descends to the river for fishing access. This large stream offers good trout fishing, as well as some cutthroat trout and steelhead.

A fine view of the river from the highway bridge near the park is worth stopping to see. Hawks are frequently sighted perched on overhanging trees. Other wildlife can be sighted in the park area.

Majestic old trees and the Luckiamute River contribute to the pleasant surroundings at Sarah Helmick State Recreation Site.

91. SILVER FALLS STATE PARK

Hours/Season: Day use (fee) and overnight (reservations available); year-round, except North Falls Group Camp and Howard Creek Horse Camp are open March 1 to October 31

Area: 8,706 acres

Attractions: Waterfalls, hiking, biking, jogging, horseback riding, photography, fishing, swimming, wildlife viewing, exhibit information, nature study, picnicking, camping

Facilities: Historic day-use lodge (snack bar in summer), picnic tables, reservable group picnic shelters, campground (47 electrical, 51 tent sites—2 accessible, maximum site 60 feet), 14 cabins, Howard Creek Horse Camp (5 sites), North Falls reservable group camping (3 group tent areas, 2 group RV areas, meeting hall, dump station), New Ranch and Old Ranch (large overnight groups), Silver Creek Youth Camp, rustic conference center group lodging, horse rentals (May through September, and weather permitting during off season), accessible restrooms with showers, public phones, firewood, horseshoe pits

Access: From Interstate 5 in Salem, take Exit 253 and head southeast on OR 22 for 7 miles to OR 214; follow signs northeast to park

Contact: (503) 873-8681; horse rentals at (503) 873-3890

Oregon's largest state park, Silver Falls, is a scenic and recreational wonderland that was once considered for national park status. It

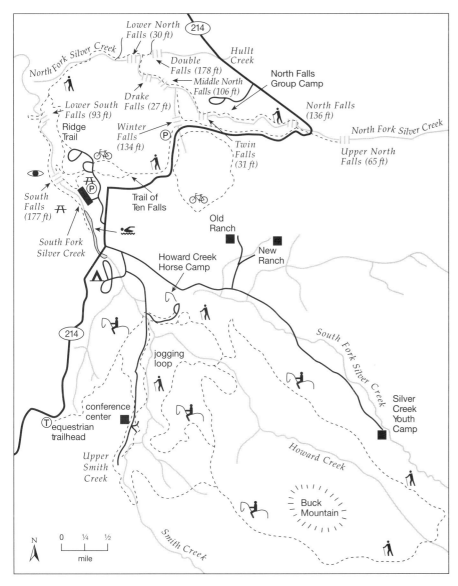

agriculture, and hunting lodges punctuated the forest. Logging was pursued enthusiastically by the Silverton Lumber Company for some time, but by 1929 only one family, that of South Falls owner D. E. Geiser, remained in town. He charged ten cents to see the falls and tried to promote this business by having a man go over the falls in a canvas-covered canoe guided by a wire. That didn't last long—the wire failed, though the man survived. Geiser's next scheme was running old cars over the falls. He charged twenty-five cents for this absurd spectacle.

Fortunately, the state came to the rescue and bought Geiser's property for park purposes. When the surrounding area was considered for national park status in both 1926 and 1935, investigation determined it too altered by man. This submarginal agriculture and logged-over forest land, however, was acquired by the federal government during the Depression years and was one of two Recreation Demonstration Areas (RDAs) in the country, with youth camps—YMCA and Girl Scouts—and other recreational facilities. The Civilian Conservation Corps constructed these camps, the Trail of Ten Falls (the Canyon Trail), the Historic South Falls Lodge, and South Falls Viewpoint. The latter two places are now on the National Register of Historic Places. South Falls Lodge was built in the 1930s as a restaurant concession with myrtlewood tables and chairs and was in business from 1946 until the late 1950s. In the late 1940s, the RDA was deeded to the state and added to their piece of parkland.

includes canyons of the North and South Forks of Silver Creek that are ribboned with a clustered series of spectacular waterfalls in the forested foothills of the Cascades.

The creeks were probably named for James "Silver" Smith, who came to this region in the 1840s with nearly a bushel of silver dollars. In the 1880s, the townsite of Silver Falls City was surveyed and a hotel built at the present location of South Falls. A sawmill was situated along the stream, tracts were cleared for

Enough time has passed that the park has recovered much of its forest and charismatic natural character. The terrain is rolling to mountainous, with an elevation range from 700 feet in the northwest corner to 3,000 feet in the southeast corner, and forested with young timber to 500-year-old Douglas firs, western hemlock, red cedar, a few yew trees, and maple, alder, and cottonwood along stream bottomland.

Geologic changes were slower, but profound. Fifteen million

On the South Fork of Silver Creek, hikers can walk under South Falls at Silver Falls State Park.

years ago, the ancestral Columbia River flowed southwesterly in a broad valley through the old Cascades, into the Salem area, and west to the sea. But then, over a period of two million years, came enormous floods of Columbia River Basalt. At least eight flows of fluid lava poured into this area from fissures to the east and began shoving the river north. Between flows, sediments and forest grew. Since then, erosion has cut deep gorges and a thick soil mantle has sprouted vegetation, but the more resistant rock has formed ledges with waterfalls. Further erosion has cut cavelike formations under both North and South Falls.

The main day-use area is adjacent to South Falls and the Nature Lodge, which has a gift shop and information on park history, wildlife, plant life, and geography. When open, a "Friends" group will answer questions and lead nature walks. Spacious picnicking lawns are located just above South Falls, with stone and log shelters. A hiker/biker trail leads to the campground and passes the play and swimming area of the creek.

The exhilarating highlight of the park is the 6.9-mile hiking loop (no pets on this trail) that descends into the canyon from the forest ledge, circles past or near ten impressive waterfalls ranging in height from 27 feet to 178 feet, and follows the two major creeks and their tributaries for a good portion of the trail. Although all the falls and bridge crossings are a joy, it is awesome to walk behind South Falls, Lower South Falls, and North Falls. Remember that spring is best for seeing powerful quantities of water, as well as a multitude of wildflowers. Look for layered lava and sediments, lava casts of trees, vesicles formed by gas bubbles, and fractures in the lava flow.

Access points are at the South Falls Viewpoint, North Falls parking, or Winter Falls parking. Several shorter circuits can be taken. Be sure to have a map of the trail system with you. Most of the trail is not difficult, but the alternate 1-mile Ridge Trail is a steep ascent.

For bikers, a 4-mile trail begins at the campground (or at the day-use area), goes along the ledge above the falls, and then makes a loop on the east side of the highway.

Horse trailheads are on the highway on the west side of the park, where there are hitching rails and a loading ramp, and at the horse camp. A 14-mile trail loops into the southeastern higher elevation of the park, circling Buck Mountain. Hikers can also use these trails.

A 3-mile jogging trail is located near the conference center. Hikers wanting to view ancient forest should access the jogging trail from the footbridge crossing Smith Creek between the meeting hall and dining hall of the conference center, and keep left as the horse trail goes right. Old-growth trees can be seen in this section of the park. Though the area was logged, the advantage of selective logging can be seen.

Wildlife sightings are frequent in the park. It is not unusual to see black-tailed deer fawns near the campground or beaver at the bottom of the falls. Diligent watchers might spot a bobcat, nutria, kingfisher, dipper, or pileated woodpecker. Black bear, coyote, and mountain lion inhabit the remote area of the park.

So vast is this park that one needs a map to realize the isolated locations and acreage that encompass the North Falls Group Camp, Howard Creek Horse Camp, the conference center, Silver Creek Youth Camp, Upper Smith Creek, and the old and new ranch structures. The latter are set on a meadow area with dormitory-style accommodations and kitchen equipment, which can be reserved for family reunions, outdoor schools, and Scout affairs. Upper Smith Creek has a meeting hall and eight cabins for a group of twenty to twenty-two people. The conference center includes lodges, dining hall, meeting hall, and a swimming pool. Silver Creek Youth Camp features accommodations, a recreational hall, craft building, infirmary, dining hall, kitchen, heated swimming pool, playfield, and a pond.

92. NORTH SANTIAM STATE RECREATION AREA

Hours/Season: Day use; year-round
Area: 119.5 acres
Attractions: Hiking, fishing, picnicking
Facilities: Picnic tables, restrooms
Access: Off OR 22, 4 miles west of Mill City

Along the north bank of the North Santiam River, the North Santiam State Recreation Area offers the prospect of some wildness bordering a well-cared-for picnic area on a grassy, open site. Trails wander in various directions toward the river, some leading to secluded picnic tables, others ending at the river's cobble beach, which is another picnic area.

This pretty section of the river includes rocks, riffles, rapids, and splits in the waterway. The clear green water and the possibility of boat or bank fishing for summer steelhead, spring chinook, and stocked rainbow trout attracts anglers. Most of the

park is natural, untrimmed, unmanicured, and heavily wooded with fir, maple, and alder, with moss hanging from trees and undergrowth vegetation.

A trail continues along the river downstream and another leads through the woods. A gravel bar along the river is accessed by a gravel road, and though there is no real boat ramp here, some put their dories into the water here and anglers cast out lines as they drift over a mile to Neal Park or 2-plus miles to Mehama Bridge. Fishermen's Bend Campground, a short distance east, provides an excellent overnight base.

The section of the river between Mill City and Mehama is an intermediate rafting run, rated from class 2 to class 3 depending on the flow of water. A good place to practice surfing, S-turns, and rolls is the play area formed by a small ledge to the right in North Santiam State Recreation Area.

The park and river bear the name of the Santiam Indians, a Calapooyan tribe that lived near the river in the surrounding territory at the time the European-Americans arrived.

93. DETROIT LAKE STATE PARK

Hours/Season: Day use (fee) and overnight (reservations available); campground closed December and January
Area: 104 acres
Attractions: Boating, waterskiing, fishing, swimming, wildlife viewing, photography, exhibit information, picnicking, camping, Detroit Lake Water Festival in August
Facilities: Visitor center, picnic tables, campground (106 full hookup, 72 electrical, 133 tent sites—2 accessible, maximum site 60 feet), accessible restrooms with showers, boat launch and courtesy dock, moorage docks, swimming areas, fishing dock, wildlife viewing area, 2 playgrounds, volleyball area and horseshoe pits (equipment available), campfire program, firewood, public phone
Access: Off OR 22, 2 miles west of Detroit
Contact: (503) 854-3346

Detroit Lake was formed by the construction of the Detroit Dam on the North Santiam River in the 1950s. The park and lake are named after the nearby town of Detroit, which was settled by several Michigan people. The Mongold day-use area is named after the highway construction work camp that was once in the vicinity but is now underwater. The park is within the Willamette National Forest and was originally a Forest Camp; the state now

Sunshine, white clouds, and mountains provide a lovely scene at Detroit Lake State Park.

popular sport here. An unsupervised swimming area with a grass "beach" is enclosed at water's edge. A combination bathhouse with restrooms is available. Though there are no specific trails, it is easy to walk along the lakefront for some distance.

The Piety Knob Island can be seen in the center of the lake. If you'd like to boat over and spend the night, primitive sites and pit toilets are available, but no water. The island is not part of the state park. You may, however, park your vehicle at Mongold if you are camping on Piety Island or along shoreline accessible only by boat.

If you visit during August, check to see if the Detroit Lake Water Festival is being held in town.

Detroit Lake State Park offers an overnight base for doing some hiking and fishing in the Mount Jefferson Wilderness, reached by driving east on OR 22 and taking good forest roads to trailheads. Scenic day hikes include the 2.3-mile hike to Pamelia Lake (via Pamelia Road 2246) and the 2.5-mile hike past Lake Ann to larger Marion Lake (via Marion Creek Road 2255), where trails disperse for more exploring. The 6-mile hike to Jefferson Park, accessed from Whitewater Road 2243, leads to expansive wildflower meadows and several lakes beneath

leases it. Forested with second-growth Douglas fir, the area was extensively logged before World War II.

Reached by fine roads and an easy hour or two from most valley population centers, Detroit Lake State Park edges the 3,900-acre reservoir and attracts many boating and fishing devotees to this North Santiam Canyon location. The campground and separate day-use area sprawl at water's edge on the north shore of the reservoir. Mongold day-use area is 1.2 miles west of the campground area off OR 22. Across the water, Mount Jefferson is seen rising above smaller peaks of the Cascades.

In the campground, boat ramps are reached from the D and G loops, the fishing dock is accessed from the F loop, and paths lead from F and H loops to the floating boat docks, where boat moorages may be rented by registered campers. Anglers can try for rainbow trout, catfish, kokanee (landlocked blueback salmon), and landlocked chinook. Teddy Timberland Playground (ages 2 through 5) is located by the F loop, while Big Bear Playground (ages 6 and over) is located in the A loop. A lakeside interpretive area fronts the lake near the visitor center. Nearby is a wildlife viewing area complete with a dock, where visitors can bring their own food to feed ducks and geese.

Mongold has widely dispersed picnic tables (lakeshore or forested, in sunshine or shade), a huge paved boat ramp, a courtesy dock, and a special takeoff and landing area for water-skiers, a

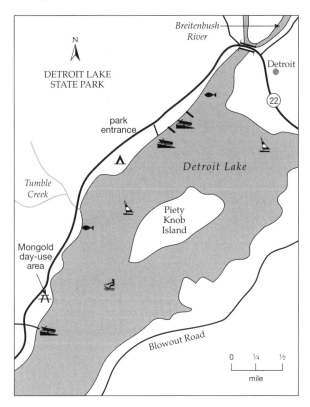

Mount Jefferson, probably the most scenic spot in the Oregon Cascades. Unfortunately, the word is out, so hike weekdays or just after Labor Day, when crowds and mosquitoes are gone, and peak wildflower bloom occurs. This hike is best done as an overnight to watch the moon rise above Mount Jefferson and sleep under the stars.

94. CASCADIA STATE PARK

Hours/Season: Day use and overnight; campground closed
    November through February
Area: 254 acres
Attractions: Soda water spring, nature trail, swimming, fish-
    ing, hiking, waterfall, ancient forest, reconstructed historic
    bridge, interpretive display, horseshoe pits, picnicking,
    camping
Facilities: Picnic tables, campground
    (25 primitive sites—maximum site
    35 feet), 2 reservable group tent ar-
    eas, 3 reservable group picnic areas
    with electricity and covered kitchen
    shelters, accessible restrooms, fire-
    wood, soda spring pump
Access: Off US 20, 14 miles east of
    Sweet Home
Contact: (541) 854-3406

Cascadia State Park was once a gathering place for Molalla and Kalapuya
Indians where they hunted, fished, and
harvested huckleberries. Later, in 1880,
a hunter was stalking deer along the
South Santiam River on the western
slope of the Cascade Mountains when
he discovered a soda spring. People
learned of this discovery and came to
drink the mineral waters, thought to
have medicinal properties, while they
hunted, fished, and camped. With as
many as 200 tents pitched at one time,
it seemed like a good piece of real estate
to George M. Geisendorfer. As a result,
he purchased 300 acres in 1895, including the mineral springs, to develop a

health spa and vacation spot. The place became a popular resort that included a post office, camp area, grocery store, water system, and the Geisendorfer Hotel, complete with dining room, tennis courts, croquet grounds, garden, and bowling alley, which he operated for about fifty years.

In 1941, the state park system purchased the property from Geisendorfer. Now 254 acres, Cascadia State Park celebrated its fiftieth anniversary on July 24, 1992, at the same time as the opening of a temporary bridge over the South Santiam River, called a Bailey Bridge, that served as the entry into the park. In 1994, a duplicate of the original bridge built in 1928 was com-pleted, the only timber-deck truss remaining in Oregon's high-way system, a 120-foot Howe Truss span. The Short Covered Bridge is 1.6 miles west of the park.

The South Santiam River flows down the western flanks of the Cascade Mountains in a steep-walled canyon and into Cascadia State Park. Its waters weave past rocks and ledges, sometimes

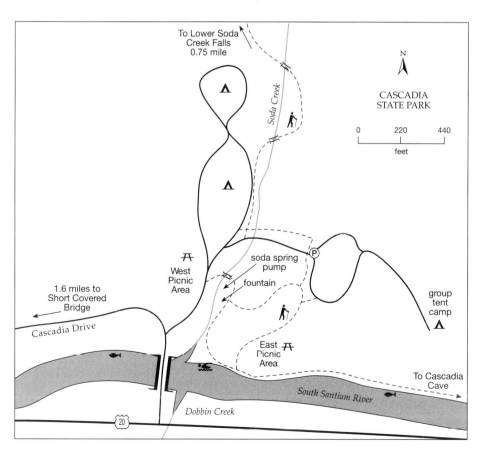

Summer days lure many people to play in the shallow pools created by rocky ledges in the South Santiam River at Cascadia State Park.

forming riffles, and offer welcome pools of cool water for summer water play and swimming. A path accesses the river from the day-use area. Anglers can walk along the bank to look for that good fishing hole. Both Soda Creek and Dobbin Creek flow into the South Santiam River in the park. A riverside trail leads southeast to Cascadia Cave. Wagon trains used the well-known springs as they traveled the Santiam Wagon Road, a route that was part of the Oregon Trail. Ruts left by these wagons can still be found in the park.

Walkways connect the soda-spring fountain area with the day-use area and with the picnic area by the campground. The separate day-use area is huge, with large meadows. Both the campground and the adjacent picnic area by the entry bridge are situated under a canopy of old-growth Douglas fir and other huge trees.

The signed 0.75-mile trail to Lower Soda Creek Falls begins along the spur road to the day-use area, but several of the easterly camp sites connect to the trail. The path follows the meandering creek moderately steeply after crossing two bridges. In several places the trail separates into two paths, which soon rejoin. Ferns abound, and trees include firs, hemlock, cedar, alder, cascara, and bigleaf maple. Mosses hang from many of the branches. This is the lowest ancient forest grove left in the South Santiam River drainage. A delicate, sometimes exuberant 150-foot waterfall, surrounded by rocky ledges and a pool, is at the terminus of the trail.

A few miles east of Cascadia, on US 20, is the designated Menagerie Wilderness, which includes a cluster of rock pinnacles that are resistant lava intrusions left after time and erosion worked on the old Cascades, which are ten million years older than the high Cascades of today. The 2.4-mile Trout Creek Trail, across the road from Trout Creek Campground, heads through forest toward Rooster Rock. The climb to the 3,570-foot-high point ends at an old lookout with a close-up view of Rooster Rock, the wilderness area, and North and Middle Sisters on the Cascade spine.

95. WASHBURNE STATE WAYSIDE

Hours/Season: Day use; year-round
Area: 37 acres
Attractions: Picnicking, hiking, exhibit information
Facilities: Picnic tables, restrooms
Access: Off OR 99W, 4 miles northwest of Junction City

When I stopped at this wayside during a spring rain, with its fine second growth Douglas fir forest anchored by a green carpet covered with tiny white flowers, the appeal of the scene was considerable. A small part of this nearly flat Willamette Valley farm woodlot has been developed as a roadside picnic area and rest stop. Trails lead off from the curving walkways into the neighboring forest lushness, an added attraction for the wanderer.

96. ALDERWOOD STATE WAYSIDE

Hours/Season: Day use; year-round
Area: 76 acres
Attractions: Fishing, hiking, picnicking
Facilities: Picnic tables, restrooms
Access: Off OR 36, 15 miles southwest of Junction City

This forested tract bordering the Long Tom River in a hollow-like setting is surprisingly delightful, though not known to many. The Civilian Conservation Corps developed the picnic facilities edging the Long Tom River about 1935. According to local lore, during the prohibition era in the 1920s, liquor was distilled clandestinely at a nearby location called Burp Holler. In 1961, the latter name was briefly considered for the wayside but the proposal was unsuccessful for obvious reasons. This riverine picnic spot is particularly lush with vegetation in spring, and a bridge over the narrow river connects to trails that reward with immediate discoveries of flow-

The lush vegetation along Long Tom River includes western dogwood at Alderwood State Wayside.

Interesting rock formations are seen along the Middle Fork of the Willamette River at Jasper State Recreation Site.

ers: bleeding hearts, yellow violets, wild currant, and trillium. Flowering dogwood trees, sword ferns, mossy rocks, and trees covered with hanging mosses attest to a well-nourished habitat.

97. JASPER STATE RECREATION SITE

Hours/Season: Day use (fee in summer); year-round walk-ins (closed to vehicles from October 1 until spring)
Area: 60 acres
Attractions: Hiking, 2 playgrounds, 2 ballfields, volleyball court, 4 reservable group picnic shelters (through park), fishing, birding, picnicking
Facilities: Picnic tables, accessible restrooms
Access: From OR 58, 12 miles southeast of Eugene, turn north at sign and follow Jasper Park Road to park turnoff
Contact: (541) 937-1173

Jasper State Recreation Site is an expansive family park on the south bank of the Middle Fork of the Willamette River. It encompasses a nice stretch of river edged by cottonwood trees and other interior trees and flower beds. Some interesting rock formations are seen on a hike along the river's edge. This stretch of river is fished mostly for summer steelhead and spring chinook, with some trout also caught.

Autumn, when the gate is closed and visitors must walk the

entry road into the park, is a lovely time to visit and enjoy the solitude and the fall foliage. The park is designed with some imagination, from sculptured walls on restrooms to a vegetable garden. The playground is out of the ordinary and an attraction for family and reunion groups who visit. Walking trails continue past the three picnic areas and loop around a wooded patch. Visiting in October, when walk-ins hike in via the entry road, I could envision a summer weekend with the group picnic areas and the playground full, perhaps even some people tending the vegetable garden.

98. ELIJAH BRISTOW STATE PARK

Hours/Season: Day use; year-round
Area: 847 acres
Attractions: Hiking, bicycling, horseback riding, fishing, nature study, wildlife viewing, picnicking
Facilities: Picnic tables, 3 reservable group picnic areas with electricity (booked through park), accessible restrooms, equestrian staging area (horse trailer parking, corrals, hitching posts, electricity, water, and toilet), horseshoe pits, wildlife-viewing platform, boat launch on north side of river
Access: Off OR 58, 15 miles southeast of Eugene
Contact: (541) 937-1173

Elijah Bristow State Park is one of the major state parks developed along the Willamette River Greenway. Along the south bank of the Middle Fork of the Willamette River, the park includes 3 miles of river frontage downstream from Dexter Dam. It includes meadows, woods, creeks, and forested bottomland along the river with mixed stands of Douglas fir, alder, oak, willow, cottonwood, and maple trees.

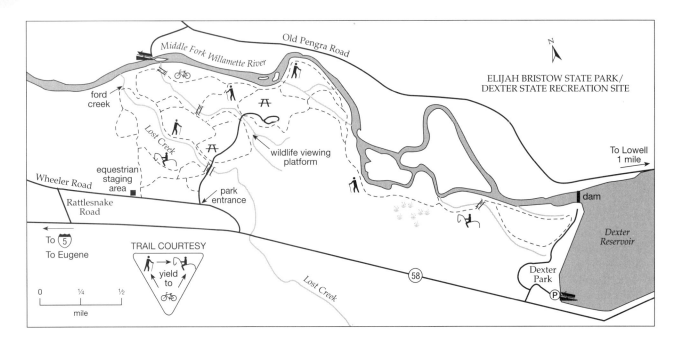

ELIJAH BRISTOW STATE PARK/
DEXTER STATE RECREATION SITE

Originally called Dexter State Park, it was renamed in 1979 to honor Elijah Bristow (1788–1872), an 1846 pioneer to the valley. He built his home because of the beauty of the area, and it is considered the first home in Lane County. He founded the community of Pleasant Hill, 10 miles west of the park. A historic marker on his home site is adjacent to a replica of Bristow's fireplace, built with the original stones. Bristow State Park captures much of the essence of a landscape that attracted so many to arrive via the Oregon Trail.

Most of the 12 miles of mostly level trails meander through wooded areas, meadows, and along the river like a tangle of intersecting puzzle pieces. Though the trails are named—Equestrian (1.5 miles), River (5 miles), Lost Creek (2 miles), Pond Loop (1 mile), and Fishermens (2 miles)—all interconnect. All except the pond loop are trails shared by hikers, mountain bikers, and equestrians. Trails may be accessed from many points, including the day-use parking area and picnic areas. Some paths are layered with chips; others are muddy after a rain. Though nearby, the river is not often in view. The River Trail is part of the Eugene to Pacific Crest Trail system that starts in Alton Baker Park in Eugene and ends near Oakridge at the Pacific Crest Trail. Lost Creek and Barley Creek traverse the park, bridged for easy crossing, except Lost Creek is forded about 0.5 mile from the equestrian trailhead. Lost Creek was reportedly named by Bristow. It is reported that Native Americans followed the creek into the woods when they needed to avoid capture.

Frogs are heard in the wetlands and creek beds. The varied wildlife includes deer, fox, beaver, great blue heron, ducks, geese, redtail hawk, osprey, raccoon, coyote, and Western pond turtle. Seasonal salmon runs provide an interesting spectacle and great fun for anglers. Plenty of intermittent blackberries offer summer snacking. A wildlife viewing platform that overlooks the pond system is located on the trail leading south from the day-use parking lot. It might not be difficult to get lost following the trails, so a map is suggested for those not familiar with the trails system.

99. DEXTER STATE RECREATION SITE

Hours/Season: Day use; year-round
Area: 100 acres
Attractions: Boating, sailing, paddling, swimming, waterskiing, fishing, picnicking
Facilities: Picnic tables, boat launch, vault toilets, *no water*
Access: Off OR 58, 16 miles southeast of Eugene

Adjacent to the Dexter Dam, Dexter State Recreation Site is primarily a place for water sports on Dexter Reservoir, whether the visitor's choice is fishing, waterskiing, jet skis, paddling, boating, or sailing across the vast surface of the reservoir. It is along the Willamette River Greenway. Views of the foothills of the Cascade Mountains edge the Reservoir.

Once a county park, Dexter was recently part of a package deal that exchanged Armitage, Ben and Kay Dorris, Hendrick's Bridge, and Jennie B. Harris State Recreations Areas—which are now managed by Lane County—for properties on the Middle Fork of the Willamette River and Dexter Reservoir. This was done to improve operational efficiency in light of the department's management of other Willamette River properties.

Picnickers will find tables overlooking the water activity. The bank along here is a nice place to throw a line into the water and catch some fish. Anglers, whether from the bank or by boat, find small- and large-mouth bass, crappie, and trout. They may also see equestrians crossing the dam to access trails in neighboring Elijah Bristow State Park. Hikers can also head west along the Middle Fork of the Willamette River on the River Trail in Bristow Park.

100. LOWELL STATE RECREATION SITE

Hours/Season: Day use; year-round
Attractions: Fishing, boating, sailing, swimming, waterskiing, picnicking
Facilities: Picnic tables, reservable group picnic area (call park), boat launch, dock, marina concession, playground, basketball court, volleyball, accessible restrooms
Access: From OR 58, 17 miles southeast of Eugene, turn north at the park sign by the covered bridge approach to Lowell, then follow signs to continue west on Old Pengra Road to the park
Contact: (541) 937-1173

Located on the north bank of Dexter Reservoir, Lowell State Recreation Site is a pleasant waterfront park in scenic surroundings complete with a marina, picturesque sailboats, surrounding foothills, and many amenities. East of a rounded point projecting into the reservoir, shaded picnic tables border the waterfront

Sailboats find moorage at the marina at Lowell State Recreation Site along Dexter Reservoir.

while geese wander about the area and waterfowl are seen off-shore. A swimming area edges the waterfront. On the west side of the point is a larger picnic area near towering oak trees that gently slopes down to where a trail edges the water. A walk to the northwest leads to the University of Oregon Crew Boathouse and dock. Besides the playground, basketball and volleyball courts are activities to enjoy.

On the point, a marina, concession, dock, and boat launch sheltered by an offshore log boom are the centerpiece of the park, with picturesque boats moored in the harbor. The reservoir is a fairly large one, about 3 miles long, and visitors wanting some aquatic action can head out in boats, some donning water skis and zigzagging around the reservoir. A variety of birds are seen near shore and in the surrounding area. It's an attractive, quiet place to spend the day.

101. FALL CREEK STATE RECREATION AREA

Hours/Season: Day use (fee at Windberry) and overnight; North Shore day use open year-round, other day-use areas and campgrounds open May 1 through September 30
Area: 1,800-acre reservoir
Attractions: Waterskiing, jet-skiing, boating, swimming, fishing, picnicking, camping
Facilities: Picnic tables, Cascara Campground (boat ramp, swimming area, vault toilets, 42 primitive sites, 5 primitive walk-in tent sites—maximum site 45 feet) reservable group tent camp with 8 sites at Fisherman's Point (contact park), Winberry Park (accessible fishing pier, accessible restroom, and two-lane boat ramp), low-water ramp at North Shore Park
Access: From the OR 58 exit on Interstate 5, continue east to Lowell covered bridge, turn north and follow park signs to Place Road, then east past covered bridge over Fall Creek to road split to park areas; Winberry Creek Road accesses Winberry Park, while Big Fall Creek Road accesses North Shore Park and Cascara Campground; 27 miles southeast of Eugene–Springfield
Contact: (541) 937-1173

Fall Creek and Winberry Creek flow west from the Cascade Mountains to form what is now the Fall Creek Reservoir, the focal point of Fall Creek State Recreation Area. Impounded by the

At Fall Creek Reservoir, only North Shore Park is open year-round; it also features a low-water ramp.

Fall Creek Dam, the Fall Creek arm of the reservoir is to the northeast while the Winberry Creek arm is southeast. The reservoir is approximately 1,800 acres when full.

The major day-use area, Winberry Park, is located not far from the dam area, near a wide area in the reservoir, shortly past a viewpoint. People with disabilities can use the accessible fishing pier and perhaps catch bass, catfish, or rainbow trout. With a two-lane boat ramp and a huge parking area, many boats can launch into the reservoir for various water sports and fishing. Winberry Park is located on a large chunk of land projecting into the water, with picnic areas spread out in many locations to take advantage of the large amount of waterfront. Winberry Creek Road continues past Winberry Park as the creek narrows and enters the Willamette National Forest after a few miles.

Big Fall Creek Road follows the wider arm of the reservoir past viewpoint parking to North Shore Park, a day-use area that is the only area open year-round. It features a low-water ramp to take advantage of reservoir use during periods of drought. A jog to the right on the entry road accesses parking for hikers to walk across the dam.

As Fall Creek narrows some miles east, another stop is at Free Meadow, then later at Lakeside I and Lakeside II. Fisherman's Point and Cascara Campground are near the upper end of this

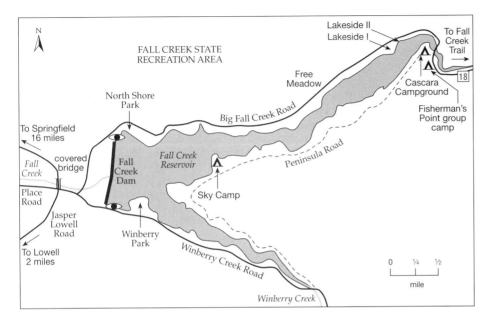

recreation area. Walk-in campsites along the water at the edge of the campground offer even more quiet and that feeling of camping in nature. Cascara should offer fine viewing of sunrises and sunsets washing over the water's surface. This site is actually situated along Peninsula Road, which branches off nearby from Big Fall Creek Road. Peninsula Road continues east to border the waterfront along the inside edges of the two arms and connects to the south with Winberry Creek Road.

For a fun day trip while camping at Cascara, consider continuing east a little more than 2 miles on Big Fall Creek Road, Forest Road 18, to the trailhead for the 12-mile Fall Creek National Recreation Trail that closely follows Fall Creek in the Willamette National Forest *(no bicycles)*. Several other trailheads allow hikers to do short day hikes or the entire distance, with an elevation gain from 960 feet to 1,385 feet. Six campgrounds are along the route. Old-growth conifers become more plentiful as one travels east and higher. The scenery includes many deep pools, some fast water, rock formations and outcroppings, and many small streams crossing the trail.

arm where the creek is small and wild and the road has just switched to the south side of the water. Fisherman's Point is a group tent camp for those wanting a serene spot that is less developed, set among a meadow surrounded by tall forest and edging the creek.

Cascara Campground sprawls along the shore of Fall Creek with several recreation choices: boating, swimming, fishing, and a

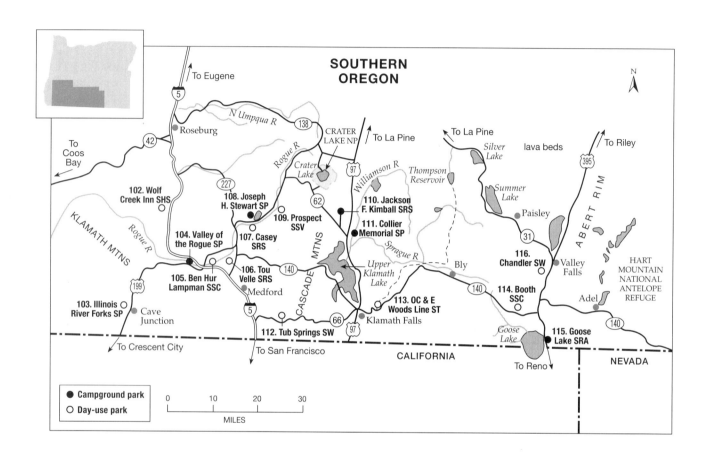

SOUTHERN OREGON

N

To Eugene

To Coos Bay

N Umpqua R

Roseburg

Rogue R

CRATER LAKE NP

To La Pine

To La Pine

To Riley

Silver Lake

lava beds

Crater Lake

Williamson R

Thompson Reservoir

Summer Lake

102. Wolf Creek Inn SHS

108. Joseph H. Stewart SP

109. Prospect SSV

110. Jackson F. Kimball SRS

111. Collier Memorial SP

Paisley

116. Chandler SW

Valley Falls

ABERT RIM

104. Valley of the Rogue SP

107. Casey SRS

Sprague R

Bly

KLAMATH MTNS

Rogue R

106. Tou Velle SRS

CASCADE MTNS

Upper Klamath Lake

114. Booth SSC

HART MOUNTAIN NATIONAL ANTELOPE REFUGE

105. Ben Hur Lampman SSC

Medford

113. OC & E Woods Line ST

Adel

103. Illinois River Forks SP

Cave Junction

112. Tub Springs SW

Klamath Falls

Goose Lake

115. Goose Lake SRA

To Crescent City

To San Francisco

CALIFORNIA

To Reno

NEVADA

● Campground park

○ Day-use park

0   10   20   30

MILES

CHAPTER SIX

SOUTHERN OREGON

The centerpiece of Southern Oregon is Crater Lake National Park, a blue jewel set in a stunning circle of jagged peaks along the spine of the Cascade Mountains. A fine supporting cast of scenic, recreational, and cultural attractions extends west to the Klamath Mountains, south to the California border, and east to the high desert terrain surrounding the Hart Mountain National Antelope Refuge, where a massive volcanic ridge is habitat for pronghorn antelope, mule deer, bighorn sheep, and birds.

In the national forest country northwest of Crater Lake, Diamond Lake is a popular recreation area along the Rogue-Umpqua Scenic Byway. The byway begins near Roseburg and follows a major river, the North Umpqua, past waterfalls, hiking trails, campgrounds, and fishing sites. Zane Grey gave up the Rogue, after it got too much publicity, to fish the Umpqua.

From Diamond Lake, the byway follows the legendary Rogue River as it flows southwest from its source in Crater Lake National Park to the Pacific. Several state parks have been developed along the river to take advantage of its natural beauty, fisheries, and hiking trails. The long-distance Upper Rogue River Trail leads from the river's headwaters downstream over lava flows, through basalt gorges, and past old-growth trees to Prospect State Scenic Viewpoint, where trails continue past waterfalls near this wild river. The river is impounded at Lost Creek Reservoir, site of Joseph H. Stewart State Park, with neighboring Casey State Recreation Site, popular for its salmon fishery, located below the dam. Downstream near Medford, Tou Velle is a fishing and picnicking spot in the valley, where the river is more sedate. Diverted more westerly now by southern mountains, the river flows near Interstate 5, where the Valley of the Rogue State Park attracts many visitors. The Rogue then heads west to find its way through the Klamath Mountains. South of the Rogue, another wild river, the Illinois, weaves through the isolated, rugged, and unique Kalmiopsis Wilderness. Illinois River Forks State Park is located near the beginning of that journey.

North along Interstate 5 is Wolf Creek Inn State Heritage Site, a historic stagecoach stop from the 1880s that has continuously provided food and lodging for weary travelers and many prominent citizens. The inn is along the Applegate Trail, an alternate branch off the Oregon Trail. Tub Springs, east of Ashland, is another state park along this trail route, and in the southeast corner of this region, pioneer wagon trains followed the Applegate Trail as it traversed the area that is now Goose Lake State Recreation Area. One drought year, emigrants found no lake, just a dry lake bed. Years later, the lake evaporated again and wagon ruts were seen entering the lake and exiting on the opposite side.

The eastern side of this region is a place of cloudless skies, alkaline lakes, and open spaces—a high desert plateau of several thousand feet elevation. A couple of state waysides, Booth and Chandler, provide nice rest stops along the Outback Scenic Byway, which edges spectacular Abert Rim and the wildlife refuge at Summer Lake.

Oregon's largest lake, Upper Klamath, is ringed by wildlife refuges with incredible numbers of migrating and resident birds of many species. At nearby Klamath Falls, the OC & E Woods Line State Trail, a 99-mile rails-to-trails conversion, heads from the urban area east into the desert, along the Sprague River, and also north to the Sycan Marsh.

North of Upper Klamath Lake, visitors to Crater Lake desiring a quiet, primitive base for visiting the national park might choose Jackson F. Kimball, near the headwaters of the Woods River. A hiking route connects that park to Collier Memorial State Park, a unique outdoor logging and pioneer museum along the Williamson River with riverside campsites.

For some cultural entertainment, attend Ashland's renowned Shakespearean Festival and the Peter Britt Music Festival at Jacksonville, a National Historic Landmark town.

For additional information on Oregon State Parks, call 1-800-551-6949, or check the official website: *www.prd.state.or.us.*

102. WOLF CREEK INN STATE HERITAGE SITE

Hours/Season: Day use and overnight lodging (reservations); year-round

Area: 3 acres

Attractions: Historic stagecoach stop, dining, lodging, historic walkway

Facilities: Nine-room hotel with dining room, outdoor exhibits, ballroom available for meetings and receptions

Access: Off Interstate 5, 18 miles north of Grants Pass at Exit 76; although you can access the inn from the north via Exit 78, you must go south to Exit 76 to return to Interstate 5

Contact: (541) 866-2474

The oldest continuously used hotel in Oregon is just as convenient today for travelers on Interstate 5 as it was for those in the early 1880s when they took the stagecoach route from California to Portland. Originally called Wolf Creek Tavern by pioneer merchant Henry Smith, who built it in 1883—though some sources report an earlier date for this—it didn't serve alcohol. (*Tavern* is an old English term describing a hotel that served food.) Today it is part of the state park system and called the Wolf Creek Inn State Heritage Site. The property includes the tavern and its immediate setting on the north bank of Wolf Creek at the community center of the village by that name. Smith had other land holdings that included orchards; the large apple and pear trees north of the inn's dining room are part of an orchard planted in 1885.

At first, the building included sixteen small guest rooms, a parlor room for men and one for ladies, a dining room, and a kitchen. A bowl and pitcher of fresh water, an oil lamp, and a comfortable bed were the furnishings. Deluxe privies were just past the back door.

One of the earliest visitors was President Hayes. Jack London stayed at the inn for several weeks in August of 1911, while he enjoyed hiking in nearby old-growth forest and wrote a short story. Ownership changed several times, and by the 1920s the inn was near the Pacific Crest Highway, which ran from San Diego,

A shaded dining patio is pleasant in summer at Wolf Creek Inn.

California, to Vancouver, British Columbia. The guest registry accumulated the names of many celebrities who stopped at the inn: Mary Pickford, Douglas Fairbanks Jr., Orson Welles, Clark Gable, Carole Lombard, and Sinclair Lewis.

Ownership continued to change hands often, with varied results and interesting histories, and although some repairs along the way saved the building from ruin, the inn was purchased by the state of Oregon in 1975. Aided by a federal grant, the inn was restored by experts in historic architecture and then operated by concessionaires. In 1998, the Oregon Parks and Recreation Department took over the daily operations of the inn, hiring their own innkeeper, chef, and operations manager. Today it is an attractive, well-kept, large wood-frame building with a colonnaded two-story front porch. It is considered an example of the dozens of similar way stations once associated with the network of early roads and trails in western Oregon.

Located in a valley of green forested hills, the inn continues to cater to overnight guests in the nine historically furnished rooms with private bath that are comfortable, but without the intrusions of television or telephones. Self-guided tours of the inn are usually available, particularly early in the day. The first room to the right on the first floor is a combination reception and recreation room, with board games and a player piano that still plays for a quarter. Guest rooms are upstairs. A ballroom, available for meetings and receptions, is above the dining room.

Meals continue to be served in the period-decorated dining room that is popular because of its excellent food. Its versatile menu uses fresh Oregon ingredients that thrive in the fertile Willamette Valley and southern Oregon. Cooked from scratch are homemade breads, soups, and desserts, plus an excellent variety of gourmet seafood and meats prepared with creativity. Salads include grilled mesquite chicken salad with walnut pesto dressing and grilled salmon or chicken Caesar. Pastas can be vegetarian, or with seafood, Italian sausage, or grilled chicken. Desserts include mouth-watering choices. Good local wines add to the appeal of the menu. The dining room is open for lunch and dinner, with reservations available. During nice weather, a patio provides outdoor dining surrounded by flowered grounds. An Octoberfest menu includes sauerbraten, goulash, bratwurst, and accompaniments of German potato salad, spaetzel, and red cabbage, along with authentic German beers and sausages. Decide between apple strudel and black forest chocolate cherry torte for dessert. Greg Meier's Umpah Band provides music for dancing.

A walk around the inn reveals many flower gardens and a pond. A circular walkway in front of the inn loops past historic exhibits. A tiny covered bridge can be seen across the street from the inn. Before the stagecoach or the highway existed here, the Applegate Trail followed the same route from Ashland north to Eugene, where it veered to the northwestern edge of the Willamette Valley (an Applegate Trail Interpretive Center is located in Corvallis).

103. ILLINOIS RIVER FORKS STATE PARK

Hours/Season: Day use; year-round
Area: 368 acres
Attractions: Fishing, picnicking
Facilities: Picnic tables, restrooms
Access: Off US 199, less than 1 mile south of Cave Junction

Illinois River Forks State Park is a pleasant, well-maintained river park, a good rest or lunch stop adjacent to US 199 along the Illinois River. Easy access to the river entices some visitors to cool off in the water on a hot day, splashing among the rocks.

Waders and paddlers are drawn to Illinois River Forks State Park during summer weather.

The confluence of the East and West Forks of the river is just beyond the picnic area. Old roads through this wilder area of the park let you explore a bit, and you can find a spot to do some angling. The river was so named because the Althouse brothers of Illinois emigrated from that state and found gold in the river in 1849.

The climate is drier on this side of the Siskiyou National Forest, which begins at the western edge of the park. Designated as a Wild and Scenic Waterway, the Illinois River has carved its way west through the Siskiyou Mountains in the Kalmiopsis Wilderness, one of the wildest and most unique natural areas in Oregon, with rare plants and rugged geology. Though also accessed from the south coast of Oregon, areas near the east side of the wilderness are accessible from two roads a short distance north of the park. The long, rough road from Selma heads toward Oak Flat, where river runners launch rafts and try their skills on the wildest of Oregon rivers all the way to Agness. Eight Dollar Road (Forest Road 3043), the best access, heads toward Onion Camp, where an easy 1-mile trail heads through the Babyfoot Lake Botanical Area to Babyfoot Lake from Forest Road 140. Past this lake are examples of one of the area's rare plants, the droopy-limbed Brewer's weeping spruce.

104. VALLEY OF THE ROGUE STATE PARK

Hours/Season: Day use and overnight (reservations available); year-round
Area: 277 acres
Attractions: Fishing, boating, interpretive trail, exhibit information, picnicking, camping, Rogue Chuck Wagon Nights
Facilities: Picnic tables, group picnicking shelter, campground (97 full hookups, 49 electrical, 21 tent sites—maximum site 75 feet), 6 yurts, group tent (3 areas), reservable group picnic areas, restrooms with showers, meeting hall, amphitheater/stage, playground, dump station, boat launch, public phone, firewood
Access: Off Interstate 5, 12 miles east of Grants Pass, or 17 miles west of Medford
Contact: (541) 582-1118

According to the former owner of this parkland, Valley of the Rogue State Park has a history of being used temporarily as a reservation by Takelma Indians. Native American artifacts and graves

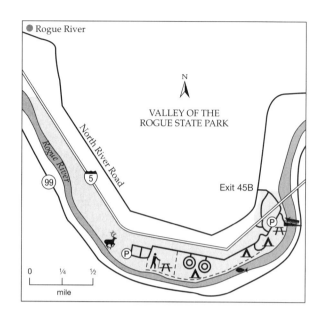

are rumored to have been found in the area, and a fort was formerly located across the river.

Located on the north side of the legendary Rogue River, and the only campground along Interstate 5, Valley of the Rogue is a popular Oregon park. The campground offers a good base camp for exploring Rogue River Valley attractions. Its day-use area is a rest stop for freeway travelers. River access for boats is at the north end of the picnic area. Though picnic tables offer a view of the river, the camping sites are a short distance from the water and have no river views. The park lies along the route of the 1846 Oregon Gold Rush and the Applegate Trail; for more information on these, see the interpretive kiosk in the day-use area.

Sheltered by fir, oaks, madrone, pine, and planted trees over green lawns, the park offers about 3 miles of river frontage for fishing. Across the river to the southwest are the Siskiyou Mountains and Siskiyou National Forest. Between two wild sections, the sedate valley section of the Rogue River experiences hot, dry, sunny summers; a number of vineyards produce respectable wines.

The campground loops are spaced some distance apart; the tent sites and group camp area are found near the beginning. The program area, phone, and another picnic area follow camp loops B, C, D, and E, with a wide landscape separating them from the F loop, which includes the yurts, meeting hall, and another public phone. Rogue Chuck Wagon Nights are scheduled on summer evenings and feature barbecued foods and music in the program area. Ask the park staff for a schedule of these events.

The river trail edges the Rogue River near the campground in Valley of the Rogue State Park.

A 1.25-mile interpretive trail follows the riverfront from the tent sites to the F loop. Entry points for the trail are also located at the program area, the playground, and near the B loop. The shaded access offers places along the river where you can fish. When I visited in 2000, a cougar had been sighted near the river, so proceed with caution; the important thing is not to run if one is seen. They can be frightened off with shouting and arm waving, but your chances of encountering one are slim.

The character of the river begins to change gradually and dramatically some miles west of Grants Pass, the largest city along the Rogue River. At Hellgate Canyon, its waters pass through a narrow slot between 250-foot-high vertical rock formations. Jet-boat excursions out of Grants Pass will take you through this canyon, or you can kayak or raft there and continue on to follow the river as it begins to spawn riffles. Indian Mary Campground offers a natural setting along the river in this area.

Good roads take you to the Grave Creek Bridge, at Galice, the eastern trailhead for the famed 40-mile Rogue River Trail, which traverses the roadless section of the "wild and scenic" river. The bridge is also the entry point for rafters and kayakers to float the challenging water downstream to Agness. Permits are required for this trip, and must be obtained well in advance. Several commercial operators will help you do the trip. The river and its environment will not disappoint you. Towering cliffs, rocky chutes, timbered slopes, waterfalls, rapids, wildlife, wildflowers, and geology move past your vision. *Be alert for rattlesnakes.* Backpackers and boaters will find several primitive camps along the route, plus a few commercial lodges. Hikers can opt to hike the trail using these lodges. Make plans for the wild section of the Rogue early; it's very popular.

105. BEN HUR LAMPMAN STATE SCENIC CORRIDOR

Hours/Season: Day use; year-round
Area: 24 acres
Attractions: Fishing
Facilities: Parking wayside
Access: 16 miles east of Grants Pass, off Lampman Road from Interstate 5

Although this park provides parking and angling access to the Rogue River along its bushy edges, it is pretty much used only by locals who know how to find it. There is no park sign indicating a turnoff from Interstate 5, nor any other facilities. From Interstate 5, Lampman Road turns off immediately to the west as it parallels the highway to the north; the wayside is reached after a short distance.

The property was acquired, as a gift from the city of Gold Hill and other owners, during construction of Interstate 5 in 1952 and 1953. Ben Hur Lampman was the editor of the *Gold Hill News* and later an editorial writer and associate editor of the *Oregonian* in Portland. He was also an avid fisherman and poet, and was named Poet Laureate of Oregon by the Oregon Legislature in 1951.

106. TOU VELLE STATE RECREATION SITE

Hours/Season: Day use (fee); year-round
Area: 54 acres
Attractions: Wildlife viewing, hiking, fishing, picnicking
Facilities: Picnic tables, group picnicking (book reservations through park), horseshoes, boat launch, restrooms
Access: From Interstate 5 at Central Point, take Exit 32 north, right to first light at Table Rock Road, then left 5 miles to park
Contact: (541) 582-1118, extension 21

Tou Velle State Recreation Site is a place for Sunday picnics, wildlife observations, and avid anglers. Many come for all three reasons. The park lies on both sides of the Rogue River by the Bybee Bridge. The take-out for boats is under the bridge on the north side of the river. A number of poplar trees and shapely oaks are found in the park. Hybrid roses add color. Several picnic areas are along the park road (one with a large stone fireplace). *No alcohol is allowed in the park.*

Follow the paved path to the east end of the picnic area, cross the bridge over a watery draw, and you will access a path along a quiet area of the river. Prime steelhead and salmon fishing is found here as the river jogs north and develops a few riffles. To the east is Mount McLoughlin.

From the upland area past the last restroom of the park, the Denman Wildlife Area can be accessed by a loop trail. This path weaves past wetland expanses and through meadows before arriving at the riverfront; it returns along the water to the picnic area. Wildlife signs alert the observer to owls and fish. Bring your binoculars. Hawks fly overhead. Great blue herons are often seen, and wading birds frequent the gravel bar in the middle of the river.

Only a few miles away, the town of Jacksonville traces its beginnings to the discovery of gold in 1851. Unlike so many such towns, it has stayed a viable city by preserving its lovely Victorian homes and historic businesses, and is now a National Historic Landmark. Saunter through town and learn about its early days. Spring is a good time, when lawns are splashed with the colors of flowering shrubs and trees. Today, Jacksonville is renowned throughout the country for its summer Peter Britt Music Festivals, named after the photographer who came here with his bulky photography gear via the Oregon Trail in 1852. Picnic on the hillside above the lights of the town while you listen to a concert under the stars. Choices include jazz, classical, folk, country, pop, dance, and musical theater. To the south, Ashland is famous for its Shakespearean Festivals.

107. CASEY STATE RECREATION SITE

Hours/Season: Day use; year-round
Area: 80.6 acres
Attractions: Hiking, boating, rafting access, fishing, picnicking
Facilities: Picnic tables, boat launch, vault toilets, *no water*
Access: Off OR 62, 29 miles northeast of Medford

Escaping from impoundment behind the Lost Creek Dam, the Rogue River recaptures some of its wild spirit as it flows through Casey State Recreation Site. A frequent stop for picnickers where they lunch under ponderosa pine, Douglas fir, and oaks, the park is situated in the midst of excellent salmon fishing during spawning migration upriver, when the waterway is often lined with anglers.

Boats of several varieties, including rafts, frequently take to the water here, sometimes combining fishing with riding the whitewater downstream. This sport varies depending on water release from the reservoir upstream, but there are usually some riffles to negotiate. Rafts sometimes launch from just below the fish hatchery and come floating past Casey.

The park was named after a squatter, J. A. Casey, who had a restaurant and other buildings on the property before the federal government transferred the land to the state.

At the eastern edge of the park is a sign for the Rogue River Trail (see map with Joseph H. Stewart State Park). The trailhead is the beginning of the 75-mile upper river section that follows the north bank of the river to its headwaters in Crater Lake National Park. Follow this paved trail to the first junction, take the right fork

Just below the Lost Creek Dam, Casey State Recreation Site is popular with anglers.

108. JOSEPH H. STEWART STATE PARK

Hours/Season: Day use and overnight; campground open
March 1 through October 31
Area: 910 acres
Attractions: Hiking trails (with connections to other trails), bicycle trails, swimming area, year-round fishing, waterskiing, boating, photography, picnicking, camping
Facilities: Picnic tables, reservable group picnicking shelters with stoves, campground (151 electrical, 50 tent sites—maximum site 80 feet), 2 reservable group tent camps, restrooms with showers, boat launch, moorage facility, fish-cleaning station, marina with store and cafe, electric kitchen shelters, dump station, playground, program area, volleyball area, public phones, horseshoe pits
Access: Off OR 62, 35 miles northeast of Medford
Contact: (541) 560-3334

that passes under McLeod Bridge, and follow the river for 0.4 mile to McGregor Park Visitor Center, with its displays about dam construction, natural history, Native American history, and early settlement of the Rogue River Valley. The center is also reached by road.

The 0.5-mile stroll along the river in McGregor Park is peppered with secluded picnic tables that are especially attractive, many overlooking the river, so why not bring lunch—perhaps some alder-smoked salmon and crackers—for your hike. This wetland habitat along the Rogue includes Oregon grape, blackberry, ferns, mock orange, and ocean spray growing beneath overhead branches of cottonwoods, California hazel, alder, dogwood, and bigleaf maple. Some spots have horsetail that are 3 feet tall. Beaver, muskrat, western gray squirrel, skunk, porcupine, chipmunk, and rabbit are at home in this ecosystem. Merganser ducks often rest atop rocks in the river.

At the spur road to the Cole M. Rivers Fish Hatchery, follow the painted paw prints on the pavement for 0.3 mile as you pass the drift boat ramp and then cross the fish diversion dam. This is the third-largest salmon and steelhead hatchery in the country.

The trail now crosses an open field (often hot) that is planted with millet to provide nutritious seeds for visiting birds. Besides ospreys, herons, kingfishers, and other birds who fish this quiet spot on the river above the hatchery dam, human fishers practice catch-and-release fly-casting.

The powerhouse for the Lost Creek Dam is 0.7 mile from the hatchery. One of the main functions of this reservoir is flood control, with low water occurring often in summers, particularly in a drought year. The temperature of released water is controlled to provide the optimum temperature for fish upstream.

For the long-distance hiker and backpacker, the North Shore Trail continues along Lost Creek Reservoir for a total of 18.3 miles to the Peyton Bridge, with several camps and side trails along the route. This canyoned side of the lake is reached only by energetic hikers and boaters, since there are no roads.

Lost Creek Reservoir is a huge expanse of blue water encircled by canyon walls on the western edge of the Cascade Mountains. It is a place of summer warmth, open spaces, cooling water, and several choices of recreation. Located along the south bank of the reservoir, and leased from the Army Corps of Engineers, the park land was once the site of a pear orchard, established by A. J. Weeks. He was the son-in-law of Joseph H. Stewart, one of this country's foremost horticulturists, who introduced the commercial orchard to this region and who is honored by this state park.

The campground is on the upper end of the lake, with some

The marina on Lost Creek Reservoir, at Joseph H. Stewart State Park, is busy in early May.

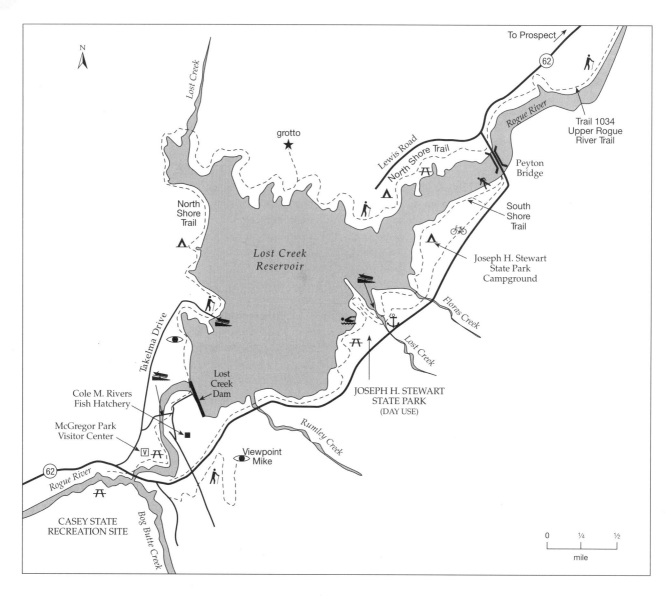

view sites overlooking the water. Trees grow along the cliffs that edge the water, but there is much open, sunny space in the campground.

The day-use area and marina are about 0.5 mile southwest of the campground, with several picnic areas that accommodate both small and large groups among the many pines and conifers. The swimming area is adjacent to the day-use area, separated from the rest of the lake by buoys and floats, but there is no lifeguard. Open to anglers year-round, the lake has excellent fishing

and is stocked with trout. Water-skiers have plenty of room to maneuver. In late summer of bad drought years, the lake can get quite low and activities on the water then have diminished access; the swimming area may even be dry.

A paved bike lane allows bicyclers to travel between the day-use area and the campground, and east to Peyton Bridge—6 miles of trail through forest and fields. The path is away from views of the lake and closer to the highway than the lake.

The 5.5 miles of hiking trails include a picturesque path that borders the lake atop the cliffs near the campground, accessed easily from many points. This trail passes viewpoints and goes through shady woods of madrone, pine, red cedar, oaks, evergreen huckleberry, and fir as it crosses creeks with bridges. It then traverses a large open, grassy meadow, with California poppies and huge salsify heads of intricate design. A few steps on OR 62, a walk across Peyton Bridge, and you can continue upstream on a trail, in fact all the way to the Pacific Crest National Scenic Trail near Crater Lake, or jog west to take the North Shore Trail around Lost Creek Lake.

Traveling west on the trail from the campground, you pass a pond, several viewpoints, the marina, and the swimming beach. From there, the South Shore Trail continues on to Casey State Recreation Site. The distance between Peyton Bridge and Casey is 8 miles; almost 4 miles of this hiking trail are within the Joseph H. Stewart State Park. Striped coral root, self-heal, Oregon grape, smilacina, wild rose, thimbleberry, vetch, fireweed, mullein, and chicory are just a few of the flora easily discovered along the trails. Butterflies are numerous, particularly monarchs and swallowtails. Habitats for frogs, toads, salamanders, and a variety of reptiles are along the trail.

The park includes a 10-kilometer Oregon State Park Volkswalk, a mapped route prepared by the Oregon Trail State Volkssport Association and graded according to difficulty.

109. PROSPECT STATE SCENIC VIEWPOINT

Hours/Season: Day use; year-round
Area: 11 acres
Attractions: Hiking, waterfalls, photography, wildlife viewing, picnicking
Facilities: Picnic tables, vault toilets, *no water*
Access: Off OR 62, 1 mile south of Prospect on Mill Creek Drive
Contact: Upper Rogue River Trail information at Prospect Ranger Station, (541) 560-3400

Although no sign is found on OR 62, exiting at Prospect easily leads you to Prospect State Scenic Viewpoint, which is signed, on Mill Creek Drive. Though the wayside itself is unimpressive, it offers parking near tall trees and access to the Pearsony Falls Trail, which connects to trails to the Rogue River, Mill Creek Falls, and the Avenue of the Boulders.

The acquisition of the state park protected roadside trees that

The Upper Rogue River Trail heads north of Prospect to the river's headwaters in Crater Lake National Park.

included sugar and ponderosa pine, Douglas fir, white fir, and madrone. The wayside is rolling land on a bench above the Rogue River lying between the present Crater Lake Highway and the old alignment. Initial development, including a stone and native wood park entrance sign, was carried out by Civilian Conservation Corps during the Depression. Originally named Deskins, the nearby community was optimistically renamed Prospect in 1889.

If you continue south on Mill Creek Drive, two other pullovers

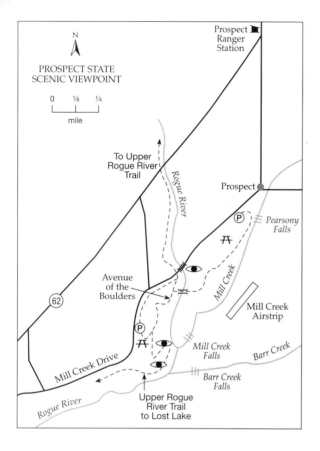

Rogue River Trail in this area can be accessed from the park, both to the north and to the south.

Though a trail follows the Rogue River from Casey State Recreation Site to the river's headwaters, the 48 miles of trail northeast of Prospect Ranger Station to the headwaters at Boundary Springs, the Upper Rogue River National Recreation Trail, are the most fascinating. The river in this area alternates between sections of wild, raging rapids and quiet pools. It is untamed here, and no kayak or raft could follow its course because of the huge trees that have fallen into the water. Yet it is a mostly undiscovered hiking trail, with charms that are unsuspected from driving OR 62. Accessed from several side roads near a string of campgrounds and picnic areas, the trail can be hiked in day-hike sections or by backpacking.

Exciting geology is found along the trail. Lava flows from the Cascade Mountains were slowly cut by the Rogue—called the "River of Flowing Rock"—forming a varied landscape, though the river still seeks an easier route shown by abandoned oxbows, peninsulas, and forested islands. At Takelma Gorge, the river twists and churns through a deep gorge fringed along its top with colorful flowers. The water is diverted into an underground maze of intact lava tubes at Natural Bridge, and emerges

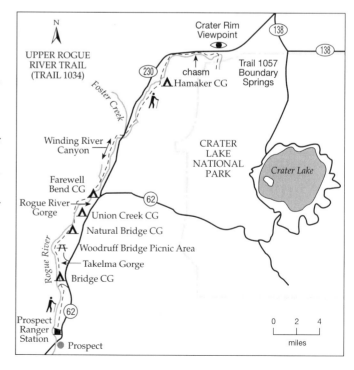

are wise stops. The first one is located where the road crosses a spectacular gorge with rapids and rocks on the Rogue River. The view from the bridge is definitely a photo opportunity.

Most hikers choose the third wayside to access the trails, where picnic tables are also found. A huge wooden sign depicts a map of the hiking area, including all the area trails. Most of these branch off a wide, easy path and become moderately difficult, mainly because of rocks strewn along the trail. Nearby are waterfalls on Mill and Barr Creeks that plunge into the spectacular canyon of the Rogue River. Head south for Mill Creek and Barr Creek waterfalls, or north for Pearsony Falls and the Avenue of the Boulders. The latter is a particularly appealing hike through an area of boulders; at one point only a small passageway lets you slip between two large boulders. Spring wildflowers, the many boulders, and a variety of trees, particularly the madrones, provide an enchanting walk to a wild section of the Rogue River. Caution is required near the river since the dam upstream sometimes releases large quantities of water that can be dangerous. The long-distance in a violent, dangerous release. At Rogue River Gorge, the roaring river is forced through a long, narrow chute left by a collapsed lava tube. In the Winding River Canyon, 250-foot vertical cliffs of pumice have been gashed by the river. Spinning rocks have left potholes in areas of lava flows. Waterfalls plunge over resistant basalt.

The flora and fauna are also impressive. Ancient forest of Douglas fir and mixed conifers—including massive sugar pines that Scottish botanist David Douglas searched for and found—as well as alder, yew, vine maple, ferns, and cow parsnip border the path. Wildflowers and mosses grow in cracks of lava rocks in the wetland and grassy meadow areas. Chiseled stumps indicate beaver activity. Log jams form pools for cutthroat trout.

110. JACKSON F. KIMBALL STATE RECREATION SITE

Hours/Season: Day use and overnight; campground open mid-April through October
Area: 19.4 acres
Attractions: Wood River headwaters, fishing, hiking, wildlife viewing, picnicking, camping
Facilities: Picnic tables, campground with 10 primitive sites (maximum site 45 feet), vault toilets, *no water*
Access: Off OR 62, 3 miles north of Fort Klamath, accessed from the highway from both north and south on a scenic loop road; follow signs to park
Contact: (541) 783-2471

A quick jog off the main route to Crater Lake leads to this quiet park: Jackson F. Kimball State Recreation Site. The primitive camp and picnic tables are nestled under pines and firs along the Wood River, a possibility for overnighting near Crater Lake National Park.

Forest birds flit among the trees. A short trail follows the river and crosses a bridge for a view of the springs that form the headwaters of the river. I startled a grouse there in the brush. The river widens quickly from its beginnings over rocks in a small pool, and in the short distance to the edge of the campsites it widens into a lakelike affair before it flows onward. This shallow lake has an appealing soft green color mingled with reflections of tall trees. Sighting downstream, a Cascade peak is seen. Swampy wetlands edge the water. Cows sometimes graze in the pasture across the water, but even so, the sensations are of a wilderness experience.

111. COLLIER MEMORIAL STATE PARK

Hours/Season: Day use and overnight; campground open mid-April through October
Area: 856 acres
Attractions: Open-air logging museum, exhibits, pioneer log cabin village, hiking, wildlife viewing, fishing, gift shop, picnicking, camping
Facilities: Two day-use areas with picnic tables and kitchen shelter, group shelter, one with a children's play area, day-use horse rest and exercise area, campground (50 full hookup, 18 tent sites—maximum site 60 feet), restrooms with showers, dump station, amphitheater, laundry facilities, firewood, public phones
Access: Off US 97, 30 miles north of Klamath Falls
Contact: (541) 783-2471

Back in 1826, Peter Skene Ogden, chief trader for the Hudson's Bay Company, passed through the area that is now Collier Memorial State Park, no doubt enjoying the attractive scenery. Though many come today to this park to see the logging exhibits, outdoor recreation urges them to linger.

Day-use areas are located on both sides of the highway. The campground area is on the east side of the highway, a short distance north. The sites are across the Williamson River from the day-use area with easy access to fishing from that side also. Connecting trails lead to all park areas, and to fishing holes east along the Williamson River.

As a memorial to their parents, 146 acres of this park were donated, in 1945, by Alfred and Andrew Collier, who then began to establish a logging museum. Hundreds of pieces of equipment, from the early days of oxen-powered logging to present time, were gathered and donated by the Collier brothers. It is recognized as one of the finest collections of logging equipment in the country.

Wander through this outdoor logging museum on the west side of the highway to see skidding equipment, steam tractors, loggers' "cats," road graders, trucks, wagons, mighty circular saws, steam-powered Dolbeer donkey engines used to skid logs to landings, and the last boat used to haul log rafts across Klamath Lake. Railroad equipment includes a narrow-gauge locomotive, a one-person handcart, a stiff-boom loader, a log buncher, a spring-boom loader, and a track-laying car, all exhibited on railroad track. The steam-generating plant produced enough electricity to run an entire sawmill. A plaque commemorates the

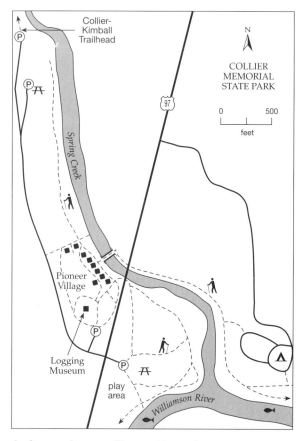

Behind the homestead is a blacksmith shed, complete with forge, anvil, bellows, drill press, a collection of harnesses and yokes, and a sling for shoeing draft animals.

Walk north of the museum to see a pioneer village. Relocated here are authentic log cabins that include a doctor's office, store, sheepherder's wagon, outhouse, explorer's cabin, and one unfinished cabin whose builder was killed before completion. These buildings vary in construction and amenities, from fire pits to cast-iron stoves, from dirt to wooden floors, from dark, crude shelters to glass-windowed homes that let you glimpse a slice of family furnishings inside. Signs along the paths identify the native vegetation.

The log cabins are at the edge of lovely, wild Spring Creek. A 1.5-mile trail follows the creek to picnic areas at both ends, passing under the highway bridge. The eastern day-use area is at the confluence of Spring Creek with the Williamson River; both waterways are excellent trout-fishing streams and open to non-motorized boating. The river is a magical sight in early morning when the sun first hits the water and hazy steam rises as the water is warmed. Great blue herons and ducks are silent stalkers along the waterfront.

A route has recently been laid out for hiking 10 miles to Jackson F. Kimball State Recreation Site, mostly following abandoned roads (nonmotorized use only). The trailhead branches off from the road to the Spring Creek Picnic Area.

Collier Memorial State Park is not far from Crater Lake

The Clatsop fir, largest to be cut in Oregon, is on exhibit at Collier Memorial State Park.

breed of men who wore "loggers' boots."

The museum includes huge sections of sugar pine and Douglas fir trees. One fir—the largest to be cut in Oregon—was a seedling when Marco Polo began his travels, 200 years before Columbus discovered America. It was toppled in one of the Oregon coast's wild winter storms in 1962, near Seaside, when it was 702 years old, 15.5 feet in diameter, and 200.5 feet high, even with a broken top. It contained 100,000 board feet, enough wood for ten two-bedroom homes.

Begin or end your logging equipment tour at the authentic logger's homestead, now an information center and gift shop staffed by volunteers from the Friends of Collier Memorial State Park. At first glance, the huge, stuffed Alaskan timber wolf in the loft looks like a bear because of its size. Other artifacts and hand tools catch your attention: felling axes, kerosene lamps, a tobacco plug cutter, a drafting table and instruments, a barbed wire display, levers with hinged hooks for rolling logs, and the saddle of Pete French, the cattle baron of Harney County.

National Park, a one-of-a-kind, more-than-a-mile-high, breathtaking blue lake formed in the caldera of a collapsed volcano. Campgrounds in the national park are often full during the tourist season, so the Collier campground is an alternative base for exploring the many trails, rim drive, and wildflower walks in the national park.

KLAMATH BASIN NATIONAL WILDLIFE REFUGES

Some of the best birdwatching in the United States is found in the Klamath Basin, which extends from southern Oregon into California. Approximately a century ago, this vast basin was dominated by 185,000 acres of shallow lakes and freshwater marshes, which attracted peak fall numbers of over 6 million waterfowl. Although much of this landscape was converted to agricultural land by the U.S. Bureau of Reclamation, the 25 percent of wetlands that remain still have the power to attract the majority of the waterfowl migrating along the Pacific Flyway, some staying for the winter, with peak fall concentrations of more than one million birds.

This wondrous bird scenario is the result of the establishment of six national wildlife refuges: Upper Klamath, Klamath Marsh, Bear Valley, Lower Klamath, Tule Lake, and Clear Lake. In fact, Theodore Roosevelt established the first waterfowl refuge in 1908 at Lower Klamath. These six refuges support 411 species of resident and migratory wildlife in a variety of habitats: freshwater marshes, open water, grassy meadows, coniferous forests, sagebrush and juniper grasslands, agricultural lands, and rocky cliffs and slopes. Each refuge has its distinctive appeal.

The Upper Klamath National Wildlife Refuge is mostly freshwater marsh and open water with excellent nesting and brood-rearing areas that attract white pelicans and several heron species, other waterfowl, and nearby nesting bald eagle and osprey. An excellent way to view this refuge is via canoe, with a brochure available on a 6-mile and 3.5-mile canoe route. The Rocky Point boat launch is on Pelican Bay on Upper Klamath Lake, Oregon's largest, with fishing available.

A short distance west of US 97, and just north of the California border, is Bear Valley National Wildlife Refuge. No public entry is allowed in this area of old-growth coniferous trees, but in late winter, birders come from far away to watch some of the nearly 300 bald eagles fly out in the morning from their overnight roost on the northeast slope. They can be viewed from an observation point not far from the highway. Several eagle pairs nest in the refuge.

Virtually all of the historic Klamath Marsh, where the Klamath Indians lived, is found in the refuge of the same name, off US 97 a short distance northeast of Collier Memorial State Park. Along the Williamson River, the marsh attracts waterfowl while the surrounding meadowlands provide nesting and feeding areas for sandhill crane, yellow rail, various shorebirds, and raptors. Pine forest supports diverse wildlife, including great gray owl and Rocky Mountain elk. Recreation includes a 10-mile trail for hiking, cross-country skiing, and mountain biking, as well as fishing and canoeing.

Lower Klamath National Wildlife Refuge, the largest of the refuges, stretches across the California border and offers diverse birdwatching along automobile tour routes, and a few photography blinds. Nearby Tule Lake also has blinds and tour routes plus canoe trails, interpretive trails, a visitor center, and headquarters for the Klamath Basin refuges. Clear Lake in California is mostly closed to public entry; it serves as a water source for agriculture for the eastern Klamath Basin.

White pelicans are frequent sightings at Lower Klamath National Wildlife Refuge.

112. TUB SPRINGS STATE WAYSIDE

Hours/Season: Day use; year-round
Area: 40 acres
Attractions: Picnicking, historic rest stop, exhibit information, freshwater springs
Facilities: Picnic tables, vault toilets, springwater pump
Access: Off OR 66, 18 miles east of Ashland

In the Cascade Mountains not far from the California-Oregon border, Tub Springs State Wayside is a forested tract lying in a shallow mountain depression, bisected by what is historically called the Greensprings Highway. This road follows the route of pioneers who took the southern route, the Applegate Trail, to Oregon. Although the travelers along the trail did not have some of the higher Cascade Mountains to contend with, today's highway reveals that this must have been a tough part of the trek. The highway is very winding, with steep drop-offs, mostly without railings, as it heads east from Ashland to the 4,895-foot Hayden Mountain Summit, which is east of the wayside. How sweet it must have been for the pioneers to arrive at Tub Springs, where springwater was available. The wayside was named for the freshwater springs that were developed with a pump and three rock tubs to hold the water.

At an elevation of 4,200 feet, the wayside is a pleasant setting for a rest stop and picnic in a forest setting, with Douglas fir, ponderosa pine, sugar pine, white fir, and an understory of manzanita and ceanothus. Exhibits relate the history of the Applegate Trail in this area. The paved trail that leads into the picnic area also continues into the woods for some distance, so today's highway traveler can stretch his or her legs in pleasant surroundings.

More recent history of the wayside involved a major timber trespass by a crafty timber thief in the early 1950s. The wayside contained large old-growth pine and Douglas fir, whereas the surrounding property had been logged. Using an erroneous harvesting permit, trees were cut, and logs were sent to both Klamath Falls and Medford. The high quality of logs and the demands for payment of woods workers prompted the receiving sawmills to make inquiries to the state park system. An investigation of the area led to a charge of criminal trespass. The case was settled out of court after several pretrial appearances of the confessed culprit. Because of this experience, a careful survey of state wayside boundaries at Tub Springs was made and iron pins were set at the boundary corners.

113. OC & E WOODS LINE STATE TRAIL

Hours/Season: Day use; year-round
Area: 99-mile railroad bed
Attractions: Hiking/biking/horse trail on old railroad bed, cross-country skiing, skating, jogging, photography, wildlife viewing
Facilities: Restrooms, parking access points
Access: From OR 140 or OR 39, take Washburn Way in Klamath Falls; signs on this street direct you to a parking area at Crosby and Avalon near the trailhead
Contact: (541) 783-2471

In 1917, Robert E. Strahorn began implementing his dream of constructing the Klamath Falls Municipal Railway. Funding was provided by bonds from the City of Klamath to build the first 19 miles to the town of Dairy. His initial dream involved a system of 400 miles of rail, but his Oregon, California, and Eastern Railway (OC & E) reached its terminus in Bly, in 1929. The portion built, however, brought growth to this basin as a logging railway that transported as much as one million board feet of pine logs a day, supplying the four mills along the line. By 1990, however, the logging railroad came to a close and railbanked the right-of-way

A railway car is on display at trailhead parking for the OC & E Woods Line State Trail in Klamath Falls.

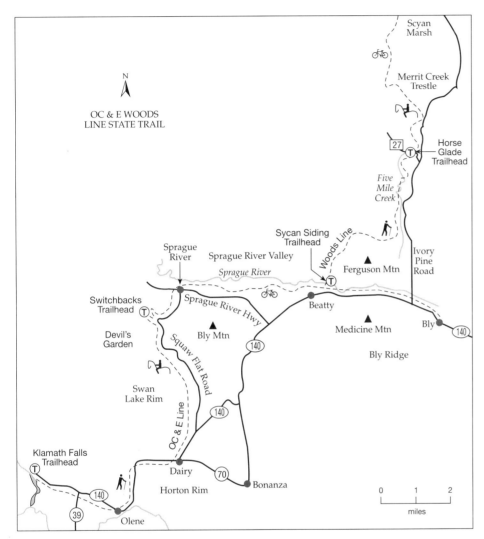

the urban setting as the surface changes to a graded and rolled path for 3.8 miles to Olene. From this point, trail users will encounter stretch and metal gates, which must be closed behind you. Along this portion, the route passes an 1898 steel railroad bridge, Wiard Park, and views of Mount Shasta to the south. Near Olene, look for the Olene Gap, where the Lost River flows through a narrow opening.

From Olene to Beatty, the surface is loose basalt and hard packed. The attractions on the 9.8 miles to the Dutch dairymen settlement of Dairy include the scenic Lost River, ranchland, Swede's Cut, and the Dairy Y Siding. The 19.9 miles between Dairy and Sprague River passes through Winema National Forest, Devil's Garden, the Switchbacks Trailhead, double switchbacks, and broad vistas. Strahorn had originally planned to construct a tunnel through Bly Mountain, but insufficient funds changed his plans and he constructed a "temporary" double switchback over this hill to allow trains to be split for navigating the hill. After the trail descends into the Sprague River Valley, the 12.5-mile portion of the trail to Beatty roughly follows the river in a scenic area that offers wildlife viewing, fishing, and the scenic Buttes of the Gods. The trail continues to follow the

Sprague River for another 14 miles, passing numerous trestles to its terminus, after 65 miles, in the once booming community of Bly. The eastern trailhead there has no sign yet, but the trail can be accessed at the west end of town, across the highway from a small park.

Just east of Beatty, the Sycan Siding Trailhead across the river heads north on cinders, basalt, and hard packed surface for 34 miles along the old Woods Line. Five Mile Creek is reached at mile 10, and the creek continues alongside and under the trail. The Horse Glade Trailhead, with restrooms and camping opportunities, is reached at mile 19. After passing through areas of the

to the Oregon Parks and Recreation Department. That was the start of the transition from a railway to 99 miles of trail on the old railroad bed.

The parking area for the trailhead is adjacent to a bright-yellow train car of the OC & E Railway. The trail begins in the middle of Klamath Falls, with 3.5 miles of paved trail between Washburn Way and OR 39. On sunny days the city trail is a fun place enjoyed by walkers, joggers, skaters, bicyclists, and equestrians. A wood chip path is provided for equestrians and joggers. The walkway crosses a canal bike path in this area. A parking area is at the intersection with OR 39. From this point, the trail leaves

Fremont National Forest, the spectacular Merritt Creek Trestle, 400 feet long and 100 feet high, is seen at mile 27. The trail ends in another 7 miles at the Sycan Marsh. The Forest Service has future plans to link this trail to one north of the marsh.

Sycan Marsh is a Nature Conservancy property, and trail hikers should not trespass; this landscape protects an array of extremely valuable wetlands. At 27,693 acres, this is the Nature Conservancy's largest Oregon preserve. Situated in the Klamath Basin's headwaters, a mile high and remote, more than 130 species of migrating and breeding birds annually use the marsh, including sensitive species that include the yellow rail, white-faced ibis, black tern, and breeding sandhill cranes. During spring migration, as many as 10,000 tundra swans visit the marsh. Sycan Marsh is the site of one of the West's largest wetland restoration projects, with the cooperation of several other agencies.

Trail users must follow certain regulations and etiquette:

1. Respect private property.
2. Motorized vehicles are prohibited.
3. Pack it in, pack it out!
4. Bicyclists and hikers must yield to equestrians and not spook the animal.
5. Equestrians must travel single file and use the wood chip trail when available.
6. Bicyclists should not startle trail users when approaching them.
7. Pets must be on a 6-foot leash and under control; remove any pet wastes.
8. Discharge of firearms is prohibited.
9. Camping is not allowed along the trail, except where designated.

114. BOOTH STATE SCENIC CORRIDOR

Hours/Season: Day use; year-round
Area: 310 acres
Attractions: Picnicking, fall color, rest stop
Facilities: Restrooms
Access: Off OR 140, 12 miles west of Lakeview

In the high desert just outside the border of Fremont National Forest, Booth State Scenic Corridor provides a pleasant picnic and rest stop among a scattering of old-growth ponderosa pines and quaking aspens, whose golden hues contrast nicely with the green needles and cinnamon-bark foliage of the pines. The pungent aroma of desert vegetation permeates the air. Huge pine cones cover the grounds where tables are spread out for privacy. Adjacent to the wayside are farms.

The park was named after Robert A. Booth, who gave the initial 50 acres of the park, and served on the Oregon State Highway Commission and Governor Patterson's State Park Commission. Booth State Scenic Corridor was developed during the Depression era with the assistance of the Civilian Conservation Corps.

Nearby Lakeview is the site of the Black Cap Hang Glider Launch Site. Adventurers interested in hang gliding can jump off a mountain above Lakeview and try for the annual cash award for the longest flight by a hang glider pilot. Participants can see an excellent overview of the Goose Lake Valley. Just north of Lakeview, at Hunter's Hot Springs, is Old Perpetual, billed as the only active geyser in Oregon; it erupts continuously.

115. GOOSE LAKE STATE RECREATION AREA

Hours/Season: Day use and overnight; campground open mid-April through October
Area: 64 acres
Attractions: Camping, picnicking, wildlife viewing, lake access
Facilities: Picnic tables, boat launch; campground (47 electrical sites—maximum site 50 feet), restrooms, showers, dump station
Access: Off US 395, 14 miles south of Lakeview, 1 mile west of New Pine Creek on State Line Road
Contact: Goose Lake State Recreation Area, (541) 947-3111; Oregon's Outback Scenic Byway, Lake County Chamber of Commerce, 126 NE Street, Lakeview, OR, (541) 947-6040

The Klamath Indian name for Goose Lake was *Newapkshi*. John Work of the Hudson's Bay Company fur brigade referred to the lake as Pit Lake when they camped near it. As pioneers settled the area, the large numbers of wild geese seen here prompted its present name.

The lake straddles the California-Oregon border, with Goose Lake State Recreation Area situated along the northeast shoreline of the lake. The lake floods the floor of a basin left by geologic action millions of years ago. Once the waters were more extensive and had an outlet in the Pit River in northeast

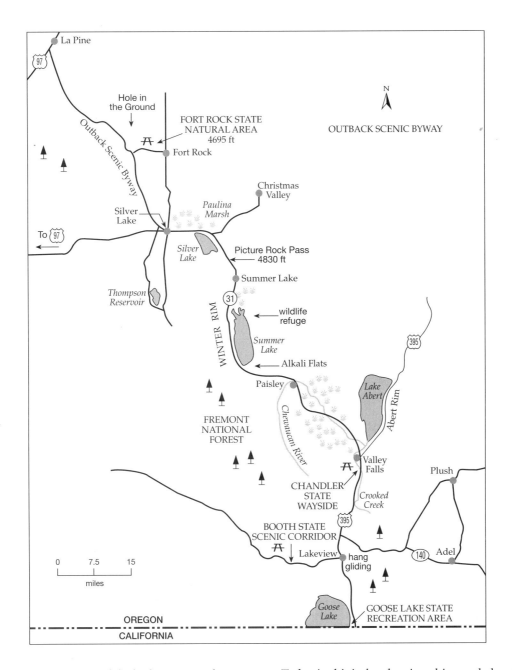

La Pine

97

Hole in
the Ground

Outback Scenic Byway

FORT ROCK STATE
NATURAL AREA
4695 ft

Fort Rock

OUTBACK SCENIC BYWAY

N

Christmas
Valley

*Paulina
Marsh*

Silver
Lake

To 97

*Silver
Lake*

Picture Rock Pass
4830 ft

Summer Lake

31

WINTER RIM

wildlife
refuge

*Thompson
Reservoir*

*Summer
Lake*

395

Alkali Flats

Paisley

*Lake
Abert*

Chewaucan River

FREMONT
NATIONAL
FOREST

Abert Rim

Plush

CHANDLER
STATE
WAYSIDE

Valley
Falls

*Crooked
Creek*

BOOTH STATE
SCENIC CORRIDOR

395

0   7.5   15

miles

Lakeview

hang
gliding

140

Adel

OREGON

*Goose
Lake*

GOOSE LAKE STATE
RECREATION AREA

CALIFORNIA

California. To the north are Ice Age lake beds. Goose Lake now has no outlet and continues to shrink, getting shallower and saltier, mostly because of irrigation uses. Pioneers settling southern Oregon followed the historic Applegate Trail that borders the southern edge of the lake.

Today, in this isolated region, this wooded and grassland tract with access to Goose Lake provides a pleasant stopover for travelers and recreation users, who can often view a large variety of waterfowl, although their numbers were higher in the past. The nice scattering of juniper, quaking aspen, weeping willow,

The waterfront along Goose Lake has views to the south, and seasonal birding.

116. CHANDLER STATE WAYSIDE

Hours/Season: Day use; year-round
Area: 85 acres
Attractions: Picnicking, rest stop
Facilities: Picnic tables, restrooms
Access: Off US 395, 16 miles north of Lakeview

Situated along Oregon's Outback Scenic Byway, Chandler State Wayside offers a pleasant picnic site at the edge of the Great Basin Desert in a lonely expanse of southern Oregon where solitude is solace for the spirit. Lying near Crooked Creek, blue jays flit among the ponderosa pines and fuller teasel edge the woods. The original land for the wayside was given to the state by S. B. and Hattie Chandler. It was once developed for overnight camping, but is now only for day use. Across from Chandler is an area of plateau basalt flows.

If the traveler continues north on the byway, the jog onto OR 31 at Valley Falls offers the first sighting of impressive Abert Rim, which runs 19 miles along the eastern edge of Lake Abert and rises 2,000 feet above the plateau. Abert Rim was raised and Abert Lake dropped along one of the big tensional faults of the past. It is one of the largest exposed faults in the world. A coating of green lichen colors the 800-foot lava cap that ends in a sheer precipice atop Abert Rim. The summit slopes to the east, and crude pictographs have been found at the base in one area. Lieutenant Fremont and his party discovered the lake and rim, and stood on top where they saw grand panoramic views of the outback country. Fossils reveal that camel and rhino roamed the lake region long ago. Between Valley Falls and Paisley, the byway follows the Chewaucan River.

Volcanic eruptions twenty-five million and ten million years ago formed this lava plateau in south central Oregon, and more recently, the area broke into blocks that moved up and down to produce mountains and valleys—basin and range country. When it rains, which is not often, water flows to the lowest area to form shallow lakes, which later dry up, leaving sediments as valleys fill and mountains erode. Dissolved mineral matter accumulates in the valleys to render the water alkaline, then glazes the ground with white deposits as the water evaporates.

Continuing northwest along OR 31 past Paisley, at the base of Winter Rim, is shallow Summer Lake. It attracts masses of ducks and other waterfowl during migrations along the Pacific Flyway. Summer Lake Wildlife Area provides 20,000 acres of

Russian olive, and ponderosa pine trees attracts songbirds that include evening grosbeak, downy woodpecker, and California quail. A line of the Great Western Railway bisects the lakeside quarter of the park.

Oregon's Outback Scenic Byway begins, or ends, near here, at the border, and continues north via US 395 and then OR 31 to its terminus at US 97 near La Pine. To avoid hot, summer weather, the best times to drive the tour are spring and fall. Geologists consider the rocks and landscapes along the basin and range country along the byway to be some of Oregon's most extraordinary ones as the route weaves through valleys between basalt mountains. North of Goose Lake, the byway follows the base of the Warner Range as it heads into Lakeview, the state's "tallest town" at 4,800 feet.

Summer Lake, with a wildlife refuge, is located along the Outback Scenic Byway.

habitat that includes marshland, pot holes, salt grass flats, and dry brush lands. It's a popular place during migrations, with parking, camping, and an automobile tour available. On rare occasions, winds cause dust storms that create dunes along the east shore of the lake, whose shoreline fluctuates greatly with the weather. Hot springs are also found in this area, with accommodations near them. Hunters inundate the Summer Lake area on the opening day of duck season, so don't come then for other recreation.

Between Summer Lake and the dry basin of Silver Lake is Picture Rock Pass, with exposed basalts and some Native American art on the rocks. The byway continues past Paulina Marsh near the community of Silver Lake. (For the remainder of the byway, see Fort Rock State Natural Area.)

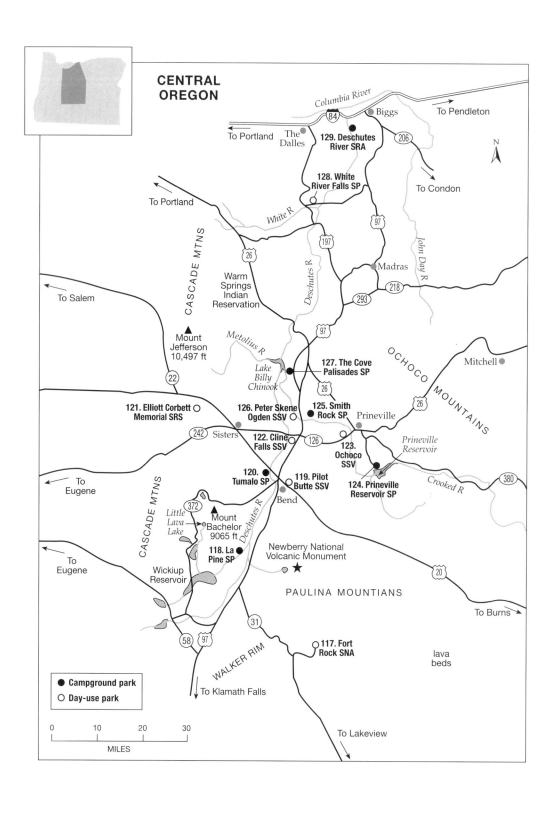

CENTRAL OREGON

Columbia River

To Portland

The Dalles

Biggs

To Pendleton

84

206

129. Deschutes River SRA

128. White River Falls SP

To Portland

White R.

To Condon

26

197

97

Warm Springs Indian Reservation

To Salem

Madras

John Day R.

293

218

CASCADE MTNS

Mount Jefferson 10,497 ft

22

Metolius R.

97

Deschutes R.

OCHOCO MOUNTAINS

Mitchell

Lake Billy Chinook

127. The Cove Palisades SP

26

26

121. Elliott Corbett Memorial SRS

126. Peter Skene Ogden SSV

125. Smith Rock SP

Prineville

Prineville Reservoir

242

Sisters

122. Cline Falls SSV

126

123. Ochoco SSV

380

120. Tumalo SP

119. Pilot Butte SSV

124. Prineville Reservoir SP

Crooked R.

To Eugene

372

Bend

Little Lava Lake

Mount Bachelor 9065 ft

CASCADE MTNS

Deschutes R.

118. La Pine SP

Newberry National Volcanic Monument

To Eugene

Wickiup Reservoir

PAULINA MOUNTAINS

20

To Burns

31

58

97

117. Fort Rock SNA

lava beds

WALKER RIM

To Klamath Falls

● Campground park
○ Day-use park

0   10   20   30

MILES

To Lakeview

CHAPTER SEVEN
CENTRAL OREGON

The heartland of Oregon begins on the pine-clad eastern slopes of the Cascades. The Cascade Lakes Scenic Byway is the best road for getting within yodeling distance of several of these snow-peaked mountains. Southwest of Bend, the tour climbs past awesome views, a string of lakes, ski resorts, hiking trails, osprey nests, and wilderness vistas. One state park along the Deschutes River, La Pine, is close enough to the byway for day excursions.

East of La Pine, the violence of volcanic action has left imprints of lava flows, cinder cones, and lava caves. Paulina and East Lakes nestle in the Newberry Crater, once a massive fire mountain of some 12,000 feet. This area attracts cross-country skiers and snowmobilers in winter, hikers and bikers in summer. For an incredible view of the Bend area and the Cascade spine, drive or hike to the top of Pilot Butte.

From La Pine, Central Oregon reaches its southern limits via the Outback Scenic Byway, which heads southeast to Fort Rock State Natural Area. This park features the remains of an ancient volcano that rises above a desert lake bed, where Native Americans camped more than ten thousand years ago and made sandals out of sagebrush.

Bounded by the John Day River, Oregon's longest, much of the east side of the region is a high, dry desert plateau with the pungent, distinctive aroma of sagebrush and juniper. Little rain falls and temperatures are in the eighties and nineties in summer, though nights are crisp and cool with low humidity. Winter climate varies greatly, depending on the elevation.

Due to geologic upheaval in the high plateau country of central Oregon, rockhounds come to the many public lands to look for thundereggs (the state rock), agates, petrified wood, obsidian, or even a rare opal or amethyst. Prineville Reservoir State Park, on the Crooked River, is one base for this activity, as well as fishing, waterskiing, and boating. Near Prineville, Ochoco State Scenic Viewpoint features a panoramic vista.

The Deschutes River heads north through the region to its northern edge at the Columbia River. Its sometimes wild nature provides a reason for several state parks: Tumalo, Cline Falls, and The Cove Palisades. At The Cove Palisades, the Deschutes is joined by Crooked River and then the Metolius River just above Round Dam, where Lake Billy Chinook spreads out as a reservoir playground among a labyrinth of canyons.

One state park, White River Falls, is located on a tributary of the Deschutes and features picnicking and a stunning waterfall. A few miles east, White River joins the Deschutes River where it is a raging torrent near Shearer Bridge, where Native Americans continue to net salmon from wooden platforms constructed above the violent current. After a wild and scenic segment of the river only seen by river runners, the river reaches the Columbia at Deschutes River State Recreation Area. Calmer now in more level, arid country, campers find wildlife and miles of trails for hiking, biking, and horseback riding.

The Crooked River has enough attractions for the development of more parks, one at a gorge wayside honoring explorer Peter Skene Ogden. Perhaps the state's most unique park is at Smith Rock, where golden rock pinnacles along the river are a magnet for rock climbers from far and wide who challenge the steep walls in this magnificent canyon.

In the less populated area between Bend and the Columbia River, ghost towns provide a window into the past, when survival was not so easy as it was in the Willamette Valley. Today, it's a fun area for history buffs, and some of the towns still have residents. Shaniko is a quaint town with a mix of abandoned buildings and a hotel that still operates. Richmond is a ghost town. An abandoned one-room schoolhouse is seen near Clarno. Yet the feel of the "Old West" still exists and resurfaces in rodeos in places like Prineville.

For additional information on Oregon State Parks, call 1-800-551-6949, or check the official website: *www.prd.state.or.us.*

117. FORT ROCK STATE NATURAL AREA

Hours/Season: Day use; year-round
Area: 190 acres
Attractions: Exhibit information, geology, picnicking, hiking trail, wildlife viewing, photography
Facilities: Picnic tables, vault toilets
Access: From OR 31, 17 miles northwest of Silver Lake; follow park signs east to community of Fort Rock, then 2 miles northwest to natural area

As the Outback Scenic Byway continues north of Silver Lake, a prominent landmark at Fort Rock State Natural Area features the remains of an ancient volcanic crater. Looking indeed like a fortification in the midst of a sagebrush plain, the rocky crater towers above shaded picnic tables. Exhibits provide geologic and human history. A 0.5-mile hiking trail begins at the parking area and climbs up a sandy slope and into the more difficult rocky terrain that is the interior of the crater.

From the air, the crater resembles a giant doughnut with one side munched off, which is where the present trail enters the imperfectly shaped crescent of the crater. During the last Ice Age, a huge, shallow lake flooded this area. When basalt magma rose beneath the lake, it generated steam that powered violent volcanic outbursts. Bits of basalt settled around the vent to form a ring of volcanic ash that became an island in the lake. Waves followed that eroded a chunk out of the ring and left wave cuts on the steep cliffs that rise as much as 325 feet above the plain.

Artifacts—weapons, tools, and even sandals—found in caves in this area are evidence that humans found shelter here some ten thousand years ago. More recently, warring Native Americans used it as a natural fortress and pioneers used it once as a place to defend themselves successfully against attackers by blocking the approach with wagons.

The nearby community of Fort Rock was once a prosperous village founded in 1908 in a dry-farming area, with three stores, two saloons, a newspaper, a creamery and cheese factory, a church, and a graded school. The struggle to farm here was finally abandoned. Consider stopping at Fort Rock Homestead Village to see the restored circa-1900 structures.

118. LA PINE STATE PARK

Hours/Season: Day use and overnight (reservations available); year-round
Area: 2,333 acres
Attractions: Oregon's largest ponderosa pine, hiking, mountain biking, horseback riding, floating the river, swimming, wildlife viewing, photography, viewpoint, snowshoeing, cross-country skiing, snowmobiling, Fall River Falls, mountain views, picnicking, camping
Facilities: Picnic tables, campground (87 full hookup, 50 electrical sites—maximum site 85 feet), 3 yurts (1 accessible), 5 log cabins (1 accessible), restrooms with showers, boat launch, dump station, public phones, slide program area, log cabin meeting hall, firewood, park store
Access: West off US 97, at signed access road to park; 27 miles southwest of Bend
Contact: (541) 536-2428

La Pine State Park includes a vast acreage along the Deschutes River that is in the midst of an area popular for both summer and winter recreation. The park itself is a gently rolling to flat pine-forested landscape that is part of a huge area where pumice and ash from Mount Mazama was deposited. La Pine is situated

A trail leads into an ancient volcanic crater at Fort Rock State Natural Area.

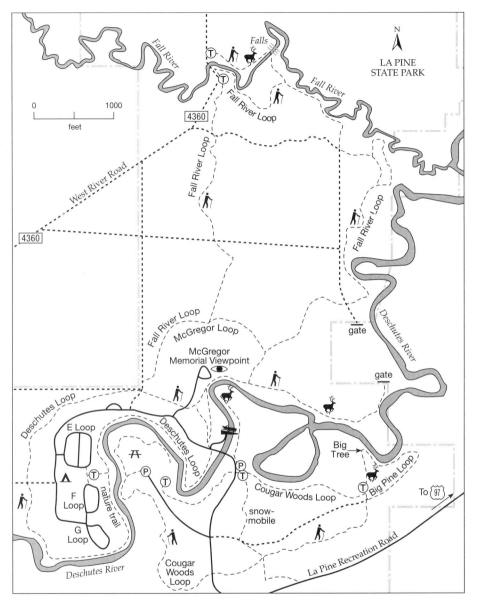

The day-use area is bracketed by a horseshoe bend in the river. Swimming is a featured activity, but remember that the river has a slight current, which requires caution. The 3.1-mile Cougar Woods Loop begins along the river near the restrooms and weaves east past the entry road to the Big Pine Loop, a loop in the river, and then back across the entry road to the day-use area.

A gravel road leads to "Big Tree" parking, where the 1-mile Big Pine Loop leads to Oregon's largest remaining ponderosa pine tree (500 years old, circumference of 326 inches, and a total height of 191 feet), which is not far from the river. It is recognized as an Oregon Heritage Tree. The trail continues along the river before returning to the parking lot.

Another road, past a bridge over the river and the boat launch area, leads to the Don McGregor Memorial Viewpoint, an excellent view of a curve in the river.

The large campground area is at road's end. The three campground loops are near the river, where a 1-mile nature trail edges the water near the campground. Much of the time, the trail is on the high bank above the river.

More trails have recently been constructed in the park. The nature trail continues past the campground as the 3.5-mile Deschutes Loop, with access points along the entry road north of the campground, the McGregor Memorial Viewpoint, and the boat launch. The 1.5-mile McGregor Loop circles the viewpoint area for some distance. The longest trail is the 4.75-mile Fall River Loop, which branches off from the McGregor Loop and heads north into the backcountry of the park to Fall River, the waterfall, and wildlife viewing before returning to the McGregor Loop. Several snowmobile trails traverse the park area in winter.

on a mule deer migration corridor between summer and winter range, and sightings are frequent. It is a favorite fishing and river-floating location, with hiking and mountain biking also available. Winter activities include snowshoeing and cross-country skiing. Fall River flows into the Deschutes River in the northern area of the park, where Fall River Falls are found.

The McGregor Memorial Viewpoint overlooks a scenic curve of the Deschutes River at La Pine State Park.

The attractions surrounding La Pine enhance the attractiveness of the park as a base for touring. To the west, it's easy to access the spectacular Cascade Lakes Scenic Byway, an up-close Cascade Mountain experience with a string of high-country lakes along the highway. You can hike, observe wildlife, ski (in winter), or just relax in wonderful surroundings where canoes slide into lakes in early morning as mist rises when sunlight warms the water. Miles and miles of trails will lead you to the Three Sisters Wilderness, or to the Pacific Crest Trail, or to waterfalls and alpine meadows of wildflowers. Backpackers and mountain climbers can access several of the Cascade peaks from this scenic byway.

To the east of the park, off US 97, the Newberry National Volcanic Monument (a year-round attraction via skis or snowmobiles) includes two high-elevation lakes within the Newberry Crater. The surrounding countryside abounds in remains of the region's vast volcanic events, and the Lava Beds Visitor Center will introduce you to them. After this preview, you can explore some of the areas that resulted from these events: Lava Butte, Lava River Caves, Lava Island Falls, Arnold Ice Cave, and Lava Cast Forest. A short distance north along US 97 is the outstanding High Desert Museum, where nature trails, live animals in natural

surroundings, and the Earle A. Chile Center on the Spirit of the West are a few of the attractions.

119. PILOT BUTTE STATE SCENIC VIEWPOINT

Hours/Season: Day use; year-round
Area: 101 acres
Attractions: View of several Cascade mountain peaks, hiking, photography
Facilities: Vault toilets, *no water*
Access: Off US 20, on the east side of Bend

Land for this park on Pilot Butte was a gift of several donors in 1927. It was dedicated with a plaque in memory of Terrance Hardington Foley, a prominent citizen of Bend. Early pioneers named the butte because it was such a conspicuous landmark as they approached from the east. It enabled them to aim their way to a safe ford among the many canyons along the Deschutes River.

The butte is a lone cinder cone that projects some 500 feet

From Pilot Butte, the view stretches past the streets of Bend to the Cascade Mountains.

above the surrounding land, at an elevation of 4,136 feet above sea level. Ponderosa pine, juniper, and sagebrush grow on its slopes. A 1-mile steep, narrow, and winding road circles around the cone, like the turnings of a spiral, to reach the top of the butte, which is level with a few trees, lava rocks, and some parking space. Watch out for pedestrians on the drive as hikers often climb the aerobic trail to access the top of the butte, especially on weekends, even in the hot desert summer.

Atop the butte, a pedestal with pointers identifies several Cascade peaks: Mount Hood, Mount Washington, Mount Jefferson, the Sisters Mountains, Broken Top Mountain, and Mount Bachelor. The view also includes a perspective of the city of Bend and the surrounding countryside. Because of the fantastic view, this site was used as an airplane observation post for a year during World War II.

120. TUMALO STATE PARK

Hours/Season: Day use (fee) and overnight (reservations available); year-round
Area: 330 acres
Attractions: Fly-fishing, swimming, hiking, picnicking, camping
Facilities: Picnic tables, 2 reservable group picnic areas (1 with stove shelter), campground (23 full hookup, 58 tent sites— 1 accessible, maximum site 44 feet), 4 yurts (1 accessible), 2 tepees, accessible restrooms with solar showers, 2 group tent areas, hiker/biker camp, firewood, playground, slide program area, public phones
Access: Off US 20, 5 miles northwest of Bend (Old McKenzie– Bend Highway), follow signs to park
Contact: (541) 382-3586

Along a scenic section of the Deschutes River, Tumalo State Park is a fine stopping place, and a quick trip for Bend residents who know about the swimming hole at a bend in the river. During spring and late summer, river fishing for German brown and rainbow trout is especially good. Basalt rock formations form a backdrop for the scenic river view. The smells are of pungent high desert plants. The name of the park derives from the Klamath Indian word *tumalo*, which means "wild plum."

The day-use area is across the road from the campground, where there are spacious lawns, paths, and shade trees (juniper,

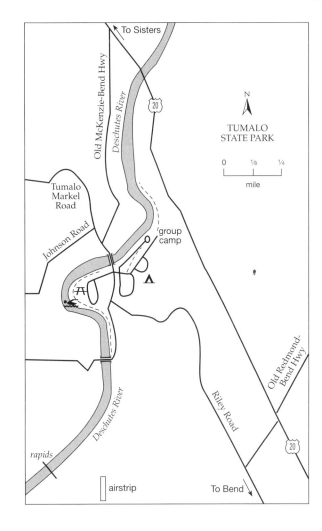

alder, ponderosa pine, willow, and poplar). The swimming area and river trail are located at the far end of the bend. Wildlife scurry about the park: golden-mantled squirrels and chipmunks dash here and there; rabbits are out in the early morning. Swallows fly in and out of homes situated in holes in the high rocks. Great blue herons silently stalk at water's edge.

In the campground area, a row of preferred tent sites is located along the riverfront, with the hiker/biker camp just behind them. A trail connects this area to two camping loops farther from the river. The group camp is at the end of the road past these loops, closer to the river along the slanting road, with a trail heading off to the river trail from Camp B. The yurts and tepees are found in Loop B.

121. ELLIOTT CORBETT MEMORIAL STATE RECREATION SITE

Hours/Season: Day use; year-round
Area: 63 acres
Attractions: Hiking, mountain biking, horseback riding, fishing, cross-country skiing
Facilities: Hiking access
Access: Off US 20, 14 miles west of Sisters, just east of the Santiam Pass, Forest Road 2076 heads south from the Corbett Sno-Park. The trailhead is 0.75 mile down this road, where a 2-mile trail leads to the park. A Sno-Park permit is required in winter.

Elliot Corbett State Recreation Site offers a different experience from most state parks. It is undeveloped, and requires at least 2 miles of trail hiking to access the acreage. The park was donated by Henry L. and Gretchen Corbett in memory of their son, Elliott Corbett II, who was lost in action during World War II. They wanted it preserved as a wilderness area, as it has been. The park includes the southern portion of Blue Lake at an elevation of 3,453 feet.

The old wagon trail over the Cascades once passed through the park where a meadow provided a stopping place to spend the night, especially with the small creek on the south side of it.

To take the trail to the park, look for the blue signs—one to Blue Lake Trail, which is the same route—on a tree at the trailhead. The signs are easily seen from Deschutes Forest Road 2076, but the E.R. CORBETT sign may not be seen. A sign on the entrance gate to old Forest Road 200 warns that the road is now to be used only for foot, horse, and mountain bike use—*no motorized vehicles*—to protect the wildlife habitat. This logged-over land is not part of the park.

Several old roads branch off from Forest Road 200, but stay on this main graveled road. You will probably follow deer tracks. Only one small Corbett Trail sign is seen some distance along the way. It is downhill to the park, through a logged forest that offers mountain, woods, and Suttle Lake views in the distance as the trail curves and switchbacks past rolling hills dotted with wildflowers blooming in the open.

Early morning is a good time to take this walk or ride, with the sounds and activities of a number of birds—juncos, woodpeckers, and vultures—overhead. When the road ends, and you are now into wild forest with lodgepole and ponderosa pine, a loop trail branches off in either direction. There are no signs. This is the outside curve of a loop, with the inner curve more closely edging Blue Lake, but you can go in either direction to complete the loop. This loop is part of the 2.5-mile Blue Lake Rim Trail, and you will see signs at certain intersections. A sign designating E.R. CORBETT STATE PARK is seen just west of an expansive meadow. Proceed west of this sign to one indicating the route to the lake, which is part of this loop and the park. Horse trails branch off from this loop. In winter, cross-country skiers use this area. Be prepared for a somewhat confusing trail-finding experience by having emergency

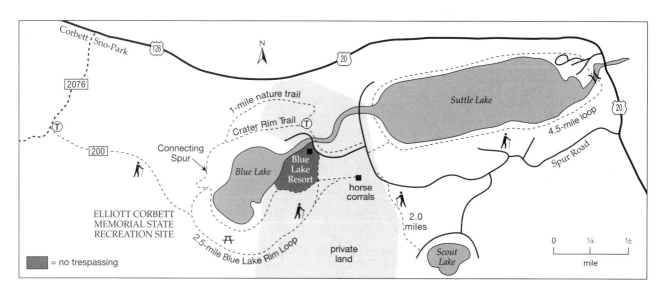

A hike to Elliott Corbett Memorial State Recreation Site includes views of Suttle Lake and the Cascade Mountains.

equipment, time, and energy. From year to year, the signing of the route may vary.

Blue Lake is a very deep, pretty lake of about 60 acres and 300 feet deep. Fishing is good for the stocked rainbow trout and kokanee, best caught by trolling. It is not easy to try to do any angling from the shore, though possible. To launch a boat for trolling, a fee must be paid at Blue Lake Resort, which is on the east side of the lake and privately owned.

There is an alternate route to the park, but it is accessed from the Blue Lake Resort, which is reached via the Suttle Lake turn-off on US 20. The attendant at the information booth may perhaps give you a day pass to the park so that you can take the Crater Rim Trail. The trail begins along a self-guiding nature walk and then connects to the rim loop on the steep slopes above the lake. Horses are available for rental at the resort.

While in the area, adjacent Suttle Lake is a popular destination with windsurfing, fishing, swimming, and Forest Camps in the Cascade Mountains. A 4.5-mile trail circles the lake and connects trails to Scout Lake and Blue Lake.

Hikers might wish to do a portion of the Pacific Crest Trail, since it's so close, and travel the spectacular Mount Jefferson Wilderness Area. This national recreation trail is accessed at Santiam Pass on US 20, approximately 2 miles west of the access road to Corbett, where there is trail parking. Obtain a map of the wilderness area at a ranger station and plan a hike that fits your needs and energy.

A quiet area of the Deschutes River invites play at Cline Falls State Scenic Viewpoint.

variety of wildlife that includes Canada geese and black-winged blackbirds perched in the cattails. A much-visited series of boulder-enclosed swimming holes is just across the highway near a bridge. The falls are a distance north of the park.

122. CLINE FALLS STATE SCENIC VIEWPOINT

Hours/Season: Day use; closed in winter
Area: 9 acres
Attractions: Fishing, swimming, picnicking
Facilities: Picnic tables, restrooms
Access: Off US 126, 4 miles west of Redmond

Cline Falls State Scenic Viewpoint includes a narrow strip of frontage along the crystal-clear Deschutes River, a pleasant place to cool off in summer, go fishing, and picnic, with tables situated along the waterway. Shading trees (mostly juniper, locust, and poplar) border it. Calm areas of the river alternate with rippling water diverted by many large boulders. Wetland areas edge both sides of the water, with vegetation attracting a

123. OCHOCO STATE SCENIC VIEWPOINT

Hours/Season: Day use; year-round
Area: 251 acres
Attractions: Hiking, photography
Facilities: Panoramic view of Prineville Valley
Access: Off US 126, 1 mile west of Prineville

As OR 126 heads off west from Prineville, it climbs a rugged butte, with a road turning off to the north near the top that leads to a viewpoint. From this site, there are distant views of the Crooked River and Ochoco Mountains, one of the ranges within the Blue Mountains, and the city of Prineville. A golf course immediately below the viewpoint is spread out like a map. The wayside is a registered Natural Heritage Site that sustains some rare and potentially endangered plants.

124. PRINEVILLE RESERVOIR STATE PARK

Hours/Season: Day use and overnight (reservations available); year-round
Area: 365 acres
Attractions: Boating, waterskiing, fishing, swimming, hiking, wildlife viewing, rockhounding, picnicking, camping
Facilities: Picnic tables and kitchen shelter, campground (22 full hookup, 23 electrical, 23 tent sites—1 accessible, maximum site 50 feet), 2 rustic cabins (1 accessible) and 3 deluxe cabins (all accessible), restrooms with showers, boat launch, 32 boat moorages, docks with access for waterskiers, fish-cleaning station, bathhouse, volleyball net, amphitheater, public phones in primary park area; Jasper Point Campground has picnic tables, campground (30 electrical sites—maximum site 35 feet), vault toilets, boat launch, dock
Access: Off US 26, 16 miles southeast of Prineville; Jasper Point Campground is 2.5 miles east of the main park area
Contact: (541) 447-4363; Jasper Point Campground, (541) 447-3875

In the midst of sagebrush, desert buttes, mesas, canyons, and alkali flats, Prineville Reservoir is 12 miles long and 1 mile wide at its widest point. Impounded in 1961 by 234-foot-high Bowman Dam, west of the park, the waters of Crooked River

Jasper Point Campground provides an alternate overnight and boat launch at Prineville Reservoir State Park.

claimed 320 acres of the desert plateau and formed many coves and turnings along the reservoir's edge. Prineville Reservoir State Park soon acquired a 50-year lease from the U.S. Bureau of Reclamation, and developed the shoreline for picnicking and camping.

The main area of the park occupies a rounded point that juts south into the water where the boat ramp is located, with considerable shoreline both to the west and east. A buoy-marked swimming area and bathhouse is along the west side of the point. On the east side is the picnic area and a kitchen shelter, above the boat moorages. The reservoir attracts anglers and boaters year-round, with good catches of largemouth bass, trout, and catfish. Waterskiing is also popular. Trails connect to the two campground loops and the deluxe cabin loop, which are situated on a slope overlooking the reservoir.

For campers wishing a more primitive area (a boat ramp and electricity are available, but no showers, nor a swimming area), Jasper Point Campground might be your choice. Fishing and boating on the reservoir are easily accessed there. Prineville Reservoir State Wildlife Area is located on a wide cove just across the water from the campground, so wildlife viewing should be interesting.

A 1.75-mile trail to Jasper Point from the main campground is accessed between sites C14 and C16, an easy to moderate hike.

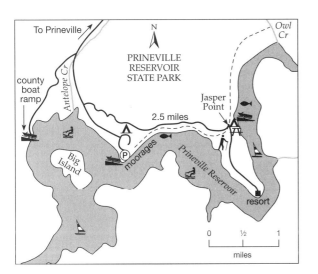

Prineville Reservoir Resort, with boat rentals, boat fuel, meals, and supplies, is 1 mile southwest from Jasper Point Campground and available to those from the main campground.

History buffs might be interested to learn that in 1845 Stephen Meek led a large group of Oregon Trail pioneers (estimated at between 1,000 and 1,500 people) across an untried Oregon route that split off near Farewell Bend on the Snake River, passed through the Prineville area, and then wandered northwest, past the Smith Rock area, to reconnect with other pioneers at The Dalles. Called the Meek Cutoff, the journey was one of near disaster, of getting lost, of insufficient supplies, of sickness and deaths beyond the average, and of trouble finding water. Many of the members of Meek's group became influential residents of the Willamette Valley, so the trip was not without some measure of accomplishment.

Along the way, while groups were out scouting for water, one pioneer found gold nuggets in an almost dry creek. Legend says that a blue bucket was filled and carried back to camp, where some tested the metal for malleability. This was possibly the first gold discovered west of the Rocky Mountains, three years before the California find. For many years, miners searched for this lost gold mine without success. Today, questions about its location are treated with a good deal of skepticism and are considered symptomatic of just plain craziness.

Rockhound Country

Prime rockhound country exists in a volcanic rock region beginning northwest of Prineville and extending to the eastern edge of the central region in the rather isolated landscape between US 26 and US 20. Rockhounds are generally collectors of stones that are classified as semiprecious gems. If you're a rockhound, this is the place to get out your tools, whether you prefer shovels, picks, mattocks, rock hammers, crowbars, or long-handled chisels. Thousands of acres of public lands offer good digging sites for a wide variety of semiprecious quartz-family stones.

Thundereggs are the most distinctive and sought-after rocks in Oregon. These deceptively drab, knobby-surfaced spherical masses, the official state rock of Oregon, sometimes have marvelous cores ranging from five-pointed stars to miniature landscapes. Theory suggests that a thunderegg initially has a central cavity, which fills with ground water carrying silica in solution. During a changing process, the filling forms a variety of colors and shapes, which accounts for a surprise when the ball or rock, usually larger than a baseball, is sawed open to reveal crystals, agate, jasper, a powdery calcite, or nothing but a cavity.

Agate is the most common gemstone. The best rocks have swirled grain such as the "angel wing," or impurities that might look like miniature trees inside the stone. Segenite, "picture jasper" (designs on cut surface), jasper interlaced with agate, limb casts, obsidian, and petrified wood (though not too colorful in Oregon) are some of the discoveries you can make, and a rare opal or amethyst is not an impossibility.

The Rockhound Code of Ethics urges diggers to respect private property, use no firearms or blasting material, leave no litter, take reasonable rock amounts, fill excavations that might be dangerous, discard no burning material, build fires in safe places, contaminate no water sources, damage no signs or structures, leave gates as found, and always use good outdoor manners. Like most outdoor activities, digging for these rocks has certain hazards. Those out digging should understand what risks are involved—road conditions, rattlesnakes, careless digging that causes rock slides, etc.—and prepare for a safe excursion. Check with authorities on current regulations (often posted at publicly managed sites) and digging areas. Some private sites are available for digging for a fee. Or these intriguing rocks may be seen or bought at many commercial rock shops in the area.

Digging is a dirty, rugged hobby, but offers enjoyment for many. This hobby has increased greatly since technology has produced the diamond-edge saw and good grinding substances. You'll find lots of fellow enthusiasts at the annual Prineville Rockhound Pow Wow. The excellent *Central Oregon Rockhound Guide*—complete with map, rock photos, and geology information—is put out by the combined efforts of the Forest Service, the Bureau of Land Management, and the Prineville–Crook County Chamber of Commerce. It points out the areas that are set aside for rock collectors.

125. SMITH ROCK STATE PARK

Hours/Season: Day use (fee) and overnight; year-round
Area: 623 acres
Attractions: Unusual rock formations along Crooked River, access routes to rock climbing, hiking, fishing, swimming, photography, wildlife viewing, picnicking, camping
Facilities: Picnic tables, walk-in bivouac camp (no RVs or fires), restrooms with showers, vault toilet along river, public phones
Access: Off US 97, 3 miles east of Terrebonne via a well-signed route

The meandering Crooked River flows through a spectacular canyon of multicolored rock pinnacles and crags, geologic features that were excellent reasons for the establishment of Smith Rock State Park, a very special place. Millions of years ago this area was a major center of volcanic action, causing the ancestral river to carve a new channel. The river eventually eroded the interior of the volcanic vent. The rock formations along the river today are of rock known as "welded tuff," volcanic ash erupted under extreme heat and pressure conditions. A rimrock plateau forms the south bank of the river. The scenic attractions of this park have lured television and movie companies to use it as a location, most recently *The Postman,* with Kevin Costner starring, in 1997.

In the U.S. Geological Survey of 1905, this area was called "Monument Canyon." The name of the state park, Smith Rock, is thought to honor John Smith, a prominent resident of the area who "discovered" the formations in 1867, although one story suggests the name arose after a soldier named Smith fell to his death in the 1860s after climbing an unstable rock to see the view.

The picnic area is located on the bluff overlooking the river canyon. A walk-in bivouac area, along the beginning of the entry road, allows hikers and rock climbers a chance to enjoy the evening and morning hours in the park. Vehicles are left in a nearby parking area and campers walk a short distance to put up tents in an area of juniper trees; restrooms with showers are nearby.

Rock climbers from around the world are attracted to the vertical rock walls of the Crooked River Canyon. The routes are shorter than the major big-wall climbs of Yosemite, but the climbs are as difficult as any in the United States. Some magazines have called these the "most challenging free climbs in North America." Several miles of trails are near the popular rock-climbing areas.

Climbers are asked to protect the fragile environment of the canyon by using existing trails to access climbs. Oregon State Parks has adopted a self-regulating rock-climbing policy; climbers should recognize that their activity involves a level of risk. Be sure to double-check climbing knots, harness, and hardware, and know practices for safe use. The use of "clean" climbing equipment (chocks, nuts, Friends, etc.) and techniques is encouraged. This is not possible on some routes, with inadequate cracks or other natural depressions, and permanent anchors have been placed. Climbers should test these fixed bolts for safety and then

A rock climber ascends the pinnacles at Smith Rock State Park.

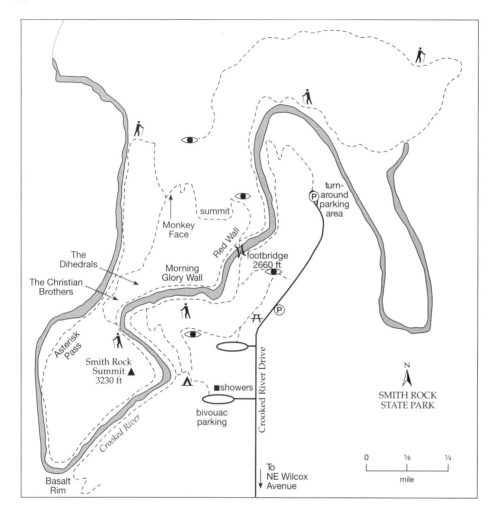

summit

Monkey
Face

The
Dihedrals

The Christian
Brothers

Morning
Glory Wall

Red Wall

footbridge
2660 ft

turn-
around
parking
area

Asterisk
Pass

Smith Rock
Summit ▲
3230 ft

showers

bivouac
parking

Crooked River

Crooked River Drive

To
NE Wilcox
Avenue

Basalt
Rim

N

SMITH ROCK
STATE PARK

0   ⅛   ¼
mile

near the bivouac area also descends to the river. From the river elevation, a tangle of paths weaves through the vegetation and skirts the water on this side of the river, with one following the river southwest to Basalt Rim.

Cross the footbridge to reach the rock-climbing area. The 4-mile Perimeter Trail loops completely around much of the climbing area, rough after the initial easy walking, so you can head either right or left. A left turn allows the closest viewing of rock climbers. Just across the footbridge a trail branches off the river trail and climbs the Red Wall via a series of steps that switchback steeply to a viewpoint. Other stair-step trails on the steep talus slopes of the north riverbank are spurs along the beginning of the Monkey Face Trail and are primarily access routes for rock climbers to the Christian Brothers, Morning Glory Wall, the Dihedrals, Asterisk Pass, and others.

In 1996, an area of the park experienced a damaging fire that necessitated a restricted area for recovery and trail changes southwest of the picnic area on the bluff. Hikers can now follow the path south from the picnic area to connect to the self-guided rim trail and memorial viewpoint, also reached from a new loop parking area. Excellent views are seen with little effort; the trail connects to the bivouac trail to the river and also returns to the new parking area. Views of the snow-topped Cascade Mountains are visible to the west, an interesting contrast to the orange and gold colors of the park pinnacles.

Exploring early in the day, before too many visitors and higher temperatures arrive, is best for wildlife viewing. Birds sing at 4:00 A.M. in May. Geese that have nested by the river in spring swim with their young following them. Ledges and overhangs high on the rocks house a variety of birds that include swallows and birds of prey. (*All hikers and climbers are asked to keep their distance from nests inhabited by birds of prey. Do not disturb the young or adults.*) Magpies fly among the tall pines along the south bank

use them. Avoid the "chipping" of climbing holds or placing additional permanent anchors so further damage to the easily scarred rock doesn't occur. No additional fixed protection is needed for any of the routes listed in *Oregon Rock: A Climber's Guide*, by Jeff Thomas.

The park is delightful for hikers who don't climb, with more than 7 miles of very scenic trails. A major trail leads downhill from the bluff to the footbridge (elevation 2,660 feet) in 0.6 mile, where trails continue for long distances on both sides of the river. If you head northeast before crossing the river, the trail continues to a climb up to the turnaround parking area, where a program area and an exhibit on golden eagles is found, a bird species with nests weighing up to 2,000 pounds. A trail and kingfishers dive into the water. *Watch for rattlesnakes in remote areas in summer.*

Scents of juniper and sage are in the air. To see wildflowers, come in early spring, though a few bloom later. Summer weather is quite hot at Smith Rock and it is not the best season for hiking and climbing, so try to visit in spring or fall when the air is invigorating and conducive to exploring.

The bronze-colored cliffs are reflected in the river in the early morning and late afternoon for good photography shots. After exploring, enjoy a huckleberry ice cream cone at the store near the park entrance.

126. PETER SKENE OGDEN STATE SCENIC VIEWPOINT

Hours/Season: Day use; year-round
Area: 97.9 acres
Attractions: Crooked River Gorge overlook, photography, picnicking
Facilities: Picnic tables, restrooms
Access: Off US 97, 9 miles north of Redmond

A few miles northwest of Smith Rock State Park, the Crooked River passes beneath both US 97 and the Burlington Northern Railway in a vertical, basaltic-walled canyon that is 304 feet deep and 400 feet wide. Peter Skene Ogden State Scenic Viewpoint lets weary travelers pull off the highway to rest and picnic or just enjoy the delightful view of the Crooked River Canyon at this site, where a masonry retaining wall borders the edge of the gorge, and allows a long walk to view the gorge. The volcanic-ash desert land rimming the rock walls is surprisingly level, with a cover of juniper and sage. To the west, the spine of the Cascade Mountains is visible.

The wayside was named for Peter Skene Ogden (1794–1854). Born in Quebec, Ogden entered Oregon in 1818 as the head of a trapping party with headquarters in Fort George, now Astoria. As the Hudson's Bay Company chief trader, he explored much of Oregon, northern California, and northern Utah. He was one of the first to describe and name many geographic features in this wide area. He named Mount Shasta in California in 1827, "discovered" Newberry Crater in central Oregon, Harney and Malheur Lakes in southern Oregon, and named the Malheur River. He was the principal explorer of the Snake River Country, and trapped multitudes of beaver in many Oregon streams. His

A walk along the flat plateau above the Crooked River Canyon offers an excellent view at Peter Skene Ogden State Scenic Viewpoint.

trips took him to the Great Salt Lake basin in Utah, and the city of Ogden, Utah, is named for him. In a noteworthy contribution to society, Ogden rescued the survivors of the Whitman Massacre in December of 1847.

127. THE COVE PALISADES STATE PARK

Hours/Season: Day use (fee) and overnight (reservations available); year-round (Crooked River Campground closes October 1 and reopens in spring)

Area: 4,130 acres

Attractions: Waterskiing, boating, sailing, kayak tours, fishing, hiking, swimming, outstanding views and geology, photography, picnicking, camping, Lake Billy Chinook Day in September, Eagle Watch in February

Facilities: 3 day-use areas with picnic tables, boat ramps, courtesy docks, beaches; Deschutes River Campground (87 full hookup, 94 tent sites, 3 group tent areas with 1 RV allowed in each—1 accessible site, maximum site 60 feet), Crooked River Campground (91 electrical sites), 3 deluxe log cabins, 4 houseboat rentals (reserve with park), restrooms with showers, amphitheater, dump station, marina/restaurant with fishing equipment, Deschutes camp store, accessible fishing pier, fish-cleaning station, 3 boat launches with waterskiing access, swimming areas, basketball hoops, firewood

Access: Off US 97, 15 miles southwest of Madras; follow signs to park

Contact: (541) 546-3412

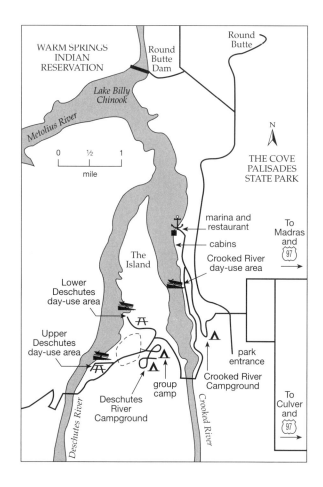

The first impression upon entering The Cove Palisades State Park is of Mount Jefferson looming over a vast labyrinth of golden canyons filled with blue water. The Cascade mountain is soon hidden from view as the road dips into the canyon and twists around the edges of Lake Billy Chinook.

This three-armed lake was formed in 1963 when Round Butte Dam confined the waters of the Metolius, Crooked, and Deschutes Rivers as they flowed out of Oregon mountains. The lake was named for Billy Chinook, a local Native American guide who helped Captain John Fremont in his Oregon explorations.

The original state park site was nearly 900 feet deep, at the bottom of Crooked River Canyon. The location had to be moved to avoid being flooded. Today, the Crooked River Campground is on the bluff above the lake, while the Deschutes River Campground and group camp are situated on the peninsula between the Crooked River and the Deschutes. To access it, descend into the canyon, turn left at the lake, and continue 5 miles to cross the bridge over Crooked River. Notice the waterfall plunging down the cliffs along the road. To prevent being flooded, a basalt boulder called

the "Crooked River Petroglyph" was relocated near the group camp, below a rock formation called "Ship Rock." Across the road from this feature, a high plateau called "The Island" projects a long finger toward the confluence of the two rivers.

The Crooked River day-use area includes a boat ramp and an accessible fishing pier. The two Deschutes River day-use areas are reached by road or hiking trails leading from the Deschutes River Campground. Trails connect the two areas so a loop path can be walked. Fourteen miles of hiking trails are found in the park, including the 7-mile upper-elevation Tam-a-Lau Trail. The marina, restaurant, and cabins are to the right of the entry road.

Since this is Central Oregon's most visited state park, don't come for solitude in the peak season. Although there are 72 miles of shoreline, land and water can get crowded in summer. Even

A sailboat is dwarfed by the immense walls above the Crooked River at The Cove Palisades State Park.

three million years ago, volcanic eruptions resulted in the basaltic cap that is visible as the rimrock palisades around Lake Billy Chinook.

As the Cascade Mountains developed, a general uplift of this land occurred, causing the Deschutes, Metolius, and Crooked Rivers to flow more swiftly and gouge canyons through the soft land. Recent lava flows entered the upper Crooked River Canyon and were then cut through by the mighty power of flowing water. Remnants of this basalt coat the canyon walls, fused to the lighter-colored rocks.

128. WHITE RIVER FALLS STATE PARK

Hours/Season: Day use; year-round
Attractions: Waterfall, history, photography, hiking, fishing, picnicking
Facilities: Picnic tables, restrooms
Access: 34 miles south of The Dalles on US 197, and east on OR 216 for 5 miles

so, deer wander into the campground, orioles flit from tree to tree, and rattlesnakes live in the surrounding territory. Fishing catches include kokanee salmon, trout, smallmouth and largemouth bass, crayfish, and especially bull trout. Waterskiing is popular, both with participants and observers. Kayak tours are scheduled frequently, with kayaks available. Sailboats and houseboats move across the water of the lake.

Most of the Metolius River is west of the park and beckons explorers, with facilities at Three Rivers Marina and a forest camp. Boaters must be familiar with park rules and regulations (brochure is available). The lake is surrounded by both private and other public land past the park boundary. The land on the north side of the Metolius River arm is the Warm Springs Indian Reservation. *Don't trespass on these private lands.*

The complex geology of the area tells us that some ten million to twelve million years ago, in the Pliocene Epoch, lava flowed from shield-type volcanoes to form the base of the Cascade Mountains, causing the land to sink in this region. In the process, the westward flow of ancient rivers was rerouted, forced into moving in north–south courses.

These ancient rivers deposited sediment—ash, cinders, and thin beds of lava—and built a layer of rock more than 1,000 feet thick along their waterways. Finally, between two million and

Arising on the south face of Mount Hood, the 50-mile White River flows through the Tygh Valley on its way to joining the Deschutes River south of Shearer Bridge. A few miles west of this merging, it descends an expanse of rocky terraces and cliffs in a 90-foot waterfall that stair-steps down these rocks in multiple falls with many horizontal ribbons, a spectacular sight in spring, and it is still quite impressive in autumn when there is less water. It is worth a visit to White River Falls State Park just to view this waterfall.

The southern route of the Oregon Trail turns south at The Dalles and heads toward Tygh Valley, where it gradually curves west to cross the south flanks of Mount Hood, following much the same descent that the river takes, but in the opposite direction. The trail misses this dramatic waterfall, which is a short distance to the east.

Picnicking in this quiet park adjacent to the falls is delightful on a fine day. Paths edge the river in this area and the visitor can wander about doing some exploring. Remnants of an old hydroelectric power station and grist pond are found below the falls.

Anglers come for early-season fishing for rainbow trout along the flatland stretch of the river above the falls, where bait is best and is legal. Below the falls, fishing is restricted to flies

A spectacular waterfall descends rocky terraces at White River Falls State Park.

or lures with barbless hooks. It's a good idea to check current regulations.

While in this area, don't miss a chance to visit Shearer Bridge on the Deschutes River, a few miles east via OR 216. This is a famous historic site on an awesome section of the Deschutes River, where Native Americans have long built wooden platforms by the river to fish for salmon. They still fish here for steelhead and salmon, and if you're lucky, as I was, you may find them fishing from the steep river bank on newly constructed platforms that are close to a wild, roaring succession of rapids.

129. DESCHUTES RIVER STATE RECREATION AREA

Hours/Season: Day use and overnight (reservations available); year-round
Area: 515 acres
Attractions: Fishing, hiking, bicycling, and equestrian trails (22-mile round-trip horse trail by reservation); wildlife viewing, photography, Oregon Trail exhibit, boat launch, picnicking, camping
Facilities: Picnic tables, campground (35 electrical, 35 primitive—maximum site 50 feet), camper covered wagon, group RV/tent (4 reservation areas), restrooms, boat launch, public phone, information building
Access: Off Interstate 84 at Exit 97; follow signs to the park, 17 miles east of The Dalles
Contact: (541) 739-2322

The warm, dry sunshine of central Oregon found along a stretch of the Deschutes River, near its mouth at the Columbia River, is a great place for Deschutes River State Recreation Area. Go in spring, before the hot summer arrives, to see wildflowers and many Canada geese with their young floating about the river.

The riverside complex includes a boat ramp located in the Heritage Landing day-use area on the west side of the Deschutes. Exhibits trace the acquisition of state land along the final 12 miles of the lower Deschutes River due to more than 10,000 contributors. Federal land extends shoreline protection to Shearer Bridge, at 42 miles. From Pelton Dam to the Columbia River, some 105 river miles was designated an Oregon Scenic Waterway in 1970 to protect and enhance scenic, recreational, fish, and wildlife values along the river while allowing public use for boating, fishing, and riverside camping. River runners ride Colorado, Rattlesnake, and Moody rapids on the last 5 miles of the river. A boat pass is required.

In late April, when spring chinook season is in progress, boats access fishing sites in the river where it is shallow enough for hip boots. The last 2-mile stretch is reserved for bank fishing. The Deschutes is famed for fly-fishing and steelhead. Anglers must observe the no-bait requirement.

The day-use area and campground are along the east side of the Deschutes, near the access from Old Highway 30. An Oregon Trail exhibit is featured. A covered wagon can be rented that will permit campers to imagine they have stopped here along the trip west, where they will soon have rapids to ride on the Columbia River. Natural vegetation is limited here, but poplar and other shade species have been planted in the developed locations. The park landscape is bounded by the high basalt cliffs of the Columbia and Deschutes Rivers, an area traversed by Lewis and Clark on April 21, 1806.

A 32-mile round-trip mountain bike trail (hikers are welcome) begins just north of the campground on an abandoned 1800s railroad bed (closed to vehicular traffic) that is fairly level and heads upstream a short distance above the river. Camping is allowed along the route, with strict regulations. In a region blessed with a profusion of blue-sky days, the panoramic views bordering the river on both sides make the ride a pleasure.

Three trails are for hikers only: the lower trail on flat terrain by the river, the up-and-down middle trail just above the river, and the more strenuous upper trail to Ferry Springs Canyon that branches off where the lower trail meets the bike route and loops around and past Ferry Springs Canyon Creek before returning to connect to the bike route. All three trails are 2 miles each and can be combined for various-length loops. Hikers might want to sample at least some, if not all, of these trails since they offer different experiences—the first through the wetlands bordering the river, the second offering panoramic river views from desert sagebrush countryside, the third offering wildlife viewing from Rattlesnake Viewpoint and Ferry Springs Canyon.

Early morning is a fine time to see anglers in the river along the hike, some floating along in inner tubes, and for birdwatching. Mergansers rest on rocks in the river, blue herons fly overhead, and chipmunks and lizards scurry before your footsteps. *Watch for rattlesnakes.* Perhaps you'll glimpse a long, green train traveling along the hills across the river. Old homestead buildings are seen at the beginning of the trail and an abandoned waterwheel once used for irrigation is along the Lower River Trail. Interpretive signs inform about the wildlife, habitat, and history of the area.

The park has a 10-kilometer Volkswalk with 4+ rating, 5 being most difficult. Detailed maps are available.

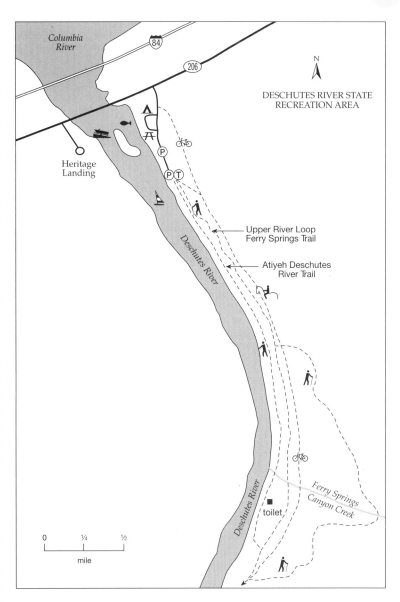

A 22-mile round-trip horse trail covers much of the terrain, available only by reservation, and numbers are limited. The trailhead branches off from the south parking area and connects to the bike trail, ending at Harris Canyon (day use only), while the bike trail continues.

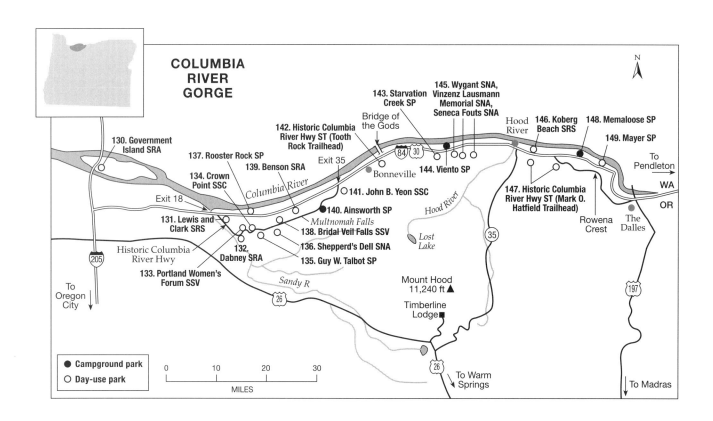

COLUMBIA RIVER GORGE

N

130. Government Island SRA

137. Rooster Rock SP

139. Benson SRA

142. Historic Columbia River Hwy ST (Tooth Rock Trailhead)

143. Starvation Creek SP

145. Wygant SNA, Vinzenz Lausmann Memorial SNA, Seneca Fouts SNA

Bridge of the Gods

146. Koberg Beach SRS

148. Memaloose SP

149. Mayer SP

Hood River

134. Crown Point SSC

Exit 35

Exit 18

Columbia River

Bonneville

144. Viento SP

To Pendleton

WA

OR

131. Lewis and Clark SRS

141. John B. Yeon SSC

140. Ainsworth SP

147. Historic Columbia River Hwy ST (Mark O. Hatfield Trailhead)

Multnomah Falls

Hood River

Historic Columbia River Hwy

138. Bridal Veil Falls SSV

136. Shepperd's Dell SNA

Rowena Crest

The Dalles

132. Dabney SRA

133. Portland Women's Forum SSV

135. Guy W. Talbot SP

Lost Lake

To Oregon City

Sandy R

Mount Hood 11,240 ft ▲

Timberline Lodge ■

To Pendleton

To Warm Springs

To Madras

● Campground park
○ Day-use park

0   10   20   30
MILES

CHAPTER EIGHT

COLUMBIA RIVER GORGE

Bounded by the Columbia River to the north, the Columbia River Gorge region extends from a few miles east of Portland to The Dalles. It encompasses all of the Columbia River Gorge National Scenic Area on the Oregon side of the river.

To the south, and rising above the gorge, in the center of the region, is an 11,245-foot composite volcano, Mount Hood, Oregon's tallest mountain. Weather often swirls violently around its summit, daring mountain climbers to predict when it's safe to climb to the summit. Glacier-fed Hood River plunges down its east slope, and side roads take skiers and hikers to Cooper Spur and Mount Hood Meadows. In summer, the meadows are boggy nurseries for wild orchids and elk.

South of the mountain's summit, past Barlow Pass and near Pioneer Woman's Grave, US 26 loops west past the spur road to Timberline Lodge. Built as a project of the Works Progress Administration, this impressive inn is an example of conservation and the creativity of Oregon craftspeople as they recycled local materials into works of art.

As blocked out on the state's map, this region south of Mount Hood is primarily within the Mount Hood National Forest, where vast choices in trails, forest camps, and fishing or canoeing the many lakes are found.

All of the region's developed state parks, however, are located in the Columbia River Gorge National Scenic Area. Even so, the climate changes dramatically from west to east as the spine of the Cascade Mountains splits the scenic area from a rainy, forested landscape to the more open and drier terrain of the Columbia River plateau. Rainfall changes from 75 inches annually to less than a foot a year near the Deschutes River.

The best way to see the gorge area is via the Historic Columbia River Highway, which begins near Troutdale. This historic highway, a National Millenium Legacy Trail, is a fascinating blend of walking, hiking, and driving trails. Two sections of the abandoned highway feature intriguing engineering sections that can be hiked on the Historic Columbia River Highway State Trails at Tooth Rock and the Twin Tunnels.

Moods change where the historic highway winds up to higher elevations, depending on the time of day or the season. Morning may bring seductive mists or a rainbow. Evening may splash distant urban lights that fringe a purple river under a cherry-colored sunset. For outstanding gorge viewpoints, visit Portland Women's Forum and Crown Point.

Images—both real and imagined—capture you with their intensity. It is not difficult to conjure up an image of a Chinook Indian poised on a rock near the river, spear over his head, waiting to stab a salmon. Parks with fishing and boating access to the Columbia River or the Sandy River are Rooster Rock, Benson (lake sports also), Lewis and Clark, and Dabney.

A web of hiking trails penetrates the forest wilderness, and the trails form connecting links with the waterfalls. One path climbs to the top of Larch Mountain as it passes singing snow-melt creeks, giant sword ferns, and wildflowers. Several parks offer both trails and waterfalls: Guy W. Talbot, Bridal Veil Falls, John B. Yeon, and Starvation Creek. Shepperd's Dell has a waterfall; Wygant has a long trail and viewpoints.

The summer wind blows strong along this stretch of river. Native Americans thought it originated from Wind Mountain where the Wind God lived, but more often it blows east from the Pacific Ocean. Windsurfers come long distances to catch a ride on the Columbia River. Several parks feature windsurfing access: Rooster Rock, Viento, Koberg Beach, and Mayer.

Only one state park has a campground along the historic highway: Ainsworth, a fine exploring base. Along Interstate 84, campgrounds are at Viento and Memaloose. Boat-in, primitive campgrounds are on Government Island, northeast of the Portland Airport.

For additional information on Oregon State Parks, call 1-800-551-6949, or check the official website: *www.prd.state.or.us.*

130. GOVERNMENT ISLAND STATE RECREATION AREA

Hours/Season: Day use and overnight; year-round

Area: 15 miles of island shoreline in Columbia River

Attractions: Boating, beach walking, wildlife viewing, swimming, fishing, water sports, picnicking, primitive camping

Facilities: Boat launch, picnic tables, primitive camping, beach access, vault toilets

Access: By boat only; located under and east of the Interstate 205 bridge

Contact: (503) 280-6844

Boaters looking for picnicking, beaches, fishing, and primitive camping on an island in the Columbia River away from the rush of the urban Portland–Vancouver area will find that possible at nearby Government Island State Recreation Area. Two docking areas, Government Island Dock and Bartletts Landing, and a floating tie-up (near Interstate 205) are located along beaches on the north side of the island, or you can head for another beach area located along the south shore. The island complex consists of Government Island's large acreage and two small nearby islands, Lemon to the northwest and McGuire to the southeast. Lemon Island provides another area to dock with primitive facilities. The 15 miles of shoreline and the Columbia River offer a variety of recreation choices that include walking the shoreline, waterskiing, swimming, fishing, and viewing wildlife in this natural area with little development. Plan on being self-sufficient and bringing what gear, food, and drink you need.

It's possible that this was the island in the Columbia River, near present-day Vancouver, where the Lewis and Clark Expedition camped in early November of 1805. They took canoes borrowed from local Native Americans to a lake on the island for an after-dark hunt that netted three swans, eight brants, and five ducks; they noted that the lake teemed with waterfowl.

From the Oregon side of the river, boaters can launch at Chinook Landing on Marine Drive or nearby Sundial near the east end of the island complex. Several launch areas are located on Marine Drive just west of Lemon Island. Other launch areas exist in the Vancouver, Washington, area.

The interior of the island is a cattle ranch and contains protected natural areas with snowberry, Indian plum, ocean spray, ferns, and cottonwood and ash trees in riverine areas; entry there is prohibited.

131. LEWIS AND CLARK STATE RECREATION SITE

Hours/Season: Day use; year-round

Area: 56 acres

Attractions: Historical exhibits, nature trail, fishing, boating, swimming, beach area, picnicking

Facilities: Picnic tables, boat launch, restrooms

Access: Off Interstate 84, take Exit 18; 16 miles east of Portland

Lewis and Clark State Recreation Site is located at the western gateway to the Historic Columbia River Highway and the Columbia River Gorge National Scenic Area, so it is an excellent starting point for explorations in this region.

Management of the resources of the Columbia River Gorge was the subject of much political discussion for many years. No other sea-level river flows through the Cascade Mountains in a spectacularly beautiful gorge. Besides its unique natural and recreational features, the area is a transportation corridor that contributes to the economy of the Pacific Northwest. The goal is to safeguard these qualities. On November 17, 1986, President Ronald Reagan signed into law the act of Congress that created the 292,000-acre Columbia River Gorge National Scenic Area. Managed in partnership by the states of Oregon and Washington, the U.S. Forest Service, the U.S. Department of Agriculture, and six local counties, the goal is to "protect and enhance scenic, cultural, recreational, and natural resources of the Gorge while encouraging compatible economic growth and development."

The first white men in this area were a boat crew from the *HMS Chatham.* When the sailors sighted Mount Hood near where the Sandy River empties into the Columbia on October 30, 1792, Lieutenant William Broughton, a British naval officer under the command of George Vancouver, named the peak in honor of Vice Admiral Samuel Lord Hood.

The state park, however, is named in honor of expedition Captains Lewis and Clark, who arrived at the mouth of this river on November 3, 1805. Though the water was only a few inches deep, "a very bad quicksand" prevented them from wading the river. Because of this, they called this stream the Quicksand River, later shortened to the Sandy River. The river upstream was explored at that time for about one and a half miles, approximately the site of this park, where they found the river to be "a very considerable stream." They returned to camp near the Columbia and shared a "sumptuous supper" with Native Americans.

On their homeward trip in April of 1806, Lewis and Clark stayed six days at a "handsome prairie" opposite the Sandy River to hunt for food, examine the river, and obtain canoes. They had hoped the Sandy might be a major navigable river, but Sergeant Pryor's scouting found it could only be canoed 6 miles upstream before encountering rapids and waterfalls as it flowed from the slopes of Mount Hood. The locals confirmed this, and Lewis and Clark discovered that they had missed the major river that watered the Willamette Valley. Clark, seven men, and a Native American guide backtracked to explore what the locals called the Multnomah, now named the Willamette River.

Lewis and Clark became acquainted with the "wapato" (from the Native American *wappatoo)* or duck potato (*Sagittaria latifolia),* common in wet places in the area. It comes up each spring from a starchy tuber with three small white petals and large arrowhead-shaped blades, and is about 40 to 50 centimeters

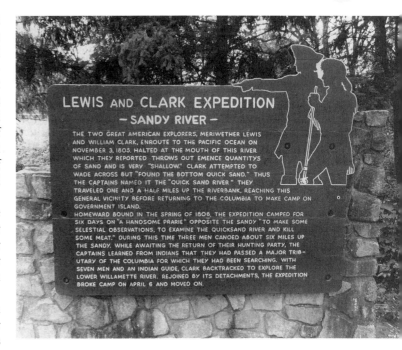

An exhibit tells about the Lewis and Clark Expedition stop in this park named for them.

tall. The abundant bulb was an important food source of the Native Americans and a major article of trade. Lewis and Clark wrote that it was the most valuable of local roots.

It seems appropriate to have a nature trail in the park named after these explorers, considering the wealth of information they acquired about the flora and fauna of the area. The Lewis and Clark Nature Trail circles the edge of a woods where an unstable rock and dirt bluff rises above the trees and vultures circle.

Lovely old trees shelter the picnic tables. In particular, huge apple and pear trees, loaded with fruit in late summer, are numerous, along with various conifers and hardwoods. A campground was once part of the park, but proximity to urban areas, and the attendant vandalism, resulted in the park being open only for day use. Signs caution against the use of alcohol and unsupervised swimming.

The Sandy River edges the park and fishermen bank fish or launch boats across the road. Depending on the season, salmon, steelhead, or shad might be your catch. In early spring, a short smelt run occurs when the silvery fish come up from the Columbia River to spawn. Nets fastened to long poles are dipped into the water to snare these small, fine-tasting fish.

132. DABNEY STATE RECREATION AREA

Hours/Season: Day use (fee); year-round
Area: 135 acres
Attractions: Hiking, fishing, swimming, boating, disc golf, picnicking *(no dogs or alcohol)*
Facilities: Picnic tables, group picnic reservations, restrooms, boat launch
Access: Off the Historic Columbia River Highway, 3.5 miles east of Exit 18 off Interstate 84

Dabney State Recreation Area occupies a considerable distance along the wooded north bank of the Sandy River. A 1.5-mile round-trip hiking path follows the water and offers a fine walk. Since the current and water height of the river vary due to upstream water control, visitors are cautioned to stay on the banks of the river. Marshy wetland areas with bigleaf maple trees border the river and invasive ivy climbs the tall Douglas fir trees of this natural area.

Trails branch off from the main path to the three parking areas, adjacent to picnicking locations. These picnic spots are spaced far apart on rolling terrain of treed lawns. The farthest one offers a shelter. A disc golf course is found in this area, one that looks quite difficult considering the many interfering trees—beautiful with spring flowers—and hilly terrain.

Not far from the last picnicking spot are two wetland areas with ponds. I surprised a great blue heron at one, side by side with a flock of Canada geese at water's edge. Chipmunks scam-

Waterfowl, including mallard ducks, are attracted to the pond at Dabney State Recreation Area.

pered across the grass. Chatterbox orchids flowered nearby and mimosa trees were in full bloom. The park is sprayed, so don't eat the berries near the parking areas.

133. PORTLAND WOMEN'S FORUM STATE SCENIC VIEWPOINT

Hours/Season: Day use; year-round
Area: 7.26 acres
Attractions: Panoramic gorge viewpoint, photography, exhibit information
Facilities: Restrooms
Access: Off Historic Columbia River Highway, 9 miles east of Exit 18 off Interstate 84, or 1.5 miles east from Exit 22 to Corbett

Portland Women's Forum State Scenic Viewpoint is the quintessential cliff-top viewpoint of this area, the place where so many photos of Vista House and the surrounding Columbia River Gorge landscape have been taken. Known as Chanticleer Lookout, at an elevation of 850 feet, the geologic landslide amphitheater in the foreground was sculptured by the catastrophic floods at the end of the Ice Age 12,800 to 15,000 years ago.

If you use the Vista House as a compass point at twelve o'clock, 850-foot-high Beacon Rock is directly above. Rooster Rock, a landslide block of Yakima Basalt, is 0.8 mile away at eleven o'clock. The Larch Mountain shield volcano is at 8.5 miles at one o'clock. Two Boring lava cinder cones, Mount Pleasant and Mount Zion, are across the river at 10:45 and 11:15, respectively.

Chanticleer Inn once occupied this site, the place where Sam Hill, Sam Lancaster, John B. Yeon, Simon Benson, and others met in 1913 to plan construction of the historic highway. After the inn burned in the 1930s, the area became a state park.

The original 3.71 acres of the park was a gift from the Portland Women's Forum, a group made up of representatives of the principal women's organizations of Portland. This group was active for many years in the preservation of the natural beauty of the gorge, under the leadership of Mrs. Gertrude Jensen. It was responsible for appointment of the first Columbia Gorge Commission in the 1950s.

At the entrance to the parking area, several historic bronze plaques are mounted on a fifty-ton granite boulder. Sam Hill, road builder, and Lewis and Clark are honored with plaques.

Columbia River Gorge: Past and Present

Imagine a scene some twelve thousand years ago when glacier-melting caused catastrophic floods and landslides. Ten times the combined flow of all the rivers of the world sluiced into a slot carved by the Columbia River through the Cascade Mountains. As the river valley was widened by this force, the tangled veins of river tributaries were cut off in midstream and left suspended on high rocky notches. The result was the greatest concentration of high waterfalls in North America. The Oregon side has at least seventy-seven waterfalls.

The cliffs looming above the mighty river are unique in character. Weathered, mossy, and textured with varied patterns of rocks juxtaposed, this geology, spewed from fiery mountains altered by landslides, is a spectacular collage of natural art forms and colors.

The Historic Columbia River Highway was the only road along the Oregon side of the Columbia River for thirty-seven years, and the history of its construction is fascinating. The spectacular beauty of the gorge inspired this ambitious undertaking in 1913, when the automobile was so recently on the scene. In fact, America's favorite car, the Model T Ford, was coming off the assembly line at the same time the historic highway was being built. Men with shovels and horses, steamrollers, and grading equipment primitive by today's standards were the tools available to road builder and engineer Samuel Lancaster. The terrain was constantly challenging, but the result was worth it. This engineering marvel climbs from farmland to rain forest and twists like a sidewinder at the edge of lichen-smeared cliffs. Because of his spiritual concern for mankind's relationship to nature, Lancaster hired Italian stonemasons who "built their souls" into the dry masonry of the moss-covered stone walls and bridges that marry the highway to the rugged terrain. Certainly, promoter and "Good Roads" advocate Sam Hill played a vital roll in the completion of this road, as he invited Lancaster to the Pacific Northwest and toured Europe with him to introduce him to exciting road-building techniques. Many other backers of great vision also were essential to the road we travel today with a sense of wonder. The historic highway is not continuous today, but that section near the many waterfalls is still intact, with another section, from Mosier to Rowena, also open to touring.

The only near–sea level passage through the Cascade Mountains, the Columbia River Gorge has provided a corridor for humans for nearly twelve thousand years, though the river itself was long a hazardous route, with numerous cascade rapids in the days before its wild beauty was ruptured and tamed by dams and locks. The metal "Bridge of the Gods," named after the natural rock bridge of Native American legend once at this location, crosses the river at the town of Cascade Locks, a National Historic Site. Transportation through the gorge was aided by the construction of a water-grade railway on the Oregon side in the 1880s, but the Historic Columbia River Highway contributed immensely to transportation in the gorge.

Road engineer Lancaster hired Italian stonemasons to do the dry masonry of the stone walls and bridges of the Historic Columbia River Highway.

The quintessential cliff-top view of Vista House and the Columbia River Gorge is at Portland Women's Forum State Scenic Viewpoint.

Another is titled "Aboriginal's Paradise," complete with Native Americans and their tepees, salmon drying, and dugout canoes against the geologic backdrop of the Columbia Gorge. Yet another illustrates "Columbia River Navigation," with stern-wheelers, steamboats, and sailing ships.

To view the area from Larch Mountain, take the turnoff from the historic highway to Larch Mountain Road just 0.4 mile east of the park. The glaciated summit and picnic area are reached by a paved road in 13 miles. This is the terminus of the 7-mile Larch Mountain Trail that climbs up the mountainside from the Multnomah Falls Lodge and passes several waterfalls (or it is the trailhead for a downhill trail, if you prefer, with pickup below). (See map under Ainsworth State Park.) A 0.3-mile trail at road's end leads to Sherrard Point, a lookout with a view of five major Cascade peaks. This is a great place to watch sunsets. It is interesting that Larch Mountain was so named because early lumbermen thought the noble fir growing there was larch. There are no western larch trees on the mountain.

134. CROWN POINT STATE SCENIC CORRIDOR

Hours/Season: Day use; view is year-round, but Vista House is open April 15 through October 15
Area: 307 acres
Attractions: Views of Columbia River Gorge, exhibits, monument to early pioneers, photography, picnicking
Facilities: Historic Vista House, exhibits and gift shop, information center, picnic tables, restrooms
Access: From the west, take Exit 18 from Interstate 84 and proceed on the Historic Columbia River Highway for 10 miles; or from the east, take Exit 35 and travel 12 miles
Contact: Friends of Vista House, (503) 695-2230

The Crown Point State Scenic Corridor features awesome views of geologic events, a cogent joining of human engineering with the natural terrain. A 720-foot promontory along the Columbia River, Crown Point was scoured by the formative Bretz floods. The dedication of the newly completed Columbia River Scenic Highway took place here on June 6, 1916.

Samuel Lancaster, chief engineer of the highway, proposed this as an ideal site for "an observatory from which the view both up and down the Columbia could be viewed in silent communion with the infinite." He wanted to inspire travelers, give them a rest stop, and share his wonder of the gorge. The name "Vista House" was his suggestion.

Construction of Vista House began in 1916, under the direction of John B. Yeon, Multnomah County roadmaster. Portland architect Edgar M. Lazarus decided on a nonhistoric design reflecting modern German architecture. The plans for interior decoration were furnished by Lancaster. It was built at a total cost of approximately $100,000 and officially dedicated as a monument to early Oregon pioneers on May 5, 1918.

Vista House is a rotunda 44 feet in diameter and 55 feet high with interior floors, stairs, and basement wainscoting of Tokeen Alaskan marble. Most of the interior is Kasota limestone, including a hand-carved drinking fountain. The dome exterior was originally matte-glazed green tiles, but it is now copper-crowned. As a tribute to the early settlers, carved panels line the interior of the dome, with these designs: chestnut, acorn, pine cone, grape, apple, wheat, Oregon grape, ginkgo, and pioneer tools and utensils.

Vista House and the original 1.71 acres were donated to the park system in 1938. It was registered as a National Historic

The view of the Columbia River Gorge from Vista House is inspiring at Crown Point.

135. GUY W. TALBOT STATE PARK

Hours/Season: Day use; year-round
Area: 378 acres
Attractions: Waterfall, hiking, interpretive signs, photography, picnicking
Facilities: Picnic tables, group picnic reservations, restrooms
Access: Off the Historic Columbia River Highway, 12 miles east of Interstate 5 from Exit 18

Continuing east on the highway, a mile past Crown Point, travelers enter the "Figure Eight Loops," an engineering marvel of road building with maximum 5 percent grades and curve radii of not less than 100 feet. This design accomplishes a 600-foot drop in elevation and parallels itself five times. At the same time,

The centerpiece of Guy W. Talbot State Park is 249-foot Latourell Falls, second highest in the gorge.

Landmark in 1974. In 1982, after the scope of the structure was expanded to include an interpretive center, a group of local Corbett residents began the Vista House Project as a way to become involved with the future of the landmark. This group became the Friends of Vista House in 1987.

The main floor has historical photos and exhibits and an information center. Posters, photographs, serigraphs, paintings, and plaques of early explorers decorate the walls. A collection of fresh flowers is an aid to native plant identification.

The basement floor has more wall displays and a gift shop that specializes in handcrafted artworks, with snacks, espresso, and complimentary coffee available. A world map pinpoints the diverse origin of visitors to Vista House. The upper outdoor level offers a panoramic vista.

Volunteers are available to assist you at the information counter, and they also coordinate Folk Art Programs on weekends: demonstrations of different handcrafted artwork—spinning wool, weaving, calligraphy, woodcarving, making baskets, and more. Profits from the gift store are used for interpretive programs and to maintain and staff Vista House.

Remodeling inside and out is in the works, with no definite date yet. If this necessitates closure of the interior in the summer of 2002, a modular interpretive unit will be available outside. And the view is always an attraction.

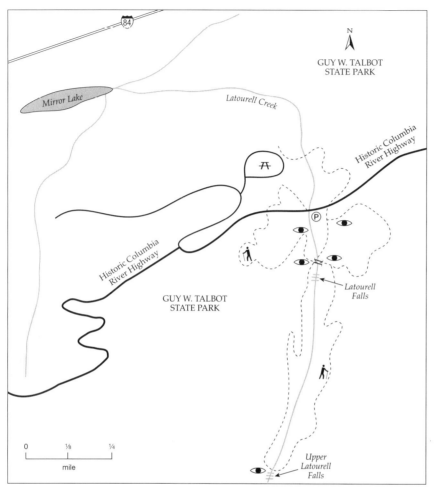

area west of the bridge via a short road.

A paved path from the highway parking lot descends quickly to the bottom of the falls. This waterfall, an example of the type called a "plunge," drops vertically and away from the cliff side, losing contact with the bedrock. It pours over a single flow of brickbat basalt with curved columns toward the base. The notch at the top is only 20 feet deep. The view is enhanced by the green of trees and the golden smear of lichen on the adjacent rock walls. A wooden bridge near the bottom of the falls allows the hiker to cross the creek and connect to another paved trail that goes under the highway bridge to the picnic area. The falls are a short hike from there also.

Another trail ascends steeply from the highway parking lot. This makes a loop that leads to the top of the falls. The falls are visible on the way up the trail through the trees, and a sunny morning will reward hikers with rainbows on the falling water. Higher up are good distant views of the area, several benches to rest on, and massive rock formations that poke above tree tops. At the top, the small creek that feeds the falls is easily crossed, but safe viewing of the falls itself is prevented by obstructions. Returning through forest on the west side of the hiking loop, you pass an old building falling down among the trees. On reaching the road, cross the bridge to parking.

a good example of western Oregon rain forest is viewed—if you're not driving.

Coming out of this design feat, you will encounter the first of a series of spectacular gorge waterfalls in Guy W. Talbot State Park. Latourell Falls, named for a pioneer settler, is 249 feet high, second highest in the Columbia River Gorge. The land for the park was donated by Guy W. Talbot, a lumber baron.

According to Native American legend, the beauty of the wife of the coyote god Speelyai was preserved for eternity when he transformed her into this waterfall to prevent her from escaping from him.

Parking on the east side of the bridge over Latourell Creek is easy to find, though parking is also available at the separate picnic

136. SHEPPERD'S DELL STATE NATURAL AREA

Hours/Season: Day use; year-round
Area: 519 acres
Attractions: Short trail to waterfall viewpoint, photography
Facilities: Restrooms, *limited parking*
Access: 13 miles east off Interstate 84 from Exit 18, on the Historic Columbia River Highway

Young Creek flows into a rocky canyon at Shepperd's Dell State Natural Area, forming a succession of small waterfalls. The water then cascades under the 100-foot concrete deck–arch highway bridge. A short paved trail descends into the fern-covered canyon for a better view of the falls. Though the park is large, it is mostly rugged, rocky, and inaccessible, bordered on the north by the Union Pacific Railroad and bisected by the scenic highway. Spectacular cliffs are nearby.

The original tract for the park was a gift from George G. Shepperd to the city of Portland in 1915, a memorial to his wife, with the land later given to the state. When the land still belonged to his family, and there were no good roads to let them attend church, this dell was a place they used to renew themselves spiritually.

The Lewis and Clark Expedition stopped at Shepperd's Dell from April 6 to 8, 1806.

East of Shepperd's Dell, just west of the Exit 28 connector to the historic highway, is an attractive new trailhead area for the 2.3-mile Angel's Rest Trail, which climbs to a viewpoint above the gorge.

137. ROOSTER ROCK STATE PARK

Hours/Season: Day use (fee); year-round
Area: 873 acres
Attractions: Unusual rock formation, fishing, boating, hiking, windsurfing, birdwatching, swimming, clothing-optional beach, exhibit information, picnicking
Facilities: Picnic tables, group picnic reservations, accessible restrooms, boat basin and launch, playground, stairs down to beach area
Access: Off Interstate 84, 22 miles east of Portland at Exit 25
Contact: (503) 695-2261

The 200-foot columnar basaltic spire that rises amid trees at the west end of Rooster Rock State Park has been officially named Rooster Rock, though the pioneers used a phallic term to designate this pinnacle, and at one time it was called Cape Eternity. The rock serves as a guide for boaters, and attracts artists, geologists, and rock climbers.

On their way west, Lewis and Clark passed through this area from October 31 to November 2, 1805. They had just brought their boats through what they called the "great chute," a wild place on the Columbia River now drowned by Bonneville Dam. They named another 800-foot volcanic remnant near this water chute on the Washington side "Beacon Rock," a unique and easily identifiable guide marker for travelers and explorers. According

The columnar basaltic spire that rises at the west end of Rooster Rock State Park is a landmark along the river.

to Lewis and Clark, "great numbers of sea otters" came up the river this far, and they wrote that Beacon Rock "may be esteemed the head of tidewater." On their return, they camped under Rooster Rock from April 6 to 9, 1806.

Before it became a state park and registered Natural Heritage Site, this land was used in connection with fish seining, and one salmon cannery was located near the present boat basin. Because problems arose during times of low water, a channel was dredged to allow boats delivering salmon to get to the cannery dock.

From high above the park, Vista House overlooks the vast array of parking lots and picnic areas that stretch along the 3.5 miles of park frontage on the Columbia River. Boat launching is to the west, with a fee for overnight use. The Columbia River

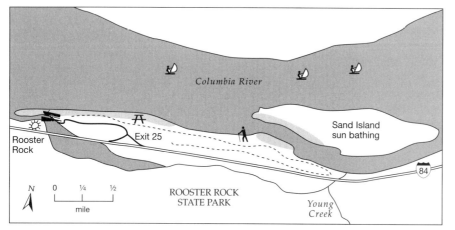

back. Winds are often strong here, although they are not assured, and sometimes they are intermittent. Experienced windsurfers have an array of different sails for these varying conditions.

Wind and wave conditions may be stronger and rougher than they appear to the uninitiated. To test your equipment and skill, use short reaches. It is best not to windsurf alone. Sailboards, considered vessels, must follow the rules of the sea. Watch for jibing and jumping. Maintain a watch for barges—which travel faster than they appear but cannot make sudden turns or stops— and other vessels.

Top-notch international competitors come to the gorge in the summer to participate in scheduled events. Check locally to see specific events and times.

A related water sport recently seen in the gorge area is called kiteboarding. The kite pulls you, even lifts you. "You fly the kite. The kite drags you. You stand on the board," explained one aficionado.

widens here and a channel winds around Rooster Rock and south to form the boat basin.

To the east are sandy beaches with fine views of the bluffs and cliffs lining the gorge to the east. Stairways lead to different sections of the beach. The water level of the river varies according to water usage, controlled by dams and periods of drought. This determines the width of the beach. Weekends usually bring lower water levels and more beach. Wetland areas punctuate the river's edge on this side of the park, rich with vegetation and food that attracts birds. At the extreme eastern end of the park, a stairway leads to paths meandering through bushy vegetation to secluded beaches where clothing-optional sunbathing is allowed. Nudity is restricted to an area 100 yards east of this stairway.

Some 3.2 miles of hiking trails weave through the park. A trail from the eastern end of the parking area leads to some natural areas as it winds along the top of the tree-covered bluff overlooking the river for some distance, through woods and blackberry patches plump with succulent berries in season, many plant species, including maroon-centered Queen Anne's lace, and wild roses. Many trails branch off, some descending to the beach, so you can wander about as you wish and not get lost. Sand Island is on the east, bordering the river.

The challenging sport of windsurfing on the Columbia River in the gorge area has become increasingly popular. Weather and the river often provide a unique set of optimal conditions. The boardsailor contends with the westward flow of the river and with winds usually coming from the opposite direction, blowing inland from the sea and being funneled through the gorge. This is an ideal situation for windsurfing across the river and

138. BRIDAL VEIL FALLS STATE SCENIC VIEWPOINT

Hours/Season: Day use; year-round
Area: 15.6 acres
Attractions: Trail to waterfall, all-abilities walkway to gorge overlook, nature study, interpretive signs, photography, picnicking
Facilities: Picnic tables, accessible restrooms
Access: Off Historic Columbia River Highway, 15 miles east of Interstate 84 from Exit 18, or from Exit 28 if you don't wish to tour the historic highway

The Bridal Veil Falls State Scenic Viewpoint was once the scene of large-scale commercial logging and a planing mill operation. The book published in 1940 by the Writers Program of the Work Projects Administration, *Oregon: End of the Trail*, notes this and remarks: "Formerly Bridal Veil Falls was noted for its beauty but the waters now are confined in a lumberflume." Fortunately, the waterfall has regained its former beauty and is now a park

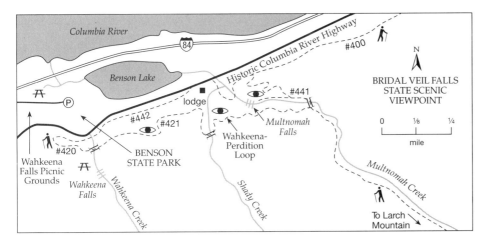

are a dark brown color and sweet, like molasses. They are made into large cakes that are slightly baked in the sun. Pioneers learned much from the Native Americans about what wild things to eat. One delicacy that resulted was camas pie.

Although there are miles and miles of wonderful hiking trails in the gorge, the nearby 3.3-mile Wahkeena-Perdition Loop is particularly fine. Start at the Wahkeena Falls Picnic Grounds, 2 miles east of Bridal Veils State Scenic Viewpoint. Hike up along the waterfall on Wahkeena Trail No. 420 and cross Wahkeena Creek on the stone bridge in 0.2 mile. *Wahkeena* is a Native American word meaning "most beautiful," and this impressive 242-foot multiple falls, lined with summer wildflower color, lives up to its name. Continue to the junction with Perdition Trail No. 421 at 0.4 mile and take this route for 1.2 miles. This trail has many stairs along the way. Short side trails to viewpoints of the gorge occur at 0.5, 0.7, and 0.9 mile, and a bridge crosses Shady Creek at 0.8 mile. The loop continues on Larch Mountain Trail No. 441, crossing Multnomah Creek almost immediately. This is the stream that flows down from Larch Mountain and feeds the 620-foot Multnomah Falls, highest in the gorge, but the stream itself is a special place here before the plunge begins. Few people think of this as a destination for a picnic, but it is. It is a wonderful place of rocks, clear flowing water, green trees, and solitude. The spur to the top of the falls is a short distance further, to the left, and it is one reason this place is missed. Most people coming from the other direction don't come quite this far.

Follow the Larch Mountain Trail for a total of 1.1 miles as it descends to Multnomah Falls Lodge and the bottom of the falls. A quarter-mile above the lodge, cross the Benson arch bridge over the water after passing a pool under the upper falls, where water sprays from its vast energy and wildflowers blow in the wet breeze. The most visited tourist attraction in Oregon, Multnomah Falls is a spectacular double falls that caused Meriwether Lewis to write how it "fell from a great height over the supendious [sic] rocks . . . the most remarkable of these cascades falls." No one is disappointed here. In winter, the falls may freeze into a suspension of giant icicles.

attraction. Following an Oregon tradition, brides often take their wedding invitations to the Bridal Veil Post Office, established in 1887, to have them postmarked; it is now open only on Saturdays.

The park's picnic tables are sheltered by trees, many laden with ripening pears in late summer, and you might want to position yourself carefully, as they frequently fall to the ground.

To view the falls, take the path behind the restrooms and descend to the falls in 1 mile. This moderately steep dirt and rock path has some switchbacking, then crosses Bridal Veil Creek before ascending a stairway to a platform with a view of the waterfall. This is a multiple falls of two tiers, full of water even in late summer of a drought year. The remains of the old mill and pond can be seen just east of the viewing platform.

The all-abilities interpretive trail offers both a nature study area and great viewpoints of the Columbia River Gorge. The round-topped cliffs drop almost vertically here, like massive oblong stones propped on their ends. The paved 0.5-mile level loop is a pleasant walk adjacent to natural wildflower meadows and camas fields backed by tall trees. The varied vegetation includes fuchsia, wild rose, blackberry, fireweed, lupine, penstemon, and native grasses. Please stay on the trail in this area to protect the vegetation.

Native Americans were well acquainted with the benefits of camas fields. This wildflower has azure blooms in April and an onion-like bulb. When boiled, the root is palatable and tastes somewhat like a potato. The traditional way to prepare it, and probably the best way, is by fermenting it for several days in underground pits filled with hot stones. When removed, the bulbs

Wahkeena Falls, just east of Bridal Veil Falls, is a trailhead for many hikes in the gorge.

Geologists might want to inspect the rocks in the walls of the lodge. If you know what to look for, you can find Yakima black basalt, Cascade or Boring gray basalt, Troutdale quartzite boulders, and Eagle Creek petrified and opalized wood.

Take Return Trail No. 442, on the west side of the lodge, for 0.6 mile back to the Wahkeena Falls Picnic Grounds.

139. BENSON STATE RECREATION AREA

Hours/Season: Day use (fee); year-round
Area: 272 acres
Attractions: Fishing, paddling, windsurfing, lake swimming, boating, disc golf, exhibit information, picnicking
Facilities: Picnic tables, reservable group picnicking, accessible fishing docks, boat ramp on the Columbia River at Dalton Point *(westbound access only from freeway)*
Access: Off Interstate 84, 30 miles east of Portland at Exit 30, *eastbound access only*

Benson State Recreation Area was named in honor of Simon Benson, a principal benefactor of the Historic Columbia River Highway and a native of Norway. The developed area lies between the freeway and the Union Pacific Railroad, although the acreage includes tracts along the Historic Columbia River Highway and east of Multnomah Falls.

The small lake that formed from Multnomah Creek is a popular place to cool off on a summer day and dominates the park. Picnic before or after a swim, or perhaps rest under cottonwood, alder, and maple trees on the level lawn. On such a day you will find the park busy with swimmers of all ages, some learning to swim, some crossing the lake, some simply on floats in the sunlight. Others hop onto rafts or into canoes and paddle around, avoiding the crowds at the edge of the water. A walk around the circumference of the lake will reveal a quiet fishing spot. New fishing piers are found along the creek that enters Benson Lake from the west, along the entry road. Those wanting to put boats into the Columbia River must approach Dalton Point from the east, where the park's boat ramp is located, with access for windsurfers.

140. AINSWORTH STATE PARK

Hours/Season: Day use and overnight; campground open mid-March through October
Area: 156 acres
Attractions: Hiking, access to gorge trails, photography, wildlife viewing, picnicking, camping
Facilities: Picnic tables, campground (45 full hookup sites— maximum site 60 feet), 4 walk-in tent sites, restrooms with showers, playground, dump station
Access: Off Historic Columbia River Highway, 21 miles east of Exit 18 from Interstate 84, or 1.2 miles west from Exit 35
Contact: (503) 695-2301

Anyone interested in camping in the waterfall area of the gorge might consider Ainsworth State Park. With more than 60 miles of trails in this area, it is an aerobic paradise of waterfalls, creeks, forested trails, and fantastic views. Large RV rigs are not suited to touring the historic highway, so use towed vehicles or walk to nearby trails, since the park has easy access from Interstate 84.

Geology is stunning in the gorge, with pinnacles of Yakima basalt seen in a 3-mile area starting at Ainsworth; some of these are visible from the campground, but are seen easily near meadows from Exit 35. These tall rocky spires are embedded with lichen and trees rooted in cracks of soil. Rising 1,500 feet above the river, Saint Peter's Dome is an erosional remnant of at least six flows of basalt. A cross section of one of the Cascade

A summer day attracts many visitors to water play at Benson Lake.

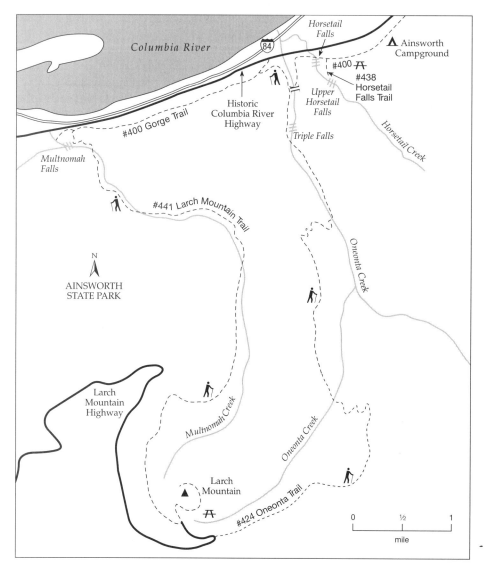

forest to the day-use restroom in 0.2 mile, and the picnic tables are a short distance farther, a quiet spot backed by lush forest growth of firs, bigleaf maples, ferns, cedar trees, mosses, and many snowberry bushes. A natural spring with elaborate stonework constructed by the Civilian Conservation Corps provides water. From here, you can connect to Gorge Trail No. 400 in 0.1 mile—a low-elevation, east-west path through the entire gorge, although some sections are not complete. This trail increases loop options. It also heads east of the campground.

The 2.7 mile Horsetail-Oneonta Loop Trail begins only 0.5 mile west of the campground, so you can either walk or drive to the 176-foot-high Horsetail Falls area to access the trailhead. Climb steep Horsetail Falls Trail No. 438 to Upper Horsetail Falls in 0.4 mile. Walk around the ledge behind the free-falling water that is edged with ferns, a waterfall nicknamed "Ponytail Falls." The water spray and rain have created lush vegetation and wildflowers past the falls.

At 0.8 mile, the trail splits and the north one offers a high viewpoint of the Columbia River. At 1.2 miles, cross the bridge over Oneonta Creek and come to a junction with Oneonta Trail No. 424 at 1.3 miles. One can continue right on the loop or first take a side trip to Triple Falls to the left, a good rest and picnic spot. This additional round-trip trail would add 1.6 miles to the loop trail. Backtracking, if necessary, to the Oneonta Trail junction, it is another 0.9 mile to the scenic highway. A 0.5-mile stroll on the road returns you to Horsetail Falls, almost immediately taking you past the Oneonta Gorge, where a creek flows between a gash in basalt rock. Another side trip possibility is to the waterfall that lies 900 feet upstream, reached by wading past rocks and round holes that are tree

volcanoes, with its vent exposed, can be seen on the upper cliffs of Nesmith Point. The Benson Plateau, the Cascade summit surface, is south of here at elevations of 3,900 to 4,300 feet where numerous small cirques on the east side have been cut by ice.

The day-use area of Ainsworth State Park is west of the campground along the scenic highway. The Ainsworth Loop Trail heads off from the southwest corner of the campground through molds left from scouring by floods. In some of these holes, pieces of opalized, carbonized, or otherwise silicified wood have been left be-hind. This small gorge has much botanical interest as well as geologic, and is quite popular.

141. JOHN B. YEON STATE SCENIC CORRIDOR

Hours/Season: Day use; year-round
Area: 284 acres
Attractions: Hiking, waterfalls, photography
Facilities: Trailheads, exhibit information, parking, *no water or restrooms*
Access: Off Interstate 84, 2 miles east of Exit 35 on Frontage Road, 37 miles east of Portland

In Mount Hood National Forest, several trails winding through quiet natural sections cut by gulches can be accessed from the trailhead in John B. Yeon State Scenic Corridor. The park honors John B. Yeon, a Portland citizen who contributed considerable energy, experience, and wealth to the development of the Historic Columbia River Highway.

Yeon is the trailhead for Elowah Falls, reached by a 0.8-mile hike. Alternately, you can go to Upper McCord Creek Falls in 1.1 miles. These two begin together and are also part of Gorge Trail No. 400. Almost immediately, 4.9-mile Nesmith Ridge Trail No. 428 branches off to the west, which climbs to 3,880-foot-high Nesmith Point. This latter trail also accesses the Gorge Trail in a short distance, taking one to the Ainsworth Campground in 4.5 miles.

The trail to Elowah Falls is easy at the beginning and becomes moderately difficult for 0.2 mile to where Upper McCord Creek Falls Trail splits off to the right. Just past this point, a pair of ospreys started squawking as I approached their nest; I looked up to see one fly to a nest at the top of a tall fir with a fish for its young, an aid in spotting the nest.

Level for a while, the path soon descends in fairly steep switchbacks to the bottom of the falls. From a height of 289 feet, Elowah Falls plunges down and reminds one of Latourell Falls, even with yellow-green lichen on the steep canyon walls. Situated in a stone-rimmed amphitheater, the water bounces off huge boulders, collects in a pretty pool, and then meanders down the creek bed under a bridge. The forest is exuberant with the growth of fir, maple, penstemon, pearly everlasting, Queen

A trail leads from Ainsworth State Park to Upper Horsetail Falls, where hikers walk on a ledge under the waterfall.

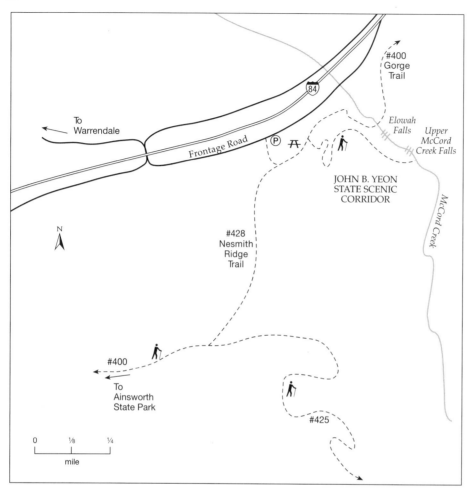

in 2.1 miles, where you can descend to the creek and explore, photograph, picnic, or fish. High Bridge crosses a deep gorge at 3.3 miles. Trekkers pass through a 30-foot tunnel blasted from solid rock near 100-foot-high Tunnel Falls in 6 miles. Camping is permitted at High Bridge. Tenas Camp is a major camp at 3.7 miles. For complete details and restrictions (because of heavy use), obtain a trail guide from the Forest Service.

Two trails with gorge views accessed from Eagle Creek Forest Camp are the moderately steep 0.6-mile Buck Point Trail and the easy 1.8-mile Wauna Trail. The Pacific Crest Trail can be accessed via Gorge Trail No. 400 in 2.5 miles.

For an appreciation of how dams have changed the lives and numbers of salmon coming up and down the river, stop at Bonneville Dam, where you can visit the fish hatchery, the fish ladder, and the visitor center on Bradford Island. Particularly fascinating is fish viewing at the center's lighted underwater windows. Besides seeing a closeup of salmon and steelhead, other curious fish— shad, sturgeon, lamprey, and others— sometimes swim by.

Anne's lace, and dripping walls with ferns. The trail continues across the bridge as Gorge Trail No. 400.

An excellent base for exploring more hiking trails is nearby Eagle Creek Forest Camp, the nation's oldest such camp, which is eastbound access only (westbound travelers can loop back from the Bonneville Dam Exit). A pair of ospreys frequently call this campground home, with their nest high in a tree, and kingfishers and great blue herons earn their meals at the creek.

The popular Eagle Creek Trailhead is just south of the picnic grounds. The 13.2-mile trail has been carved into basaltic cliffs above forested Eagle Creek. Worthwhile intermediate destinations can be hiked for a shorter hike. The first one is at Punchbowl Falls

142. HISTORIC COLUMBIA RIVER HIGHWAY STATE TRAIL (TOOTH ROCK TRAILHEAD)

Hours/Season: Day use; year-round
Attractions: Hiking, bicycling, wildlife viewing, exhibit information, photography, picnicking
Facilities: Trailhead, picnic tables, vault toilets, restrooms
Access: Off Interstate 84 at Exit 40, Exit 41 (eastbound only, others go west to Exit 40 and then east), and Exit 44

An abandoned section of the Historic Columbia River Highway, the Tooth Rock segment of the state trail, can be hiked between

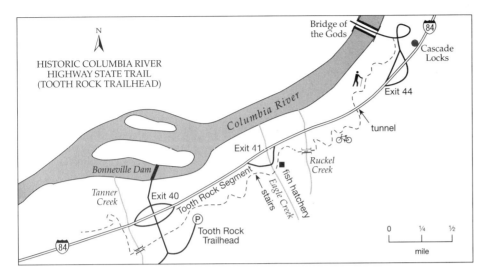

HISTORIC COLUMBIA RIVER
HIGHWAY STATE TRAIL
(TOOTH ROCK TRAILHEAD)

people with disabilities. Several forest trails intersect the old highway route.

In 1848, Tooth Rock was the greatest obstacle to improving the pack trail for a wagon road. When Lancaster designed the historic highway, his engineering solution to cutting through the steep unstable rock resulted in construction of viaducts at both Tooth Rock and Eagle Creek between 1913 and 1915. The Tooth Rock Viaduct was abandoned in 1936 when the Tooth Rock Tunnel, necessitated by highway changes due to the construction of the Bonneville Dam, was drilled through a landslide of Yakima basalt.

Cascade Locks and the Bonneville Dam intersection, with parking available at Cascade Locks (under the Bridge of the Gods), the Eagle Creek Fish Hatchery at Exit 41, and south of the Bonneville Dam Exit 40 interchange. At Cascade Locks, the trail heads west near the entry road to Interstate 84, tunnels under the freeway after less than a mile, and weaves through a lush, green landscape of ferns, moss-covered rocks, and wildflowers for 2.5 miles to Eagle Creek. The Tooth Rock segment continues west for another mile, with views overlooking the Bonneville Dam and locks, and a chance to walk or bicycle the Historic Highway Tooth Rock Viaduct. The only difficult stretch is a steep set of stairs (sixty-two steps with six landings) just west of Eagle Creek, impassable to wheelchairs but bikers should be able to carry their bikes. A trail continues from the Tooth Rock Trailhead over a mile to Bonneville Dam. The trail is rated moderate to difficult for

The eastern Tooth Rock Trailhead is in Cascade Locks, where a river excursion can be taken on the stern-wheeler Columbia Gorge.

143. STARVATION CREEK STATE PARK

Hours/Season: Day use; year-round
Area: 153 acres
Attractions: Hiking, waterfall, exhibit information, photography, picnicking
Facilities: Highway rest stop, picnic tables, restrooms
Access: Off Interstate 84, 10 miles west of Hood River, *eastbound access only*

Winter in the Columbia River Gorge is often mild, but occasionally a storm blows in and dumps snow. This happened in the winter of 1884–1885, and passengers on an Oregon-Washington Railroad & Navigation train were snowbound for several days in 30-foot snow drifts in the vicinity of Starvation Creek State Park.

Getting food and keeping warm were priorities. According to newspaper reports, seats were burned to keep people from freezing. Men from Hood River were employed to carry food using homemade skis. A relief train finally got through from the west. Though no one starved, lack of food did earn the name "Starvation" for the park, creek, and its waterfall.

A short trail leads to 186-foot Starvation Creek Falls. You can picnic at tables positioned beside the creek among trees below the falls. To the left of the restroom is the trailhead to Viento State Park, a 1-mile trail that quickly crosses a new bridge over the creek and then traverses a section of the old Historic Columbia River Highway.

The trail to Lancaster Falls begins at Starvation Creek State Park.

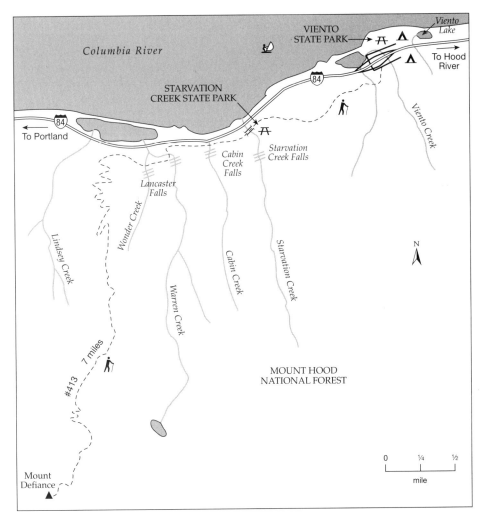

Starvation
Creek Falls

Cabin
Creek
Falls

Lancaster
Falls

MOUNT HOOD
NATIONAL FOREST

N

0   ¼   ½

mile

144. VIENTO STATE PARK

Hours/Season: Day use (fee) and overnight; campground open mid-March through October
Area: 248 acres
Attractions: Windsurfing, Viento Lake, bank fishing, sunbathing, river swimming, wildlife viewing, nature trail, picnicking, camping
Facilities: Picnic tables, river access, campground (58 electrical, 18 tent sites—1 accessible, maximum site 30 feet), accessible restrooms with showers, playground, public phone, program area, connection to gorge trails
Access: Off Interstate 84 at Exit 56, 8 miles west of Hood River
Contact: (503) 374-8811

The name for this state park and the creek that flows through it, Viento, means "wind." The name, however, actually arose from that of a nearby railroad station which combined the letters of railroad builder Henry Villard, capitalist William Endicott, and a contractor named Tolman. The Civilian Conservation Corps built a rustic footbridge across the creek. The picnic area is a grassy meadow with some trees next to the camping area.

Mountain Defiance Trail No. 413 begins west of the park, alongside the entry road. If you want to see more waterfalls, hike the easy beginning of the trail, 1 mile on an old wagon road before it becomes a trail. Cabin Creek Falls is seen at 0.3 mile, followed by falls on Warren Creek at 0.6 mile—named for a Portland fish packer who died aboard the *Titanic*. At 1.3 miles, Lancaster Falls honors the engineering wizard of the historic highway.

Mountain Defiance Trail changes after this easy jaunt. Only the fittest will want to attempt the 7-mile climb to the summit of 4,960-foot Mount Defiance, "The Guardian of the Gorge." This trail has the most elevation gain of any in the gorge, a rugged, challenging climb that is used by local mountain climbers to get in shape for climbing Mount Hood.

Viento is beautiful in spring—even in a light rain—with its lush mix of green vegetation, wildflowers, and flowering trees. From the northeast edge of the campground, between sites A27 and A29, a 0.25-mile nature trail leads to Viento Lake. This pretty little lake is a quiet place to meditate, with a wetland area around it that nourishes cattails and other water-loving plants.

A 1-mile paved trail, with trailhead parking and access on the south side of the freeway, allows campers to walk to Starvation Creek Falls, and to access other trailheads at that park. Thirteen of the tent sites are also in this area, near Viento Creek.

Many of those who visit the park are windsurfing enthusiasts, which, ironically, fits the name of the park. The Columbia River in this area provides a good practice area and also a camp for those

Windsurfers and swimmers are attracted to water activities and camping at Viento State Park.

means of travel, and the thrilling entertainment of races among the stern-wheelers, with passengers cheering them on. The stern-wheeler *Harvest Queen* caused some excitement in 1890 when she shot the Cascade Rapids. Today, passengers don't have to furnish their own food and blankets, as some did on early rides.

145. WYGANT STATE NATURAL AREA, VINZENZ LAUSMANN MEMORIAL STATE NATURAL AREA, AND SENECA FOUTS STATE NATURAL AREA

Hours/Season: Day use; year-round
Area: Wygant, 667.7 acres; Vinzenz Lausmann Memorial, 126 acres; Seneca Fouts, 425.5 acres
Attractions: Viewpoints, hiking, picnicking, photography
Facilities: Trailhead, picnic tables, pit toilets, *no water*
Access: Off Interstate 84 at Exit 58, 6 miles west of Hood River, *eastbound access only*

participating in the many competitive events in this windy gorge. Windsurfing access is across railroad tracks between the park and the Columbia River (carry no rigged sails); use caution. Recent improvements include river access parking, a rigging area, and better beach access. Trails lead through a wooded area to the beach along the river. A nice view of the wind-swept gorge is seen from the driftwood-strewn beach, where swimmers play in summer.

Consider a day trip to Cascade Locks and board the *Columbia Gorge*, a 145-foot stern-wheeler at the Marine Park of Cascade Locks National Historic Site, for a 2-hour narrated tour of the river to Bonneville Dam and Stevenson, Washington.

The diesel-powered *Columbia Gorge* is a reminder of the importance of the steam-driven paddle-wheelers of the past, when their arrival was an exciting event, bringing goods, news, a

Exit 58 has a sign for the Mitchell Point Overlook, but there is no mention of the three parks, although the road only leads to

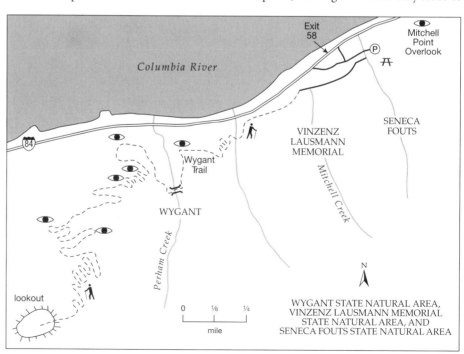

the overlook and these parks, which are contiguous parcels beginning from the parking area and extending west. Construction of Interstate 84 cut off public access to Wygant State Natural Area, now reached only by a trail. Seneca Fouts State Natural Area is at the eastern end where the overlook is located, adjacent to a parking area. A picnic table overlooks the view.

The Mitchell Point Tunnel was once located near this overlook, a famous engineering feature of the Historic Columbia River Highway. Sam Lancaster was inspired by the three-windowed Axenstrass Tunnel, which he viewed with Sam Hill in Switzerland, and he designed a five-windowed tunnel cut out of solid rock. He thought the view across the Columbia to the Cascade Mountains surpassed the beauty of the Rhine River in Germany. Workers "were lowered on ropes as much as 200 feet where they hung like spiders" while they built this tunnel. Bypassed for safety reasons in 1953, the tunnel was destroyed in 1966. One remaining rock wall fragment rests on a ledge. The old scenic highway used the route through this tunnel, now 50 feet above the interstate. A wonderful old black-and-white photo of this windowed tunnel is found in the book *Oregon: End of the Trail* published by the Writers Program of the Work Projects Administration.

A memorial plaque in a circle of trees near the western edge of the parking space locates the beginning of Vinzenz Lausmann Memorial State Natural Area.

The primary attraction is the 6-mile Wygant Trail, in the third park. This mostly unknown hiking trail is accessed from the old road that branches off west from the entry road, closed now to vehicular traffic. There is a sign pointing in that direction, plus signs along the way at crucial points. Follow the old pavement for a short distance through Vinzenz Lausmann Memorial State Natural Area until it leaves the road to cross Mitchell Creek and then returns to pavement again. The hiking trail soon takes off to the left through the forest and begins to climb moderately. Just after you see a sign for the Chetwoot Trail, which branches off to the left, there is a spur from the Wygant Trail to the first Columbia River Gorge viewpoint.

Back on the main trail, descend to a bridge over the fast-moving waters of Perham Creek. The trail is fairly easy and level as it switches back toward the river and the second gorge viewpoint. In the distance is the freeway curving around Mitchell Point, the river, and the Washington side of the gorge. This could be your destination if you want a short hike with an incredible view, perhaps a place to bring a picnic and savor the scenery. Thick, soft moss edges some huge boulders that are perched on the steep edge of the gorge. *Use caution near this vertical cliff.*

A vista point on the Wygant Trail shows Mitchell Point and a panoramic view of the Columbia River Gorge.

There are many areas of tanoak woods along the trail, but also sections of tall conifers, mushrooms, ferns, mosses, and habitat for ospreys. These birds are easy to spot because they start whistling a frenzied *cheereek!* if you get near a nest.

There are three more viewpoints before switchbacks climb up to the summit lookout, plus water views through the trees. The Washington side of the gorge looks like a three-dimensional map as one spots Dog Mountain and the Little White Salmon River flowing out into Drano Lake, and then into the Columbia. Washington Highway 14 and a bridge are situated on the narrow arm of land between the lake and the river.

Sometimes the last 0.5 mile of the trail to the summit is not negotiable because of downed trees adjacent to steep drop-offs. The trail is eroded in this area and little used. By backtracking a short distance, a sign is found on a tree that points to the down-hill Chetwoot ("Black Bear") Trail, and this route can be taken back, though you might prefer the easier Wygant Trail. Near the beginning of the Chetwoot, a view of the gorge reveals the snowy peak of Mount Adams. The path then follows a narrow ledge to the bridge over Perham Creek and descends through woods to the intersection with the Wygant Trail.

Both trails have a section in the middle where they cross an old road near power poles. This disturbed area hides the trails with heavy bushy vegetation for a short distance, but the trail is easy to follow. The Wygant Trail goes directly across the road. The Chetwoot Trail jogs slightly to the right.

146. KOBERG BEACH STATE RECREATION SITE

Hours/Season: Day use; year-round
Area: 87.5 acres
Attractions: Windsurfing, fishing, picnicking, rest stop
Facilities: Picnic tables, restrooms, beach and river access
Access: Off Interstate 84, 3 miles east of Hood River, *westbound access only*

When Interstate 84 was constructed, the state park system purchased three widely separated parcels located on the north side of the interstate between Hood River and Mosier. The western-most tract of 22.57 acres contains a prominent basalt outcrop that provided material for highway construction and, in addition, a swimming beach, which was operated for many years by the Koberg family as a recreational site complete with dance pavilion. In 1962, this was developed for picnicking and rest area facilities as the Koberg Beach State Recreation Site.

Besides serving as an interstate rest stop, the easy access to the Columbia River has made this a favored windsurfing area. A short path west of enormous Stanley Rock leads to a rather nice stretch of gravel beach for launching into the wind that is more prevalent on this side of the rock that projects out into the river some distance. From the beach, you can see a Native American fishing platform attached to the rock's tip. No trespassing is allowed at the government property to the east of the parking area, where only treaty fishing access is allowed.

Koberg Beach is a windsurfing launch area near Hood River.

147. HISTORIC COLUMBIA RIVER HIGHWAY STATE TRAIL (MARK O. HATFIELD TRAILHEAD)

Hours/Season: Day use (fee); year-round
Attractions: Hiking, bicycling, wildlife viewing, exhibit information, photography, picnicking
Facilities: Hood River Visitor Center (restrooms), vault toilets, picnic tables
Access: Mark O. Hatfield West Trailhead (Hood River) is off Interstate 84, 2.5 miles east of Exit 64 via OR 35 to US 30; Mark O. Hatfield East Trailhead (Mosier) is off Interstate 84, at Exit 69 to Rock Creek Road

The recent opening of a section of the Historic Columbia River Highway State Trail between Hood River and Mosier provides a fascinating hiking or bicycling excursion. Five miles of trail connect two diverse ecosystems and allow the traveler to walk or bike through the reopened Mosier "Twin Tunnels."

Once, Model T automobiles drove this cliff-hanging Historic Columbia River Highway from Hood River to Mosier and traveled through the Twin Tunnels that rose 250 feet above the river. The 17-foot-wide roadway accommodated two-way traffic until larger autos began to cause accidents, necessitating traffic lights for one-way traffic, which caused problems with falling rock while stopped. After the new water-grade interstate highway opened, the historic highway remained intact except for the closure of the two tunnels, which were filled with rock. Thanks to many dedicated advocates of the historic highway, the tunnels were reopened in 1996. Since rockfalls had always presented a hazard on the western end of the tunnels, a uniquely designed rock catchment was constructed before the grand reopening of the tunnels, a two-million-dollar, 700-foot-long, column and deck structure.

Facilities are found at both the Mark O. Hatfield West Trailhead near Hood River and the Mark O. Hatfield East Trailhead in Mosier. Visitors drive a mile of the historic highway to parking at the Hood River Visitor Center and head east on foot or by

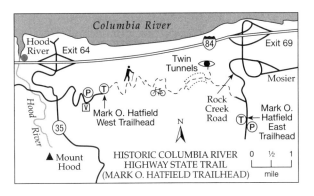

A car travels the Twin Tunnels in the early days. (Photo courtesy of the Oregon Department of Transportation)

bicycle to the Twin Tunnels as the 3.5-mile paved walkway climbs gently through a tree-shaded landscape typical of western Oregon. Watch for wildflowers, ospreys, hawks, and views of mountains, rock formations, the Columbia River, and into Washington. After passing through the intriguing open shelter of the long catchment tunnel and the connecting rock-walled and windowed Twin Tunnels, the traveler emerges as if by magic into a semiarid terrain dotted with ponderosa pines and lit by brilliant sunlight. Vistas are incredible along the way, and a short spur leads to an overlook before the downhill 1.2-mile walk to the east trailhead. Choose to do the entire trail, the east end, or the west end, depending on the season and weather. Flowering trees and wildflowers are impressive in spring.

148. MEMALOOSE STATE PARK

Hours/Season: Day use and overnight (reservations available); campground open mid-March through October
Attractions: Sacred Native American burial ground on offshore island, exhibit information, photography, picnicking, camping
Facilities: Picnic tables, river access, campground (43 full hookup, 67 tent sites—maximum site 60 feet), accessible restrooms with showers, dump station, playground
Access: Off Interstate 84, 11 miles west of The Dalles; direct westbound access through rest stop—eastbound take Exit 76 and backtrack
Contact: (541) 478-3008

Situated on a sloping hillside overlooking the Columbia River and the rugged, picturesque bluffs of Washington, Memaloose State Park narrowly escaped being destroyed by a raging forest fire in July of the extreme drought year of 1992. Although black, burnt ground edged the camping area and ground squirrels poked their heads out of black holes, the campground survived after the people were evacuated. Considering the handsome large trees—tanoak, weeping willows, maples, and other species—that still stand among the campsites, this was fortunate.

The campground area is entered via the day-use rest stop on Interstate 84. The park was named "Memaloose," which means "island of the dead," in honor of the two nearby islands in the Columbia River that were sacred Native American burial places. The Columbia River's huge runs of salmon supported vast numbers of people in the past. Since all things about the river were sacred, it is understandable that islands were chosen as burial places. Big Memaloose Island, above The Dalles, is now covered by The Dalles Dam pool. Lower Memaloose Island is seen from the state park, where a white monument marks the burial spot of Victor Trevitt, a pioneer and resident of The Dalles, who wanted his resting place to be "among honest men."

Also buried by The Dalles Dam was Celilo Falls, extraordinary fishing grounds of the Native Americans. When salmon and steelhead trout migrated upriver to spawn, these falls poured through the many cracks and fissures in the basaltic rock obstructions in the river and concentrated the efforts of the fish. Fisherman positioned themselves on platforms built on rocks jutting into the water and caught the anadromous fish with nets on long poles. Because this place was the heart of Native American life, it was called the Tumwater, or Tum Tum, to reflect the sound of a heartbeat. It was a happy place during the good fishing from spring to fall, when spring chinook weighed over seventy pounds and early June steelhead were over thirty pounds. Native Americans feasted and offered thanks to the Giver during this time.

Fishing sites were a valued possession, controlled by families and handed down from father to son, or by marrying into the family. When fish canneries sprang up, cable cars were built to let native fishermen have access to otherwise unreachable fishing spots. But then settlers started using fishing wheels that were capable of catching eight tons of salmon per day, lowering the resource drastically until they were outlawed in 1926. For more than ten thousand years, Native Americans have lived and fished on the banks of this river. Some still use platforms to fish today, but with the influx of settlers, the Columbia River salmon fishery has declined.

The traditional Native American salmon bake that was so closely tied to fishing the Columbia River is continued today.

149. MAYER STATE PARK

Hours/Season: Day use (fee at East Mayer); year-round
Area: 677 acres
Attractions: Windsurfing, swimming, fishing, beach, birding, boating, photography, picnicking, hiking, bicycling, auto tour of Rowena Crest Overlook and Rowena Loops along segment of Historic Columbia River Highway, nearby McCall Nature Preserve
Facilities: Picnic tables, river access, boat launch at West Mayer, restrooms
Access: Off Interstate 84 at Exit 76, 10 miles west of The Dalles

Mayer State Park consists of three different areas, and was named for Mark A. Mayer, who contributed 260 acres to the park. In times past, its varied terrain was valued by the Wasco Indians, who caught fish from the Columbia River and went to the Rowena Plateau to gather edible plants.

From the interstate exit, follow the sign to East Mayer on the river. This is essentially a day-use parking area with many spaces for windsurfers, a popular place for launching into the strong wind along the river.

To reach West Mayer, from the same freeway exit, backtrack on a parallel road west a short distance to a park sign before

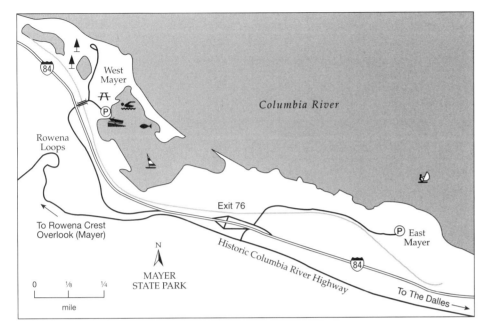

Columbia River

West Mayer

84

Rowena Loops

To Rowena Crest Overlook (Mayer)

Exit 76

Historic Columbia River Highway

East Mayer

84

To The Dalles

N

MAYER STATE PARK

0 · 1/8 · 1/4
mile

and manages the preserve to maintain its biodiversity. This place offers premier wildflower blooms occurring from late February through May, with masses of yellow balsamroot dotting the meadows. State Park Director David G. Talbot wrote that he spent a day there when "the wildflowers were so beautiful, the display knocked my eyes out." The wildlife includes golden eagles, red-tailed hawks, and rattlesnakes, so use caution. Trails wind among the flowers and along cliffs.

Continuing west on the Historic Highway from Rowena Crest, stop at the Memaloose Overlook for a view of Memaloose Island and the Memaloose Campground with nearby McClure Lake. Farther west are vast fruit orchards that are dazzling in spring blossom.

The Historic Columbia River Highway in this area offers some challenging bicycling, with less traffic than the highway near the waterfalls. It is still a place for caution, however, particularly with the steep downhills. Have good brakes and wear a helmet. The route can be expanded considerably by including the Seven Mile Hill Road and making a 22-mile loop.

crossing under the interstate and then over a small wooden bridge (limit six tons, *no trailers or motor homes*). The park is wetland habitat with lakes, vegetated channels, adjoining woods, and small islands at the edge of the Columbia River. This landscape offers fine birding, fishing, and boating—a quiet place to spend some time. You might don your swimsuit in the warmer summer weather on this eastern side of the Cascades.

The third area of Mayer State Park, the Rowena Crest Overlook, is along the 9-mile portion of the Historic Columbia River Highway between Mosier and Rowena (heading south from Exit 76 or east from Exit 69 at Mosier). The historic highway climbs uphill from Rowena, along loops in the road designed by Lancaster, to an elevation of 1,000 feet. Bretz floodwaters topped this mesa-like bench called the Rowena Plateau and stripped off most of The Dalles Formation, which originally covered it. The park's Rowena Crest Overlook hints at what an eagle sees as it flies above the land, including the incredible vista of Lancaster's loops and the route of the mighty river. (Please be aware that the park does not include property all along this drive, though you'll want to travel the entire distance of the highway).

The Rowena Crest area is also the site of the Tom McCall Nature Preserve, more than 219 acres on the Rowena Plateau dedicated as a memorial to Governor McCall's commitment to preserve the Oregon landscape. The Nature Conservancy owns

Balsamroot is one of the many wildflowers found in the Rowena Crest area.

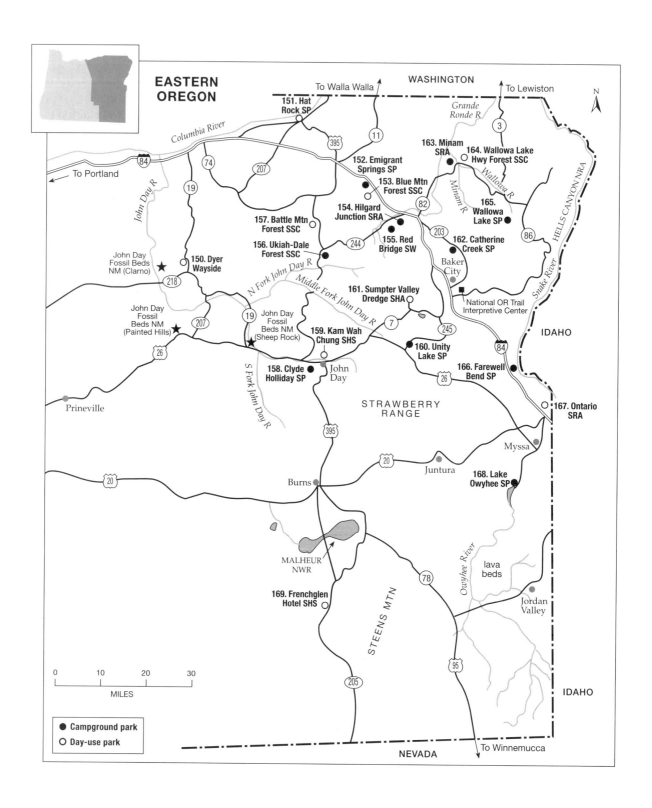

EASTERN OREGON

WASHINGTON

To Walla Walla · To Lewiston

N

151. Hat Rock SP

Columbia River

Grande Ronde R

To Portland

John Day R

163. Minam SRA
164. Wallowa Lake Hwy Forest SSC

152. Emigrant Springs SP

153. Blue Mtn Forest SSC

165. Wallowa Lake SP

154. Hilgard Junction SRA

157. Battle Mtn Forest SSC

156. Ukiah-Dale Forest SSC

155. Red Bridge SW

162. Catherine Creek SP

John Day Fossil Beds NM (Clarno)

150. Dyer Wayside

N Fork John Day R

Baker City

National OR Trail Interpretive Center

161. Sumpter Valley Dredge SHA

Middle Fork John Day R

IDAHO

John Day Fossil Beds NM (Painted Hills)

John Day Fossil Beds NM (Sheep Rock)

159. Kam Wah Chung SHS

160. Unity Lake SP

166. Farewell Bend SP

158. Clyde Holliday SP

John Day

167. Ontario SRA

Prineville

S Fork John Day R

STRAWBERRY RANGE

Myssa

Burns

Juntura

168. Lake Owyhee SP

MALHEUR NWR

Owyhee River

lava beds

Jordan Valley

STEENS MTN

169. Frenchglen Hotel SHS

0   10   20   30
MILES

● Campground park
○ Day-use park

NEVADA

To Winnemucca

HELLS CANYON NRA

Wallowa R

Minam R

Snake River

CHAPTER NINE

EASTERN OREGON

Eastern Oregon is a vast region that extends from the Washington border south along the Idaho border to Nevada. It reaches west to where the John Day River meets the Columbia River. With the exception of some terrain edging the Columbia River, where Hat Rock State Park is found, the landscapes are high desert or mountainous.

Many people never get to the northeastern corner of Oregon, yet it is a place of superlatives. Along the Idaho border, the Snake River has gouged the deepest gorge in the United States: Hells Canyon. The Wallowa Mountains dominate the terrain to the west of the gorge, magnificent forested peaks that loom above Lake Wallowa and the state park at its edge. Nicknamed "Little Switzerland," this landscape was once the summer home of the Nez Perce Indians. Also in this corner are three quiet state parks along waterways: Minam, Wallowa Lake Highway Forest, and Catherine Creek.

The Blue Mountains tower to the west, covering vast distances and many ranges. These steep and rocky mountains were a trial to the pioneers on the Oregon Trail. Today a freeway follows their old route northwest from its entry into the state, near Ontario State Recreation Area, to the Columbia River. Along the way, several of their camp sites are now state parks: Farewell Bend, Hilgard Junction, and Emigrant Springs.

Southwest of the Oregon Trail route, still within the Blue Mountains, are more state parks: Red Bridge, Ukiah-Dale Forest, Battle Mountain Forest, Unity Lake, and Clyde Holiday. Kam Wah Chung State Heritage Site in John Day preserves a historic building from the area's mining days. The Sumpter Valley Dredge is another heritage park, a relic of gold mining in these mountains.

The John Day River drains the western slopes of the Blue Mountains and has cut its way through basalt cliffs at Picture Gorge near Dayville. Three fascinating units of the John Day Fossil Beds National Monument are not far from the river.

Southeastern Oregon is a sprawling high-desert plateau punctuated with rugged canyons, huge ranches, green meadows, alkaline lakes, craters, and mountains. Owyhee country, near the Idaho border, is full of lava beds, river gorges, and sheer walls and pinnacles splashed with colors from pink to chocolate brown—rockhunting terrain. Lake Owyhee is downstream of the Scenic Waterway area of the Owyhee River. Colors here are similar to the warm-tone canyons of Utah, punctuated by greens and blue contributed by the river. Geology buffs will love the area. Temperatures in summer are downright hot. This is the lonely corner of the state, a place where all is not yet explored.

An interesting auto tour is routed through the historic Blitzen Valley, south of the Strawberry Mountains and the city of Burns, where the senses are flooded with nature's input and the brain with human history. Cattle Baron Peter French came to Blitzen Valley in 1872. His round barn and P Ranch headquarters are here, and the Frenchglen Hotel is still signing in guests. Malheur National Wildlife Refuge is along the route, with marshes, alkaline lakes, and grasslands that attract more than 280 species of birds, including sandhill crane nesting habitat. Oregon's highest road—though not the easiest to travel—loops up into Steens Mountain, a massive fault block with splendid valleys, wildflowers, creeks, and trails.

For additional information on Oregon State Parks, call 1-800-551-6949, or check the official website: *www.prd.state.or.us.*

150. DYER WAYSIDE

Hours/Season: Day use; year-round
Area: 0.6 acre
Attractions: Picnicking, rest stop
Facilities: Picnic tables, vault toilets, *no water*
Access: Off OR 19, 10 miles south of Condon

Dyer Wayside is located off the beaten track in Patill Canyon, along a branch of Thirty Mile Creek, where it occupies a narrow gorge of the canyon. The park was a gift from J. W. Dyer to the state of Oregon in 1931. The wayside was closed for a time during relocation of the John Day Highway (OR 19) in the 1960s. It provides a rest stop, perhaps for a picnic, for those traveling in the area.

151. HAT ROCK STATE PARK

Hours/Season: Day use; year-round
Area: 756 acres
Attractions: Unusual rock formation, hiking, swimming, fishing, waterskiing, boating, picnicking
Facilities: Picnic tables, boat launch, restrooms
Access: Off US 730, 9 miles east of Umatilla
Contact: (541) 567-5032

Hat Rock was the first distinctive Oregon landmark passed by Lewis and Clark on their outbound journey. Clark recorded the sighting in his journal entry for October 19, 1805. The name "Hat Rock" is quite appropriate, as it does resemble a man's silk top hat. The rock has not changed a great deal, but the state park would certainly have surprised the explorers with its uncharacteristic well-watered lushness. It is located on the shore of an arm of Lake Wallulu, which was formed after construction of McNary Dam on the Columbia River.

A boat dock provides access to the river. This sheltered arm of the lake provides an area for swimming and fishing. A large natural spring on the southern tip of the this arm forms a large pond. This large pond—which is stocked with rainbow trout—is a highlight of the park, with its varied wetland associations and cool comfort. Trees shade the walkways that border the pond, cross bridges, pass a water fountain, and access the wooded picnic areas. A multitude of resident ducks and geese are quite friendly. Not so easily approached are the great blue herons, although I saw one heron that was so harassed by a crow

With Hat Rock in the background, young fishermen relax with poles at edge of the large pond in Hat Rock State Park.

punching its rump repeatedly (why, I have no idea) that he might not have noticed me. Kingfishers dive into the water and goldfinches sing in the trees.

The countryside was originally a rolling sagebrush area sloping to the south bank of the river. That type of habitat still surrounds the developed area of the park with Hat Rock looming above, an exposed remnant of a 12-million-year-old basalt flow now speckled with lichen colors. Several foot paths leave the green area from various locations and weave haphazardly up to circle Hat Rock, where I spied several deer—three does and three bucks with forked antlers—in mid-July.

To the west of the boat ramp, an undeveloped landscape invites exploration as it meanders on bluffs above the river. Summers are hot and dry here with temperatures often above 100 degrees for several weeks. For those who want to stay in the area longer, a private campground with swimming pool is located across from the park.

Nature enthusiasts might want to visit the nearby Umatilla Wildlife Refuge, west on US 730 through Umatilla and past the town of Irrigon to Peterson Ferry Road, where you'll see a sign for this 8-mile wildlife refuge with public access and space to roam. This is the McCormack Slough Unit. When the John Day Dam destroyed critical wildlife habitat, other wetlands were created that are managed extensively to support bird populations. An informative area map is found here, with roads and hiking trails designated; walking is permitted in all open areas. Canoeing is an excellent way to quietly approach wildlife, enjoy the wetland surroundings, and observe vegetation varieties. The more than 180 species of birds include mallard ducks, Canada geese, bald eagles, long-billed curlews, and burrowing owls. Other wildlife include deer, coyote, beaver, muskrat, raccoon, porcupine, and an infrequent rattlesnake.

152. EMIGRANT SPRINGS STATE PARK

Hours/Season: Day use and overnight; cabins and 4 sites available year-round, all sites open mid-April through October
Area: 23 acres
Attractions: Oregon Trail exhibit, hiking, horseback riding, picnicking, camping
Facilities: Picnic tables, kitchen shelter, campground (18 full hookup, 33 tent sites—1 accessible, maximum site 60 feet), Totem Cabin and 6 reservable rustic log cabins (2 accessible), horse camp (7 sites and corrals), restrooms with showers, reservable community building (call park), slide program area, firewood
Access: Off Interstate 84, 26 miles southeast of Pendleton
Contact: (541) 983-2277

In January of 1812, trappers and traders with the Astor Overland Expedition, under the leadership of Wilson Price Hunt, crossed the Blue Mountains in the vicinity of Emigrant Springs State Park, afoot in waist-deep snow, and established the route later used by Oregon Trail emigrants. Thousands of pioneers later traveled this way and it was the first forest of evergreen trees seen on their westward trek. In order to avoid heavy snowfall, travelers tried to start in spring so that transit through the mountains was between late August and early October. These rugged mountains, named for their color when seen from a distance, were difficult enough to cross in good weather. Routes established by horseback were another matter for wagons burdened with heavy loads. To cross the forbidding Blue Mountains, wagons were lifted with ropes and pulleys, and sheer muscle power was needed to slow their descent and keep them from being smashed to pieces.

Emigrant Springs State Park is named for the spring to the west and the fact that emigrants often camped in this area north of the 4,193-foot summit of the Blue Mountain Pass. Besides taking time to refill their water barrels, the pioneers easily found firewood in this pine forest watered by mountain rainfall. Wild berries, edible

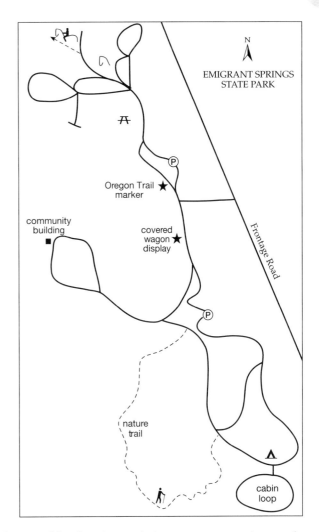

plants, and fine hunting made it even more attractive, a welcome change after the arid stretches of trail. To honor these brave pioneer travelers, a monument was erected at this location and dedicated by President Warren G. Harding on July 3, 1923.

In the 1880s, the trail was replaced by the Oregon Railway and Navigation Company (now the Union Pacific) railroad. During interstate highway construction in the 1950s, trail artifacts were found in the gulch south of the park.

Modern travelers pull into Emigrant Springs to camp or picnic under the canopy of yellow, ponderosa, and lodgepole pine trees. Extensive day-use projects were completed by the Civilian Conservation Corps in the 1930s, and an overnight camp was added in the 1950s. Oregon Trail information and a display are seen on

Covered wagons once overnighted near a spring in the Emigrant Springs State Park area.

the north spur from the entry road, which leads to the horse camp and horse trail. The south spur leads to the overnight campground and the new cabin loop. The community building is centrally located. A self-guided nature trail begins near the registration booth and circles through the woods to the service road. Watch for the plentiful wildlife inhabiting the Blue Mountain area: elk, deer, bear, ducks, geese, pheasants, chukar, and a variety of other birds.

Nearby Pendleton features the Pendelton Round-up in mid-September, a western rodeo that attracts some of the country's most accomplished cowboys. After a cowboy breakfast in Stillman Park, visitors can watch rodeo riders compete in calf roping, saddle-bronc riding, bull dogging, bareback riding, steer roping, and Brahma bull riding. In addition, local tribes set up tepees and present ceremonial dancing and the Happy Canyon Pageant.

153. BLUE MOUNTAIN FOREST STATE SCENIC CORRIDOR

Hours/Season: Day use; year-round
Area: 2,150 acres
Attractions: Viewpoint in Blue Mountains, wildlife viewing, photography
Facilities: Vault toilets, *no water*
Access: Off Interstate 84, 4 miles northwest of Meacham

This large acreage in both Umatilla and Union Counties, the Blue Mountain Forest State Scenic Corridor, is located near Emigrant Springs State Park. Situated on a long mountain ridge, the forest contains intermittent stands of old-growth ponderosa pine, western larch, Engelmann spruce, lodgepole pine, and white fir. It is one of the few examples of mature evergreen forests along Interstate 84 between Ogden, Utah, and The Dalles, Oregon. Spectacular vistas of the surrounding mountain country are seen along the corridor, with the major viewpoint 4 miles northwest of Meacham.

The Blue Mountains are said to have been named about 1811 by explorer and fur trader David Thompson of the North West Company, who noted their bluish cast against the sky while descending the Columbia River. The Blue Mountains represent one of the largest uplifts in the state, with the main range together with its spurs and offshoots extending into several counties. These mountains consist largely of sedimentary and metamorphic rocks and are divided into five general ranges from west to east: Ochoco, Aldrich, Strawberry, Greenhorn, and Elkhorn. The Blue Mountains are separated from the Wallowa Mountains by the Powder and Grande Ronde Rivers. Their highest elevation is reached at 9,097 foot Rock Creek Butte, a few miles west of Baker. Strawberry Mountain, near Prairie City, is almost as high at 9,052 feet.

The springs and cooling shade of this forest were much appreciated by overland emigrants who passed through the area on the Oregon Trail.

154. HILGARD JUNCTION STATE RECREATION AREA

Hours/Season: Day use and overnight; campground open March through October
Area: 232.5 acres
Attractions: River rafting access, Oregon Trail exhibit, fishing, wildlife viewing, fall colors, picnicking, camping
Facilities: Picnic tables, group picnic shelter, campground (18 primitive sites—maximum site 30 feet), restrooms, nearby dump station, horseshoe pits, firewood
Access: Off Interstate 84, 8 miles west of La Grande

The Grande Ronde River begins in the high elevations of the Blue Mountains southwest of Hilgard Junction State Recreation Area, and enters a fairly quiet stretch here in the valley before it continues northeast to its junction with the Snake River just north of the Oregon border. It's an easy place to launch a raft into the water and float the river.

Hilgard Junction is along the Oregon Trail route, a place to water and rest before challenging the mountain summit to the northwest. An Oregon Trail exhibit is informative. A walk along the road west of the park reveals views of the type of landscape traveled by the pioneers.

The park takes its name from a nearby junction of the Union Pacific Railroad line that was named after E. W. Hilgard, former dean of the College of Agriculture of the University of California. A logging railroad of the Mount Emily Lumber Company once passed through the park area before connecting with the Union Pacific en route to La Grande.

The picnic and camping areas are quite appealing and relaxing along this fine, slow-flowing stream bordered by cottonwood, willow, and some ponderosa pine trees. Children fish and play in the shallow river while hip-booted fly anglers cast long lines into the green water of morning. Swallows glide over the water surface to catch insects, ducks swim by, and deer come to drink in early morning quiet.

An Oregon Trail Interpretive Park at Blue Mountain Crossing is just a few miles west of Hilgard Junction at Exit 248 off Interstate 84. Signs for the park will guide you onto OR 30 toward Kamela for 0.5 mile, then on Forest Road 1843 for 2.5 miles to the park trailhead. The Blue Mountain Trail is an accessible half-mile paved path with colorful interpretive panels. Two additional interpreted trails are an option for those with more time and energy. All of these trails provide views of the historic Oregon Trail. A picnic area is available along the forest road.

155. RED BRIDGE STATE WAYSIDE

Hours/Season: Day use and overnight; campground open March through October
Area: 37 acres
Attractions: Fishing, picnicking, camping
Facilities: Picnic tables, campground (10 primitive sites—maximum site 45 feet for RVs), 10 primitive walk-in tent sites, accessible restrooms, group RV camp, firewood, horseshoe pits
Access: Off OR 244, 16 miles southwest of La Grande

Just a few miles west of Hilgard Junction, Red Bridge State Wayside is another shady stop along the Grande Ronde River on the Starkey Highway. The land along the road is generally flat and sprinkled with yellow violets in spring, with a steep-canyoned

wall across the river. Trees are predominantly ponderosa pine, but there is also an abundance of cottonwood, poplar, and willows near the stream, where buffleheads are frequently seen in spring. National forest is across the highway. The park early included a campground, then reverted to just a day-use area, and is again available for camping, which should please anglers. The old highway bridge was maintained in red paint by Union County, but the new and present bridge is quite unobtrusive.

156. UKIAH-DALE FOREST STATE SCENIC CORRIDOR

Hours/Season: Overnight (no developed day-use area); campground open mid-April through October
Area: 2,987 acres
Attractions: Fishing, paddling, nature study, picnicking, camping
Facilities: Picnic tables, campground (27 primitive sites that can accommodate RVs—maximum site 50 feet), restrooms, artesian well water, firewood
Access: Off US 395, 3 miles southwest of Ukiah, and extending 14 miles south

The only developed area in this huge, protected forest acreage is at the north end of Ukiah-Dale Forest, a nice peaceful setting on Camas Creek where you can camp by the water and get out your fishing rod. The aroma of wild roses fills the summer air near the water, where many tiny fish and crawfish can be seen. The steep and narrow canyon of the creek with its grass-covered banks is flanked by forested hillsides that attract many species of wildlife. Ponderosa pine and Douglas fir are found in the lower areas and larch or tamarack on higher slopes.

The park continues south along the road for 11 miles past the crossing of the North Fork of the John Day River just before ending at the junction with Meadow Creek. The headquarters of a logging camp once occupied this area.

According to geologists, the Ukiah area was once covered by a large lake. That changed when Native Americans heard "a great rumbling" and the lake vanished "many moons ago," according to legend. For many years, Native Americans came to the area around the park to gather the root of wild blue camas for food, which explains the creek's name.

You might wish to access Ukiah-Dale Forest by following the 130-mile Blue Mountain Scenic Byway from its beginning at

Along Camas Creek, the campground is located in a scenic area of the Ukiah-Dale State Scenic Corridor.

the Heppner Junction on Interstate 84, and then continuing on past Ukiah to the Elkhorn Drive at Granite. Stop at the ranger station in Heppner or nearby Ukiah for an informative brochure and map of the byway.

157. BATTLE MOUNTAIN FOREST STATE SCENIC CORRIDOR

Hours/Season: Day use; closed in winter due to snow
Area: 420 acres
Attractions: Historic site, wildlife viewing, picnicking
Facilities: Picnic tables, restrooms, outdoor stone fireplace
Access: Off US 395, 9 miles north of Ukiah

A stop at this 4,270-foot summit, alongside a highway less traveled, often finds visitors alone at Battle Mountain. As you read the plaque about the battle fought in this vicinity on July 8, 1878, you can almost feel the presence of Native Americans among the rolling golden-green fields that drop to the valley below. Surely there are still artifacts here beneath the soil of the decisive battle of the Bannock War, a war reported to be the last major uprising of Native Americans in the Pacific Northwest. The war was started by the Bannock Indians as a protest against white encroachment,

The picnic area at Battle Mountain Forest State Scenic Corridor includes a stone fireplace constructed by the Civilian Conservation Corps.

but Egan, a Piute, inherited command and led the Bannock, Piute, and Snake tribes on a wide sweep out of Idaho and through eastern Oregon into the Blue Mountains at this site, where troops under General Oliver O. Howard defeated them.

The picnic facilities lie on a ridge at the edge of a spur of the Blue Mountains with a view of rolling terrain, a deep canyon to the north, and small draws at the south end of the park. In 1935, Civilian Conservation Corps workers constructed tables, stoves, and a water system. One outdoor stone fireplace attracts group use during summer when this forested elevation is a good place for gatherings of relatives and friends.

This acreage includes a preserve of forest land that is primarily ponderosa pine, larch, douglas fir, and spruce on both sides of the highway. Scattered wildflowers are those of the high desert. Though there are no established trails, it is easy to do some wandering and not get lost.

158. CLYDE HOLLIDAY STATE PARK

Hours/Season: Day use and overnight; campground open March 1 through November
Area: 20 acres
Attractions: Fishing, geology, exhibit information, wildlife viewing, hiking, picnicking, camping
Facilities: Picnic tables, campground (31 electrical sites—maximum site 60 feet), 2 reservable tepees, hiker/biker camp, restrooms with showers, amphitheater, dump station, horseshoe pits, public phone, newspapers
Access: Off US 26, 7 miles west of John Day
Contact: (541) 932-4453

Situated along an Oregon Scenic Byway, Clyde Holliday State Park is in the midst of Grant County's gold and cattle country. The discovery of gold in nearby Canyon Creek in 1862 resulted in 26 million dollars in gold being mined in the John Day/Canyon City area. Cattle ranching started about the same time and is still a mainstay of the local economy. If you're here when cattle are being moved between winter and summer pastures, you might see them along the highways and even moving through main streets of local communities.

The park is along a tree-shaded stretch of the John Day River with well-watered lawns; the park has its own water source for this. The picnic area includes a short river access trail that heads east from the restrooms. Picnic tables and restful benches for

John Day Fossil Beds National Monument

In the 1860s, when paleontology was still a relatively new science, a young frontier minister named Thomas Condon (later the first state geologist of Oregon) recognized the potential of the John Day Basin as an important site for finding fossils. Today, three units make up the John Day Fossil Beds National Monument: Sheep Rock, Painted Hills, and Clarno. Together, these 14,000 acres have yielded diverse plant and animal fossils that span 40 million years. Paleontologist R. W. Chaney wrote that "no region in the world shows more complete sequences of tertiary land populations . . . than the John Day Basin."

Environments of the monument evolved from tropical and subtropical forests to a time of deciduous forests and great biological diversity along with multiple volcanic events, followed by a weathering into soil that nourished grasses and mixed hardwood forest in a moderate climate. This area is now at the northwest edge of the Great Basin Desert, which evolved between twelve thousand and five thousand years ago.

Sheep Rock Unit: Five miles northwest of Dayville, past 1,300-foot-deep Picture Gorge and north on OR 19, Sheep Rock Overlook is adjacent to the Cant Ranch Visitor Center, which provides a comprehensive orientation to the monument, an introductory video, and fossil and geology exhibits. In midsummer months, a ranger explains fossil preparation in a small rustic laboratory behind the center. Bring a picnic and enjoy the spacious grounds of the ranch. North of the center is Cathedral Rock, a huge block of John Day Formation that slid down a high bluff and caused the river to change course. Interpretive trails are located in the Blue Basin and Foree areas.

Painted Hills Unit: Six miles northwest of Mitchell, photographers are drawn to the surrealistic colors of the rounded hills in this unit when washed with light, often with a bloom of spring flowers at the foot of these badlands. I still remember the emotional pull of this place shortly after sunrise when coyotes were howling in the distance. Claystone is the distinguishing component of these hills, with colors ranging from bronze, tan, red, pink, and black, which result from the presence of twelve elements, plus seventeen trace ones. Several varied trails are found along the road through the unit.

Clarno Unit: Off OR 218, 20 miles west of Fossil, the rock palisades at Clarno are the oldest in the monument. From an ancient landscape of tropical to subtropical forest, unique fossils of seeds, nuts, fruits, and leaves (from more than 300 plant species found here) are viewed along two different trails. Ancient fauna continue to be found and identified in the Hancock Mammal Quarry, which is operated by the Oregon Museum of Science and Industry and offers several programs for those interested.

The John Day River heads north into the Sheep Rock Unit of John Day Fossil Beds National Monument at Picture Gorge.

Views of the Aldrich Mountains across the John Day River are seen at Clyde Holliday State Park.

contemplation overlook the river and its riparian vegetation. The Aldrich Mountains are in the background to the south, an impressive site in spring with thick snow lingering on their summits. Two tepees have pretty sites facing the river and mountains. A few of the sites in the campground have the same view. Lovely shade trees include huge cottonwoods and willows, with birdhouses attached to several of them. Flowering trees and shrubs add to the park's appeal. Birdwatchers will no doubt find several species easily. Horseshoe pits are found in the hiker/biker camp area and in the day-use area.

North across the highway is 4,000-foot Mount Vernon Butte, whose southern slopes are eroded on Picture Gorge basalt flows, which slope southwest. The low hill in the foreground, which slopes northwest, is rudely bedded volcanic breccias of the Clarno Formation. The difference in angles is caused by fault movements. A much larger fault, the John Day Fault, is believed to be buried under river gravel just south of the day-use area and runs 50 miles east to west along the north foot of the Strawberry Range and along the John Day Valley near Dayville. The principal movement here was eight to ten million years ago, long before the river eroded this wide valley. The movement raised older rock more than 1,000 feet, so the two faults have stair-stepped the rocks.

159. KAM WAH CHUNG STATE HERITAGE SITE

Hours/Season: Day use; open May through October, daily except Fridays
Area: 0.42 acres
Attractions: Historic Chinese apothecary, exhibit information
Facilities: Museum, *no restrooms*
Access: Off US 26, on Canton Street in John Day adjacent to John Day City Park

To learn some pioneer history, visit the Kam Wah Chung Museum in the city of John Day. The structure was erected as a trading post on The Dalles Military Road in 1866–1867. This park preserves the building that served Chinese miners as a general store, trading post, bank and assay office, cultural center, dispensary of herbal medicines, Chinese Temple, and home until the early 1940s.

Two young Chinese immigrants, Ing Hay and Lung On, purchased the Kam Wah Chung and Company building in 1887, when a large Chinese population was engaged in gold mining. The Grant County census for 1879 shows 2,468 Chinese miners and only 960 Caucasians. When acquired by the state, the stone structure was restored and opened to the public with its intact cultural collection. The museum is maintained for the park system by a lease arrangement with the city of John Day, with picnic tables in the adjacent city park.

Kam Wah Chung Museum is an historic building that served Chinese miners as a general store, trading post, temple, dispensary of herbal medicines, and home.

Ing Hay, a Chinese herbalist, and Lung On came to America seeking a fortune in gold mining and stayed on to become an important part of Grant County. The Kam Wah Chung State Heritage Site preserves their contribution to American history. Thousands of artifacts and relics illustrate the many former uses of the site.

160. UNITY LAKE STATE PARK

Hours/Season: Day use and overnight; campground open mid-April through October

Area: 39 acres

Attractions: Fishing, swimming, windsurfing, waterskiing, boating, wildlife viewing, picnicking, camping

Facilities: Picnic tables, campground (35 electrical sites—maximum site 40 feet), 2 tepees, hiker/biker camp, accessible restrooms and solar showers, boat launch, dump station, firewood, public phones

Access: 46 miles east of John Day on US 26, and 4 miles north of Unity on OR 245

A dam was constructed on the Burnt River to provide agricultural irrigation water. On a peninsula on the south shore of the lake that formed, Unity Lake State Park was created to provide public access for anglers, boaters, picnickers, and campers. At an elevation of approximately 4,000 feet, this reservoir is a mini-oasis

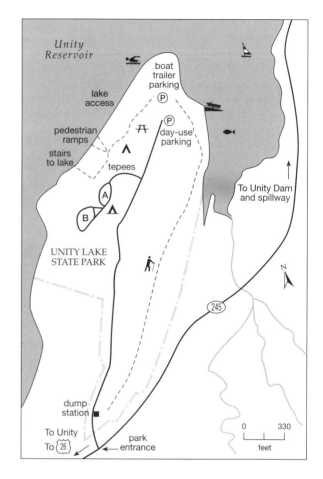

Tepees with Native American designs are located at lakeside at Unity Lake State Park.

surrounded by a fairly barren landscape, with mountains to the north. Trees have been planted to enhance the park area, and these have grown to a nice size and hold several birdhouses. Unity Lake State Park is used frequently by people who live in the area, a good gathering place for reunions under the shady trees at water's edge. The large boat-launch area is a short distance north along the lake. To the south of the day-use area, the campground also fronts the reservoir. Steps lead down to access the lake from the campsites, and a hiking trail leads through the day-use area to the boat launch area. A swimming area is located near boat trailer parking.

The lake offers fishing for trout, bass, and crappie, which is best during spring and fall. Boating, waterskiing, and sailboarding are popular on the reservoir. Many campers find the park a good base in October, when they can combine some fishing with hunting for both big game and upland birds in nearby public land. (Hunting is not allowed within the park boundary.) Other visitors enjoy wildlife viewing in the park area.

A drive northeast along the Burnt River offers wildlife sightings plus unusual rock formations. Three wilderness areas lie within 30 miles of Unity: Strawberry Mountain, North Fork John Day, and Monument Rock, beautiful in spring with snow-covered mountains.

161. SUMPTER VALLEY DREDGE STATE HERITAGE AREA

Hours/Season: Day use; visitor center and dredge open to touring from late April through October
Attractions: Nature trail, historic gold-mining dredge, historical exhibit, tours of dredge, fishing, picnicking, wildlife viewing, Sumpter Valley Railroad excursions to park
Facilities: Picnic tables, accessible restrooms, visitor center
Access: Off OR 7, 30 miles west of Baker City

The highlight of Sumpter Valley Dredge State Heritage Area is a historic gold-mining dredge at the base of the snow-covered Elkhorn Range of the Blue Mountains. It is located along the Elkhorn Drive National Forest Scenic Byway.

The park features a nature trail that loops around the historic dredge through tailings, with spurs to the Powder River, private picnic tables, and past a maze of ponds that form premier wetlands. Watch for beaver, river otter, and a variety of waterfowl. The visitor center, with information, books, and gifts, is a good place to begin your tour of the area.

The Sumpter Valley Dredge was the last dredge to work the Powder River in the main part of Sumpter Valley. Built by the Sumpter Valley Dredging Company, it began dredging in 1935. Although the five-story, 1,255-foot, 1,240-ton piece of equipment didn't dredge during World War II from 1942 to 1945, it did dredge the valley under various owners until 1954. During its operation, the dredge recovered more than 4.5 million dollars in gold, then priced at 35 dollars an ounce. In all, Sumpter Valley recovered more than 10 million dollars in gold from its dredging operations. The dredge now spends its final days resting on the outskirts of Sumpter in a small pond. A rehabilitation project restored the dredge to its original condition and it is now open to public tours, when curious people access the interior of the dredge via ramps and walk around it to check out its various components.

Visitors check out the components of the Sumpter Valley Dredge that recovered 4.5 million dollars in gold from the Powder River.

From Memorial Day through September, the Sumpter Valley Railroad, a restored narrow-gauge railway, travels between McEven Station, 7 miles southeast off OR 7, and the Sumpter Depot. Daily excursion trips go through the dredge tailings and end near the visitor center by the historic dredge. Near the turnoff for McEven Station, watch for a high nesting platform built for ospreys who raise young there in spring.

The town of Sumpter has a history that includes a fort, mining, lumber production, and ranching activities. The boom ended with the shutdown of the gold mines and a fire in the town; the population now is about 175. Several special events are scheduled from May through February in the Sumpter area.

Consider exploring more of the 106-mile Elkhorn Drive National Forest Scenic Byway that heads south and then west from Baker City before arriving at Sumpter. Northwest of Sumpter, the loop passes reminders of the gold rush and logging days, views of the Elkhorn Mountains, and trailheads into the mountains. Summer and winter recreation includes the Anthony Lakes ski area, fishing lakes, and more trailheads before the byway drops downhill to Baker. Stop at a Wallowa-Whitman National Forest ranger station and pick up a detailed brochure of the byway.

162. CATHERINE CREEK STATE PARK

Hours/Season: Day use and overnight; campground open
   mid-April through October
Area: 168 acres
Attractions: Fishing, hiking, picnicking, camping
Facilities: Picnic tables, campground (20 primitive sites that
   accommodate RVs—maximum site 50 feet), restrooms,
   firewood, horseshoe pits
Access: Off OR 203, 8 miles southeast of Union

Tenters and RVers who believe in self-sufficiency will find
Catherine Creek State Park a place to pull up on the grass beside a clear-flowing mountain stream edged by forest land. It's
a quiet place, with considerable charm, a place to relax and
fish. The drive to the park is scenic, with views of the foothills
of the Wallowa Mountains. Early mornings are often punctuated with splintered sunlight shining through the trees onto
south-facing slopes that are covered with sunflowers as wisps
of clouds move slowly over fuzzy slopes and lichen-smeared
rocky projections.

Located near the western fringe of the Wallowa-Whitman
National Forest—almost within shouting distance of the Eagle
Cap Wilderness—the park is bisected by Catherine Creek and
extends high on timbered slopes of pine, larch, and cottonwood.

The park focuses on creek accessibility, with two picnic areas
along its edge. One area is adjacent to the campsites; the upper
picnic spot is about a mile up the road with its own facilities. A
trail heads there from the campground, where I heard kids say,
"Let's go over the bridge." The path crosses an arched wooden
bridge over the water and continues along the creek for a bit.
Horseshoes can be played under the trees as Steller's jays and
kingfishers go about the business of life.

The mountain-rimmed valley to the west is a pastoral feast
for the eyes as one drives north or south on OR 237 from Union,
with its museum and historic homes.

A trail from the campground to the picnic area crosses the arched bridge over Catherine Creek.

163. MINAM STATE RECREATION AREA

Hours/Season: Day use and overnight; campground open mid-April through October
Area: 602 acres
Attractions: Fishing, river rafting, picnicking, camping
Facilities: Picnic tables, campground (12 primitive sites—maximum site 71 feet), vault toilets, rafting access, horseshoe pits
Access: Off OR 82, 15 miles northeast of Elgin

For 2 miles along the Wallowa River, below its junction with the Minam River, Minam State Recreation Area has primitive sites edging the river, which is an Oregon Scenic Waterway. A riverside trail is used by anglers to toss lines from the bank and catch some trout. River runners can launch their rafts. Campers wanting a place for some quality relaxation listening to the river, while perhaps reading and enjoying the surroundings, will find this a fine place off the beaten track. Some flat land along the river makes this possible with simple amenities amid the sometimes steep, pine-forested banks of the Wallowa River. A few miles to the north, the Wallowa merges with another Scenic Waterway, the Grande Ronde River, which runs northeast into the state of Washington.

Sockeye and coho salmon once migrated down the Wallowa River in great numbers, but the sockeye became extinct in the early 1900s and the coho in the 1970s, after dams were built on the Columbia River. The rivers of northeast Oregon do, however, still offer fine fishing—thirty-nine fish species are found here—including spring steelhead. This corner of the state also offers great hiking trails.

The drive north from La Grande to Minam State Recreation Area is delightful through the Grande Ronde Valley, first settled by European-Americans when gold was discovered in the region in 1861. An old wooden church is seen in Imbler and checkerboard fields in the valley are fringed by mountains, the Blue Mountains to the west and the Wallowas to the east. OR 82 climbs gradually along the Grande Ronde River, and wildflower-flecked meadows suggest that this is good camping country with its quiet ambiance. The Grande Ronde heads off north at Elgin, where the historic Elgin Opera House was built in 1912. Beautifully restored now, it offers movies, plays, and opera. It also features a museum and art displays, with tours available. The highway reaches the 3,538-foot summit pass at the town of Minam, where the road leads north 2 miles to the state recreation area. Keep an eye out for bald eagles and other raptors.

164. WALLOWA LAKE HIGHWAY FOREST STATE SCENIC CORRIDOR

Hours/Season: Day use; year-round
Area: 314 acres
Attractions: Picnicking, fishing, wildlife viewing
Facilities: Picnic tables, restrooms
Access: Off OR 82, 12 miles west of Enterprise

The Wallowa Lake Highway Forest State Scenic Corridor is a large tract of land located on both sides of the highway, starting 2 miles east of Minam and extending for 5 miles along the banks of the Wallowa River. The forested landscape includes ponderosa pine and some Douglas fir that is native to the steep-sloping river canyon. Primarily a rest stop with picnicking facilities for highway travelers, knowledgeable anglers will find fishing spots nearby. The wildness of the surroundings might include some wildlife sightings.

165. WALLOWA LAKE STATE PARK

Hours/Season: Day use (fee) and overnight (reservations available); year-round
Area: 166 acres
Attractions: Hiking, horseback riding, nature trail, boating, paddling, fishing, swimming, photography, wildlife viewing, picnicking, camping, Jazz at the Lake Festival and Alpenfest
Facilities: Picnic tables, group picnicking, boat launch, campground (121 full hookups, 89 tent sites—2 accessible, maximum site 90 feet), 2 yurts, 1 deluxe (6-room) cabin, group tent (3 areas), hiker/biker camp, accessible restrooms with showers, slide program, playground, firewood, dump station, boat launch, marina with reservable boat moorage, concessionaire with water sports rental equipment, swimming area, laundry facilities; *no water at full hookup sites in winter*
Access: Off OR 82, 6 miles south of Joseph
Contact: (541) 432-4185; phone (541) 426-4978 for information about Hells Canyon National Recreation Area

Among Oregon parks, Wallowa Lake is unchallenged in its combination of uniqueness and charisma. *National Geographic* chose it as one of six outstanding state parks in the Far West, and that included Alaska and Hawaii. As visitors drive along the lake to

A short walk from Wallowa Lake State Park accesses a gondola to the top of Howard Mountain, where the mountain views are beautiful.

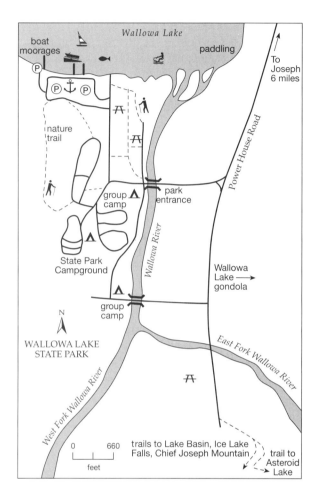

that continental drift caused ancient groups of tropical islands in the middle of the Pacific Ocean—displaced terrains—to attach to coastlines.

The name of the lake and park, Wallowa, is a Nez Perce Indian word for a fish trap for trout and salmon. Tripods of stakes were set on opposite sides of a stream to support a network of sticks in the water that trapped the fish, which Native Americans then caught by hand.

The Wallowa Lake area was the cherished summer home of the Nez Perce Indians where they fished, hunted, and raised pinto ponies in the "land of winding waters." They thought the Treaty of 1855, which reserved the Wallowa country for their tribe, would protect their land, so they were friendly with the first white settlers. Confusion arose in 1877 from other Nez Perce agreements and uprisings, however, and caused young Chief Joseph to try to flee with his tribe to Canada. This long, arduous, thousand-mile journey was only a short distance from success when he was forced to surrender in a snowstorm in Montana.

The park is in two units. The campground and one day-use area are on the lake with a swimming area; the second day-use area is a mile south between the East and West Forks of the swift-flowing Wallowa River that feeds into the lake. Nature trails weave through the park area by the lake and the river. A 10-kilometer Volkswalk is located here, with a 3 rating (5 being the most difficult). Ask for a map at the park.

Deer and golden-mantled squirrels wander among the campsites and the surrounding cottonwood, spruce, western larch, ponderosa pine, and grand and Douglas fir trees. A checklist for the many birds of Wallowa Lake is available in the park. Summer weather is often perfect, though a thunderstorm may blow in. Late September can be surprisingly nice. At that time of year, Rocky Mountain elk wander through the park in the early morning trying to scrounge a lick of a bacon-smeared frying pan, pose for photographs, or just relax on the grass between campsites. Though they are beautiful animals, their wildness must be respected. This is their habitat and they are quite at home.

The two yurts in the park are of different construction than those found in more temperate areas of the state. Constructed of wood inside and out, they are octagon shaped, with lots of windows and a large skylight to watch the stars. The heating unit immediately becomes a simulated flaming stove after switching on the thermostat. The yurts offer magnificent views of the Wallowa Mountains.

Paddlers can launch canoes into the lake and weave among

the park, past the burial site of old Chief Joseph of the Nez Perce Indians, they are soon dazzled by the setting of this hidden valley. The snow-peaked Wallowa Mountains hug the southern end of this 4-mile glacial lake at the edge of the Wallow-Whitman National Forest. These mountains include twenty-eight peaks over 8,000 feet and sixteen peaks over 9,000 feet; the Matterhorn is the highest at 9,845 feet.

Glaciation occurred here during the late Pleistocene Age, about one million years ago. The great mass of ice dug deep into sediments and pushed up lateral moraines to the east and west of the lake, with a terminal moraine to the north. The lake formed in the large, deep hole when the ice receded. The Wallowa Mountains contain tropical fossil corals, mollusks, algae, and sponges that are identical to those found in the European Alps. One theory suggests that they may have common origins and the picturesque white tree skeletons that have drowned with their roots in the watery tangle of river inlets. The lake invites a variety of water sports, and many fishers use bait and hook (instead of *wallowa* techniques) to catch kokanee (landlocked salmon) and several varieties of trout.

Two longer trails begin by the south day-use area. One heads up the side of Chief Joseph Mountain for 7 miles, but fine lake views are seen by hiking 2.2 miles, with an elevation gain of 600 feet. The West Fork Wallowa River Trail leads into the Eagle Cap Wilderness and an area of alpine lakes—Lake Basin—in 9 miles, but day-trippers can sample segments of the scenic terrain. The Ice Lake Trail that branches off from this trail is one possibility. This is horse country, and nearby facilities will rent you a mount and guide you for extended pack trips. Obtain trail information at the ranger station in Joseph. A trailhead pass is required for the day or year, obtained at national forest offices, not at trailheads, and displayed on your windshield.

A wonderful hike awaits visitors in summer atop 8,200-foot Mount Howard. A short walk from the park accesses the steepest vertical lift for a four-passenger gondola in North America. Fifteen minutes of scenery later, passengers walk out onto more than 2 miles of alpine trails that loop around the summit in the crisp mountain air. Views stretch into four states as you pinpoint a row of peaks that includes Eagle Cap, Chief Joseph, Matterhorn, and Bonneville. Wallowa Lake is jewel-like in the western distance, backed by colorful squares of valley farmland.

Two special events are held annually at Wallowa Lake. The Jazz at the Lake Festival is held in mid-July; Alpenfest (with German food) is featured in September. The town of Joseph celebrates Chief Joseph Days annually during the last weekend in July, when a major attraction is a top-notch rodeo.

A short distance east of Wallowa Lake, Hells Canyon National Recreation Area preserves Snake River country that includes North America's deepest gorge. Most of this area is rugged, undeveloped, varied landscapes. River runners with permits can choose the 31.5-mile "Wild" section or the 36-mile "Scenic" section. Nearly 1,000 miles of trails challenge the hiker. About a third of the acreage is designated wilderness that edges much of the gorge area, but those unwilling or unable to penetrate these wild areas will find much to be recommended in the drives, campgrounds, and hikes of the Imnaha River west of the gorge.

Good roads access shoreline views of the Snake River north from Oxbow Crossing to Hells Canyon Dam. One seasonal road leads 54 miles northeast from Wallowa Lake to a precipitous viewpoint of the gorge at Hat Point. Do check on current road conditions for these seasonal roads. Headquarters for the Hells Canyon National Recreation Area is Box 490, Enterprise, OR 97828; phone (541) 426-4978.

166. FAREWELL BEND STATE PARK

Hours/Season: Day use (fee) and overnight (reservations available); year-round
Area: 72 acres
Attractions: Oregon Trail exhibit, fishing, boating, bird-watching, swimming, waterskiing, hiking, wildlife viewing, picnicking, camping
Facilities: Picnic tables, campground (91 electrical, 45 primitive sites—1 accessible, maximum site 56 feet), 3 walk-in tent sites, 3 covered wagons (seasonal), 4 tepees (seasonal), 2 log cabins (seasonal), 2 group tent areas, accessible restrooms with showers, amphitheater, lighted boat/fishing dock, boat launch, swimming area, dump station, public phones, fish-cleaning house, volleyball court, basketball hoops, horseshoe pits, firewood
Access: Off Interstate 84, 4 miles southeast of Huntington
Contact: (541) 869-2365; Oregon Trail Interpretive Center, 1-800-523-1235

Farewell Bend State Park, along the Snake River not far from the Idaho border, is the place where one diarist on the Oregon Trail wrote "bid hur a due forever" of the river that had been the visible route for more than 300 miles, a fitting spot for a modern campsite. It was also the site where Captain Bonneville, N. J. Wyeth, John C. Fremont, and Wilson Price Hunt sometimes camped from 1811 to 1843. The missionary Marcus Whitman guided the first large wagon train through the area of Farewell Bend in 1836. At the entrance to the park is an old pioneer wagon, and a nearby Oregon Trail Shelter features a historic exhibit.

A ferry to cross the river from Idaho into Oregon was operated by R. P. Olds from 1862 to 1882. The west landing was located 0.5 mile south of the park. Some emigrants stayed in eastern Oregon when they heard of the gold discoveries in the Blue Mountains in 1862, but the gold rush was not long-term. This precipitated many abandoned homes, though some stayed on to farm or log.

When the park was acquired, the open river bank supported a crop of alfalfa, but that reverted back to sagebrush and tumbleweed except for the watered and landscaped picnicking and

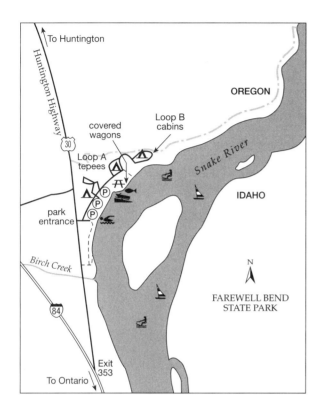

of river against a backdrop of mountains. Fronted by a deck complete with propane grill and a table with an umbrella, these include a heater and an air conditioner. Walk-in campsites near the river offer views and fewer neighbors. The primitive camping area near the park entrance has been upgraded with new slab sites and better restrooms. The group tent area has new barbecue areas. Three electrical campsites have brick patios, shaded tables, and gas barbecues. Campers should be able to view spectacular sunrises and sunsets with the openness of the views bordering the river.

The day-use area includes plenty of picnic tables and recreation areas: basketball, volleyball, badminton, and a variety of sports equipment are available for the asking. Anglers and boaters will be delighted with the improvements in the boat launch and fishing dock area, which is now lighted. A lovely area next to the boat ramp has flowers along the steps and a trail overlooking the river. Many paths within the park permit wandering in the natural areas and often lead to the water, where they edge it for some distance, offering visitors a chance to find quiet fishing spots along the river's shore. Some call this the "catfish capital," but bass fishing is also good. A fish-cleaning house is available for your fresh catch. Benches are found along the river for relaxation, enjoying the scenery, and observing nature and people. Water-skiers put on an exciting show.

camping areas. Steep hills are seen across the river, a prelude to the rugged country to the north. Wildflowers add color in spring and summer, and a diversity of rocks can be found in any season. Chipmunks and ground squirrels are abundant, and wildlife observers can sometimes glimpse deer, antelope, eagles, chukar, and Hungarian partridge. Canada geese are frequently seen with their young in spring, and during late summer— especially in summers of drought—large numbers of geese and ducks are attracted to the edible vegetation growing along the low, nutrient-rich banks of the water and the wetlands across the road. Killdeer flit among them.

The park has undergone considerable recent development. The campground now offers a variety of camping choices. Situated in a grove of sunlit trees, four attractive tepees (three different sizes) look almost authentic, decorated with colorful designs that include buffalo and antelope. Covered wagons are near the river. With their iron tripod holding a coffeepot over an outdoor firepit, you can pretend you're an Oregon Trail pioneer camped here, or perhaps just ponder the courage of their endeavor. Two cabins have spectacular locations overlooking a curving stretch

Mountain terrain edges the Snake River in Farewell Bend State Park, where camping choices are varied and day-use activities numerous.

Those interested in other sites along the Oregon Trail might want to check out an Oregon Trail Interpretive Site managed by the Bureau of Land Management a short distance away, at the Birch Creek Site just south of interstate Exit 353. Only 4 miles from the Snake River, ruts left by the iron-rimmed wagon wheels of the pioneers can still be seen.

Commemorating the importance of the Oregon Trail in the settling of Oregon, the impressive National Historic Oregon Trail Interpretive Center opened its doors to the public on May 25, 1992, as a celebration of the 150th birthday of the Oregon Trail (which was actually in 1993). Follow the well-signed route from Interstate 84 north of Baker City on OR 86 to Flagstaff Hill. The view is a stunning one and gives the visitor a good perspective of the land traveled in this area by the emigrants, with the lush Powder River Valley backed by the Elkhorn Mountains to the west. For the pioneer traveler, the land began to show its promise for settlement. By 1869, close to 250,000 Americans had made the journey from Independence, Missouri, to Oregon Territory destinations. Follow the footsteps of early pioneers by walking the 4.2 miles of the interpretive trail system as it passes an encampment of covered wagons, drops into the valley to a rutted campsite, and passes a lode mine.

167. ONTARIO STATE RECREATION AREA

Hours/Season: Day use; year-round
Area: 35 acres
Attractions: Picnicking, fishing, boating, wildlife viewing
Facilities: Picnic tables, accessible restrooms, boat launch
Access: Off Interstate 84, 1 mile north of Ontario

The attraction at Ontario State Recreation Area, not far from the Idaho border, is the mile of river frontage on the Snake River, which includes Johnson Island with its lush green vegetation and trees. The riverbank is generally level and easily accessed, making boating appealing in the hot summer climate of this area. A boat launch is available. The most popular angling in this area of the river is for channel catfish, with smallmouth bass being taken in growing numbers, as well as crappie.

It's cooler along the river for pleasant picnicking. But, as one radio announcer remarked when I visited in summer when it was approximately 100 degrees Fahrenheit: "If you're near the river, jump in and cool off." I'm not sure I'd recommend that here, since

there is no swimming area. At the right time of day, in the cool of morning or evening, binoculars and quiet observation should result in some wildlife sightings. Easily viewed from the riverbank, Johnson Island should attract numbers of birds.

The Washoe Ferry crossed near here in the 1860s, north of the mouth of Malheur River, where it flows into the Snake. With six oarsmen to power the ferry, fees of a thousand dollars a day were sometimes earned.

168. LAKE OWYHEE STATE PARK

Hours/Season: Day use and overnight; campground open April 15 through October
Area: 730 acres
Attractions: 53-mile-long reservoir, fishing, waterskiing, boating, horseback riding, hiking, wildlife viewing, photography, picnicking, camping
Facilities: Picnic tables, V. H. McCormack Campground (31 electrical, 8 tent sites—maximum site 55 feet), 2 reservable tepees (canoes with life jackets included, no electricity), Indian Creek Campground (50 primitive sites for RVs and tents—accessible sites, fuel sales and supplies), boat launch at day-use area and both campgrounds, dock at Indian Creek Campground, restrooms with showers, dump station, fish-cleaning house
Access: 33 miles southwest of Nyssa, off OR 201, follow signs to park on road that branches off a few miles south of Nyssa
Contact: (541) 339-2331

Plan your trip to Lake Owyhee State Park to allow time to enjoy the drive to the park along the paved backcountry road. The road passes striking sculptured rock formations bordering the greenery and wetlands along the Owyhee River and passes through a one-lane tunnel, a particularly colorful tour in early morning or late afternoon. Watch for blue herons, cormorants, and fawns drinking in the river. Two recently upgraded waysides managed by the Bureau of Land Management, the Owyhee River Watchable Wildlife Interpretive Site and Snively Hot Springs, are located along the route at appealing sites.

Once past the dam at the northern end of 53-mile-long Lake Owyhee, however, concentrate on driving the winding, narrow road along the edge of the canyon for a few more miles to the park. It's a bit tricky with RVs and boat trailers, but people do it.

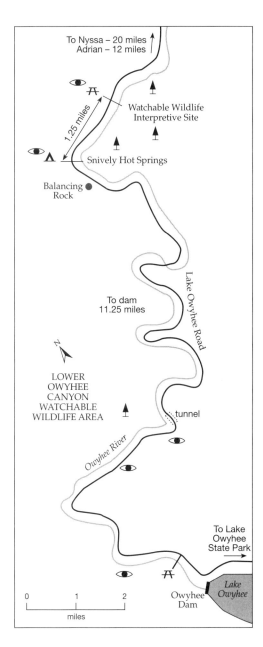

A major tributary of the Snake, the river became known as the Owyhee after two Hawaiians, on a fur-trapping expedition for the Hudson's Bay Company in 1819, were attacked and killed by Snake Indians. The spelling is a variation of Hawaii used in that era.

The Gordon Gulch picnic area is separate and reached first, about 1 mile north of V. H. McCormack Campground, which is

on a point jutting out into the lake. Two tepees with canoes edge the waterfront. Weather will determine campsite choices. The lower sites along the river have green shade trees and watered lawns; the upper ones have incredible views, but are scorchers on a hot day. Water access is found on both sides of this campground, with the boat ramp west along the water and trails on the east that lead to three fishing coves. A nearby resort site, a short distance south, is now part of the park: Indian Creek Campground. Primitive sites here are less individually delineated, and are rather part of large areas.

The terrain in the park is rough, steep, and arid, with sagebrush, but the canyon vistas are inspiring with colors of purple, brown, gold, rose, tan, and red. You can roam on foot over the hills and into coves on the beach. Rockhounds can find agate and jasper in nearby canyons.

Boaters and water-skiers merge into a video simulation against the rainbow towers, colorful side canyons, and promontories of the canyon walls across from the park, which spurs many visitors to boat just for a visual tour of the geologic features of this impressive canyon. Anglers throw out lines for trophy largemouth bass, rainbow trout, black crappie, and catfish. Scan the surroundings for deer, antelope, bighorn sheep, pheasant, chukar, quail, and hawks circling above.

This southeastern sliver of Oregon adjacent to the Idaho border is the oldest land area of the state, and probably was the coastal edge approximately 200 million years ago. Oregon's most active volcanic period helped structure eastern Oregon, fourteen million to twenty-eight million years ago, as enormous flows of basalt lava covered most of Oregon east of the Cascades. Later, the runoff from the glacial period and concurrent heavy precipitation accelerated erosion. The Owyhee River was one of the major rivers that sliced through the lava plains, creating the large valleys, canyons, and gorges we see today.

A fault, or perhaps a major earth fracture, may have determined the channel of this scenic river, which has cut one of the deepest canyons in the west in a rhyolite flow. Today the Owyhee carries a sizable amount of water only during the spring runoff, yet it is an erosive river at the bottom of a massive granite gorge.

During a short season in most springs—usually April and May—when there is sufficient snowmelt to make the wild part of the upper river navigable, whitewater rafters can run this most remote of Oregon rivers, with its spectacular canyon walls, abundant birds and wildlife, desert flowers, riverside hot springs, and Native American petroglyphs. Most floaters put boats into the

In addition to boating, waterskiing, and fishing at Lake Owyhee, the steep cliffs edging the water reveal fascinating geology.

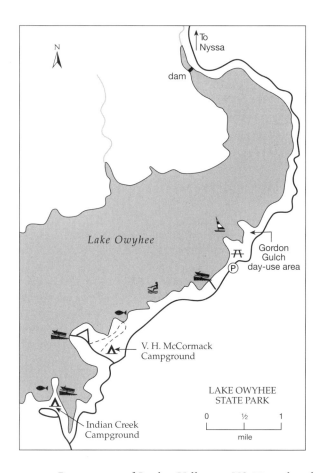

water near Rome, west of Jordan Valley on US 95, and end at Leslie Gulch south of Lake Owyhee, about 63 miles and five days later (class 4 rapids are encountered). Rafters should always check the water flow; it can be too dangerous even during that season.

Anyone in the Rome area should head 3 miles north of Rome on an unpaved road to see the Walls of Rome, located on a dry side canyon of the Owyhee. Walk about 100 yards to the base of mile-long cliffs of eroded lake sediments capped with lava.

Oregon Trail aficionados might consider heading west 1 mile south of Nyssa and then northwest to reach the Keeney Pass along the Oregon Trail, which was reached shortly after the emigrants crossed into what is now Oregon. The site includes visible ruts, trail, and exhibit information. Though sagebrush has regrown over the ruts left by their wheels, some 4 miles of the original trail can still be walked south of the exhibit. The overlook provides a panorama of a day's trip from Fort Boise on the Snake River to the Malheur River near Vale.

169. FRENCHGLEN HOTEL STATE HERITAGE SITE

Hours/Season: Day use and overnight (reservations available); open March 15 to November 15
Area: 2.37 acres
Attractions: Historic hotel with dining area, exhibit information, wildlife viewing, picnicking, lodging, adjacent to Steens Mountain and Malheur National Wildlife Refuge
Facilities: Picnic tables, 8-room hotel, dining room, restrooms
Access: Off OR 205, 60 miles south of Burns
Contact: For reservations, call (541) 493-2825

In 1917, when travelers were beginning to discover the wonders of Malheur National Wildlife Refuge, Steens Mountain, and the surrounding high-desert cattle country, Frenchglen Hotel was built to provide accommodations and dining in this isolated area of Oregon. Frenchglen, Oregon, may not have many human residents, but it does have a zip code. The name Frenchglen derives from combining the names Peter French, who established the first cattle empire in Blitzen Valley in 1872, and Dr. Hugh Glenn, financial backer and father-in-law to French.

The hotel has changed considerably since that time, primarily

The historic Frenchglen Hotel continues to provide accommodations and dining in this isolated area of southeastern Oregon

after significant additions by the Civilian Conservation Corps in the 1930s. The state park system now preserves this historic hotel and outbuildings as Frenchglen Hotel State Heritage Site, as it continues to fulfill its primary intent: food and lodging for travelers.

The eight rooms of the hotel are comfortable, but without the intrusion of television or telephones, which makes it possible to hear natural noises, such as the honking of Canada geese flying in for the night at the refuge. The hotel has an attractive rustic appeal, with varied quilts, photographs, paintings, and accessories in the rooms that reflect the surroundings. Bathrooms are down the hall. Pets are not allowed, nor is smoking, except on the pleasant front porch.

The hotel serves breakfast, lunch (sack lunches are available), and family-style dinners, which are promptly served at 6:30 P.M. and seat twenty-four people, with reservations a must. Operated by John Ross, this friendly place is committed to imaginatively prepared, simple fare that includes such favorites as herb-baked chicken, down-home pot roast with garlicky, roasted potatoes, or honey-glazed pork chops. Save room for the homemade desserts; marionberry cobbler with ice cream is a specialty. An evening spent in the dining and living rooms is a time to get acquainted and share the day's discoveries.

A day-use area offers picnicking as well as exhibit information. Picnic tables are scattered about the spacious lawn, where tall shade trees support a variety of birdhouses that attract some of the many birds in the area.

The hotel is located across the highway from the beginning of the demanding and difficult loop road that ascends Steens Mountain—Oregon's highest road—a favorite access for viewing the mountain's scenery and accessing trailheads for hikers. An easier 42-mile self-guided auto tour (shorter tours are also suggested) has been laid out (a brochure is available, complete with history details); incredible wildlife viewing at Malheur National Wildlife Refuge is part of the appeal of the drive. The tour covers the major sites of interest from Frenchglen north to Burns. A Migratory Bird Festival and Art Show is held in Burns each year, usually during the first week in April, with workshops, tours, and many other programs, but visiting the refuge during migrations just to view the many birds and perhaps do some photography is an excellent activity. The refuge is managed primarily for nesting and migrating birds, with excellent habitat for marsh birds, greater sandhill cranes, shorebirds, and raptors. Trumpeter swans are there year-round. Resident species include pheasant and wintering mule deer. A museum with bird and mammal specimens is part of the refuge.

Several Oregon beaches offer razor clamming.

APPENDIX

STATE PARK OFFICES

Oregon Parks and Recreation Department: 1115 Commercial Street NE, Suite 1, Salem, OR 97310-1002; (503) 378-6305; TT/voice, 1-800-735-2900; *www.prd.state.or.us*

North Coast (Area 1): (541) 994-8152

Willamette Valley/Portland/Columbia Gorge (Area 2): (503) 731-3293

Central/Western Oregon (Area 3): (541) 997-5755

South/Western Oregon (Area 4): (541) 888-3778, extension 26

Central Oregon (Area 5): (541) 388-6212

Eastern Oregon (Area 6): (541) 523-2499, extension 3

OTHER STATE INFORMATION SOURCES

Oregon Tourism Information: (503) 986-0000; (800) 547-7842 (United States and Canada); *www.traveloregon.com*

Oregon Department of Fish and Wildlife: (503) 872-5268; Newport office, (541) 867-4741; *www.dfw.state.or.us*

Oregon Marine Board: (503) 378-8587; *www.boatoregon.com*

Oregon Department of Forestry: (503) 945-7200; *www.odf.state.or.us*

Oregon Department of Geology: (503) 872-2750

Oregon Bicycle Program: (503) 986-3556

Oregon Outdoors Association: 1-800-747-9552, (541) 382-9758

FEDERAL AGENCIES

U.S. Bureau of Land Management: (503) 952-6002; *www.or.blm.gov*

U.S. Fish and Wildlife Service: (503) 231-6828

National Park Service/Pacific Northwest Regional Office: (206) 220-4000

U.S.D.A. Forest Service Recreation Information: (503) 872-2750; *www.fs.fed.us*

A cascading stream near Multnomah Falls, Mount Hood National Forest

INDEX

Page numbers of photographs are set in *italics*.

ABOUT THE AUTHOR

After working indoors for several years as a research biochemist, Jan Bannan became a professional outdoor writer and photographer and has explored the West for twenty-four years. Her credits include the *New York Times Sophisticated Traveler,* the *Oregonian,* the *Seattle Times, Wilderness Magazine, Wildlife Conservation, Motor Home,* and many others. She is the photographer and author of four other books: *Great Western RV Trips, The West Less Traveled, Utah State Parks,* and *Sand Dunes,* a children's book that adults enjoy also. As a member of several environmental organizations and as a wanderer, she chose this career to inspire readers to be better stewards of our treasured landscapes and ecosystems of the West. Visiting them should inspire action.

Writing the first edition of *Oregon State Parks* required traveling thousands of miles in Oregon, exploring the parks and hiking all the trails. For this edition, almost every park was revisited, including sixty additional parks, to update the text to reflect numerous changes in the park system and to do more photography.

ABOUT THE MOUNTAINEERS

THE MOUNTAINEERS, founded in 1906, is a nonprofit outdoor activity and conservation club, whose mission is "to explore, study, preserve, and enjoy the natural beauty of the outdoors. . . ." Based in Seattle, Washington, the club is now the third-largest such organization in the United States, with 15,000 members and five branches throughout Washington State.

The Mountaineers sponsors both classes and year-round outdoor activities in the Pacific Northwest, which include hiking, mountain climbing, ski-touring, snowshoeing, bicycling, camping, kayaking and canoeing, nature study, sailing, and adventure travel. The club's conservation division supports environmental causes through educational activities, sponsoring legislation, and presenting informational programs. All club activities are led by skilled, experienced volunteers, who are dedicated to promoting safe and responsible enjoyment and preservation of the outdoors.

If you would like to participate in these organized outdoor activities or the club's programs, consider a membership in The Mountaineers. For information and an application, write or call The Mountaineers, Club Headquarters, 300 Third Avenue West, Seattle, Washington 98119; 206-284-6310.

The Mountaineers Books, an active, nonprofit publishing program of the club, produces guidebooks, instructional texts, historical works, natural history guides, and works on environmental conservation. All books produced by The Mountaineers fulfill the club's mission.

Send or call for our catalog of more than 450 outdoor titles:

The Mountaineers Books
1001 SW Klickitat Way, Suite 201
Seattle, WA 98134
800-553-4453
mbooks@mountaineersbooks.org
www.mountaineersbooks.org

The Mountaineers Books is proud to be a corporate sponsor of Leave No Trace, whose mission is to promote and inspire responsible outdoor recreation through education, research, and partnerships. The Leave No Trace program is focused specifically on human-powered (nonmotorized) recreation.

Leave No Trace strives to educate visitors about the nature of their recreational impacts, as well as offer techniques to prevent and minimize such impacts. Leave No Trace is best understood as an educational and ethical program, not as a set of rules and regulations.

For more information, visit *www.lnt.org,* or call 800-332-4100.